NEGOTIATING IN THE PRESS

MEDIA & PUBLIC AFFAIRS
Robert Mann, Series Editor

Media & Public Affairs, a book series published by Louisiana State University Press and the Reilly Center for Media & Public Affairs at the Manship School of Mass Communication, LSU, explores the complex relationship between knowledge and power in our democracy. Books in this series examine what citizens and public officials know, where they get their information, and how they use that information to act. For more information, visit www.lsu.edu/mpabookseries.

NEGOTIATING
IN THE PRESS

AMERICAN JOURNALISM AND DIPLOMACY, 1918–1919

❧ JOSEPH R. HAYDEN ❧

LOUISIANA STATE UNIVERSITY PRESS

BATON ROUGE

Published by Louisiana State University Press
Copyright © 2010 by Louisiana State University Press
All rights reserved
Manufactured in the United States of America
First printing

DESIGNER: Michelle A. Neustrom
TYPEFACES: Adobe Garamond Pro, Marcel
PRINTER AND BINDER: Thomson-Shore, Inc.

LIBRARY OF CONGRESS CATALOGING-IN-PUBLICATION DATA

Hayden, Joseph, 1964–
    Negotiating in the press : American journalism and diplomacy, 1918–1919 / Joseph R.
Hayden.
        p. cm. — (Media & public affairs)
    Includes bibliographical references and index.
    ISBN 978-0-8071-3515-0 (cloth : alk. paper)
    1. Journalism—Political aspects—United States—History—20th century. 2.
Government and the press—United States. 3. Press and politics—United States—
History—20th century. 4. World War, 1914–1918—Public opinion. 5. United States—
Foreign relations—1913–1921. I. Title. II. Series.
    PN4738.H39 2010
    070.4'4932773—dc22
                                                                    2009020003

CONTENTS

ACKNOWLEDGMENTS

Two decades ago in a lecture hall packed with students, I heard Indiana University professor George Juergens tell the following story about Woodrow Wilson. It seems the president was vacationing in Bermuda and had just returned from a bicycle trip with his daughter Jessie. The two were tired and sweaty and perhaps not in the most sociable of moods when a flock of reporters descended on them, a few snapping photographs to record the occasion. Wilson testily asked that they stop, saying he didn't so much mind the pictures of him but believed his daughter was a private figure who did not deserve the intrusion. When one photographer continued anyway, Wilson lost his temper and started for him angrily: "I want to give you the worst thrashing you ever had in your life, and what's more, I'm perfectly able to do it."

I knew then I had to learn more about this president. The result was a paper, a dissertation, and ultimately this book. Thus my earliest debt is to Dr. Juergens, who showed me the passionate side to Wilson, nourished my professional interest in journalism history, and served as an adviser and dissertation committee member.

I have known David Nord of Indiana University almost as long and owe him quite as much. His thoughtful seminar on the history of the press is the kind of graduate school experience you dream about, one that encourages both learning and creativity, analysis and play. Professor Nord was also kind enough to take over full-time duty as dissertation chair, and without him this project might not have been completed. Through the years, then, we have both persevered. But above all he has been my friend, whose sense of humor made this long process less lonesome.

I am indebted to two other scholars as well. Nick Cullather of Indiana University and Ulf Jonas Bjork of Indiana University-Purdue University Indianapolis read versions of this manuscript, asking questions and offering suggestions that have improved various drafts.

Several dedicated librarians provided important assistance to me. The staffs at the Library of Congress, the Newberry Library, and the Lilly Library all performed brilliantly, while the Interlibrary Loan Department at the University of North Carolina at Charlotte warrants special mention for rounding up more aging microfilm reels than either of us cares to recall. Judy Bramlett of the Chester County (S.C.) Public Library enabled me to finish my research by procuring books faster and more dependably than I thought humanly possible. And Amy Inskeep of the Archives Department of the *Louisville Courier-Journal* rendered service that would have made Arthur Krock proud.

It has been a delight to work with the superb staff at LSU Press, particularly acquisitions editor Alisa Plant and Media and Public Affairs Series editor Bob Mann. They have helped make the entire process amazingly smooth. I would also like to thank Derik Shelor for his painstaking copy editing.

Alexia Bock of the History Department at Indiana University deserves a paragraph all to herself. No one completes a dissertation there without leaning heavily on her good graces.

In Bloomington I also benefited from an inimitable network of support —friends like Andrew Cheung, Andy Draheim, Patrick Hayden, John Hibbard, Gregor Koso, David Roper, Mike Schreiner, and Helen Walsh, with whom I shared voluble conversations over pitchers of beer or during walks in Bryan Park.

I must thank my parents, Raymond and Violetta Hayden, for their unflinching encouragement and criticism. The only thing more inspiring than their ability to challenge their children has been their unrivaled work ethic. That, or their tomatoes.

Most of all, I want to acknowledge the love and patience of my wife, who right along with me lived and breathed and brooded over this book for so many years. Gloria, this is for you.

NEGOTIATING IN THE PRESS

INTRODUCTION

Progressivism, Journalism, and Diplomacy

How do mass media institutions affect the making of peace? What happens when reporters and diplomats cross paths during international summitry? This study examines the role of the American press at the Paris Peace Conference of 1919, looking at journalists' influence on the peace process and their relationship to heads of state and other delegation members. Most historians seem to assume that the press was peripheral to the peace process. This book presents the opposite argument. Indeed, it lays out how journalism and diplomacy were inextricably linked during the latter stages of the progressive period, linked by a shared faith in information and expertise, in the "authority of facts," as a reformer of that period described it.[1]

Journalism and diplomacy shared something else, too, during those years. They were also equally driven by a compulsion to serve, and to justify themselves before, public opinion. As paradoxical as it may seem, reporters and diplomats sought simultaneously to manipulate *and* conciliate popular sentiment, for the simple reason that they did not always understand what it was.[2] The Paris Peace Conference of 1919 was the site on which these two groups struggled to reconcile their progressive obsession with facts with their democratic veneration of public participation. In the end, though, they could not harmonize these competing objectives. Journalism and diplomacy proved to be too fractious as bedfellows.

Yet they were not too fractious for an astonishing degree of fellowship, for in making the attempt the two vocations embarked on an unprecedented experiment in peace via publicity. Scholars have focused relentlessly on the disappointing results of that endeavor without justly acknowledging the remarkable nature of the experiment. At what other time have journalists and diplomats wrestled so awkwardly and yet so grandly over the composition of a treaty? Their work regularly involved demonstrations of information-based expertise, passionate rhetoric about the primacy of public opinion, and, finally, frequent and extraordinary efforts at publicity, all of which made journalism and diplomacy sometimes appear to be strangely similar enterprises, with reporters occasionally assuming diplomatic duties and statesmen occasionally making public appeals in newspapers and magazines. This little-known aspect of progressive peacemaking constitutes the heart of my story.

Why is the peculiar commingling of journalism and diplomacy important? First, it tells us that the progressive years could accommodate such anomalous circumstances because of the fluidity still present then in American public life, in social institutions, in the newborn professions. And in politics, too: this was, after all, the decade that produced probably the most influential third party in American history. The professions' mutability was not accidental, but rather the result of a determined effort to balance the ubiquitous influence of science with the elusive ideal of democracy, to unite faith in facts with faith in forums.

Second, we see how dominant journalism and mass communication generally were in the thinking of American reformers early in the century, that something inherent in the dissemination of news appealed powerfully to progressives. Media technology loomed as a way to introduce democracy to the masses. And journalism often served as the language of reform even when diplomacy was the target for change. In trying to democratize peacemaking in Paris, that is, some Americans spoke and acted as though what was needed was first to journal-ize diplomacy. Journalism supposedly held the cure because, in addition to its zeal for expert information (however imperfectly realized), it purportedly communed with public opinion, with the sentiment of the masses. As the situation was typically the reverse for diplomacy, an injection of journalism might in theory offer it the press's contact with the public and therefore some semblance of accountability. Diplomatic reformers promised to shine light on the process of peacemaking, and news correspondents understandably believed they would be the illuminating instrument.

Finally, the entwined relationship between diplomacy and journalism is important because it helps clarify a crucial aspect of the controversy surrounding Woodrow Wilson's part in the peace. Because he was the most prominent diplomatic reformer in the world at the end of the war, a progressive who led journalists to believe in the possibility of an expanded role, the question obviously arises: how did the American president's own relations with the press, particularly his methods of managing publicity, lead to diplomatic trouble in Paris, as well as the treaty's eventual defeat in the U.S. Senate? It is a commonplace assertion in historical scholarship that one of the reasons the Senate rejected the treaty was Wilson's inability to "educate" the public about his vision of a post-war international order.[3] Unfortunately, most historians stop short of telling us exactly how and why Wilson failed, or, if they do, they slight journalists' achievements at Paris or miss that perspective altogether.[4] What is needed, then, is closer scrutiny of the interaction between the press and Wilson. But, more than that, we need a broader perspective, one which encompasses the relationship between the press and other negotiators. Such a focus would give us insight into a persistent historical controversy: Did Woodrow Wilson "lose" the peace? Did he forsake the first of his Fourteen Points, the principle of "open diplomacy"? Answering either question makes little sense without informed reference to journalism, but the usual concentration on Wilson tends to prejudice assessments of the press. It did so in 1919 and still does today.

How did the making of peace affect the press? It is my contention that the peace conference of 1919 marked a decisive stage in the history of American journalism, a coming of age for many news organizations, which, like numerous other occupations in the Unites States, were wrestling with the internal propulsion toward professionalization. I place my topic squarely in that context. How did consorting with the world's statesmen and with other premier journalists in the exotic locale of Paris change or confirm the way others saw them? Perceptions of journalism are important because they inevitably reveal beliefs about public opinion, democracy, and diplomacy. Understanding what journalists did before, during, and after the Paris talks can tell us a great deal about how the negotiators and the Wilson administration worked throughout 1919 and gives us a richer integrative view of peacemaking as a whole.

The impact of the peace process on the press and that of the press on the peace process were phenomena unique to early twentieth-century America, a bizarre relationship never before or since witnessed. Below I outline briefly just how American journalists and diplomats were brought together by the logic of the progressive era. In this confrontation both groups grappled with their respective understanding of, and commitment to, "the authority of facts," while trying to balance that objective with their respect for the legitimacy of public forums. To appreciate that tension between information and participation more fully, we need to turn first to the climate that produced it.

PROGRESSIVISM

The progressive era got underway during the last decade of the nineteenth century—that much is certain or, at least, is more or less the consensus.[5] The precise nature of that era, though, has been the subject of a half-century of vigorous debate among historians. Whether progressivism was a movement, a mood, a morality, or a method is not altogether clear, though most scholars generally concede that it bore some characteristics of each, and that is how the term is employed here, as a loose amalgamation of ideas and behaviors distinctive for their concentration at that time, a thirty-year phenomenon of varying intensity.[6]

But my conclusions are based on the belief that method was the most salient characteristic of the progressive spirit. Indeed, reformers' passion for communication—the means and media they used to publicize their aims—strikes me as the strongest force capable of connecting Robert La Follette and Teddy Roosevelt, John Dewey and Walter Lippmann, Hiram Johnson and Jane Addams. Progressivism entailed a measure of liberal reform—in politics, the primary, the initiative, the referendum, and the recall; in business, legislation against fraud, danger, exploitation, and monopoly—that might well have gone unenacted without the means of publicity.[7] In the very act of publication, moreover, progressives seemed to be calling forth a democratic ritual whose communal nature helped them confront modernity. To an extent greatly underappreciated today, progressivism hinged on publicity.

Defining who the progressives were is more difficult, however, since people of all stripes were at one time or another drawn toward their various causes. Certainly many were middle-class men and women of the cities, taxpayers and consumers assuredly, who were alarmed by the evidence of widespread government ineptitude or corruption and by the bewildering consequences of industrialization and immigration.[8] Scholars may debate the severity of the "crisis" perceived then, but there seems little doubt that many people perceived one. Democracy appeared under assault, and Americans struggled to find a combination of remedies to restore order and stability. An essay by Woodrow Wilson in 1901, "Democracy and Efficiency," captures both

the angst and the source of hope from that time. The political science professor from Princeton argued that the issue was not the "excellence of self-
government" but "the method of self-government."[9] As the article's title itself
suggests, progressives saw the challenge of their era as one of balancing democracy and science, participation with "efficiency."

A prominent element of the former was the outburst of information and
opinion: the explosive growth of pulp printing, of magazines and newspapers,
particularly the rapidly growing foreign-language press with its cacophony of
corrieres and *Zeitungs*. These burgeoning mass media overwhelmed large urban areas with sheer quantity, yet seemingly failed to inform or instruct the
whole of society adequately. But the problem for Wilson as for many other
progressives was not information *per se*. Indeed, just the opposite: information beckoned as a solution. Within and between nations, the exchange of
information made progressive action likelier and thus more achievable.[10] The
problem appeared to be a void of "proper" information management, an absence of civic-minded leaders to organize that information, a lack of attention to "the public interest."[11]

Pointing to anachronistic inefficiencies still besetting the United States,
Wilson insisted that the country could surmount these difficulties in time
and with expert guidance. Wilson's recommendation was professionalism. A
more professional civil service and diplomatic corps, along with improvements
in administration and legislation, could lead the way to a better-informed
public and to more sensible choices. Make no mistake: Wilson believed that
"constitutional government" came down to "understandings," which in turn
meant active discussion and the exchange of popular opinion. And, no doubt,
he bore a persistent distrust of career men in the State Department, believing,
not altogether unfairly, that it was a haven for Republicans then. But Wilson
was adamant that "the best opinion" emerge to influence decision making.
There was simply too much vagrant opinion rambling about. "Leadership
and expert organization have become imperative," the future president wrote.

Few members of the urban middle class required Wilson's exhortation
then. As historians Richard Hofstadter and Robert Wiebe have argued per-
suasively, rhetoric about "expert opinion" permeated the first two decades of
the twentieth century, and such demands became enmeshed with progressive
calls for reform.[12] Where science offered hope for improving society, managing
the application of that science naturally implied the need for knowledgeable
practitioners. And all the social sciences at that time—especially economics,

sociology, and anthropology, but including fast-evolving fields like library science, psychology, and statistics—were embracing the tenets and language of the physical sciences. Psychology, for example, sampled heavily from engineering and medicine; statistics borrowed from mathematics.[13] Both to enhance occupational credibility and to keep "outsiders" at bay, advocates of professionalization warmed to quantification and objectivity.[14] Knowledge, in this view, had to be verifiable by certified experts for society to benefit, but benefit it would in the progressive's dream of efficient democracy.[15]

According to this ideology, in fact, reformation followed information; American society had to undergo education before experiencing redemption. And that was an attractive formula for Americans worried about the pace of urban growth. Privilege and opportunity could be shared with the new citizens, that is, but only as such persons gained in maturity, wisdom, and experience. Immigrants would be "taught" to be good citizens, it was often said, which meant more than simple naturalization. Stressing the need for instruction, as most progressives did, underlined the importance of the educator (the expert) as well as the education itself, and implied that without it immigrants, minorities, and poor whites were nothing more than aliens undeserving of full citizenship. Somehow civic education would have to be harnessed to the power of information. By the same token, though, sources of information would be expected to serve a more constructive or at least didactic role.

The progressives' literature of disclosure fueled protest against public corruption and intrigue and, eventually, led to localized experiments in democratic governing. Neither the anxiety about the cities nor the experiments were new. Between 1897 and 1904 a couple of cities had implemented a variety of reforms, most having to do with corporate taxation and rules concerning utility franchises.[16] The events that took place immediately after this period, however, represented a seismic change: "The first fifteen years of the twentieth century witnessed most of the changes; more precisely, the brief period from 1904 to 1908 saw a remarkably compressed political transformation. During these years the regulatory revolution peaked; new and powerful agencies of government came into being everywhere."[17] The legislative peak for statewide reforms took place between 1906 and 1907, most of these introducing direct primaries and creating utility and transportation regulation as well as commissions with broad powers. And state courts generally approved this reform.[18]

A great deal of Victorian moralism hovered over these campaigns, and religiosity, according to Paul Boyer, was never very far away from progressive planning.[19] The fact is the reformers required a wide array of tactics to achieve their goals because the course of public policy often followed a twisting path whose bends were as unpredictable as the stones along the way. Numerous scholars have documented the necessarily eclectic manner and achievements of progressive activists,[20] a manner whose focus probably sharpened as the possibilities of publicity suggested techniques for escaping drift. "Next to political activity, journalism was the most visible progressive profession," the historian Robert Crunden has written.[21] But even this is an understatement: progressive politics actually depended upon journalism to thrive.

JOURNALISM

The consequence of this orderly commitment to manage information on behalf of democracy was twofold. First, it encountered democratic rhetoric and inevitably produced certain reforms (such as direct elections). Second, it fostered experiments in journalism, muckraking being the most famous example. But muckraking was not the only manifestation of this progressive quest to use information as a pedagogical tool. An additional sign was the tendency toward professionalization. Still another aspect was the publicly ritualized nature of all reform campaigns of that time. Men and women bent on social and political change undertook the rites of publication in order to draw attention to perceived problems and to agitate legislators to enact laws.

The hallmark of the literature of the progressive era was a combination of themes, then: community, paternalism, expertly directed improvement. It was literature characterized by middle- and upper-class outreach. Progressivism was not a grass-roots movement but a highly self-conscious effort by the haves, who supposedly knew better, to help the have-nots, who supposedly did not. The exclusive possession of certain kinds of knowledge was thus a key underpinning of progressive leadership. Reformers looked to the enlightened management of information as the way to make American democracy work.

"It is hardly an exaggeration to say that the Progressive mind was characteristically a journalistic mind," Richard Hofstadter wrote two generations ago.[22] In journalism social activists and political philosophers at the turn of the century had discovered a middle way, a compromise, between science and democracy (between science and religion, for that matter). Muckraking journalism in particular was a morally rooted and philosophically idealistic method of social betterment through the power of relentless empirical observation. "Betterment," however, might be overstating it, for these reformers were really critics more than they were doctors. They demonstrated a knack for cataloguing the ills of American society, without necessarily proposing practical remedies to cure the patient.[23] Nonetheless, they toiled diligently toward a diagnosis in the hope that their efforts would eventually produce the appropriate antidotes. Faith in journalism, or in mass communication expertly improved, at any rate, gave progressives confidence in their country, confidence to say, "Destiny . . . chose America to be the greatest laboratory, the greatest testing-ground of democracy in the world."[24] Progressive journalism was not characterized by muckraking alone, but muckraking was probably that journalism's most representative embodiment. It demonstrated for reformers that most powerful and pragmatic of weapons: method.

Progressive writers began by examining, as never before, the country's problems and, as never before, lobbying hard for change. Calls for reform filled the air. It was "an era of shifting, ideologically fluid, issue-focused coalitions, all competing for the reshaping of American society," Daniel T. Rodgers writes.[25] Pamphleteers and later magazines joined a growing chorus of dissidence and began recording an inventory of some of the nation's uglier warts. In the famous January 1903 issue of *McClure's* Lincoln Steffens, Ida Tarbell, and Ray Stannard Baker documented, in withering detail, numerous instances of municipal graft and unchecked business greed. For another half dozen years muckraking magazines ruled America's print culture, focusing the national agenda and drawing the full attention of a least one American president, Theodore Roosevelt, while powerfully influencing two others, Taft and Wilson.

Shepherding the political experimentation during the early years of the twentieth century, muckrakers were the "watchdogs," Ronald Steel says, but other historians go further, saying these journalists sparked the entire movement.[26] Muckraking stirred strong emotions, sold well, and addressed the serious problems of living in the modern American city. According to Steel, progressivism focused on what the metropolis had become and thus "directed its anger at the industrial trusts, the political bosses, and robber barons beyond the reach of law. This loose and disparate coalition of reformers believed that men are essentially good and that a just society could be legislated into existence. To do this they sought wider public participation through such electoral changes as initiative, referendum, and recall, the regulation or public ownership of utilities, and the destruction of the urban political machines."[27]

Cities, therefore, were mainly the problem. But urban life also contained the implements for its own restoration and improvement—mass media, namely.

Communication embodied a crucial front in the movement to adapt a large, heterogeneous society to democratic principles. For reformers both in and out of the news business, initiating improvements in journalism seemed like a good place to start. In fact, a dramatic segment of the culture of the press in the United States was flirting with the idea of professionalization at the turn of the century. At that time American journalism was in the midst of a thoroughgoing transformation, one distinguished by rising social status and increased job security. And yet journalists also faced stricter demands, duties, and constraints as a result of heightened competition. These last elements were largely the result of a transformed literary marketplace. The change in journalists' status was the complex result of that marketplace as well as a number of other factors, including the influence of science, realism, and muckraking; the emergence of writer-celebrities like Ida Tarbell or Upton Sinclair; and the example of other professionalizing occupations.

Journalism was remaking itself, and at the same time being remade by societal forces that were also shaping other white-collar enterprises. Michael Schudson has described the attraction that self-described professionals felt for the concept of objectivity, an attraction shared by people from many different fields.[28] Attachment to that concept may not have been brand new at the beginning of the twentieth century, but it had become particularly intense, and in an era when realism was already well established, writers celebrated the scientific authority surrounding "facts."[29] Reporters and editors alike often spoke in a tone that echoed that of the scientific and quasi-scientific professions. Writers increasingly mentioned "responsibility" and "standards," "training" and "education." They singled out and contrasted less seemly practitioners with worthier colleagues—the good and bad among them. They discussed and experimented with proposals for improving their work where it suffered and enshrining it where it succeeded, but otherwise augmented their respectability and autonomy.[30] In the three decades prior to World War I, journalists were witnessing and gradually coming to understand the slow, subtle evolution of the jobs they did. The changes in the literary marketplace brought dramatic new opportunities as well as awkward restrictions. Writers invariably grumbled about the latter, while taking quick advantage of the former.

But journalists did not just react to a reconfiguration imposed upon them. To a significant extent they joined in and shaped the change. It is not a coincidence that newspaper correspondents were enjoying the greatest access and the richest rewards they had ever known while writing impassioned columns about what it took to be exemplary journalists.[31] Most journalists engaged in continual self-promotion. This was after all a time when the word "publicists" was so loosely thrown about that individuals as different as Lincoln Steffens, Norman Angell, even Woodrow Wilson and Georges Clemenceau, occasionally earned the label.[32] In essence, the modern publicist was born at the turn of the century because popular media like newspapers and magazines had only recently become mass media (capable, that is, of reaching masses—hundreds of thousands of people). Public relations was born at the same time, as were mass communication theory, crowd psychology, and demography. Within a decade following the end of Word War I, sophisticated public opinion polling likewise began. In any case, the press was at the heart of this political and intellectual revolution, an era in which many contemporaries believed information management could unlock the puzzles of governance, a time when news gathering could be said to be "one of the truly sacred and priestly offices in a democracy," "the newspaper . . . in all literalness the bible of democracy."[33] Journalists endeavored to sell their expertise as publicity professionals.[34]

What one sees happening during the progressive era, in short, is the systematic development of what might be called "democracy science." Observers from around the country sallied forth to offer detailed analyses of America's ills, most of them agreeing that the dissemination of information was critical to the functioning of popular government, and therefore that that dissemination had to be scientifically managed. The solution, in other words, was more expertise, but expertise leavened by a democratic sensibility. In this alloy of an idea—democracy science—lay the linchpin of progressive reform. In expertly engineered communication, American elites had found their magic formula; in the press, they found their instrument. Journalism, or as it was more broadly conceived at the time, publicity, thus represented the vanguard of progressive politics, philosophy, and creativity. In that era and in that movement, the medium was the message. It was this fact that made the critical difference in the higher prestige that newspaper and magazine reporters came to enjoy in the twentieth century, for more money and job security alone would not have sufficed to give them glory. Only the perception that what they did for a living was important could enhance their social status. In the bustle of wartime, moreover, that prestige became interwoven with both expertise and patriotism.

Newsmen and -women acquired real cachet by their occupation. Observers may have identified numerous faults with journalism at the time, but almost no one disputed the power of the press then. Indeed, in the midst of international propaganda battles, no institution seemed more important. A typical writer rhapsodized thus about journalism: "We can say . . . without exaggeration that, in a democratic state, the fate of the nation is in the hands of the newspapers"; "that the most reliable medium of influence in democratic countries is the press."[35] This admirer of the Fourth Estate also stressed its necessary responsibilities, its duties to society, and to the principles of democracy. What was clear in testaments like these was the hope Americans held in journalism as the fulcrum for managing information efficiently and democratically. If journalism needed to professionalize in order to stay abreast of the modern world, other professions needed a dose of journalism to aid democracy.

DIPLOMACY

A critical part of the progressive equation was democratic accountability, and not even statecraft was immune from this rambunctious ethos. In the early twentieth century, diplomacy also experienced an array of social and intellectual pressures sufficient to alter the way it was both perceived and practiced. A rarified world of cultivated manners, aging sages, and tight-lipped gamesmanship, diplomacy must have seemed an unlikely candidate for democratic change. Traditionally in Europe the province of seasoned old students of world affairs, its practitioners were men who as a rule had had the benefit of classical training in history, literature, and languages at prestigious schools, who had paid their dues for years in laborious middle-management foreign office functions, and who had slowly climbed their way past committee posts and expert panels to senior advisory roles and negotiator status, where they brokered agreements with a jeweler's eye for detail.

In America the situation was sharply different. An informal foreign service existed, but until the twentieth century it had not been subjected to any systematic bureaucratic overhaul, nor put through a rigorous set of codified procedures, protocols, or promotion standards. The "American diplomatic tradition" up to that time provided scarcely any professional tradition at all.[36] A century and a half after its formal independence, the United States was, in short, a diplomatic amateur, "continuously stepping on its own feet," one reporter remarked in 1919.[37] But the country could ill afford such seeming ineptitude when it was clear following the Spanish-American War that the United States was becoming a world power, an imperial power, in fact, and one which henceforth would finds its affairs increasingly tangled with those of other nations. In the first few years of World War I, too, America slowly climbed its way to the top of the international economic order, and by war's end was the world's foremost banker.

U.S. diplomacy at the turn of the century simply followed in the footsteps of its gigantic economy: laissez-faire and lightly regulated. By the end of the war with Spain, critics within and outside the government were clamoring for merit-based standards for the State Department, yet simultaneously demanding diplomacy to be more responsive to popular will. This centrifugal combination of emphases on a professional diplomacy and on an open diplomacy constituted the chief components of a distinctive new phase of *progressive* diplomacy, a dimension less well known or understood today than "dollar diplomacy" and big-stick activism.[38] Though flashing elements of this story appear in many different accounts of the period, on the whole it remains a largely untold story, which is especially curious considering the amount of scholarly attention paid to the Wilson era.[39] But this quest for both a democratic and an expert management of foreign affairs lay at the heart of Wilsonian diplomacy in the waning years of World War I.

The presidency of Woodrow Wilson heightened the internal tensions within American diplomacy. Wilson welcomed professionalism in principle but regarded professional diplomats with considerable ambivalence and mistrust, and, perhaps because of that suspicion, subscribed wholeheartedly to the idea of diplomatic reform along democratic lines. The influence of public opinion on peacemaking threatened diplomats' independence and challenged their expertise; it crowded the field of negotiation yet raised the stakes frightfully. In the last gasp of progressivism, then, diplomats were put in an impossible position: they were expected to be both elite information brokers and representative public servants; deal-makers and democrats. While encountering these demands, diplomats also experienced stressful relationships with journalists with whom they were thrust into often challenging circumstances.

What American journalism and American diplomacy both came to share in the early twentieth century was an awakened appreciation for the power of information. The two occupations represented nearly opposite poles on the communication spectrum, with journalists the traditional advocates for openness, access, and publicity, and diplomats the traditional custodians of state secrets. Reporters and diplomats alike revered the authority conferred by important information, journalists because it underscored their critical democratic partnership with the people, diplomats because in reinforced their vital relationship with government policy. For both groups, information management bespoke their expertise. And the self-conscious possession of that specialty, the recognition by themselves and by others of that elite status, helped mark their professional standing. Many American journalists and American diplomats in the early twentieth century viewed their occupations as important professions, even though technically those occupations in the United States had heretofore displayed few of the trappings typically associated with the professions.

That professional ethos helped power the transformation of American society during the progressive era because professionalism's emphasis on reform-minded scientific regulation and elite, socially responsible leadership gave to that period its distinctive tenor and pace. Even more, professionalism's natural gravitation toward white-collar information management found direct release as well as purpose in the field of communication. It should therefore come as no surprise that one of the greatest slogans of the first two decades of the century was "open covenants, openly arrived at"—the first of Wilson's Fourteen Points and a quintessentially progressive maxim, for this saying truly embodied both the idea of a democratic reform of diplomacy and the implication that communication experts would be necessary to convey the content of those covenants. Woodrow Wilson was throwing down the final gauntlet of the progressive era: a blueprint for democratic communication between nations.

In the pages that follow I explore the relationship between journalism and diplomacy and argue that the intersection at which both encountered the other was precisely the juncture where the importance of public opinion appeared. It was a most peculiar intersection. That two enterprises so sharply different could share such a singular dimension underscores the basic nature of the progressive era itself, for in no other time in American history has the work of reporters and statesmen overlapped in such dramatic fashion. The spirit of those years pervaded and altered both occupations profoundly. It also intermingled the two, and in ways that sometimes made their interests seem strikingly, even paradoxically, similar. One of the most significant stories of the peace conference, indeed, is the extent to which journalists and diplomats did in fact share such a remarkably cooperative foundation while nonetheless experiencing powerful tensions between them. The existence of acrimony might not be surprising, but the two occupations' peculiar symbiosis surely is, for that is not generally the way scholars depict their relationship. And that is my overall point in telling this story—that the culture of progressivism forced an improbable conflation of roles during the peace process. Journalists were sometimes diplomats in 1919, and diplomats were sometimes publicists.

After examining the traffic in information from two perspectives—government and journalism—this book then focuses on the broaching of peace by each sector. From there the narrative describes journalists' experiences and reportage while covering the Paris Peace Conference and, finally, analyzes the relationship between journalists and diplomats in Paris, as well as the consequences of that relationship both abroad and at home. Because these experiences are central to my main arguments, I have scoured the vast array of memoirs and other personal accounts left behind by the individuals involved and pored over thousands of pages of newspaper and magazine articles (most of the major magazines from that period). These non-official primary sources tell a different story from that typically told in diplomatic histories, and they supply a crucial dimension missing from some otherwise excellent accounts of the era.

Like all evidence, such sources have their limitations, but read with discernment they can provide vital insights toward understanding the role of public opinion in foreign affairs. And, more important, that role simply cannot be understood without them because the entire process of peacemaking involved publicity at the outset. That connection is a complicated story, one which begins well before the 1919 peace conference, before even 1918, for American journalists first had to cope with the world's largest information bureau (set up in 1917), the Committee on Public Information, and an administration determined to see that that bureau dominated wartime communication. The particular ways in which that other war made itself felt is the subject of the next part of the book.

PART ONE

THE WAR OF WORDS

Government Publicity during World War I

∽ 1 ∾
FEDERAL POWER AND PUBLICITY

America's entrance into the Great War required a concerted national effort to prepare citizens for a level of bloodshed not seen since the days of the Civil War and for technological and logistical challenges simply without parallel in human history. World War I was the world's first experience with "total war," with conflict that would demand the entire resources of every nation involved. One such crucial resource was public opinion. "What . . . men and women think about the war is all important," wrote one journalist in the summer of 1917.[1] Indeed, many Americans so valued the will of the people that they regarded the war itself as a "gigantic struggle of morale."[2] As early as 1914, in fact, some were already dubbing the Great War the "first press agents' war."[3] Political and intellectual leaders therefore believed it was up to them to "cultivate," "lead," or "educate" public opinion, a sentiment that for many democratic rhetoricians had already become deeply ingrained by the early twentieth century. The urgent task of mobilization made the management of public opinion especially critical in 1917.

Men like George Creel understood that fact as well. The future director of the Committee on Public Information, Creel was a progressive newspaperman from Denver, Colorado, who early in 1917 wrote letters to Secretary of the Navy Josephus Daniels in which he argued that the establishment of a public opinion bureau was essential. Creel's view was straightforward: effective mobilization necessitated that the government supervise the flow of information; the Wilson administration must direct publicity itself. This war would hinge on propaganda, then, one of the most important weapons in the arsenal of the modern state. And in 1917 propaganda bore a very progressive stamp—no accident, as it turned out. The heart of Creel's new organization, the CPI, was comprised of muckrakers and socialists, political activists and reform-minded publicists. Their version of mobilization thus took on a uniquely energetic and constructive dimension.[4] Eventually that emphasis on progress and productivity seeped into the national consciousness, and did so because for two years the United States ran a war of words in the language of progressivism.

The management of information had become not just an indispensable means to fight but generally to govern, not just a dangerous weapon but a glorified ideal, almost a dogma, whose adherents passionately believed that mass communication, progressively run, could make democracy work. Or diplomacy, for that matter: One writer claimed, for example, that "[t]en years of propaganda of general education along international lines will do more to eradicate ignorance and misunderstanding between peoples than has heretofore been accomplished in one hundred years."[5] This chapter explains how the federal government wielded information according to that prescription, and how in adopting the methods and values of publicity experts, as well as in hiring experienced practitioners, the Wilson administration transformed the nature of government by essentially converting it into another mass medium, the first, the largest, and perhaps the most successful of its kind.

Conventional wisdom describes the topography of wartime discourse as a valley of darkness.[6] Certainly there was breathtaking repression (to be detailed later in this chapter), as the Wilson administration clamped down hard on dissent. But that picture is only partly correct. In other respects, news and publicity flourished as never before. Not only did the CPI lead the way in generating unprecedented amounts of information, but newspapers and magazines found that the war had created a vast hunger for ever more information. Writers had to turn down assignments or did double duty for the extra money; female correspondents were actively recruited; the range of subjects exploded; issues sold out. If criticism of the war was silenced, interest in topics evoked by the war spoke volumes.

But it wasn't just journalists who initiated publicity. The government did as well; indeed, Washington invited it. Progressive attitudes about publicity made it impossible for Wilson, or the correspondents who covered him, to resist the promotional possibilities of either the new presidency or the new diplomacy. Such subjects demanded attention and warranted inquiry, and they got them. That was the tension inherent in progressivism, for it conspired to control but also inspired others to participate. It simultaneously suppressed and informed. Progressivism contained both democratic and undemocratic tendencies. The spirit of the age thus had not one dimension but several, and the importance of communication was central to each. Though the administration cracked down on sources of protest, the U.S. government did *not* as a rule constrict information. It unleashed it.

In 1917 the federal government swiftly took measures to keep itself better informed and also to communicate directly to citizens. Prosecuting the war, in short order, meant publicizing it—advertising its cause, its aims, its needs. Because Woodrow Wilson became a professional administrator and a politician in the immediate aftermath of the muckraking era, it is not surprising that he and other progressives applied the journalistic spirit of that time to the business of war. Wilson had long believed that publicity was indispensable for executive success. As the author of *Constitutional Government in the United States,* with its emphasis on the leadership of public sentiment, Wilson was not the kind of executive who could leave opinion-making to chance.[7] Like the writer Walter Lippmann, the president thought there was already too much leaving to chance, too much drift, in the world.[8] Censorship might be necessary, yes, but censoring alone was considered both primitive and inefficient. Publicity, on the other hand, was a progressive's first line of attack—active, creative, educational. While censorship could be made to fit within the progressive framework, the framework itself was quite impossible without publicity. "For Progressive reformers particularly," says David Kennedy, "faith in publicity as the chief instrument of reform was axiomatic."[9] Above all, Wilson wanted order. And for that he needed to involve the government in the business—and science—of information.

Toward these goals, it was necessary for various government agencies charged with collecting information to step up their efforts, maximize efficiency and productivity, prepare to share their findings with other agencies, and expand their basic services. Policy makers and administrators were already learning to accept publicity as a crucial part of their jobs.[10] In time of war, many in fact regarded information management as their paramount function. Numerous departments, permanent or temporary, contained both research and publicity offices. The State Department, for example, already had its Division of Information, which was established in 1909. Those organizations that didn't, like the Attorney General's Office, promptly hired reporters, editors, or press agents.[11] And the administration itself directly launched its own famous experiment in hands-on publishing with the *Official Bulletin,* "the official daily newspaper of the United States government," which was sent regularly to more than a hundred thousand subscribers between May 1917 and March 1919.[12] Such enterprises in publicity demonstrated Wilson's acknowledgment of the power of advertising and propaganda.[13]

The degree to which reports were shared with the general public varied greatly, of course, but at some instance every department approved information for popular consumption. Even the Army was overrun with publications, the journalism historian Frank Luther Mott observed: "Nearly every large camp and cantonment in the United States had its soldiers' newspaper, while various branches of the A.E.F. published such papers abroad; after the armistice, some were established in hospitals and soldiers' homes."[14] We might question Mott's assertion that "the American people were better informed of the progress of the war than those of any other country in the world," but there seems little question that the public was always in the minds of agency officials, who treated the population at large as readers and viewers and listeners, as media consumers, as prospective members of an audience.[15]

This appreciation for marketing and this sensibility toward the work of communication were truly characteristic contributions of the progressive era, for students of government in that time believed that the most cutting-edge methods of administration were practiced by American business,[16] and American business seemed consumed then with talk of public relations. The progressives' love-hate relationship with the large corporation blended admiration of the dynamic organization with distrust of the power in a behemoth like U.S. Steel.[17] Aware of the increasing use by corporations of public relations counsels, government leaders believed that they, too, had to "sell" themselves to the American people. Toward that end "every means then known was tried in swaying public opinion and in silencing those whose views differed radically from the unified majority."[18] Administrators saw the benefits of releasing positive news about the jobs they did and of combating negative news with explanations and counterattacks. At any rate, publicity was widely regarded as the *sine qua non* of executive efficiency.[19] Both during the war and at the peace conference it was considered a crucial weapon for success. Publicity occupied one side of the progressive coin; suppression, the other. Most progressives who supported the war chose to focus on the first, but whichever side made more of an impression, the currency itself was always based on information.

"UNCLE SAM'S MEGAPHONE":
THE COMMITTEE ON PUBLIC INFORMATION

Progressives paid the highest possible compliment to the value of publicity by creating the Committee on Public Information. No government had ever before devoted itself so intensely and elaborately to the management of mass communication. The organization was without parallel. Vast, resourceful, and inexhaustible, the CPI represented in myriad ways the administration's mightiest muscle. "Uncle Sam's Megaphone," the trade magazine *Printers' Ink* declared, "is a great new organization for molding the minds of masses of citizens."[20] Without question, that megaphone was loud and made itself heard. So effective was the CPI's publicity and so "infectious" its "salesmanship," one scholar notes, that "the spirit spread, and the home front became giddy, especially during bond drives."[21]

News and education constituted two of CPI's primary activities, but beyond that description characterization is difficult because the organization evolved rapidly and spontaneously. The CPI, the best study concludes, "defie[d] blue printing . . . was developed according to no careful plan . . . was improvised on the job."[22] Creel and his staff simply expanded the organization's duties as essential functions made themselves apparent. The plainest summary might be that the Committee was an information bureau with a foreign division and a domestic one, its audience to be both American and European, allied and enemy. Structural categories are otherwise elusive. From a basic clearinghouse of information to a great generator of information, the Committee published its own newspaper (the *Official Bulletin*), issued innumerable pamphlets in the *Red, White, and Blue Series,* the *War Information Series,* and the *Loyalty Leaflets*; commissioned posters and cartoons, sponsored films, organized public speakers, and, of course, distributed tons of press releases to newspapers and magazines around the country. In short, the government of the United States had reinvented itself as a multimedia conglomerate decades before the arrival of a private counterpart and on a scale nearly unimaginable even today.

With World War I, the federal government itself became a mass medium. Indeed, it became the country's largest publisher, filmmaker, art foundation, and speech organizer. In the area of print alone, Washington set astounding records:

> Throughout the twenty-four hours of the day and night more than five thousand employees manipulate the hundreds of type-setting machines, run

presses which print tons upon tons of white paper, and bind mountainous piles of books. There is more type set in a year in the Government Printing-Office—more than two billion 'ems'—than is required for the entire output of Scribner's, Harper's, Doran's, Putnam's, Appleton's, and Macmillan's, or any other half-dozen book-publishing houses combined.[23]

The Committee's desired domestic audience was every American—young or old, male or female, literate or not—and toward that ambiguous end staff members enlisted business leaders, educators and public school systems, churches, writers, journalists, and advertisers to spread the word. Persons who were private publicists before the war often became government-subsidized publicists during the war, so much so that it was sometimes difficult to discern the employer behind a particular writer. Both the nature of the work and the patriotism of the endeavor attracted the literati. During the war, writer Will Irwin said, "most eminent American authors not in uniform contributed the free copy which the Committee on Public Information handed out to the newspapers."[24] The CPI gave them steady work and a passionate cause.

By the end of 1917 the CPI's publicity machinery was reaching virtually every corner of America, thanks to its legions of professional communicators. In much the same way that private publicists entered public service, public servants now dallied in activity that had been previously considered private enterprise. The two realms were subsumed under the pressing need to manage information. The importance of publicity to executive leadership and its role during a time of national emergency imbued the white-collar workers of the war years with an unsurpassed sense of patriotism, expertise, and self-worth. One writer casually boasted of America's "absolute faith in popular education," a compliment intended for the country's educators, not its people: "While the response of America was slow, it was steady, it was powerful. The leadership of the thoughtful classes was accepted. The solidarity of the country was revealed. Intellect triumphed."[25]

The employment of "the thoughtful classes" by the federal government and specifically by the president—in the service of the CPI or The Inquiry, his traveling band of professors—made the second Wilson administration synonymous with brain-trust government, government by elites, infused though they were with progressive rhetoric about the people. In one critical respect, then, this war was a white-collar war, the first to engage an army of clerks, secretaries, writers, and assorted functionaries whose primary duty was the endless trafficking in mainly public records. "The Federal Government has started a big drive for stenographers and typewriter operators," reported the *Literary Digest*.[26] Writers talked of the crucial service performed by "mental workers," men and women who produced "brain sweat."[27] Their demand naturally brought forth a sea of paper. The minutes, files, statistics, lists, memoranda, reports, bulletins, rosters, and registries compiled by government workers between 1917 and 1919 were probably ample enough to fill every newspaper in the country for the duration of the war.

Such a prodigious amount of publicity was necessary to combat dissent at home and abroad. This was the world's first experience, after all, with *de facto* propaganda debates conducted according to pseudo-scholarly formats: the famous position papers that Britain, France, the United States, and Germany all produced during hostilities. These documents were war records put together to aid historians and public policy experts after the war, but they were also manifestly intended during the war to put forth a country's best argument in defense of a particular policy so as to "assist" people around the world in making up their minds about various issues. They represented a merging of the progressive impulse for pedagogy and the wartime obsession with publicity.[28] "How the nation's brains are being mobilized" was a question probably every publisher in America asked at the time.[29] "Already, on all sides," novelist Gertrude Atherton observed, "one sees women reading instructive books for the first time. The appetite was created by the war books."[30] There were many such documents to choose from. In 1917 alone, journalist/statesman Arthur Bullard griped, "we have had Blue Books and White Papers thrust down our throats."[31] Governments competed with one another for the moral and intellectual sanction of the international community.[32] World opinion mattered acutely to all the nations making war. It mattered not just because every ally won meant extra muscle in the field but because in the context of a "total war" every neutral converted to sympathy meant a possible future supplier of food and munitions, a potential coaling station or naval base, perhaps a money lender or fellow propagandist. After the war, some among the Allies thought that Germany should be compelled to issue a "White Book" admitting its responsibility for starting the war.[33] For some Americans, Allied propaganda was actually democratic peacemaking at work.[34] No less significant than the trench skirmishes in France, therefore, were the public opinion battles waged around the world. As federal propagandist Guy Stanton Ford later explained it, the "thing that had to be built up was the morale of the fighting nations. To do this, new instrumentalities, comparable in their way to the new types of armament, were brought into play—the printing press, the platform, the public schools, the advertising columns, the poster, the moving picture, the telegraph, the cable, and the wireless. All these had to be mobilized, directed, and inspired, so that the common man, the hope and support of self-government, felt clearly that the battle line of democracy ran straight from the fields of Flanders to every home and forge and farm."[35]

Behind the American effort to publicize and propagandize was the Committee on Public Information, and by most accounts that organization was enormously effective. With a budget of from $1.6 million (in its first year) to $1.2 million (in its second)—or about "one two-hundredth of one per cent of the total war expenditures"[36]—the organization achieved its goals of explaining and justifying the war to the American people, bringing forth the war whoops Wilson had said were necessary before he could lead the country through years of bloodshed. To some extent, also, the bureau's ubiquitous presence obscured the impact, and political fallout, of censorship.[37] Finally, the CPI enhanced Wilson's reputation with the public. Mentioning him by name, praising his leadership, extolling the cause for which he fought, the huge volume of propaganda that the CPI produced made Wilson look good.

Creel's Committee was for Wilson the perfect tool: it mediated his relations with the press, which made personal meetings less necessary and gave him time for other duties as well as respite from the unsavory business of consorting with journalists. It was structured, formal, and hierarchical, which conformed to his views of optimal executive efficiency. Its progressive principles (concerning, e.g., education of the masses or the assimilation of immigrants) appealed to liberals, on whose political support the president depended.[38]

Wilson's confidence in Creel's organization was evident in his faith in Creel: Wilson possibly met with him more than with any other man during the war.[39] The CPI made press conferences superfluous yet kept journalists informed. In effect, the Committee exerted a nearly irresistible influence on the press, fully flooding newsrooms around the country with all manner of material suitable for publication. The infinite minutiae inevitably generated by war-making bureaucracies kept reporters busy just trying to stay abreast of the paperwork. Offering extensive information to newspapers and magazines forced journalists to focus on the details that the administration was happy to share, while diverting them from those issues the administration preferred to keep silent about.

It thus confirmed in Wilson's mind the ideal method of leadership—not democratic counsel, public referenda, or even the improvizational wizardry of charismatic individuals—but bureaucratic management by experts. It was a leadership style that not only carefully managed press relations but prefigured the role of The Inquiry, his own hand-picked panel of experts, at the Paris Peace Conference. Wilson spoke passionately about his regard for the people, for democratic processes. But he was really more a democratic theoretician than a democrat, more a teacher of democratic values than a dedicated student of democratic practice.

Wilson did not originally see the CPI at war's beginning as a publicity machine so much as a censorship machine. His advisers, Secretary of War Newton Baker, Secretary of the Navy Josephus Daniels (a former newspaper editor), and indirectly George Creel and Arthur Bullard, argued the opposite. For them the idea of a propaganda bureau arose from the same "general explosion of interest in democratic methods" that inspired so many other progressive social engineers.[40] Wilson had always understood the role of the president in directing public opinion. "His is the only national voice in affairs," he wrote in 1908. "Let [the President] once win the admiration and confidence of the country, and no other single force can withstand him, no combination of forces will easily overpower him."[41] But Wilson had also always struggled to reconcile his appreciation of presidential public relations with his strong distaste for personal encounters with reporters, and so Creel does deserve praise for at least discouraging the president's authoritarian tendencies. Robert Hilderbrand summarizes Creel's record well:

> It remained one of Creel's fondest contentions that the CPI represented a force for moderation in the troubled years of 1917–1918. To some extent this rings true. Most CPI divisions attempted to avoid the worst wartime excesses, and Creel himself supplied the strongest and most consistent voice in Wilson's administration against overzealous application of censorship laws. The CPI had its dark side, however. It seemed occasionally guilty of repeating, if not promoting, the most vicious examples of anti-German propaganda, and it surely helped to create a domestic atmosphere favorable to the persecution of individuals not sharing its enthusiasm for war.[42]

Not surprisingly, the CPI's legacy remains a controversial issue. While historians like Stephen Vaughn and David Kennedy have emphasized the bureau's accomplishments and liberal influence on Wilson's administration,[43] other scholars take a more pessimistic view. William Graebner paints a darker portrait. Both Wilson and Creel, he writes, were fully aware that "the tools of the C.P.I. . . .were the product of 20th-century social science; that 'democratic' social engineering, far from being an ineffective, lesser version of coercive state power, was a powerful device for shaping opinion and behavior; that 'democracy' as Creel and Bullard understood it, was every bit as potent a system of authority as Prussian autocracy."[44]

However much Wilson, Creel, and others grasped the dictatorial dimensions of a national propaganda bureau—and it is questionable whether they viewed it that way, for progressivism drew its energy from faith in democracy—there seems little doubt that all the people behind the organization of the Committee on Public Information did strive aggressively to control the media marketplace during World War I. They did so, of course, in ways that conferred to them status as experts and authority as administration agents. In a guest column in the *Advocate of Peace,* Creel pled essentially for silent obedience. "Let no one ask, 'when will the war end?' for it is a question that tears at the very heart of resolve. The war will end when we win and not until then. . . . It remains only for the American people to support their President."[45]

But it is important to note that Creel and his colleagues additionally strove to procure a soothing democratic legitimacy, a legitimacy that was formless and fleeting but nonetheless fundamental in the American context. Since no one on the CPI was elected by the people, the Committee had to highlight its effectiveness in working *for* the people, specifically by mobilizing millions of individuals to participate in various wartime projects and campaigns. The way they would mobilize Americans was through the scientific management of information, through a logology informed by public relations, propaganda, and diplomacy by cliché.[46] Creel and the Committee stressed publicity, not secrecy.[47] They encouraged self-censorship, not government repression.[48] In some circumstances George Creel even defended publications like the notorious magazine *The Masses* when it was suspended for violating the Espionage Act,[49] a detail generally left out of most histories of the period, which like to cast Creel as a power-hungry heavy. Most significant, the very notion of publicity exuded an aura of democratic accountability and thus the potential for public participation. As three of Wilson's cabinet members described that power in a memo to the president in 1917, an information bureau would provide people with "the feeling of partnership that comes with full, frank statements concerning the conduct of the public business."[50]

Then as now, the Committee has frequently been mischaracterized and misunderstood. The organization was elitist and relentless, intolerant of dissent and protest—all true. But it was never a disingenuous ploy to brainwash people. The progressives were too optimistic for such an attitude; they believed that most citizens were basically educable and reasonable if trained to be. The new scientific bureau of words was above all pedagogical, for the CPI was the logical application of the idea of progressive publicity to the situation of war, and progressivism reveled in teaching citizens their proper duties. In the line from muckraking to state-sponsored propaganda, then, the constant element throughout both was the reverent validation of the role of social educator, the person who communicated knowledge. The subject of public education, in fact, pervaded the literature of that time.[51] "The democratic countries are not only fighting for their own freedom, but also for the chance to educate the world," a writer for *The World's Work* explained.[52] And in America, progressives believed, the challenge was no less formidable. Wilson, George Creel wrote, "has been, in truth, a schoolmaster, and not all that we get from a teacher ever softens humanity's curious resentment at having to be taught."[53] Creel's apt metaphor for Wilson explains much about Wilson, Creel himself, and the progressive era. The essential problem in democracy, as they saw it, was the natural proclivity of the public toward ignorance and superficiality.

In the CPI the Wilson administration displayed not only a wariness about the press but also about the American people as well. And the reason for caution was not a flattering one: policy makers perceived the electorate as a dim-witted giant, slow to think and act but unalterably powerful when it did so, thus the necessity for a proper public education. "By education," one writer said, "we shall create a protective power more potent than that of armies and navies."[54] And after all, why create the nation's first official propaganda bureau unless one thought that public opinion mattered greatly? The irony for progressives was the importance of public opinion coupled with the belief that unorganized public opinion was usually an embarrassment. The "Great American Public," Creel sarcastically remarked concerning the apparent popular misunderstanding of Wilson, "has never been particularly in love with analysis."[55] Other progressives involved in war work were coming to the same conclusion, Walter Lippmann probably the most famous example. Lippmann's later writings were grounded in a low estimate of public opinion, and his proposed solution—the organization of information experts—strove to fix the problem by educating the masses. Creel and Lippmann, with more subtlety than Wilson, represented an increasingly publicity-conscious political and intellectual elite.

The sudden emergence of pedagogical thinking in wartime literature thus came alongside, and partly stemmed from, the awakened recognition that public opinion was of inestimable importance in America. The concept and the words "public opinion" were hardly new in those years, but the phrase echoed continually then. To a large extent, such lip service increased as Westerners began to talk about and debate the essence of propaganda, and as they tried to add scientific sophistication to their understanding of how public opinion was manipulated. The U.S. government itself warned Americans to be on the lookout for enemy-inspired information and those spreading it. In dark, sinister-looking CPI pictures like the one entitled "Have You Met This Kaiserite?" reprinted in countless magazines, readers were alerted to traitorous citizens wittingly or unwittingly "helping German propagandists to sow the seeds of discontent."[56] "Spies and Lies," another such poster, shows two chatty women discussing the contents of what appears to be a letter (from a serviceman?), while a few feet away a man listens intently. It, too, instilled in readers the urgent need to be cautious and even suspicious. "Make no mistake," the text reads, "German agents are everywhere." An astounding irony: the world's most formidable propaganda agency was telling its citizens to beware of becoming a propaganda tool.

Of course, the CPI meant to red flag the *enemy's* propaganda, not its own. Most Committee employees did not, in fact, consider their work propaganda because they believed it truthful and righteous, or if they did consider it such, duly distinguished between good and bad propaganda. Nonetheless, they had no doubt that controlling public opinion was a crucial element in winning the war. Quite explicit is the CPI poster entitled "I Am Public Opinion," an appeal for the fourth liberty loan drive. The image depicts a strong, young woman (Public Opinion) who resembles the Statue of Liberty, with clenched fist, her other hand raised as if in alarm. "All men fear me!" the caption begins. It continues by stating that people are judged by actions not words, then ends on a most ominous note: "I warn you—don't talk patriotism over here unless your money is talking victory Over There. I am Public Opinion! As I judge, all men stand or fall!"[57]

The role of public opinion in the First World War was sufficiently valued and, at the same time, sufficiently feared that government leaders also sought to implement propaganda's more conspicuous sister, censorship. Both endeavors actually constitute two sides of the same enterprise: the control of information. In the case of censorship, authorities negatively and usually reactively stifle certain ideas; in the case of propaganda, those leaders positively and actively promulgate them. With each, the purpose is to supervise selectively the flow of news. With propaganda, however, the government undertakes a much more constructive role, a more creative function than simply the suppression of objectionable material. Here the government nearly competes with traditionally private news organizations to generate news of its own choosing, thus both supplanting and co-opting those it fears. The CPI, therefore, was America's progressive institution *par excellence,* a manifestation of the reformer's spirit at the turn of the century commingled with the challenge of winning a war. By contrast, censorship was a throwback to an old system of information control. It was the un-progressive formula used as a fallback measure in case propaganda proved insufficient. That hardly meant it lacked teeth, however. Quite the contrary, America's organization of censorship during World War I was at least as sweeping as its organization of propaganda and no less unprecedented.

CENSORSHIP

Early in 1917 George Creel and Secretary of the Navy Josephus Daniels won Wilson's approval of a system of a voluntary censorship in which journalists would police themselves, but the president nonetheless believed censorship laws were imperative. In censorship the president found a convenient means to net whatever managed to evade the tentacles of propaganda. He quickly signed a number of bills into law: the Espionage Act (June 15, 1917), the Trading with the Enemy Act (October 16, 1917), and the Sedition Act (May 21, 1918). After the Espionage Act in particular, "the shadow of force lurked behind censorship of the press."[58] These laws threatened publishers with $10,000 fines and long-term imprisonments should they undercut America's effectiveness in winning the war. Statements and reports challenging the validity of Allied war aims or allegedly hampering military recruitment fell under the first law. The second contained even more punishing restrictions, especially in the imposition of prior restraint upon the foreign language press, henceforth making it responsible for submitting translations of all political news and opinion. The Sedition Act was supposed to clarify the Espionage

Act; instead, it broadened it by expanding the range of criminal speech and print. All three acts gave the president more arbitrary control over communication than any president had had since John Adams through the Alien and Sedition Acts of 1798. Worse, the laws invested so much discretionary authority in the Post Office that normal means of redress were impossible. Even uncharacteristic transgressions could be fatal, because in withdrawing questionable publications from the mails a postmaster could also revoke a paper's second-class mailing privileges if it were suspended long enough: "By a Kafkaesque logic, dissenters were thus held responsible for not coming out with issues [of the publication] the government itself suppressed."[59] The war years definitely marked "the low point in protection of press freedoms."[60]

Perhaps the worst aspect of censorship during World War I was its murky and arbitrary application—the "official delay," complained one writer.[61] Postmaster General Albert Burleson, arguably the worst censor in American history, was an enthusiastic harasser of periodicals he happened not to like, and he believed it unnecessary to explain his reasons in particular cases, even denying Congress the right to read his criteria because he thought such clarification "incompatible with the public interest."[62] Single issues of *The Nation,* the *Christian Monitor* ("a newspaper certainly not radical in its editorial policy and usually conservative in its news policy"),[63] the *World Tomorrow,* and Theodore Roosevelt's pet publication, *Metropolitan Magazine,* were temporarily held up, even through the nature of their violations was far from obvious. Roosevelt protested that he and the latter magazine had always stood "'squarely behind the National Government in all things which are essential to bring the present war to a successful end; and to support 'the righteousness of the nation's cause.'"[64]

Yet Burleson was not the sole czar of suppression in 1917 and 1918; hundreds of postal employees could on their own authority pull questionable matter from the mails. That Burleson made the final decision did not alter the fact that journalists could find their publications (and their livelihoods) interrupted by a host of individuals around the country. Thus, censorship proliferated because of a proliferation of potential censors. Through the Espionage, Sedition, and Trading with the Enemy Acts, the dangers for journalists had multiplied, as censorship was democratically delegated.

The trilogy of repression resulted in more than two thousand cases, most involving quick convictions.[65] The majority of the defendants were little-known journalists, publicists, and activists, as Wilson's laws apparently did not target the larger, mainstream publications, which might explain their complacency in accepting some controls and their apathy toward the fate of less fortunate colleagues. "One has the feeling," writes home front historian Robert Ferrell, "that repression of Socialist publications may have been to keep larger publications in line."[66] Not that the press and Congress did not gripe about Wilson, Creel, and Postmaster General Burleson. But by and large the press acquiesced in the censorship, and by and large the public also approved.[67] The result was the loss of an unusually large and feisty faction of American journalism. "We killed 1,954 publications during the war," *Editor & Publisher* announced, noting that some were the victims of consolidation and the high cost of newsprint, but that the reduction was twice as large as the previous year and that the Espionage and Sedition Act had unmistakably hurt the press. The German-language press was cut by one-third.[68] Another writer keeping an eye on press casualties estimated that the federal government directly "interfered with" some seventy-five papers, the majority of them socialist publications.[69]

Bad as government censorship was at the time—and it was even stricter elsewhere[70]—in many ways, the forgotten cornerstone of World War I censorship was self-censorship, both by the press and the public. American vigilantes took it upon themselves to curtail the use of German in the schools, even though Wilson himself and Department of Education Commissioner Philander P. Claxton fought the movement.[71] Other pressure groups heaped abuse on "hyphenated" Americans, who intentionally or unintentionally played Germany's "game." Even a famous ex-president contributed to this atmosphere of intolerance. "[W]e shall tolerate no kind of divided allegiance in this country," Theodore Roosevelt declared in the summer of 1918.[72]

The situation concerning the press was similar. One angry editor labeled the whole of American journalism during the war as "reactionary and servile."[73] Gus Karger, the *Cincinnati Times-Star*'s Washington correspondent, crowed that there was "no greater achievement in self-government on record than the self-censorship of the American press during the emergency now happily passed."[74] Within days of America's declaration of war, organizations and individuals unconnected to the Wilson administration outdid themselves trying to formulate the most effective methods for communicating the country's reasons for joining the fray and its objectives in doing so. Columbia

University was one of many institutions that offered suggestions to journalists, the first line in its War Papers Series on the press being "Teamwork and teamwork only can win this war."[75] The document went on to emphasize the role that news reports, not editorial columns, would play in transmitting the progress of the war and thus the direction of public morale. The writer recommended stressing "our" allies and "our" forces rather than referring impersonally to troops stationed somewhere afar; keeping all war news on the front page; taking pains to mention American involvement at every turn.

While the Sedition, Espionage, and Trading with the Enemy Acts were crucial aspects of wartime communication, far more pervasive was journalists' willingness to censor themselves. Editors "sweated to do their part," Ida Tarbell wrote.[76] And a statement issued by the Associated Press in late April 1917 was a case in point: "That as loyal citizens of the Untied States, we hereby pledge our hearty support of the effort of the executives of the government to carry out effectively the mandate of the nation as expressed in the war resolution adopted by Congress."[77] A *New York Times* editorial in May revealed the personal insult and "stigma" attached to the press by necessity of an imposed censorship. "Why apply compulsion when voluntary service, spontaneously offered, is loyally performed?"[78] Did the president not know how to ask journalists for help or not think they would?

The fact that war correspondents often adopted a soldier-style uniform, which except for rank was identical to a commissioned officer's, should indicate the close affinity many in the press felt toward their government.[79] Whether for fear, for patriotism, for circulations, or out of caution, the majority of American newspaper and magazine staffs submitted voluntarily to a circumscribed sphere of writing and reportage. As dissident intellectual Randolph Bourne had warned, the individual was being subsumed by "the power of the collective community"; he was on the way toward becoming "almost identical with his society."[80] The might of the federal government was wielded through its leaders, its machinery, its execution of the nation's laws, and its influence subtle and not-so-subtle, all combined to demand not only loyalty but active involvement in the successful prosecution of the war. The government targeted citizens in a variety of venues, but its most important strategy depended on co-opting the most prominent channels of public communication—namely, the press. Like them or not, Woodrow Wilson needed journalists in 1917. They needed him, too. By the end of the second decade of the twentieth century, the executive branch in America had become fully enmeshed in a system of political discourse that put the administrator and the journalist in an uneasy yet often overlapping relationship. In calmer days Roosevelt had understood that reality and excelled at the challenge. Wilson recognized it, too, but despite occasional exhibitions of genuine flair, he only grudgingly played the game. War complicated the presidential-press relationship.

❧ 2 ❧

THE NEW PRESIDENCY

Numerous signs—Wilson's creation of the CPI, the unprecedented growth of executive publicity generally, the auxiliary diplomatic group known as The Inquiry, even the establishment of censorship —all exemplified the progressive zeal for bold executive action in the realm of information management. Most historians have excelled in disregarding that aspect, have vastly understated it, or—perhaps with an eye toward Hitler or Stalin—have chosen to emphasize its diabolical ramifications.[1] But totalitarian abuses in the post-Depression West were no more logically inevitable than moments of courage in the nationalistic movement of post-war India. Rather, each understood the power of the media in shaping opinion and claiming authority.

The language of progressivism—its emphasis especially on the rights of the people and the needs of the citizenry—justified and legitimated, for many, the aggressive presidential leadership displayed in the war years. If, as Benjamin Ginsburg has argued, elite opinion disguises itself as mass opinion, American leaders in World War I were neither so Machiavellian nor so uninterested in public participation.[2] To be sure, the Wilson administration acted in an authoritarian manner. Yet even in the midst of such encompassing controls, the president, his cabinet, Creel's Committee, and indeed virtually all progressives paid an ironic tribute to democracy by seeking to influence it. It may not have yet been "government by publicity," observed of America in the 1950s, but it wasn't far off, and these were after all the seminal years of its establishment.[3]

Publicity was the means by which progressives sought to reconcile their democratic sympathies with the authoritarian needs of war. They trumpeted "the pen of democracy versus the sword of autocracy."[4] The wielder of that pen—the federal government—however, was a bully of a new writer. And Woodrow Wilson himself was personally disposed toward being "as big a man as he can."[5] Like McKinley, Roosevelt, and even Taft, Wilson lived in a very different time, culturally and technologically, from The Three Forgettables —Rutherford B. Hayes, James A. Garfield, and Chester A. Arthur. Even had Hayes and Arthur wanted to assert themselves, they did not really possess the means. Absent extraordinary circumstances, they waited for Congress to act. By the 1900s, however, the means were well in place. According to historian Lewis L. Gould, the "mechanisms of publicity and mass information . . . at their disposal" was one of four major changes in authority or opportunity enjoyed by twentieth-century presidents.[6]

Of course, Wilson was not the first executive to interpret liberally his powers of office. Theodore Roosevelt endeavored to be a "big" man himself and almost alone ushered in the age of the imperial presidency with his bully pulpit tactics, his exquisite command of presidential public relations, and such big-stick gambits as the American intervention in Panama. Roosevelt's "corollary" to the Monroe Doctrine, his zest in pursuing goals aggressively in America's backyard, put a definitive stamp on how the United States would conduct foreign policy in the Western Hemisphere. His role in settling the Russo-Japanese War established him as one of the important figures in early twentieth-century world history. And yet, unfortunately for his publicity ambitions, the country went through relatively uneventful times during his watch.

Wilson's confidence in executive leadership matched Roosevelt's, but Wilson was president when the greatest war in history up to that point erupted. Not surprisingly, he soon became the most powerful president in the history of his country. More powerful than that perhaps, according to one writer at the time: "It may be doubted whether any human being in *all* history has been called upon to exercise power so vast and comprehensive, and to make decisions so many-sided and so momentous."[7] Still, Republican critics mainly went along with the administration's expansive powers. As one editor paraphrased Senator Irvine Lenroot (R-Wisc.), who had virtually complied with every executive request during the war, "there was more danger to the country of failing to win the war by not giving the President enough power than there was of imposing upon the country a dictatorship by giving the President too much power."[8] The country opted to give Wilson more power.

In the Overman law, Congress essentially ceded some of its functions to the president in order to expedite war-making decisions.

Progressives' ambivalence about bigness (they feared but admired it) coincided with the Great War to provide President Wilson unprecedented control over both foreign affairs and domestic developments. Already by the 1910s Americans had reached a "turning point," historian Richard McCormick finds, a time "when the weight of public opinion changed, when the forces of localism and opposition to governmental authority that had sustained the distribution of privileges but opposed regulation and administration now lost the upper hand to the forces of centralization, bureaucratization, and government actions to recognize and adjust group differences."[9] And now, in addition, there was the conflagration of war. Wilson thus enjoyed a unique opportunity to acquire extraordinary power at a time when that acquisition would be most likely to win enthusiastic approval. As the *Des Moines Register* intoned, "the President must be sustained in every possible way."[10] "Give the President Plenty of Power," chimed an editor for *The World's Work.*[11] There were wary critics, to be sure—citizens uneasy about the prospect of a leader with supreme authority. But louder still and more insistent were the voices calling for Wilson to take decisive action and to employ emergency-style efficiency. Many Americans wanted a "warlord."[12] "There is every reason for giving him the freedom of executive organization which he desires," one editor confirmed. "Since that is the way he wants to work, he should be given fullest opportunity so to work. In no other way can we get out of him on the side of administrative performance and leadership the best of which he is capable. We must not be satisfied with less."[13]

In the atmosphere of war, countless critics were arguing for the president to do whatever he thought would bring victory most quickly. Indeed, in the face of some Senate criticism that the War Department was not functioning well, Wilson's call for more wartime authority was difficult to reject. Imperial presidency or not, most Americans just wanted to win and end the war. Wilson obliged, paying surprisingly little attention to his cabinet and even less to Congress. One reader of *Leslie's* wrote to columnist Norman Hapgood that he was worried about the president's newfound power. Hapgood disagreed strongly: "My correspondent seems to feel that the President takes too exclusive charge of diplomacy. My criticism would be, on the contrary, that he has not been ruthless enough administratively."[14]

Wilson's second term accordingly brought the White House a strength it had never before possessed. Most of that strength rested on his position as commander-in-chief, but a crucial part of it lay in Wilson's role as the nation's premier representative and the country's first spokesperson and publicist: America's communicator-in-chief. The president's stature personified the country at war yet transcended that image, too. War simply made the average citizen's association with Wilson more personal and more important. It intensified the relationship. The "publicity spotlight" that in America was normally reserved in the nineteenth century for Congress was in the twentieth focused intensely on the White House, then dramatically amplified.[15] With the United States and the world at war, attention was positively riveted on the president.

World war was thus the ingredient missing from the Roosevelt years that would have elevated the former New York governor to the heights shared by Wilson in 1918. World war made Wilson a world leader, a figure of eminence and power and authority. But global conflict by itself could not have been sufficient to make Wilson the world leader he became. The other necessary component, one which Roosevelt did appreciate and in fact thrived on, was the use of publicity. Information management, in short, was an indispensable part of an imperial presidency. "To an extent unimaginable before the end of the nineteenth century," one historian has written, "the executive became a dominant force in the leadership of public opinion."[16] To be successful the executive actually had little other choice. The modern American leader was forced to influence if not direct the news about him. In a political culture characterized by massive numbers of voters (roughly twice as many in 1920 as in 1880) and the unrivaled potential of mass media (metropolitan papers, e.g., with nearly a half million daily readers), a leader's options were limited. As Walter Lippmann wrote, "The reason why we trust one man, rather than many, is because one man can negotiate and many men can't. Two masses of people have no way of dealing with each other."[17]

In the United States, writers and politicians could not simply glory in talk of powerful rulers, so defenders of the new presidency consequently emphasized efficiency and businesslike administration, and, above all, paid regular homage to the people. "It has been that relationship between President and public that has given this office its power and importance," an early student of the subject observed.[18] Rhetoric about government of the masses and for the masses followed as a matter of course. Democratic politicking in the twentieth century involved paying close attention to what the newspapers and magazines were saying and, more significantly, trying to influence what they were saying. A common progressive rallying cry called for "the expression of expert opinion."[19] Leaders in the White House, moreover, had few constitutional powers other than "hortatory" ones; their skills of persuasion, inspiration, and image-making increasingly affected their popularity and effectiveness.[20] When Wilson told a group of correspondents that he believed "a large part of the success of public affairs depends on the newspapermen . . . because the news is the atmosphere of public affairs," he truly meant it.[21] Presidents who neglected public relations—presidents like William Howard Taft—hurt themselves and their party and wound up losers in November. "[W]e are done in this day, gentlemen, with private arrangements," Wilson proclaimed as governor of New Jersey; "every man who wants to make out his case has to make it out in public."[22]

And at publicity Wilson proved a natural. A terrific speechmaker, a gifted orator, a genuine man of letters with an interest in history and literature,[23] the president was a wordsmith in an era when that counted for much.[24] He also thirsted to be a famous spokesperson. As he wrote to the woman who would become his second wife, in the early 1910s, "I have a passion for interpreting great thoughts to the world. I should be complete if I could inspire a great movement of opinion and so communicate with the minds of the great mass of the people as to impel them to great political achievement."[25] This was the type of leader Robert Wiebe has described so memorably in *The Search for Order*: "the public man . . . an educator-extraordinary . . . [who] bore the greatest responsibility for raising mass intelligence to the level of true public opinion."[26]

Wilson is now well-known and rightfully regarded as a pioneer in presidential communication. He resumed the practice, abandoned by Jefferson, of delivering major addresses to Congress in person. The first occasion was a speech on tariff reform, its impact "stunning,"[27] which he gave before the Senate and House on April 8, 1913. Wilson also started a new tradition by holding regular press conferences—approximately twice weekly between April 1913 and August 1914, once a week from then until the summer of 1915, and sporadically thereafter. Especially in those first encounters, Wilson signaled a sharp departure from presidential precedent: "He made the conferences a normal part of White House routine, scheduled them during business hours, and treated them as official appointments."[28] Wilson's vigorous and orderly relations with the press, indeed, signaled a different type of presidency—one that was active, organized, and at the dependable hub of national news. Despite their more jaded recollections of later years, the correspondents deeply appreciated the change in policy at the time.[29]

Wilson was by no means done, however. Toward the end of the decade he would undertake two monumental communication challenges: the effort to mobilize support for a war in Europe and the campaign to change diplomacy. His ability during the war years to "crystallize" world opinion, "the world's ideals," broad concepts like internationalism, pacifism, and so on, was the talent that most journalists paraded on their pages.[30] Mesmerized by the president's "universally recognized genius for expressing lofty ideas," writers both American and overseas created an almost mythical persona in the White House: Wilson the Articulator. Even editorial foes acknowledged his impressive mastery of rhetoric.[31] The *Chicago Tribune* congratulated Wilson for his expert command of public opinion and his incorporation of popular sentiment into a diplomatic campaign to win over the German people.[32] The president had expressed the Allies' moral ideals in compelling, unifying language, observers explained.[33] He stood "as the world's foremost democrat and statesman," an editorial in *The Independent* proclaimed, "because he articulates the very conscience of the American people."[34] He had "expressed the mind and soul of the people."[35] And thousands of journalists paid tribute to the president's powerful rhetorical influence, referring to various of his speeches, for example, as "hammer blows" to the enemy, his words in certain messages "worth a million men in France."[36] In the same way that Theodore Roosevelt enjoyed a manly reputation for public expression, Wilson, too, because of the war, acquired a heroic status for his powers of communication. As Senator Lee Slater Overman boasted after the armistice, "Every leaflet containing his speeches dropped from aeroplane or balloon on enemy soil no doubt served our cause as well as a hundred cannon."[37] The rhetorical presidency had arrived in America.[38] The "media presidency" had too, for rhetorical leadership was not possible without the means to carry it out.[39]

Those developments also put the Wilson presidency at the pinnacle of expansive executive action. In all the many agencies and the thousands of workers utilized by them, President Wilson exhibited extraordinary government responsibility and a measure of initiative that fundamentally hinged on the power of information management. Executives like Roosevelt and Wilson, one historian writes, "sought supportive public opinion to expand their governing authority."[40] The president acted and simultaneously explained in printed sheaves to the correspondents how and why. The imperial presidency depended on the constant direction of public relations. This meant a combination of censorship and propaganda, the two often complementing one another. In December 1918, for example, when the White House announced its intention to commandeer overseas cables in preparation for the upcoming peace conference, President Wilson characterized the authoritarian step as a service to facilitate information. "Seizure of Cables, He Says, Aids in Keeping Members Posted on Parleys," the *Chicago Daily News* reported.[41] Most journalists were unhappy with the decision, and some quite irate, yet since it was plausible that temporary federal control could minimize inefficiency, many who might have grumbled more loudly than they did felt forced to extend the administration the benefit of the doubt. Wilson's unprecedented executive power pivoted on his use of publicity, on propaganda. And these tools were not inherently punitive, brutal, or bad. Publicity rationalized and justified presidential power, and also suggested inherent reforms for the misuse of executive power in and between other countries.

➣ 3 ➢

THE NEW DIPLOMACY

Publicity and public opinion, indeed democratic rhetoric generally, would come to matter much even to as improbable a group of citizens as diplomats, a class of folk with an obviously precarious "image problem" during the war. High casualties, scant progress, and escalating costs tempted Westerners in 1915 and 1916 to blame their diplomats for the cessation of peace in 1914. Statesmen, in this view, had not worked hard enough, selflessly enough, wisely enough. Instead of intelligently trying to avert war, they had seemed to resign themselves to its irresistible pull or, worse, conspired indifferently with belligerent compatriots. The war, in short, gave diplomacy a black eye. American and European writers alike shared little faith in the ability of traditional statesmen to put the world back together again in 1919, but even before the armistice they had started to construct a critique of diplomacy, and European diplomacy, needless to say, received the bulk of critics' animus.

Yet even for American writers the real villain was not diplomats merely residing on the Continent or in the British Isles, although coincidentally they were indeed to blame. The surer target of critics' disapproval had less to do with nationality than it did with occupation. What these writers were condemning was, in short, professional diplomacy and professional diplomats, or at least what professionalism in that occupation had come to mean. As one writer put it dourly: "Professional diplomats have reason to feel chagrined over the fact that the longer the war lasts the less are their arts prized."[1] Philosopher John Dewey blamed statesmen for their love of secrecy, saying such men were members of "a class so personally and professionally set apart that it moves in a high, inaccessible realm whose doings are no concern of the vulgar mass. It breathes contempt of publicity because it springs from contempt for the public."[2] Reform, then, was much in the air. And in "this general scrutiny the methods and machinery of Diplomacy cannot hope to escape."[3] Architects of the new diplomacy were fascinated with the idea of a league of nations, something akin to the Hague Conferences—a vehicle for discussion, consultation, and arbitration—and with the principle of publicity or "open diplomacy." The latter component was crucial. In fact, since reformers seemed to be hoping for more professional diplomacy in America and a more democratic diplomacy in Europe, the new diplomacy represented a balancing act—diplomacy that was both efficient and democratic—and only possible through mass communication.

The first half of that reform movement, American professionalism of diplomacy, was well under way. Succeeding earlier efforts to bring order to the Foreign Services, executive orders and congressional acts in 1905, 1906, and 1909 placed the diplomatic and consular services under civil service restrictions. That meant that all positions under the level of minister were generally filled by internal promotion or transfer, and contingent upon entrance examinations. American diplomacy made tremendous strides during the progressive era. In 1913, Joseph Grew, a young American embassy secretary stationed in Berlin, wrote a letter to the editor of his alma mater's newspaper, the *Harvard Crimson,* defending his profession's recent improvements: "It is unfortunately true that the positions of ambassador and minister are still regarded as excepted from these Civil Service principles, but it must be remembered that the great progress already made in the permanency of both the Diplomatic and Consular Services has been effected within the last few years, after over a century of the spoils system, and that perfection cannot be expected overnight."[4] During the nineteenth and early twentieth centuries, in fact, the spoils system sometimes extended to presidents' favorite writers or publishers, who received plum commissions to travel overseas as diplomats. They rarely maintained their journalistic duties, however; for most, it was a prestigious career move simply granted to individuals holding timely political positions.[5] Bureaucratic reforms, in addition to calls for education, training, and testable knowledge (international law, languages, and economics were the subjects usually cited), would supposedly make diplomacy more empirical, more expert. Wilson often told his press aide, Joseph Tumulty, that he desired a "scientific settlement" after the war.[6]

But that emphasis on expertise clashed with the second half of diplomatic reform, which centered on democratization. Here the main, if vaguely stated, target was European diplomacy (not that America's burgeoning corps of young statesmen would not benefit as well). Democratizing diplomacy for the progressive meant one thing above all else: publicity. And publicity did not necessarily mean propaganda, though both efforts might certainly overlap. The former signified verifiable information relatively undistorted by ulterior motives—a *public* diplomacy.[7] It was an article of faith among reformers that the reasons war had come in 1914 were that ordinary citizens were kept out of the political loop, that their opinion was not sufficiently respected and consulted before hostilities commenced, and that some kind of stronger connection between the public and the peacemakers needed to be made. Mass communication provided the link.

A seminal theoretician who advanced the cause of this new diplomacy was Arthur Bullard. Part of the inspiration behind the Committee on Public Information, Bullard was a restless critic who constantly emphasized the need for more government openness and robust publicity. In a handful of articles and a book published in 1917, *The Diplomacy of the Great War,* Bullard counterposed such historic conclaves as the 1878 Congress of Berlin with what he considered a more idealistic and progressive conference. "The Congress of Berlin," he wrote, "was the last important diplomatic conference which entirely ignored public opinion. It was the end of an epoch."[8] Bullard did not think that publicity was necessarily a simple matter for governments, in Europe, the United States, or anywhere else, and America, he believed, posed a unique set of challenges. "This is the crux of the problem—as yet unsolved— of how to develop a democratic diplomacy. The tradition of secrecy is bad. It breeds suspicion and encourages aggression. It is essentially aristocratic. But the real difficulty lies deeper. It is that the democracy tends to be self-centered, absorbed in domestic problems, indifferent to foreign affairs."[9]

Bullard labored to bring attention to the problem, to heighten understanding of both diplomatic challenges and democratic ideals. He was no patriotic patsy, maintaining that the "veil of secrecy which shields Downing Street and Wilhelmstrasse and the Quai D'Orsay is no denser that that which enshrouds our State Department."[10] But he nonetheless held great faith in the curative powers of publicity—it "will have the same salutary effect on diplomacy that we are finding it has on politics and business"[11]—and believed that eventually governments would pay more heed to what the people wanted with respect to foreign policy. Even Bismarck, he noted, had appreciated the increasing influence of public opinion. Its "force . . . which the Iron Chancellor recognized a generation ago, has grown immensely. All the governments of Europe, by various means and with various degrees of success spend considerable energy in 'preparing' it."[12] He also insisted that the end of the war would demonstrate the culmination of that influence.

While Bullard's contributions were critical, the individual most responsible for marketing the dichotomy between the old and the new diplomacy was none other than President Wilson. Wilson's offer to mediate between the belligerents before April 1917 naturally made him appear more peace loving than other nations' leaders. But Wilson had structural changes in mind, too, at least in the last year of the war. He had picked up on the idea of a worldwide association of nations, a league of nations. The league would be more than an international gentlemen's club. It would have a substantive constitution, a vital purpose, and it might forever change the face of foreign relations. Wilson's foreign policy ideals were not unpragmatic ambitions totally removed from reality, contrary to the claims of George Kennan, but "responsive and flexible."[13] Indeed, as Klaus Schwabe has argued, Germany would soon enough find out how much of a realist prepared to compromise Woodrow Wilson could be.[14] But in line with progressive thinking generally, the White House understood that the country "was not simply powerful . . . would not just 'muddle through' the twentieth century, so much as it should be possessed of a dynamic character that gave it purpose and direction in a world filled with deadly challenge."[15] The president and his supporters were determined to change diplomacy so that countries would not just be helpless bits of paper blown by the winds of war. A worldwide tribunal, publicized and documented treaties, open negotiations—these were the reforms by which Wilson and others believed they could bring a rational, orderly stability to foreign relations.[16] Democracy had to be extended across the globe and "invoked from above."[17] Wilson's diplomatic ideals were not, therefore, so much the quixotic idealism of a dreamer but the overly expressive enthusiasm of a pragmatic progressive publicist. In any case, the by-now sterile debate over whether Wilsonian diplomacy was idealistic or realistic misses a larger point: the extent to which it was focused on method, organization, and creativity. Wilsonian diplomacy was intended to be constructive.

Not surprisingly, Wilson's forays into foreign relations were marked by an orientation toward educative diplomacy. He spoke, for example, of wanting to "teach" the Filipinos self-government.[18] His attitude toward Latin America generally, as well as toward the "undemocratic" peoples of Europe, Germany included, received the brunt of his attention. During the war he promised to save the German people from their rulers by bringing them an end to autocracy. The progressive impulse toward reform imposed from above breathed through all of Wilson's foreign policy for both terms of his administration and reached its climax during America's involvement in the First World War.

On January 8, 1918, the president delivered an address to a joint session of Congress, outlining a dozen-odd principles that detailed America's war aims and a new vision of the postwar international order. These "Fourteen Points" were a package of diplomatic reforms and international adjustments that had been prepared by journalistic advisers to The Inquiry, most importantly Walter Lippmann. The principles included provisions for specific territorial adjustments, free trade and navigation, arms reductions, and a league of nations. But aside from the last principle, the proposed "association of nations," the two most publicized elements in Wilson's package were the first and fifth points, which dealt with open diplomacy and with colonial claims. Some writers even interpreted Wilson's speech as an inspiration for the new open diplomacy, because they were "negotiations . . . conducted in *public*."[19]

The first of Wilson's principles declared America's commitment to "open covenants of peace, openly arrived at, after which there shall be no private international understandings of any kind, but diplomacy shall proceed always frankly and in the public view." The idea behind the phrase "open covenants" came as a direct response to Russia's publication of the secret wartime treaties in November 1917 after Leon Trotsky discovered the documents in the Foreign Affairs Ministry. By these arrangements Britain would be granted lands in the Middle East; France would receive the same, along with European concessions like Alsace-Lorraine, Rhineland territory, and the Saar Valley; Italy would obtain the Trentino, the Dodecanese, and a slice of Dalmatian real estate—among other compensations. All three countries were to divvy up Germany's former colonies. And, finally, Rumania, Russia, Serbia, and Montenegro would each get a number of territorial rewards.

Wilson later said he knew nothing of these terms until he went to Paris, a claim many people challenged. "Up to November, 1917," one reporter remembered, "governments and diplomatists alone knew of [them]. Journalists knew something about them, but could not publish what they knew."[20] Whatever the truth regarding the president's assertion, clearly the speech he crafted in 1918 was meant to rebuke the diplomacy that produced such backstage dealmaking. He also meant to distance himself, and the United States, from the thunderous aspersions let loose by Trotsky the previous fall, when the Russian revolutionary exclaimed that "the methods of secret diplomacy are as international in character as the rapacity of imperialism itself."[21] Trotsky's words made effective propaganda, and Wilson knew it. So in renouncing imperialism, Wilson also had to renounce secret diplomacy, rhetoric far more easily expressed than fulfilled, as the president would eventually discover. Of course, Wilson was not altogether opposed to secret diplomatic initiatives. His authorization of the House-Grey Memorandum in 1916 stood as proof, but that document was written to persuade warring nations to stop fighting.[22] Besides, Wilson also made comparable peace-aims discussions in the open, too. In fact, the failure of the House-Grey Memorandum convinced him to "publicize" his views to get the warring nations to publicize theirs.[23] By then the president's diplomatic philosophy had been fully enveloped by the fashionable ideas bandied about in the press by Bullard and other intellectuals.

The rhetoric of open diplomacy became a full-fledged political fetish in the United States in 1918, a darling phrase in the press made all the more adorable because of its nice ring. It did not hurt, either, that rhetoric about open diplomacy also spawned a wave of condemnation for its theoretical nemesis, secret diplomacy. The old diplomacy was blamed for ignoring God and the people.[24] "The peace of exultation of the strong over the weak," one writer explained, "of exploitation, of revenge, of mere compromise, of secret diplomacy, of intrigue, of a subjection of small nations against their will, of greed and selfishness, or of any dicker with German war lords would be no peace at all."[25] Alliances between countries came under attack as the underlying cause of the Great War, because they were said to "belong to the realm of secret diplomacy and all the international abuses from Machiavelli to Metternich."[26] Journalists set up as their straw man the stereotype of "bourgeois oligarchies who have no thought in their heads but that of national self-aggrandizement."[27]

Despite its superficiality, many American publicists nonetheless became ardent champions of the idea, and not a few diplomats embraced it for its progressive, democratic qualities. More was expected of diplomats in the future. They would have to respond to their countrymen's demands: "The next few years will show whether our statesmanship can satisfy the spirit created by the war among the millions of men and women who have learned to ask of their common life that it should satisfy the spiritual needs of men and women."[28] The image of citizens eagerly reading about the honest compromises concluded in their behalf by conscientious negotiators (negotiators kept conscientious by public accountability) was evidently too appealing to dismiss. America's propaganda visionary described this alluring scenario in 1917:

> No diplomat, returning from this congress, will ride up the avenue of his capital, waving his silk hat to an . . . admiring crowd, who shout approbation to such a vague and bombastic phrase as "peace with honor." The coachman will turn about in his seat and say: "Your Excellency, why did you annex all that African swamp?" a newsboy from the sidewalk will cry: "why did you abandon that railroad concession in China?" the papers of the opposition, and hostile members of Parliament will ask similar and more searching questions. The diplomat who cannot answer them will be in a bad way.[29]

Henceforth, foreign policy would be kept properly harnessed to domestic policy; people in and out of government might exert influence on its formation.[30] But they could only do so with information.

Like all the reformers of that age, journalists and political leaders alike believed in the mystical power of mass communication, in publicity, to answer the challenges of modern democracy. Shortly after America's declaration of war on Germany, Wilson's adviser Colonel Edward House proposed that the *New York World* and the *Berliner Tageblatt* conduct a discussion of war aims as a way to short-circuit both countries' generals and diplomats—statecraft via international forum.[31] Hyperbole aside, there was something to the notion. The laying of transoceanic cables in the 1860s, 1870s, and 1880s had stimulated both journalists' attention to other countries and a drastic improvement in diplomatic services. Indeed, a "new journalism helped prepare the way for the New [diplomatic] Paradigm."[32] The two spheres were implicitly connected in the new diplomacy.

At any rate, well before the Paris Peace Conference, publicists were hailing democratic diplomacy as essential and achievable, even though most stopped short of describing the particular means for bringing it about. Yet clearly some instrument "enabling the minds of the peoples to meet" would have to be put into place.[33] By the end of the war, journalists had convinced themselves that they were the integral and perhaps most important part of that mechanism of democratic peacemaking. Whether their contribution would mean prominent roles as negotiators or entail something more akin to advisory editing,[34] members of the American press took the idea of new diplomacy to heart.

CONCLUSION TO PART ONE

In 1917 the American government undertook a war that involved a deeper commitment and more of the nation's resources than any other war in its history. To organize, train, and sustain such a military machine also required the most formidable level of public support ever needed, and garnering that support meant direct involvement in publicity work. With the First World War the Wilson administration became the premier publisher, publicist, and public relations agent in the world, outdoing not only its own limited past experience with such activity but even that of other nations. In the Great War the distinction between government and mass media became blurred, too. "Dollar-a-year" businessmen who worked cheaply for the War Industries Board; journalists and novelists who wrote copy for the CPI; scholars who volunteered their research skills on behalf of The Inquiry; statesmen who publicized their nations' political aims—this blending of economic and occupational sectors was a hallmark of total war, the distinguishing stamp of the twentieth century's world wars.

But these examples also point to something subtler and, in many ways, more astonishing: the pervasive use of mass communication by governments involved in those wars. The active management of publicity was essential to mobilize nations, indispensable for modulating public morale and involvement, influential even in affecting the course and manner of diplomacy. In fact, it is not too much to say that the so-called new diplomacy was impossible without publicity, without, therefore, the press. This ideal was the final legacy of the progressive movement: a widespread crusade to reform statesmanship and thus diminish the possibility of future war. This was a crusade whose most important component was perhaps its evangelism, its zealous dissemination of the "good news."

The new or progressive diplomacy, like the new warfare of the twentieth century, required a fervent publicity; governments would presumably make available for public consumption a continuous supply of information and ideals. It would, in theory, be both more democratic and more orderly, the perfect remedy for most people in the progressive era.[35] But the new diplomacy promised information to journalists in a context over which government now had more influence and control. While the Committee on Public Information thus beckoned as a promising ally in the quest for enlightened statesmanship, it also represented a competitive threat to the press, and along with heavy-handed censorship threatened to undermine the government's liberal credentials.

Information management, nonetheless, was a crucial gauge with which to evaluate the president's political effectiveness, for although not everyone was comfortable with the ways in which the Wilson administration carried out its communication responsibilities, virtually no one questioned that it did have a duty to communicate with its citizens. And *in* communication many people put their faith that a number of seemingly insoluble challenges could be overcome: the welfare of diplomacy amid global warfare, the fate of democracy in a very undemocratic world, the future of traditional institutions in a society growing larger and more complicated all the time. Publicity was often perceived as an omnipotent political solution, one that journalists were as quick to appreciate as were politicians.

PART TWO

PROFESSIONALIZING JOURNALISM

The Democratic Control of Public Opinion

↬ 4 ↬

THE PROFESSIONALIZATION OF JOURNALISM

Excitement about the new diplomacy spread quickly among journalists, who could not fail to notice the self-serving benefits in a cult of publicity. But writers and reporters also sincerely believed in the democratic value of such a movement. At the heart of diplomatic reform, in other words, lay an acknowledged tribute to public opinion and public accountability. Both concepts were experiencing vital re-evaluations in the twentieth century, as Americans struggled to balance their faith in republican virtues with their anxiety over disruptive socioeconomic changes. Professionalization was one way to balance these competing impulses, a solution that centered on the promise of access (under certain conditions) to privileged knowledge—or, in other words, on the democratic control of public opinion. Through professionalism, progressives could combine "the authority of facts" with the idea of public accountability. In the United States, professionalization made its most conspicuous mark in the years 1890–1920. The professionalization of journalism, to a large extent, also dovetailed with progressivism, and most scholars so characterize that era.[1]

But that connection involves more than a mere coincidence. The impulse to professionalize among members of the press was not only sudden and intense at the turn of the century but, indeed, never more so than with the resurgence of progressivism during the First World War. Journalists fully absorbed the spirit of professionalism in those years because that spirit helped them to resolve the fundamental progressive tensions between democracy and expertise, between community and authority. Like the progressive era itself, the professional movement afoot in journalism was both democratic and undemocratic. Professionalism allowed reporters to market their knowledge and dissemination of the "facts" as a civic service. The press's greatest impetus toward professionalization therefore depended on the progressive obsession with expertise and its embrace of publicity.

Since it is often said that one of journalism's rewards is its potential impact, that the journalist "helps shape his own times," it should not surprise us that writers of the turbulent twentieth century came to think differently about their work.[2] Professionalism in America was strongly stimulated in the mid-1910s by intellectuals' ambivalence toward the masses and public opinion in an age when civilization itself seemed threatened. Journalists' professional ethos drew strength rapidly in a service-oriented, merit-based, expertise-hyped culture geared toward winning a world war. More significantly, talk of the new diplomacy promised journalists a key new political role, one which was potentially greater than even that of diplomats. Finally, the particular way the press interacted with the president was itself a professional contest over who should speak for public opinion. At a time when the federal government's communication operations suddenly dwarfed even the largest news organizations, that tension was pronounced. Yet the press's occasional resentment against Washington often receded amid waves of patriotism and the sense of professional pride reinvigorated by a new presidency and calls for a new diplomacy.

Several factors contributed to the development of journalists' professional ethos in the years leading up to World War I: technological innovations; the experience of muckraking; progressive forays into the science of democracy; the general cult of expertise that helped to define so much of that era, especially during the war itself; and, finally, the new presidency of the early 1900s. These elements did not work in domino fashion to bring about a linear and climactic result, however. Nor were all of them necessary to produce full-fledged professionalization. Some, like the advent of a stronger executive, did not precede the movement. But each furthered the cause, and each came rife with tensions, ambivalence, and confusion over what to do about the masses.

TECHNOLOGY

In an occupation without an esoteric body of knowledge, where college education was not an obvious requirement, and in which even the apprentice system was, for writers, becoming largely unnecessary, journalism bore few of the telltale signs of esteemed, high-skill trades. What it could offer, though, were social significance, power, influence, and even celebrity. And all these were impossible without mass media, without the technological innovations that could bring publicity to the masses.

So much has already been written about the dramatic mechanical improvements in the news business at the turn of the century, we need not describe them here, except to say that in terms of its appearance, rapid production, and availability to huge numbers of people, the modern American newspaper was born during the 1890s.[3] Newspapers and magazines by the twentieth century would be able to satisfy an enormous readership and thus potentially influence a substantial part of the public. It was new technology, then, that most vividly demonstrated the power of the press to move millions, new technology that alerted American progressives to journalism's tremendous potential.[4] According to historian Andrew Abbott, "a characteristic story in the system of professions begins with a disturbance—a new technology requiring professional judgment or a new technique for old professional work. Those disturbances . . . lead to a variety of readjustments."[5] A "disturbance" journalism certainly had in the bona fide emergence of mass media and their influence over national politics. After the 1890s, Americans seldom doubted the press's power.

What the wonders of technology also did was to temper harsher assessments of journalism by suggesting glamorous ways it might be used constructively. During the progressive era both journalists and their critics sounded more optimistic—both about the public and about America. While early on they had implied that society's institutions might require fundamental change, the availability of technology seemed to offer hope of at least alleviating those institutions' more unpleasant symptoms through gradual remedy. "For progressive reformers and press defenders alike," Douglas Birkhead says, "the most compelling spectacle of the press going into the twentieth century was not its economic configuration but the marvel of its mechanics."[6] Its assets promised an astonishing new energy and effectiveness with which to institute reforms. Hence, the "tantalizing solution to the problem of industrialization was perhaps a deeper commitment to the machine."[7] Technological innovations in the news business simply imbued members of the press with a nameless sense of power and an elusive sense of responsibility. These conditions thus made professionalism a plausible and attractive means both to improve the occupation and to benefit society.

MUCKRAKING AND REFORM

Americans gasped at the revelations of malfeasance, greed, and corruption that such writers as Ray Stannard Baker, Ida Tarbell, Upton Sinclair, and Lincoln Steffens told at the turn of the century. "Muckraking" was the term used to describe this journalistic literature of insider exposé, and for several years the genre completely dominated magazine writing and powerfully influenced the urban news business in general. That dominance may have come at a price, however. As Thomas Leonard insists, the journalism of progressivism "undermined the ritual of political participation" because progressivism was essentially elitist. Muckrakers "scoffed at politics as they labored to make politics better," so their tough criticism of crooked political bosses and ruthless financiers went hand in hand with a condescending cynicism toward the gullible masses the bosses and financiers so easily duped and exploited, a snobbery anyone would have trouble disguising.[8] By contrast, other scholars contend that muckrakers' emphasis on investigation, inquiry, and research helped inject a dose of democracy, or at least meritocracy, into American literature by blasting Victorian grandiloquence with realism and raw data.[9]

The two views, it can be argued, are not quite mutually exclusive. Muckrakers did want to awaken the public, did want to improve politics, did want to encourage democratic responsibility. And a commitment to professionalism and to expertise was one way to negotiate the compromise. It was natural, then, that muckrakers eventually trained their sights on journalism itself as an industry in need of reform. Muckraking magazines had already begun motivating traditional newspapers to re-examine the way they covered news and related to sources. Some papers "escalated their rhetoric, even as many magazines were cooling theirs."[10] The press did not escape America's reforming rhetoric. In 1909 Edwin Ross described how most dailies were apt to be "mouthpieces of the financial powers," and two years later Will Irwin published a long series entitled "The American Newspaper" in *Collier's* that also detailed the array of monetary temptations to which newspaper reporters and editors were routinely subjected.[11]

Their timing seemed appropriate, considering the fact that William Randolph Hearst had already gained fame as the publisher who in 1898 "created" a war in order to boost his newspapers' circulation. His precise part in promoting what came to be known as the Spanish-American War has been the subject of much debate, but that role was, in any case, viewed with ever-harsher contempt. War sold papers, everyone knew, and Hearst wanted to make money, so the third part of the syllogism was obvious. Even the sociologist Charles Cooley, at first ecstatic about the colorful reporting of the war with Spain, came to loathe the papers he eventually felt were instilling an unthinking jingoism in Americans. To many observers, that disturbing perception seemed to cry out for redress. At the same time, though, it meant journalism was worth thinking about. "It is, in a way, a form of flattery," one writer concluded, that "modern journalism . . . should be put on its defense—added to the fascinating list of 'problems.' This is a tribute to its importance."[12] Journalism's political power inspired hope but also invited reform. And in the context of changing views about the public and public opinion, such talk took on a keen urgency.

PUBLIC OPINION, EXPERTISE, AND
THE SCIENCE OF DEMOCRACY

As the growing and dramatic presence of printing technologies transformed the mechanism of journalistic practice, it fueled a faith in science and progress. The excitement about technology also inspired enthusiasm for putting science to work in the cause of democracy. As one magazine article proudly teased, "Card-Indexing Your Politics: The Great Political Campaigns of Today Are Scientifically Planned."[13] Somewhere in science seemed to loom the solution to the challenges of democracy, and something about journalism beckoned as a critical key in that solution. Three political scientists, John Dewey, Charles Cooley, and Walter Lippmann, can be considered the most important representatives of that second great wave of American political philosophers, active at the turn of the century, who wrestled with those challenges. They, along with many lesser lights, struggled to reconcile their political beliefs with their newfound progressive appreciation of scientific efficiency and corporate-style organization. How was democracy supposed to work in such a large, unwieldy nation of heterogeneous cultures? How was the public supposed to exercise its civic duties when the scope and complexity of the day's choices seemed ever vaster? These thinkers recognized that public opinion ought to reign supreme in a society that called itself democratic (representative government was said not to exist in Central Europe).[14] The problem was whether public opinion was sufficiently well-informed. The tensions caused by the subject of public opinion formed most of what has been called the "epistemological crisis" of the progressive era.[15]

The best solution appeared to be the proper training of the public, the education of public opinion, the "democratization of knowledge."[16] In the so-called science of democracy, therefore, expertly directed mass communication was essential. "The professional classes," Michael Schudson has written, "took public opinion to be irrational and therefore something to study, direct, manipulate, and control. The professions developed a proprietary attitude toward 'reason' and a paternalistic attitude toward the public."[17] As one writer urged during the war, "American public opinion needs training, education, cultivation."[18] Consequently, much was expected of journalists. Theirs would be a role as important as the schools' and churches' had been traditionally. The press had, in fact, one writer declared, now superseded the State's power—"indeed, the governing power of the State is the creature of that mightier power of publicity."[19] In the progressive era journalists would be expected to perform a crucial civic function: providing the people with the information they needed to make their most important political decisions. The American press often went one step further, believing its function was purely pedagogical, too—disseminating knowledge for the sake of knowledge. Magazines like *The Independent* and *The Outlook* included guidelines on how to use each issue, complete with a "lesson plan," or, like *The World's Work,* offered outline studies of the current history they discussed.[20] Teachers used copies of *Red Cross Magazine* to combine lessons in patriotism with reading practice.[21] Newspapers, too, issued Sunday supplements brimming with background on important stories, primers on international politics and history, mini-biographies of important figures in the news, key documents currently under discussion. The *New York Times* won a Pulitzer Prize in 1918 precisely because of such reports.[22]

Before the 1890s other institutions had apparently sufficed to educate; now, many thought, it was up to the press. So cleaning up American journalism seemed a necessary step for preparing reporters and editors for their newfound function. Professionalization therefore stressed responsibility. Responsibility was a virtue grounded in paternalism, which nonetheless paid tribute to the power of the people. And, indeed, without respect for that power, the movement for professionalization would have been far more seriously hampered than it was. Professionalization, in short, epitomized the paradox of a society that valued public opinion more than anything else but also distrusted it more than anything else. A representative article from that time, for example, suggested that public opinion settle strikes—a democratic notion, certainly—but only after an investigatory tribunal had first looked into the controversy and established the "facts."[23]

"The future of public opinion," wrote one political philosopher, "is the future of civilization."[24] Public relations counsel Edward Bernays explained it more concretely: "Perhaps the most significant social, political and industrial fact about the present century is the increased attention which is paid to public opinion," especially by those who used not to care, he wrote. "The public to-day demands information and expects also to be accepted as judge and jury in matters that have a wide public import."[25]

Bernays was not alone. In the two decades preceding the First World War a remarkable number of writers hailed the public or public opinion as the undisputed king of the jungle. All that remained was to find qualified lion tamers. And amid this growing circus of publicity—including an incredible profusion of public relations specialists such as Bernays—hopeful professionalizers clutched science as a way to counter the conspiratorial influence of press agents.[26] Without the "expert" guidance of journalists, it was thought, ordinary people would be helpless to resist self-interested publicists.

The experience of the war seemed to validate journalists' assessment of the public's dependence on them. A sense of modern community only seemed possible through the press. "When the United States entered the ranks of the belligerents," *Editor & Publisher* announced, "the demand for daily newspapers became well-nigh universal among our people, extending even to the remote country homes where, in times past, a weekly newspaper filled every need."[27] Reporters and editors filled a need deeply felt by Americans to know and somehow participate in the war overseas. By virtue of what they *did,* journalists were qualified to report and comment, not so much because of any specific training they might have had. Journalists' credentials primarily stemmed from firsthand experience: they interviewed the nations' leaders, traveled to or near the battlefields, observed the troops. Ironically, their main qualification as communicators might have been simply their superior access to transportation. But it was more than that, too. The expanded executive branch—the imperial presidency—also increased the importance of the correspondents who covered the man in the White House. In Stephen Ponder's words, "The emergence of the president as the First Source for the news media also encouraged the professionalization of political journalism."[28] The possibility of a new diplomacy dependent upon journalists' cooperation promised additional uplift. For the time being, journalists often stressed their powers of observation, their understanding of the way things usually worked, their interviewing experience, their tireless productivity as writers. They had not gotten where they were by accident or luck, they said, but by diligent work, by ethical standards, and by pride in excellence. They constantly emphasized their specialized knowledge and skills. "Everybody wants the specialist, the man who does one thing superbly," an editorial writer declared near the end of the war.[29]

The rise of the expert was one of the key social changes under way between 1890 and 1920, an occurrence that coincided with the apotheosis of mass communication in America. The conjunction of both stimulated the drive for the professionalization of journalism, which in turn underscored the gap between high expectations and a less-lofty reality. If, as Dewey, Cooley, and Lippmann maintained, the transmission of information was the single most important function in a democracy, then it made sense that those doing the transmitting should be supremely well prepared. Education, in fact, was a recurring theme in much of the writing of the early twentieth century. Progressives' prose was utterly suffused with the significance of pedagogy. Most tracts dealt with how to educate the public, or public opinion, or new citizens, or all citizens, or the lower classes, or "the masses." Instruction was the thing. Much of this quest for edification was grating and paternalistic. "At its worst," Christopher Lasch notes, "the idea that education was the answer to all social problems degenerated into the jargon of the efficiency experts."[30] But that jargon was precisely the mechanism progressive elites used to distance themselves from the common people they had vowed to help. Most mass communication theorists at the turn of the century took the view that they and a select group of specialists had knowledge to transmit to the public, not that the public might have knowledge to share with them.

At the heart of this apotheosis of the expert was, of course, the glorification of science. Men and women needed something to believe in at this time when so many old assumptions had already been either shattered or shaken. Quantification and the scientific method held out hope for people that there were indeed certitudes about them. "We do believe in the divine right of democracy," one magazine writer said, "and in the infallibility of science."[31] But fear abounded, too. Many middle-class Americans brooded over the feeling that society, commerce, and certain trades in particular had grown too complicated for the usual oversight. Swelling ranks within occupations added to the anxiety that competition would spiral out of control and thus undermine prestige, since society could hardly value lawyers, say, if they became as numerous as ditch diggers.[32] The prospect of coping with throngs of rivals who were allegedly incompetent but above all foreign-born or possibly female prompted urgent calls for professional reform. "The untrained amateur may mean well, but he knows not how to do well. Why should he?" Walter Lippmann asked, when the amateur had no "qualifications."[33] According to scholar Nathan O. Hatch, the ideal of expertise was a means to restore order: "Progressive reformers viewed the rise of bureaucratic organizations staffed by trained experts and employing scientific objectivity as the only way to sustain and renew the best of American democracy."[34] This was a time when the American Red Cross could be referred to as "the Army's expert in the strategy of compassion,"[35] when journalists heralded sundry "new professions,"[36] when a newspaper like the *New York Tribune* featured regular columns on "Professional Housekeeping."[37] Talk of expertise by journalists was a way of claiming authority democratically. And faith in the heralded objectivities of science was "the dominant ideal," Michael Schudson has written, "that legitimates knowledge and authority in all contemporary professions."[38]

By 1900 objectivity was the ruling ethic in American journalistic practice,[39] and that was an important ingredient in journalists' quest for professionalization. For without it, they had little to stand on except their social and political influence, which was far from guaranteed for many young reporters. Objectivity clothed journalists' correspondence in the quasi-scientific language of discovery, impartial observation, and careful data-gathering. Political sympathies hardly disappeared, and at critical times such subjectivity might gravitate toward the old partisan networks.[40] But overt political bias was considered disreputable. More importantly, objectivity was a way for journalists to distinguish themselves from the growing number of press agents and lobbyists whose partisan motives were said to be narrow and selfish—and also a way to reduce the competition for jobs that the presence of those outsiders ultimately implied. Objectivity thus gave weight to journalists' claims of expertise but also indicated their sense of political independence and public responsibility. Both brought them close to a systematic reorganization of their life's work.

PROFESSIONALIZING JOURNALISM

Enthusiasm over advances in printing technology, experience with muckraking, the heady progressive theories surrounding the promise of the press and the management of publicity, and, finally, the glorification of the expert—all these factors stimulated demand for journalists to join the ranks of other self-reforming white-collar workers in the United States and to professionalize.[41] Criticism of journalism continued, but journalists themselves had taken over the impulse for reform and for social responsibility and directed that pressure inward. A rise in the number of journalists, particularly women, also fueled the reform movement.[42] The result was the creation of journalism schools, codes of ethics, even calls for licensing and legislation. Perhaps more important than all these things was the simple rhetoric, the publicized ideology, of professionalism and its value—"a less threatening and more credible means of press accountability for journalistic insiders than either the endowed press or legal restraints."[43] Professionalization, we are coming to realize, seldom comes all at once, but certain eras are capable of ushering in sudden change: "Many professions do have periods in which they actively move toward a given cultural model of 'how to be a profession.'"[44] The progressive era appears to be one such period, probably the most important one, and maybe the last, for journalism.

In the first decade of the twentieth century a number of universities organized two- and four-year journalism curricula. Just as professional social scientists in such disciplines as economics were beginning to "put down roots" in a more inclusive and middle-class academia, so, too, were journalism educators and historians.[45] In 1908 Walter Williams founded the nation's first journalism school in Missouri, and a slew of other midwestern and northern land-grant institutions soon followed suit. Columbia University opened its Pulitzer School in 1912, Northwestern the Medill School in 1921.[46] Clearly, journalism was perceived to be a re-emerging occupation of greater importance, one that demanded more and better-trained practitioners: At a time when England's press tycoon Lord Northcliffe was hailed as "the most powerful man who has lived since Oliver Cromwell's day," educating journalists seemed like a good idea.[47] Where college graduates in the newsroom were once seen exclusively as intruding oddballs, in the twentieth century they were quickly becoming the norm. Even in the 1870s and 1880s, for example, they had made their presence felt. Whitelaw Reid, editor of the *New York Tribune,* recalled at the time that "there is scarcely a writer who is not a college graduate; while, indeed, two thirds or more of its reporters are, to use the vague phrase, men of liberal education."[48] Newspaper and magazine editors had already begun recruiting more college graduates by 1910, but the presence of firmly established schools of journalism now brought a self-serving reason as well: university training for aspiring reporters paid faculty salaries. Though the old apprentice system never did die out altogether, it quickly came to seem antiquated and even somewhat irrelevant in the early 1900s, considering the corporatization of metropolitan newsrooms, with their innumerable departments and intricate divisions of labor. The distinction between the literary and mechanical realms within a single organization grew sharper, removing the original reason for apprenticeships and making them far less necessary for anyone but typesetters.[49] The new journalistic experts did not need experience running presses; they needed a broad range of knowledge, writing ability, and, better yet, well-placed contacts in business and government.

If specialized education was still not essential in the 1900s, it was more easily accepted because it had become much more common.[50] By the end of the war a writer could remark that the "college man is, as a rule, good reportorial timber."[51] Like other callings seeking to reform themselves, journalism recognized education as a way to broaden a future practitioner's experience, which some writers insisted was the critical distinction between a profession and a mere trade.[52] They also understood professionalization as a way to increase their own financial compensation. Journalists were already beginning to see a rise in reporter income by the twentieth century. Established writers made pay that was comparable to the rewards of other professions, and the "salaries on the metropolitan papers are liberal, and are becoming greater each year as the business of news-purveying becomes better systematized and more profitable."[53] Yet, despite rising incomes, increased opportunities, and more frequent by-lines, Christopher Wilson says, journalism's reputation was hardly more impressive in 1900 than in 1850.[54] Changes in the press's social context, however, raised expectations in the twentieth century.

The founding of Sigma Delta Chi, a professional society established at DePauw University in 1909, even bore one of the important trappings of upper-middle class education: the Greek-lettered fraternity. But Sigma Delta Chi's mission went beyond mere social recreation; in the distribution of prizes for meritorious practice it and other societies conferred recognition and approval of newspapers practicing what they considered to be exemplary journalism. Clubs like Sigma Delta Chi, Kappa Tau Alpha, and Theta Sigma Phi rewarded individuals and organizations for conforming to specified standards. More and more in the early 1900s, journalists were demonstrating a marked inclination toward social organization and informal association. The Gridiron Club and the Standing Committee of Correspondents were founded in the 1870s and 1880s but became national institutions only after the Cleveland administration.[55] The following decade brought an explosion of press clubs, and in 1908 a national version was founded in Washington.[56]

By the turn of the century, the International Congress of the Press had been established and was soon drawing members of the press from two dozen countries.[57] The growing sense of solidarity was sufficient to elicit international calls for a worldwide summit, and one was planned for the first anniversary of the armistice, November 11, 1919, in Sydney, Australia. Walter Williams selected the date for the conclave.[58] American correspondents also bonded with their British counterparts immediately after the war, in Paris, an alliance that created both formal and informal professional ties between the two groups.[59]

The other significant professional area of concern was the subject of licensing and legislation for journalists. There had been calls for such action in the 1890s, when the excesses of the yellow press stirred much righteous indignation, but the first real concerted flurry of agitation occurred in the 1910s. Then, many working journalists warmed to the idea itself but not the practical or immediate implementation. In the fall of 1915, after Talcott Williams of the Columbia University School of Journalism had strongly endorsed licensing exams, the trade magazine *Editor & Publisher* gently recommended otherwise. Testing was fine and certainly appropriate in a journalism school class, the writer pointed out. "The young man who has taken a course in journalism under capable and experienced teachers, such as Dr. Williams and many others, stands a much better chance for making good in a newspaper office than one who has not had this preliminary training." But not everyone was so fortunate. "It should not be forgotten . . . that there are many young men who have in them the material for the making of successful journalists who could not pass an academic test for a newspaper license. Should these be shut out of the profession?" The writer of the article then proceeded to explain further that newspapers would fight any bill that involved such "interference," that threatened to violate "the spirit of independence that has hitherto characterized the American press."[60]

A Connecticut congressman proposed licensing journalists in that state in 1917, a step that would have involved a test, six months of experience, and a $10 licensing fee. A *Chicago Herald* writer had great fun toying with possible test questions:

> Write an editorial for a Republican paper congratulating Wilson on settling the European War.

Compose a head-line for the front page without use of any of the following words: "Graft," "Probe," "Raid," "Fleet," "Peace," "Lloyd George," "Mike the Pike," "Landis," "Gold Coast," or "Murder."

How many high-balls does it take to turn a prominent clubman into a well-known figure in the city's night-life?

. . . How much must a father leave before his daughter may be called an heiress, and how long after forty-two may she still be young and beautiful?

When is the last analysis in hand?

Write a sentence with the words "It is alleged" in such a manner that the reader will have no doubt the allegation is true.

. . . How long after a woman is arrested for shoplifting does she become a former actress?[61]

Clearly, many journalists still entertained doubts about licensing.

Other steps were less controversial. The press sought and secured certain trade restrictions. The Washington corps that covered Congress banned press agents from the gallery in late 1919—"at last," commented *Editor & Publisher*.[62] Journalists also fought to win legal respect for the work they did. The Associated Press sued the International News Service for stealing its material, a suit that in December 1918 went all the way to the Supreme Court, where it was decided that news was an important commodity deserving the same protections as other business property.[63] There were also calls for newspaper foundations, for endowed papers along the lines of Dewey's "Thought News," though perhaps less intellectually ambitious. Victor S. Yarros pushed this idea during the war because he said that reform would not otherwise come. The "evils and vices of contemporary commercial journalism," as he put it, demanded that Americans give the experiment a chance.[64] Finally, other suggestions for professional change included "making deliberate falsification a misdemeanor, reserving columns for a public defender, compelling journals to answer questions put to them by competent and duly qualified investigators, and publishing official newspapers."[65]

THE PROGRESSIVE PRESIDENCY

This, then, was the status of American journalism when Woodrow Wilson was elected president, an atmosphere characterized both by internal tensions and high expectations. In the first two decades of the twentieth century American journalists were enjoying more opportunities and greater compensation than they had ever before experienced. They were also witnessing real growth in social stature, growth made all the greater in the years following 1917, because suddenly what they did for a living dramatically affected the hearts and minds of people all over the nation. The ethos of professionalization was not halted during the war, as some scholars have suggested.[66] Indeed, that spirit positively blossomed as journalists covering the war in Europe or the home front saw the immediate value of their work to readers with loved ones in uniform, as they reflected on gradually awakening First Amendment concerns, and as they came into contact with correspondents from across the United States and around the globe. This burgeoning solidarity may not have been instantly translated into specific changes in training or education, but it enhanced journalists' social status in an unprecedented way that was necessary if not sufficient for those occupational changes to take place.

Part of that rising stature was surely the result of the expansive new American presidency of the twentieth century. Before the progressive presidents, there were plenty of famous editors but not many famous reporters, unless they were lucky enough and talented enough to distinguish themselves as war correspondents. The reporters assigned to Washington generally focused on Capitol Hill, because that is where most of the news originated. Yet the average correspondent was so tied in with and dependent upon particular congressmen, he oftentimes advanced as much by the secrets he kept as the scoops he scored. But a keeper of secrets was less likely to make a name for himself, and without a promising reputation it was hard to make much of a full-time living in journalism.

The presidencies of McKinley, Roosevelt, and Wilson offered the Washington correspondent a real chance for success because these activist executives made front-page news anytime they chose. They also kindled in members of the press a sense that what they did was of vital national significance, and something which carried substantial civic and political responsibility. The first twentieth-century presidents, except Taft, reached out to journalists, curried favor with them, accommodated them, and verified their importance. Wilson told the correspondents gathered to hear him for his second press conference as much in 1913, inviting them into a "partnership" with him to keep the country informed of what he was thinking and the president informed of what the country was thinking.[67]

The businesslike regularity of these early conferences underscored in journalists' minds that they were key players in the game of politics. As Stephen Ponder has concluded, "The opportunity to meet with the President regularly and to hear his pronouncements not only gave the correspondents something to write about, it raised their stature professionally."[68] Wilson's frustration with occasional indiscretions only made them redouble their efforts to continue playing. When one correspondent used the president's words without permission following a press conference, Wilson threatened to end the weekly practice unless journalists policed themselves. This they did, and the result was the White House Correspondents Association, which forbade unauthorized quotation of the president and insisted upon accreditation. Steps like these took journalists further along the path toward professionalization.

World war and its immediate aftermath redirected but nonetheless sustained interest in professionalism if not actual reform. A progressive president's advocacy of a progressive diplomacy—the new diplomacy of openness and public accountability—broadened journalists' vision beyond America's borders. Oswald Garrison Villard made probably the most impassioned case for change: "A free press after the war is as badly needed as freedom of the seas and freedom from conscienceless Kaisers and autocrats." Otherwise, the people would revolt when war with Germany ended because dissatisfaction with the nation's journalists was intense, Villard said. "When that day [of peace] comes here, the deep smouldering distrust of our press will make itself felt. Our Fourth Estate is to have its day of overhauling."[69] The country could not tolerate "untrained accidental witnesses" any longer. The proliferation of propaganda and the suspicion that some correspondents (particularly foreign ones) might really be press agents in disguise made professionalism seem a sound idea. In the midst of diplomatic reform, too, "expert organized reporters" would be needed.[70] American leaders wanted much more from journalists, and journalists expected more and often better, too. This anticipation sharpened acutely during the war, with fears of "propagandists," "publicity men," and writers for hire on the rise, and as a consummate professional man in the White House began talking about open diplomacy.

≈ 5 ≈
WOODROW WILSON
AND THE PRESS

No President has ever had a good press from the point of view of the President.
His privacy is invaded, his word is openly doubted and his motives habitually
suspected. No pigeon ever had a good hunter.

Saturday Evening Post, January 9, 1932

At this height of the movement for professionalization in journalism,
a select group of professional hopefuls and a pedigreed former college professor embarked on an often difficult working relationship.
Wilson's attitude toward public information was ambivalent, and his relationship with the press was a complicated one. Despite his approval of the
harshest laws restricting the First Amendment since the Alien and Sedition
Acts of 1798, he was no tyrant. Yet despite his espousal of ringing phrases
like "open covenants, openly arrived at," "open diplomacy," and "making the
world safe for democracy," he had hardly proved himself a champion of liberality. America's twenty-eighth president probably possessed the most complex
personality of the century, perhaps in the whole history of the presidency. His
relationship to journalism and publicity was accordingly marked by ironic
twists and enigmatic contradictions. It was made all the more difficult during
the war, when the administration and the press competed as authorities on
the subject of public opinion.

WILSON AND THE PRESS GO TO WAR

Wilson had always envisioned a strong presidency, but the path to war inevitably magnified the power of the office he held. While war with Germany
added immeasurable responsibilities and raised the stakes for failing, Wilson
knew, too, that the nation's crisis imbued him with an unusual prestige—

commander-in-chief—a stature which naturally discourages public complaints and confrontations. There was criticism of Wilson through 1917 and 1918, to be sure, muted complaints, for example, that he had not specified America's war aims.[1] And minor crises arose in the omission of General Leonard Wood from assignment overseas,[2] the refusal to grant Theodore Roosevelt a commission and a force of volunteers, the occasional perception that the administration was not deploying American troops as efficiently as possible,[3] or Wilson's estrangement from Congress.[4] Despite the presence of censorship, politics was never adjourned during the war.[5]

Yet the White House managed to avoid the brunt of many attacks—partly because of censorship, partly because of the oceanic deluge of positive information generated by the administration's publicity machine, the Committee on Public Information, but mainly because of the patriotic upswelling the president inherited when war began (an atmosphere that inhibited criticism).[6] "Probably most newspaper owners and editors honestly believed in the righteousness of the American and Allied cause, a belief partly generated by their own and the Government's propaganda."[7] It was not so much by way of calculated responses and detailed defenses, then, but by going on the offensive that the White House managed its public relations during the war. The Committee saturated America's cultural climate with positive data about the country, the war effort, and, by extension, the administration itself. Finally, the use of censorship, and the tendency toward self-censorship that ensued from fear of government reprisal, also kept murmurs of dissent quiet or under wraps.

On the whole, then, Wilson fared well in the press during two years of war. As one magazine writer summarized it, "No President has ever had more power or been less subjected to criticism, either by his own party or the opposition, than President Wilson,"[8] an exaggeration, perhaps, but not a totally implausible claim. Based on a survey of magazines and newspapers during 1918, it is safe to conclude that the president generally received favorable coverage. That is not to say that he had no critics or that journalists treated him reverently. Wilson had his enemies, notably the Hearst papers and Republican institutions like the *Chicago Tribune*.[9] And some periodicals were certainly less forgiving, patient, or sympathetic than others, but many of these expressed anger toward the president indirectly by assailing his advisers, War Secretary Newton Baker in particular.[10]

And even traditionally partisan critics changed their tone slightly once war began, many, in fact, warming gradually to their nation's wartime administration and their commander-in-chief personally. By the spring of 1918 *Leslie's* could finally applaud the president for speaking "as a real war leader."[11] Wilson was congratulated for putting down the pen and taking up the sword.[12] An editorial in *Collier's,* at about the same time, acknowledged that "[h]aving differed with the Administration on matters of policy, Collier's is only too pleased to report that at last the departments of the Government are coordinating, authority is centralizing, and officials of the Government, paid and unpaid, are working with tireless energy.."[13] Some six months later, the magazine further conceded the president his due: "We are dealing now with a different Wilson from the philanthropist and philosopher of two years ago. And it would be a poor sort of American who would deny him grateful praise for the whole-hearted energy and the stern sense of purpose with which he has thrown himself into the war."[14] The writer noted Wilson's "intellectual" leadership internationally and praised him specifically for his democratic rhetoric, which seemed at that time to be undermining the institutions of German autocracy, the equivalent of "twelve army corps and a regiment of angels."[15] A host of newspapers also applauded the president's perceived improvement as commander-in-chief, but many emphasized in particular his "power of utterance" and ability to lead public opinion.[16]

While the war went on, therefore, Wilson's personal reputation swelled amply. It certainly helped his cause that editors like Edwin A. Grozier of the *Boston Post* publicly pledged their allegiance to the administration and urged others to do likewise: "The duty of the American press henceforward is to uphold the President in his efforts to assist in the reconstruction of the world."[17] Or that editors like John A. Sleicher of *Leslie's* declared that "[t]his is no time for caviling or unnecessary disputation,"[18] or that *McClure's* styled itself a "Win-the-War" magazine.[19] Wilson therefore reaped the most from this patriotic windfall that put both pacifism and pessimism in the disloyal category.[20] His vaunted progressive reputation also won numerous admirers. As a contributing writer to *The World Tomorrow* quipped: "I think I can qualify as a liberal—I swear by President Wilson and at *The New York Times.*"[21] Though Wilson never lacked for critics, or criticism, he had little to complain about in his treatment by the press.

For that, he had to thank not so much the Committee on Public Information or the censorship but, rather, the beneficent impact of a strong presidency on a professionalizing press, plus an expert press adviser in Joseph P.

Tumulty. Tumulty had been with Wilson ever since the latter had entered politics, in New Jersey. Reporters loved the quiet, amiable Irish-American, who returned this affection with hard work, dutiful service, and a gentle camaraderie.[22] Tumulty never forgot the personal side of presidential-press relations, and if he sometimes spent time on small details, journalists never forgot such kindnesses: "At one time or another Tumulty convinced Wilson to send friendly letters of appreciation to Frank Noyes and Melville Stone of the Associated Press, Henry Watterson of the *Louisville Courier-Journal,* J. Frederick Essary of the *Baltimore Sun,* and Arthur Brisbane of the *Washington Times.*"[23] One of the president's bitterest critics at the end of the decade, Colonel George Harvey, never stopped liking Tumulty, whom he called "[t]he man who has rendered by far the greatest service to Mr. Wilson."[24] Some writers thought that "assistant President of the United States" was a fitting title for someone who got such important things done so reliably. According to the *New York Times,* Wilson "stands or falls by the qualities of his secretary more than he does by those of any other appointee, cabinet ministers included."[25]

The CPI era, April 1917 to November 1918, unfortunately witnessed the diminishment of Tumulty's influence on Wilson.[26] What this meant was the growing distance between the president and journalists. This fact is not, however, a reflection of George Creel's political views or the natural tendencies of his personality. He opposed censorship and encouraged Wilson to meet more often with reporters. But whatever his own personal disposition, the form and function of the Committee widened the gap between Wilson and journalists. Wartime duties kept the president constantly and intensively preoccupied, so much that he, in consultation with his physician, devised a meticulous schedule of work and exercise, the former in such preponderance that five-, ten-, and fifteen-minute meetings were planned and held with unerring discipline. Creel said that when he himself met with the president, he would prepare "just as a lawyer prepares a brief" in order not to waste time.[27] With the advent of war, Wilson increasingly found meetings with journalists inefficient and frustrating. When he discontinued such sessions temporarily in 1915 he told Creel it was because he thought them "futile." Correspondents often dwelled on the unimportant, the president claimed; they urged him to make predictions and distracted time and attention away from the major points he was trying to stress.[28] Once in May 1916 he met the correspondents as a group, but he ceased even these occasional encounters until the war ended. In fact, between 1917 and 1918 Wilson supposedly did not meet with any one correspondent individually.[29]

Whether the Committee on Public Information also widened the gap between the president and the public at large is another matter. One can make a good argument that it did, for despite a proliferation of information about the war and America's fighting men and women, the CPI did not (and by law could not) generally make more than superficial mention of Wilson himself. Had journalists enjoyed more personal contact with the president they would almost certainly have been able to transmit more revealing insight about him to the American people. As it was, they were confined to regurgitating CPI handiwork and consulting with fellow correspondents, which tended to demarcate more clearly the interests of the administration from the interests of the press.

Wilson's increasingly icy treatment had one unintended consequence, however. It fanned journalists' desire for political independence, for professional distinction. If the president became too busy to spend time with reporters, they at least had each other for company, and in time of war that was notable company indeed. Had Wilson been more predisposed toward personal favorites, as Roosevelt had, news correspondents might have gone to Paris more divided by competitive jealousies and more split along party lines. On the eve of their trip to Europe, they were instead more impressed with their own professional potential than they were with any personal estimation of the president or their practical access to him. Considering the conspicuous absence of an American agenda at the upcoming peace conference, it is little wonder that the attention of American journalists was turned inward at the end of the war.

THE PRESS'S REACTION TO THE CPI

As detailed in Part One, the Committee on Public Information epitomized the Wilson administration's progressive effort to communicate with the American public during the war, with all the problems and opportunities such an orchestrated campaign entailed. The CPI's primary beneficiary, the federal government, enjoyed improved public relations during the war, but the organization's director did not fare so well personally. Indeed, Creel, "the *enfante terrible* of the Administration,"[30] was often subjected to withering abuse from all sides and constant ridicule or suspicion from the press. As the *Literary Digest* summarized his reputation, Creel had "probably provoked more slings and arrows from raging editors than any other Government official connected with our war-time activities."[31] The CPI director was the "vicarious target of pages of editorial ooze," Will Durant wrote.[32] *The Liberator* complained after the war: "We do not want our knowledge of current events strained through the brain of George Creel any longer."[33]

And criticism came not just from journalists: "Jumping on George" was a favored game in congressional circles as well.[34] While Creel was a careful administrator, someone who did not normally make obvious, prominent mistakes in public, when he did slip up, critics seized on such episodes with voracious glee. One such stumble occurred early in 1918 when Creel boasted that the country's unpreparedness for war proved it was truly neutral until the last minute.[35] Praise of unreadiness could hardly go over well while American soldiers were currently fighting and dying in European trenches. It did not seem to matter that Creel was hardworking, that he sympathized with journalists' plight, that he genuinely favored maximum publicity. He made countless enemies, and, though he had his supporters,[36] "neutrality toward him has been the one impossible attitude."[37]

The press quickly grew to dislike both Creel and the CPI. Even as reporters depended on and benefited from the organization's services—newspapers and magazines were not obligated to carry Committee releases and screamed if they did not get their fair share—they resented the presence of an intermediary between themselves and the president, its impediment to access, and the implication that they couldn't be trusted to do their jobs adequately. The fact that not a few journalists had joined the organization's staff did not seem to deter others in their animosity. Will Irwin, a popular and respected writer, conceded widespread journalistic hostility to the organization he had joined, noting that reporters often took out their ill will against Creel: "At one time in 1918, we could count on the Washington correspondents to suppress or 'queer' any story handed out from our office."[38]

During Roosevelt's term in office, presidential-press relations could be characterized as predominantly personal encounters, sometimes between the president and one or two correspondents, sometimes between him and fifty correspondents. But they were personal encounters, with all the color and variety such meetings involve. Wilson's more formalized press conferences may have routinized the work, even added to their institutional prestige, but they also removed the personal dynamism between the president and reporters. The CPI went one step further by removing the president altogether from the podium. Creel's bureau was blocking the door to personal access to the White House, and journalists did not hide the bitter indignation they felt.[39]

But writers also sensed that the Committee represented something potentially dangerous to democracy. The "real menace of propaganda," Robert Herrick observed, "is the discovery by governments and other interested agencies that this extension of advertising—for that is what propaganda essentially is—can be readily utilized to sway and control democratic masses."[40] However benign it might appear, however constructive its work in hastening the end of the war, however much the press might rely on its supply of news and information, the Committee on Public Information posed a threat to newspapers and magazines by making them dependent upon the government, increasingly dependent. Criticizing Creel was therefore a safe way for the press to challenge the administration and to defend itself against charges of incompetence or disloyalty. The existence of the Committee indirectly signaled the existence of censorship, which greatly troubled many writers, even when they did not protest publicly. Journalists often attributed the problems of censorship to Creel's influence—he sat on the Censorship Board, after all—unfairly suspecting him of advocating suppression or autocratic control, as when the government seized the cables at the end of 1918.[41] *The New Republic,* one of the administration's strongest supporters and probably one of the CPI's fairest critics, attested in 1918 to the organization's worth: "We trust Mr. Creel's committee will be liberally supported during the war, for in spite of a few mistakes, its work of propaganda has been conducted with increasing effectiveness, discrimination, and imagination." Then the editor added this chilling qualification: "But we trust also it will be ruthlessly suppressed just as soon as the war is over."[42] Succinctly in that sentence one friendly observer captured the collective fear felt by journalists toward the government's propaganda bureau: it was a behemoth they distrusted.

THE PRESS'S RESPONSE TO CENSORSHIP

Censorship gave radicals two reasons to criticize the administration—for the war itself and for the oppressive measures the war brought. Far less radical critics were also much displeased with the censorship laws, particularly the clumsy, reactionary methods and attitude of the Post Office, and writers weighed in publicly on the war's burdensome censorship restrictions. "Until yesterday," Norman Angell wrote after the war, "any discussion of peace, save in terms of 'Hun-roasting' was likely to bring one within the scope of the Espionage Act."[43] Most of these critics expressed their discomfort with the state of civil liberties in publications like *The Nation* and *The New Republic*, although staunch political adversaries of Wilson took heart from senators who attacked George Creel or the CPI. Ironically, the main thrust of liberals' complaints echoed the fears that Creel and Bullard had originally had before the war started. Taking issue with the apparent crackdown on foreign language newspapers, one person asked: "Why be hot and stupid when the times demand coolness and wisdom?"[44] The position of the German press in America was an extremely delicate issue, with virtually all commentators expressing discomfort with its operations. Without question, however, "German-language newspapers have been dying fast since we entered the war," the *Literary Digest* observed.[45]

An article on newsgathering difficulties in *The Nation* quietly mentioned censorship as one of the wartime obstacles, but failed to elaborate on exactly how it so impeded reporting.[46] Instead, the writer spelled out the burdens caused by cable crowding and delays, then spent most of the remainder of the essay discussing the prevalence of unwilling sources in the Wilson administration. Far from dominating the author's analysis, censorship here emits little more than a token squeak.

Before the end of the year, however, *The Nation* would have much to complain about, its September 14 issue pulled by Post Office solicitor William Lamar for the essay "The One Thing Needful," which included personal criticism of labor leader Samuel Gompers.[47] After protests by Oswald Garrison Villard to Tumulty, Wilson effectively reversed the Post Office decision, one of only a few times he so challenged his censors. Two weeks later the publication warned of the damage unrestrained censorship could cause "if the liberal elements in this country and abroad were to discover that there is less freedom of utterance and criticism here than in Europe."[48] An editorial writer for *The New Republic* agreed: "Why is it that the British government, after four years of the most desperate responsibility, still observes a toleration of criticism which seems dangerous to us?"[49] A week later that magazine went further in castigating the Post Office for its excessive zeal in policing the press.[50]

But editorials before *The Nation*'s scuffle with Burleson also faithfully defended the right of free speech, expressed disbelief and dismay over passage of the Espionage and Sedition Acts, and rebuked all instances of mob or police repression of pacifists, socialists, and other protestors. Moreover, the magazine implored Wilson to loosen the government leash on dissent. "The President should lose no time in making his opposition to the new bill to amend the Espionage Act as clear as he did his repugnance to the bill to turn over all trials for sedition to courts-martial," one writer declared.[51] *The Nation* pointed to more relaxed standards in other countries, such as in England and in France, and even ventured to applaud Republican criticism of the censorship laws.[52] The unceasing implication: if allegedly less democratic nations and less liberal politicians could tolerate protest, why not the United States and the Wilson administration? Interestingly, however, the complaint was most often about inadequate or unintelligent censorship, not censorship itself, and some journalists pled for the establishment of a war publicity bureau.[53]

Not a few journalists, however, paraded their own patriotism during and after the war, including their willingness to censor themselves, to be trustworthy, to be loyal foot soldiers for the government. Frederick Palmer, an experienced war correspondent who accepted a roving commission from General John J. Pershing, remarked that reporters made the best news censors, meaning that the vast majority could be relied on not to tell too much.[54] Creel himself thought that journalists condemning the censorship in America were succumbing to the temptation to find a scapegoat for their anxieties, and censorship was "too good a 'goat' to lose."[55] In any case, it was probably true that, as Norman Hapgood concluded, "In the last few years many liberal publications have ceased to exist, and others have ceased to be liberal."[56] The vast majority certainly made much ado of their loyalty to the nation. The jingoes of American journalism were loud and insistent then, and many preferred to look the other way when competitors were harassed. Recalled one writer, "We believe that it is well within bounds of truth and temperance to say that never was a President supported by the nation regardless of partisanship or of personality more loyally or more unanimously than Mr. Wilson has been."[57] Scholars have found little evidence to the contrary. "Probably most newspaper owners and editors believed in the righteousness of the American and Allied cause."[58] Still, a low, murmuring discontent was always present. Field correspondents, for example, did not always see things eye to eye with their editors. And exposed to the censorship employed by other governments abroad, these reporters demonstrated more sensitivity to the subject when it arose at home. Whether from political radicals, left-leaning editors, Republican congressmen, or rank-and-file reporters, protest against the administration's authoritarianism continued through the end of the decade.

The result of this criticism against wartime censorship was a sudden burst of libertarian energy, for, ironically, one of the unintended fruits of censorship is often louder, more insistent demands for additional freedom. The American Civil Liberties Union was founded in 1920. Legal theorists and judicial advocates began lobbying for wider latitude for the First Amendment. Justice Oliver Wendell Holmes began rethinking his Schenck decision of 1919. After the war years the significance of the First Amendment "would remain intimately connected with the protection of minority rights,"[59] and writers would henceforth be much more sensitive to incursions by government on their work. Civil liberties had at last become "a public policy issue" in America.[60]

CONCLUSION TO PART TWO

The continual tension journalists felt between pitching in patriotically and exercising a critical independence from government reached its height in the last several months of the war. The war had strengthened and accelerated the drive for professionalization, for serving in elite, specialized roles as government-subsidized or -inspired publicists. This drive revealed journalists' self-conscious attempt to distance themselves from regular civilians while essaying to speak for and to them. They wanted to distance themselves from the people yet also to influence them directly in a paternalistic fashion. The end of the war, however, undermined the paternalistic philosophy, for as reporters wrote about the upcoming peace conference and its anticipated experiment with the new diplomacy, they found themselves constantly bandying about sentences hailing the people and the public. They found themselves pushed by the logic of their own rhetoric toward trying to be wary watchdogs of government, bona fide public ambassadors.

By the end of the Great War, the press nurtured great professional aspirations. Politically, socially, and emotionally for journalists, a lot rode on the peace conference. Many journalists were already referring to themselves as professionals—some loosely, to mean the "better" class of people,[61] others more precisely, to indicate either a better trained or more educated sort of worker. Charles Grasty, a *New York Times* correspondent during the peace conference, concluded that an American reporter "should belong to the same general class as statesmen and diplomats, and he really is a greater influence in the world than many diplomats and statesmen."[62] Journalists made exhaustive mention of their own service and influence during the war.[63] Self-servingly, perhaps, many writers expressed their belief that the press was a crucial institution then, one that had successfully "educated the public mind on the issues of the war," such as the need for a draft.[64] Just as the war had helped to make other professions more respectable—college teaching, for example[65]—so, too, did World War I inflate the significance of journalism, even if it did not altogether end the disagreement over what to do about professional reform.

Of course, many newspaper and magazine editors successfully resisted this impulse, and journalism never did become a white-collar sanctuary for highly paid, highly educated practitioners. What it did become, what in fact it had already become, was a refurbished enterprise that fit somewhere in the middle between the most prestigious professions and the more mundane trades. Journalism had been transformed by the end of the progressive period— and urban journalism, in particular, became more specialized—but all press operations more or less succumbed to the logic of industrial America, too: they generally grew or folded, monopolized at every opportunity, tended toward corporate bureaucracies. They gravitated more toward "a business basis."[66] In the end, journalism was not a more difficult business for a reporter to break into, nor was it endowed with substantially more prestige, at least not until 1917.

World War I, however, sharply transformed the symbolic importance of the press, putting its members at the center of vital world affairs. They no longer held exclusive possession of the culture of publicity, but they still stood at the heart of it, and for a few years journalists seemed poised not only to enjoy the trappings possessed by other professions but to acquire a crucial new political function. "Whether journalism's inability to monopolize makes it 'not a profession' is not particularly interesting," Andrew Abbott writes. "What matters is that interprofessional competition in fact shaped it decisively."[67] Abbott refers here (and only briefly) to the competition produced by publicity agents. He omits, however, the rapacious competition generated by the federal government. And this was what most shaped journalists' self-conception during World War I. Rhetoric about the new diplomacy represented a trade-off for journalists: it ceded leadership of public opinion to a new kind of American president, an executive communicator, in exchange for an influential professional role in facilitating that communication.

PART THREE

REKINDLING PROFESSIONALISM

The Atlantic Transition

⚛ 6 ⚛

"THE GREAT ADVENTURE"

The convening of the Peace Conference at Versailles will be the greatest international event in history. There is not a living man who would not be glad to be present either as a participant or an observer.

The Outlook, November 27, 1918

Wartime tensions between the president and the press made the Paris Peace Conference appear to be something of a respite and, at the same time, a thrilling new opportunity as well. Journalists who were tired of the war, the restrictions, the rhetoric, the same old scenery, could look forward to a striking departure from the ordinary. Those who were energized by the war's demands and exhilarated by the president's lofty ideas on democratic peacemaking were excited about the prospect of witnessing, and possibly even participating in, a historic moment. The challenge to identify and influence public opinion was now more wide open than ever, with the prospective dismantling of the CPI and with the pantheon of American journalists poised to travel overseas in December 1918. But it was also more complicated than ever, too, with so many of the world's political leaders and their retinues in attendance. The American press had boasted of both its patriotism and its professionalism during the war, though more the former than the latter. Now it was eager to showcase its professionalism. While in theory that stance suggests a more adversarial relationship between Wilson and the correspondents, in practice a professional ethos needed not antagonize anyone, so long as the president maintained harmonious relations with some reporters. Unfortunately, however, the president's track record was not encouraging in that matter. But that was war, this was peace, and many journalists believed that things might now be different.

The experience of traveling overseas to cover the peace conference was indeed different for American correspondents. Led to believe in their future participation in peacemaking, many reporters braced themselves for what they thought might be a new epoch in democratic publicity and thus a new beginning for journalism itself. In a sense, both hunches proved correct, if not in the form anticipated. Indeed, the transformation on both counts had already begun. By the second decade of the twentieth century, publicity was considered essential for democracy, integral to the new presidency, and irresistible to progressive diplomacy. But journalism had changed, too, and the peace conference following World War I epitomized those changes. In 1919, the press did feel a robust sense of professionalism. In fact, in the letters they wrote home, in their diaries and memoirs, most correspondents truly regarded the Paris summit as almost a professional conclave—a chance to work, learn, socialize, and enjoy the collegiality of one's peers. This was their chance to bask in the spotlight, to feel that they'd made it both individually and collectively. The latter, their sense of themselves as a group, was an important shift in their perspective, one made considerably stronger by contact with foreign journalists and foreign governments. Even the self-absorbed correspondent William Allen White, for example, moved in this direction. But well before the conference started, pride and expectations ran high. As described in this chapter, the American reporters who went to Paris in 1918–1919 "arrived" in Europe in more ways than one.

"INTERESTS TUGGING AT US FROM ACROSS THE SEAS"

The Paris Peace Conference was a plum assignment for American correspondents—the reporting opportunity of a lifetime and the progressive political moment, perhaps, of all time. Writers of various backgrounds, with any credentials whatsoever, hastily sought to go. Age and experience did not matter. Connections helped but were not essential. At any rate, the initial emphasis in most reporters' accounts is what they as *individual* journalists went through and experienced before leaving the country.

William Allen White offers the best illustration. At the end of 1918 White was almost fifty-one years old. He could reflect proudly on a distinguished career, a hefty salary, and a national reputation that seemed out of all proportion to his position as editor of the *Emporia Gazette*. With friends on Capitol Hill, in the Navy, the Supreme Court, and even the White House, the Kansas editor was supremely well connected. He had authored several novels. His recent nonfiction book about the war remained popular. And he enjoyed a healthy marriage and supportive home life. Some men his age may have thought about retirement. But as news of an impending armistice gradually made its way across the land, White had but two wishes: he wanted to go to Europe, and he wanted to go as a diplomat.

Such an ambition presented few qualms for White, as it would have for many other journalists at the time. Being a "newspaper man" did not rule out work for the government or, for that matter, service to a political party, certainly not in small-town America. White had long been active in Republican Party politics in Kansas and never showed concern about occupational conflicts of interest. But politics probably had less to do with White's motives than other factors. Actually, running a newspaper was for him a vehicle through which to pursue community involvement and to do so aggressively and with confidence. For White, newspaper work was not so much a political venue as it was a civic endeavor, a creative public expression of his progressive sympathies. And his interest in diplomacy was but an international extension of this need to be involved in politics and in reform generally. But even more than that, it simply reflected his desire to be in the fast lane. Journalism was White's stepping stone to bigger and better things, even if temporarily. Diplomacy was one such attraction. And besides, other writers had followed similar career paths. The most prominent example at the time might have been ambassador to England Walter Hines Page, who had formerly been the editor of *The Forum*, the *Atlantic Monthly*, and *The World's Work* before being named to the Court of St. James in 1913, a post he held for over five years.[1]

An alternative way to view White's diplomatic ambitions is to construe it as the logical reaction by a journalist to the progressive campaign for a more open diplomacy. If publicity was second-nature to American leaders, organizers, and opinion-makers in the early twentieth century, it is not surprising that a call for diplomatic reform might invite the participation of men and women who wrote for a living. White is perhaps too complex to pigeonhole so neatly. Nonetheless, he could not have been immune to the temptation to create a new world order among nations, and this was in fact one of his motivations to go then.

And yet, as part of the internal tensions journalists faced in the early twentieth century, decisions like White's would not necessarily go uncriticized. Herbert Bayard Swope, of the *New York World*, agonized repeatedly over whether to join the military during the war and actually toyed with a couple of different offers before finally deciding against a commission. But he did volunteer for the War Industries Board, where he met and befriended Bernard Baruch, a financier who would prove to be a powerful source in Paris. And he did cozy up to Wilson, which triggered concern on the part of his New York editor, John O'Hara Cosgrave. Cosgrave scolded Swope repeatedly for letting his guard down and succumbing to the temptations of power. Swope was risking "journalistic accomplishment" by getting too friendly with those he was supposed to be writing about honestly.[2]

Regardless, Swope and countless colleagues intended on going to Paris to cover the conference. Walter Weyl, a co-founder of *The New Republic,* also endeavored to travel there—first as a delegate, then when that did not work out, as a writer and observer.[3] With peace at hand, William Allen White wasted no time either. He wrote friends, acquaintances—any contact that might prove useful in securing a diplomatic post. An early target was Woodrow Wilson's right-hand man, George Creel. White sent America's first official propagandist a letter filled with a lot of bait yet an unmistakable hook:

> I am sending you an editorial about your beloved President—I suppose I might as well confess he is also mine. . . .
>
> It is indeed a bit funny that we are not together. We who hold 80% of our political opinions in common. I suppose that each of us is repelled by the crooks that the other runs with. You don't like mine and I don't like yours. I hope the day will come when there will be a thorough-going radical party, with a thorough-going radical program. I weary of promises and repression, and all the mummery of pretended agreement with smug conservatism. I have written a dynamiting, hell-raising book that has just been published, and I am sending it to you herewith. I wish I could persuade our beloved President to give me a JOB in the organization of the Peace commission. I don't want to be a high commissioner but I would like to be somewhere where I could stick my eye to the keyhole and see what was going on inside.[4]

Within a week White cabled telegrams to Republican Party chairman Will Hays, Senators William Borah, Hiram Johnson, and Henry Cabot Lodge, U.S. Representative Medill McCormick, Secretary of the Navy Josephus Daniels, Secretary of the Interior Franklin Lane, Assistant Secretary of Agriculture Carl Vrooman, and Supreme Court Justice Louis Brandeis. White wrote Lodge a second time, explaining that he wanted "not a job as commissioner but something."[5] White's friend Mark Sullivan shared his colleague's enthusiasm. "I hear that you are going to the Peace Conference," Sullivan wrote. "I think it is very probable that I shall go, too. I suppose it will be the most important meeting of men's minds in your lifetime or mine."[6] In response, White continued to importune unabashedly: "Now about the peace commission. I want to go in some minor place in the organization. If you know how to get me there, I wish you would waltz up to Washington and do it. If I cannot do that, I want to go representing the syndicate, but I would lots rather go for less money as a member of the organization."[7]

White did not end his efforts there. Having contacted congressmen, White House officials, and military officers, he cabled at least thirty newspaper publishers, using the same basic format each time. Addressing the editor of the *New York World* he wired the following message: "I am going to conference. Would be mightily glad to serve World. . . . I am exceedingly anxious to represent World."[8] White's next tactic was to appeal to the Red Cross, the former sponsor of his 1917 trip to Europe. Here he enumerated exactly what he wanted:

When you are in Washington, see about my passport. I want to go early in Dec. I wish you would ask the Red Cross people to give me some sort of a roving commission, with such brevet military status as they can afford. I have a perfectly good RC uniform that I can use. So long as I am paying my own expenses, and shall not charge the RC Magazine for what I contribute, I assume that I will be permitted to write for such American newspapers and magazines as I please. This permission was given to me on my other trip, and I assume that it will be satisfactory this time. I shall make my copy help the RC drive next spring, in your magazine and in other papers.

P.S. I want to take Billy with me as my Sec. 18-years-old, member of US Army Student Training Corps.[9]

Not everyone approved of White's particular ambition. Medill McCormick was somewhat taken aback by his request for an official position in the U.S. mission, and he sent White a sardonic reply, surprised at White's accommodating political disposition:

Your final telegram—which I find in Washington upon my return here, puzzled us all. One of my young men insists that you are serious in suggesting that you might go as a member of the presidential mission. . . . Unless you have joined the chorus of concurrence I cannot see how you dare hope to be one of the presidential parasites. When you suggest that I be the vehicle of your application,—like the darkey from whom someone sought to borrow a dollar—"I haven't got it but I thank you for the compliment just the same."[10]

White quickly clarified his position:

I did not want to be one of the blushing peace commissioners. I wanted a job as under third assistant secretary to the Republican member, a job to which I might almost honorably aspire. I am now going to Europe about the 10th for the Red Cross, and the Wheeler Syndicate, and I want you to do something for me. I am applying for passport through the RC. Mr. Belknap Millett of the RC Personnel Bureau has charge of my application. If it is entirely proper, and if it is not asking too much of you, I would be pleased if you would send over to Mr. M. of the RC, a request to the State Department to make my passport a diplomatic passport. I expect to go to France, Italy, Serbia, possibly Russia, and surely England, and I notice that at frontiers I can get around better if I have a diplomatic passport.[11]

What William Allen White lacked in subtlety, he made up for in perseverance. He went to Europe, was awarded diplomatic papers and a special State Department assignment on February 7, 1919, and amid his various duties represented and wrote for a slew of American newspapers in the McClure Syndicate.

White may have been more industrious, with more resources, than the average correspondent, but he was not alone in wanting fervently to attend the peace conference. Other journalists had caught the travel bug as well and were eager to witness the upcoming deliberations.[12] The novelist Edna Ferber, for example, was itching to go and tried to get White to pull some strings: "I see by the papers of yesterday that you're going to France for Wheeler's. Well! Some folks have all the luck. God, but I'd love it! Can't you work me in, somehow? I'm a swell reporter, and I've got a stunning new suit and hat (despite my family calamities) and Paris needs me."[13] Former magazine editor Charles F. Lummis begged muckraking titan S. S. McClure in a similar vein, only more desperately: "You know me! Why have you forgotten about it? I expected, long before this, to have a commission from you to send me Over There to do some Real Stuff for your magazine and syndicates and things. I was with you in your very first ventures, and think you found me always making good."[14] Edward Bellamy Partridge, a novelist and historian, was more successful, and he took great pride in his new overseas assignment and correspondent's uniform, expressing enthusiasm with a typical wisecrack: "Somehow I couldn't see that uniform going to the moth balls without the smell of powder or the red stains of—well, of the wine of France, at least."[15]

Trade magazines like *Editor & Publisher* no doubt stimulated the frenzied impulse to go to the conference with its close, enthusiastic coverage of the upcoming event and its hailing of designated conference correspondents as pseudo-celebrities.[16] Newspapers and magazines took out advertisements in publications like *Editor & Publisher* to boast of the talented personnel they were sending overseas. "A Staff of Stars," Universal Service dubbed its crew.[17] For men and women then in the business of news gathering and writing, covering the Paris Peace Conference was simply the world's premier assignment, with untold professional rewards awaiting those chosen to go.

Who were these "stars"? Raymond Stannard Baker, the famous muckraker, Wilson watcher, and, by some accounts, "America's Greatest Reporter," for one.[18] May Birkhead, probably the English-speaking world's most famous "society writer," and Winifred Black, "a name greatly revered in newspaper circles," went as representatives, respectively, of the *New York Herald* and the *San Francisco Examiner*.[19] Writer/editor Mark Sullivan, hailed as "a national asset," went to Europe.[20] Accomplished war correspondents like Lincoln Eyre of the *New York World*, who had made a rare trip to Germany right after the armistice, traveled overseas then,[21] as did Frazier Hunt, of the *Chicago Tribune*, one of the few journalists to have journeyed to Russia.[22] Other well-known writers, besides White, who made the trip included *Crisis* editor W. E. B. Du Bois, muckraker Ida Tarbell, and newspaper writers John F. Bass and Paul Scott Mowrer. Bass and Mowrer were both experienced war correspondents for the *Chicago Daily News,* Mowrer actually a Legion of Honor winner.[23] Ida Tarbell, a household name after her history of Standard Oil, accepted an assignment from *Red Cross Magazine* to report on what French women were going through now that the war was over. Gertrude Atherton was a successful novelist whose works had been made into movies. Now she became a credentialed correspondent for the *New York Times*.[24]

W. E. B. Du Bois likewise engaged in a frantic attempt to attend the conference, though his motives went far beyond the usual ambitions. Du Bois wanted to orchestrate a small, ancillary assembly made up of "colored men of ability and high character, from all parts of the world."[25] This "Pan-African Congress" would represent the interests of black people everywhere, and would discuss and defend those interests as needed throughout the Conference. These were the issues that moved him; professionalism was the least of his concerns. Du Bois's vision reflected a widespread sentiment held by public figures in America during the First World War, a zestful curiosity about things foreign that spoke to both the causes of the war and the prospective solutions for ending it. Du Bois had also been prepared in mid-1918 to accept a captaincy in military intelligence, a post he appears to have been quietly auditioning for in his journal, *The Crisis,* by urging American blacks to support the president and the war.[26] Like other writers, nonetheless, Du Bois was impatient to get to Paris. Politically, socially, culturally, and diplomatically, that city beckoned progressives as an important testing ground for liberal activism of all sorts.

When pacifist journalist A. D. Call described how "the verdict of the gathering [would be] the most memorable in the history of international assemblies," his announcement crackled with excitement and possibility. Call, the announcement read, would have "the unprecedented opportunity of meeting not only the members and staffs of the commissions sent by the nations, but also the large number of important personages from all quarters of the world."[27] A magazine editorial published just before the war's end also perfectly captured that international spirit. It might take a few years yet to beat Germany, the writer said.

> Until that time there will be a constant stream of Americans crossing the ocean to take their part in ridding the world of a pestilential theory of government. A million of them are there now; millions more will follow. The most interesting spot in the world for us is France. There is not only the hope of the world; our boys are there, too. They'll follow all the tides of life—fighting, dying, living, loving. They'll change France, and be changed themselves. We at home are not satisfied with the little we hear from them or about them from the papers and returning visitors; we want a complete picture. So Good Housekeeping has sent a member of its staff to live in France and keep in touch with our boys and the French people and the whole gamut of interests tugging at us from across the sea. She will send back monthly just the things you want to know. Those who remember Miss Savage's brilliant work as our "Washington correspondent" early in the year will be glad to know that it is she who has been sent as our representative to this bigger field.[28]

"[I]nterests tugging at us from across the sea" is a phrase that helps to explain journalists' urgent desire to go abroad in 1918. So does White's expression, "eye to the keyhole." American newsmen and -women not only wanted to witness the changes the world was about to undergo, they wanted to take part in those changes. They wanted to be present at the conference that would "assemble the world's keenest minds and most experienced diplomats."[29] Their quest was both physical and intellectual, a phenomenon observed by Edward Price Bell, the London bureau chief for the *Chicago Daily News*. Speaking of two foreign correspondents already at work for the *Daily News* in Switzerland and Siberia, Bell wrote to Charles Dennis, saying: "These men if they travel about, if they are good men, nearly always do fresh and forceful work. There is something about physical movement, as you well know, that stimulates mental movement." Bell went on to say that people were becoming more broad-minded as the world witnessed the growth of institutions and the development of economic interdependence. Such expansiveness would keep journalists on the move: "There is scarcely an important human center on the globe where our paper ought not to be completely represented."[30]

Adventure, mission, the future—these ideas animated the correspondents sailing to Europe and filled them with tremendous anticipation. So, too, did professional aspirations: Journalists were led to believe by the administration that in Paris Wilson would meet the American press every day to discuss the peace talks.[31] There would be much to do in Europe, much that would supposedly bring in a new age of journalism, diplomacy, and world politics. Mass communication itself seemed on the verge of something profound. As several newspaper headlines trumpeted the president's journey: "Wilson Trip News Comes by Wireless, Pigeons and Ship"; "President by Radio Directs Government."[32] Wilson himself appeared in the role of publicist, or quasi-journalist perhaps, at least according to one description of his voyage aboard ship to Europe: "The President has his own typewriter on board and is using it at intervals in working upon the speeches he expects to deliver in France."[33] Expectations, jubilation, and pressure ran high. Simeon Strunsky described how he felt knowing he would soon behold the end of an era by saying his shipmates were nervous but hopeful. "In this seemingly mixed and inadequate mood we approach Europe and the Peace—frivolous, and yet a little frightened, gay but not outside the echo of a sense of tears. Europe looms up ahead of us, the laboratory in which is to be fashioned a new world."[34] America was on the verge of the most complex foreign entanglement in its history. So was its press.

ARRANGEMENTS

War is unpredictable. Agreements falter, cease-fires break down, individuals do not always act as they are ordered. Subsequently, it is difficult for a newspaper or magazine with a circumscribed budget to be able to plan very far in advance, to send correspondents ahead of their proposed subjects, to prepare those reporters adequately for the logistics of covering global politics. The work of the press has always been a mainly extemporaneous enterprise. And so when it was clear in the fall of 1918 that it was time to transport journalists overseas, a kind of mad scramble ensued. Some correspondents knew before November that they were to cover the eventual peace conference. Others found out late. For both groups uncertainty always loomed. Would they, in fact, be the ones, or among the ones, from their news organization actually to sail to Europe? Would last-minute changes be made? If they were to go overseas, how long would they stay?

Given these anxious concerns, when journalists were informed of their assignment, they made arrangements as best, and as quickly, as they could. The Wilson administration took the unprecedented step of offering to transport many of the major magazine and newspaper correspondents on the Navy-crewed *Orizaba,* which left the United States a few days ahead of the president. Despite the generous gesture, preparing to leave the country was a complicated affair, and most members of the press left in haste and often with rattled nerves. Even S. S. McClure, an independent syndicate operator of considerable means, felt the rush, as his diary entry for December 1, 1918, shows: "Sun. noon. Am sailing presently. Awfully driven. Just got my passport in the last moment. I got $300 from William Kent, my California friend. Address 1925 F. Street, Washington, D.C. The honorable William Kent. I got $200 from Harry."[35]

Quick cash was an immediate concern, too, as McClure's note above illustrates. Journalists borrowed from friends, they used their own money, and sometimes when they were lucky their newspaper or magazine advanced them the necessary funds. Haste in departure made for haste in settling financial affairs, a subject that would concern them throughout their stay overseas. Correspondents acquired what cash they could and carried it along with their other belongings. For Simeon Strunsky these included a trunk, suitcase, shawl-roll, and typewriter.[36]

The most serious obstacle in leaving the country was in securing the necessary papers. A. D. Call described his experience in a humorous but none-theless obviously frustrated vein:

> If one wishes to go to France one must take one's hard-earned United States passport to the French Consulate in New York where one finds to one's surprise that it is wholly inadequate. Here one finds to one's astonishment that one's photograph is far more popular than had been surmised in one's moments of greatest conceit. Three had been furnished at Washington. Four were asked for by the flattering consulate at New York. One hasn't them, and the time is short, but one goes out and gets them. One then goes to a notary and swears all over again to things one knows nothing about, such as the birthdays of relatives long beyond the reach of consulates. One signs, and swears in triplicate and higher multiples; one waits and fears the moment, the grand climacteric, when a final something will happen to one's passport and the column marked "Visas" shall be satisfied. That moment never arrives. It is skeptically examined at the port of debarkation, stamped upon, written upon, frowned upon.[37]

Clearly, making arrangements to cover the conference was fraught with bureaucratic traps, frustrations, and delays, and the sooner a correspondent undertook preparations the less frazzled he would be en route to Europe. Most journalists, however, were not allowed the luxury of organizing their trip months in advance, so, like Call, they rushed to get what they needed in a frantically compressed amount of time, many dashing to Washington to obtain passports in late November or early December. And sometimes not even that was sufficient: Creel at first told Du Bois at the dock that he would not be able to board the ship because he had not been notified of his plans to go to Europe and because there wasn't room. After a long wait, however, Du Bois was allowed on.[38]

Herbert Bayard Swope, the thirty-six-year-old reporter for the *New York World,* arrived at the dock two hours late and "almost didn't make the voyage." As his biographer, E. J. Kahn Jr., tells it, Swope made up for the tardiness with his usual brash style: "At twelve-thirty, just as the last lines were being cast loose, a baggage wagon thundered down the pier like a Roman chariot, propelled by two fleet longshoremen. Swope was on the cart, astride his luggage, and as he approached the gangplank he was shouting last-minute instructions to Alex Schlosser, trotting along at his side."[39] According to Kahn, the ship's captain actually delayed embarkation to give Swope a chance to get there. If Swope was not your typical correspondent, it nonetheless seems characteristic of that age of publicity that a journalist would be so indulged.

DEPARTURE

Several hundred American journalists traveled to Paris between December 1918 and June 1919. The *New York Tribune* counted 350 journalists on board the *Orizaba,* but the exact figure is not known because the only official record kept was the list of 142 correspondents who registered with the American Peace Delegation at the Hôtel de Crillon in January. Not all who went registered, however. And many journalists continued to arrive throughout the winter and spring of 1919, coming and going as they pleased. *Editor & Publisher* tallied the American correspondents in Paris in May 1919; it listed 131 reporters, fifty-five of whom were not on the earlier list. Two hundred, therefore, is probably a very conservative estimate.[40]

American correspondents chosen to cover the peace process in Europe left the United States in two conspicuous waves. One group, Swope's, composed of one or two hundred journalists (all of them male on this passage), traveled on the *Orizaba,* which set sail on December 1, 1918, and arrived in Brest, France, on December 9, 1918.[41] Another group traveled a few days later with the president aboard the *George Washington.*[42] The remainder caught passage on ships as they could, often in the company of soldiers and YMCA volunteers. Whoever their companions were, these traveling journalists felt moved by the experience. For virtually all of them, leaving their country to observe the postwar meeting of statesmen stirred feelings of excitement, grand purpose, and national pride. "The Army and Navy did everything in their power to enable the correspondents victoriously to enter Paris," A. D. Call wrote. "The Navy transported us to France with all the royalty Americans can muster."[43] *Atlantic Monthly* writer Simeon Strunsky entitled the journey "*voyage sentimale*" and declared, "We are on our way to the last act of the biggest show in history."[44] Woodrow Wilson's own passage was especially significant, Strunsky wrote, "probably the most momentous trans-Atlantic voyage . . . in the last four hundred years. . . . Time, the major-domo, draws aside the portières of Europe and announces, 'If you please, madam, America!'" In his self-congratulating nationalism, Strunsky portrayed the United States as "a member of the family" come home in Europe's hour of need. "Fate speed the George Washington and her freight! She carries with the President a good share of the hope of the world."[45]

With so inspiring a mission, most journalists found the trip invigorating, and for several reasons, because in addition to the political and diplomatic circumstances of the voyage, and in addition to Bell's theory that travel stimulates the mind, the correspondents who went to Europe shared a festive camaraderie and a growing solidarity that underscored their own social significance. "One always feels a fraternity towards one's fellow-voyagers quite as if they together had been mystically initiated by their experiences into a secret order," A. D. Call wrote on board the *Orizaba*.[46] Simeon Strunsky put it this way: "There is a spirit of adventure giving glow to the fundamental fidelity to one's job."[47] "Delightful" and "lovely" W. E. B. Du Bois called the voyage.[48] President Wilson inaugurated journalists' sense of identity with a joke he wired the *Orizaba* at the beginning of the journey. He saluted the correspondents: "One of my Fourteen Points is to make the world safe for the press (evidently intended to read 'safe from the press')."[49]

Such mirthful fanfare characterized the trip as journalists' fraternity began, not surprisingly, as recreation. "There were the usual games," Call remembered, "some gambling, and a series of sparring exhibits among members of the crew."[50] Veteran Associated Press reporter E. M. Hood described one particularly vivid memory in a letter home to his wife. During an evening of drinking, a number of correspondents suddenly broke into song, playing instruments they had brought or borrowed, and crooning with gusto. The journalistic jamboree featured "DL [David Lawrence] picking the mandolin banjo; Wolfe [Edgar T. Wolfe] accompanied on same; Larry Hills pianist, Herbert Swope drum and cymbals etc. Sang 'Over There' with great success, judging from the applause."[51]

But journalists' attachment to each other took on a more high-minded tone, too, as they endeavored to prepare each other for the serious business awaiting them in France. Several correspondents offered to tutor colleagues in subjects that might benefit all. Informal help-sessions became full-fledged courses. Daniel Bidwell of the *Hartford Courant* taught French classes, while W. E. B. Du Bois lectured on African colonies, and S. S. McClure lectured on French politics.[52] The ship had become a floating Chautauqua, and teaching seemed to renew journalists' sense of community. It also made them feel useful. McClure recalled: "I gave them all lectures. They were very cordial and appreciative and whenever any of them see [me] they smile and call my name. The ship's officers are also extremely pleasant."[53] Simeon Strunsky was glad to receive foreign-language instruction, although he sensed a growing disparity: "Like the minds of Mr. Wilson and the late German government, the minds of our shipload and the minds of the old textbook makers do not meet. *Voulez-vous la parapluie de votre belle-soeur?* Not on your life, monsieur; greater things draw us. *Je veux un billet pour le Conference de Paix,* and there is nothing about conferences de paix in the textbook."[54]

From late-night bull sessions to mid-day lecture series, journalists were getting to know each other in a way impossible at home. They were meeting more colleagues and having more time to become acquainted with them than perhaps at any time in American history. This was, in a variety of ways, their first *convention*. And they loved it. "Remarkable gathering of valuable newspapermen there," E. M. Hood wrote, "and I have made many acquaintances among people whose names stand high in the profession, like S. S. McClure, Lincoln of World, Ralph Pulitzer, H. Swope . . . Glass (my table neighbor), Jim Montague and others."[55] A. D. Call beamed as he described the way the "men of this craft look upon their work as a profession, and on the whole there is a fine ethics among them."[56] Shortly before landing in Europe, the group on board the *Orizaba* pushed their fellowship one step further by organizing as the United States Press Delegation to the peace conference. "We are to look after the welfare of and secure proper recognition and facilities for the correspondents," E. M. Hood wrote.[57] To no one's surprise, journalists chose Swope to be president of the professional organization.

Passage to Europe thus combined both serious and not-so-serious opportunities for group cohesion. The trip reinforced in the minds of journalists that they were important people who mattered, whose work could change the world. And many of them thought the world was on the verge of epic change. To be part of that was stirring indeed. In December 1918 Howard Wheeler, a correspondent for *Everybody's Magazine,* wrote about the spirit of the times with heady optimism. The present was bursting at the seams, he believed, and change for the better lay ahead:

> [T]here it was, the future, demanding to be recognized. It had to be considered. How else could the day's work be managed? How else could the present be directed? Those statesmen with their old vision, their old traditions and their agonizing business—they had to look at it and try to make out the features of the future that was staring them out of countenance. So they are doing it.
>
> How? To get at and give the answer to that is going to be the work of many world reporters for many months to come. We are working hard, we reporters here in France, harder than we ever worked before. We have been trying

to get at fact. Not surface facts, no impression of facts, but deep, fundamental, substratum facts that will remain facts through Versailles—and after.[58]

Wheeler quoted a respected statesman overseas who when asked about the distinctive nature of the future answered without hesitation: "'Adventure,' he said, like a shot, as though he had long ago thought out his answer."

> Romance and adventure. Not the old sort, mind you, not the ruthless, half-conscious gambling, each man and each nation for himself or itself, with the devil at last getting all of us, foremost and hindmost, too, but adventure where the risk will be real, open-eyed, deliberate—high adventure with bold plunges into the mysteries of science, daring grappling with the unsolved problems of thought, art and social living. We shall dare to marry the spiritual with the material. The men of our future will not say: "These evils always existed; therefore they will always exist." The modest adventurer will demand—he is already demanding: "This evil is the oldest and most difficult in the world? Very well, we will defeat that evil first." That is what President Wilson is saying.[59]

McClure's managing editor, Charles Hanson Towne, shared that feeling as well. "Everybody was bent on a serious errand," he wrote; "yet there were happy greetings and laughter everywhere. . . . Always they [soldiers on board] said but one thing—they were glad to be off on the great adventure." No doubt this enthusiasm for adventure spilled over onto Towne: "People who would not have interested you then [before the war], strangely interest you now. Everyone has had an adventure, at least an experience in the United States which gives him plenty to talk about. There are more backgrounds, more contrasts in all our lives. The exchange of stories is limitless, and tea-time becomes a different function, followed always by a thrilling lecture. The Great Adventure had begun. Yes, indeed, they are getting us over!"[60] The American press corps covering the Paris Peace Conference reached the shores of Europe under a swirl of high emotions—feeling, sometimes all at once, proud, inspired, hopeful, anxious. There would be much to do, and much would be expected of them.

ARRIVAL

When journalists made it to France they were upbeat but understandably nervous. The Orizaba's passengers were relieved to discover that Wilson's ship had not beaten them to Europe, as some feared when they departed the United States.[61] They wanted to see the popular reception given the president. But there were other anxieties as well. Word had spread during the ocean voyage that lodging was hard to come by in Paris, so upon landing the travelers' first order of business was to find their bearings and then obtain transportation to the capital. Again, the U.S. government stepped in to assist the correspondents in overcoming many of the more taxing obstacles. One journalist noted: "It was the Army that arranged that we should have accommodations over the crowded and crippled road to Paris, obtaining two special cars for the purpose. It was the Army that spared us the common ordeal of being vaccinated against a half-dozen diseases, and of being bothered greatly over passport and other details."[62] But reporters did not know ahead of time that their country would help them until Creel finally informed them so, hours after arriving in Brest.[63] And the initial days on the Continent still proved trying. Hood detailed his trek:

> [S]pent two days trying to get through quaint Breton town to Paris. Night of 10 finally got into day coach and sat us all night without heat until reached Paris next day, Dec. 11, 1919, about 10 am. Found a bedroom and bath (15 francs a day) reserved for me at Hotel Wagram, Rue du Rivoli and Rue 29th July, old fashioned place lacking most conveniences. In over six months stay, I never had any heat in my room. But it was central, between AP Office—13 Place de la Bourse—and the Hotel Crillon, American Peace Commsn headquarters & fronting beautiful Tuilleries Gardens & Louvre, in best part of Paris.[64]

If Brest was stressful, Paris was chaotic. At the railway station in Montparnasse, Du Bois wrote, "the confusion was the worst I ever conceived of in well-ordered France: no one to collect tickets, no porters, no cabs and a surging crowd."[65] And Du Bois was one of the rare registered American correspondents who were fluent in French.

Much of their worry soon passed as the days progressed and the reporters became more accustomed to being in a foreign country. Hood himself was "delighted with Brest" and positively overwhelmed by Paris: "I seem to be in a dream; the names of the avenues and streets are familiar from my past reading, but the reality is all so strange; I am not sure yet how I will like it when I get down to earth again." Return to earth he did, though, and while Hood remained optimistic he also recognized the challenges he would face: "Looks like a big job ahead of me here, made very difficult by my lack of knowledge of the language and ability to get about freely. Perhaps all these difficulties will diminish as the days pass."[66] Part of the anxiety was caused by President Wilson's absence. Awaiting Wilson's arrival, Hood remarked, "I must say that I never have had less time to do anything while accomplishing nothing."[67] Delay gave correspondents time to hear things they did not like, such as a nickname chosen for them by the French press: "Creel's Trained Fleas." Hood noted it dourly in a letter home: "rather unfortunate and may be embarrassing if we meet with ridicule at the outset."[68]

Despite the teasing, most reporters basked in the attention of performing high-profile roles at an important place. Even so trivial a thing as the passport many journalists worked so hard to get in the United States gave them pleasure or at least amusement in Paris, as policemen and other authorities asked to see identification. "The owner begins to feel that he has a thing of value and permanent significance. He takes it out in secret and looks at it lovingly. It is all his, this visible expression of international suspicion and ultimate approval, this evidence, real and palpable, of various nations' kindly interest in his intimate affairs. He keeps it religiously about his person. Surely it will be of great value to him some how, some day."[69] It was also necessary to obtain further identification cards, as well as "passes" for specific events and access to particular places. As Harry Hansen later reported, "Nobody can get far in Paris without a pass of some kind."[70]

Woodrow Wilson did finally arrive. On December 14, the *George Washington* sailed into Brest, bringing an incumbent American president to foreign shores for the first time. Wilson's presence electrified the masses and set off one tumultuous welcome after another in cities across Europe. His reception in France was especially moving, Howard Wheeler wrote, with "gay, eager, cheering crowds; bands, bugles, the rumble of guns. It was a brave spectacle, without pomp. It was human, real, throat-gripping. It was great to be a Frenchman that day. . . . *And it was great to be an American.*"[71] The fact that Wheeler had been a journalist during the war did not take away from his appreciation for the cheering. To the contrary, he accepted it proudly and gratefully, for the crowds were extolling more than him and his colleagues—in fact, more than Wilson; they were also paying tribute to America, its ideals, and its part in ending the war.

We could not have been mistaken for soldiers, we three reporters, but wherever we went—and it was the same at Strassbourg, Colmar, Mulhouse and

Belfort—they cheered us with the same spontaneous whole-heartedness as they cheered when they saw the autos carrying Pershing, or their own military leaders. All day and every day as we worked our way through the crowds, it was the same: *"Les Americains! Vive Wilson! Vive l'Amerique!"* It was seldom "President Wilson," almost always just "Wilson." Americans—any Americans, soldiers or not—meant Wilson. And Wilson meant America. And American meant something very big and full of comfort and happiness to those simple, happy people. I didn't get it into words until I got back to Paris. And then I got it from the lips of a French financier, who had generously given me much of his time to inform me concerning the French merchant marine and its problems. As I was leaving, I told him of my trip to Metz and through Alsace, and of the enthusiasm toward Americans. "Ah, yes!" He said. "You must remember that the people of Alsace as well as all other French people are passionately liberty loving. You will find that America is very close to the hearts of the little people of France. There are many reasons. One of them is that your President has a rare gift of taking an ordinary discussion of statesmanship, or world politics, and making it sound like a prayer—a prayer which French people understand, one which gives expression to their deepest desires."[72]

The French were also celebrating change—the heralded beginning of a new era, Wheeler wrote. He believed he and his progressive-minded countrymen symbolized that change by their very presence in the Old World. Reform was on the way:

Paris to-day is full of peoples. . . . And Americans—thousands of us; not the tourists of the old days, but officials, military and civil, commissions, missions, troops, reporters. . . . The reason, of course, is that the Peace Conference will be the first Congress of the World. It will decide the fate of the nations. "Armistice" is only a word. The war is over, the fighting. Two of the great old empires have been beaten to pieces. The balance of power is broken. The whole world is to be rearranged. The earth's surface is to be redistributed.[73]

Even the soberer *New York Tribune* chimed in in an admiring editorial: "We congratulate [the president] upon a gorgeous human experience."[74] And the *Tribune*'s correspondent confirmed that French officials also thought Wilson's reception was extraordinary and unprecedented.[75]

Soon after the public ballyhoo came the private homage—honors, courtesies, invitations—a courtship, really, that took place as governments one by one tried to woo the press successfully. It did not happen right away. In fact, it seems that American correspondents were initially disappointed by inflexible American and French bureaucrats.[76] But government officials gradually learned to be accommodating, and between Wilson's arrival and the start of the conference, conditions improved. The apex of good treatment came in England in late December when journalists crossed the Channel to cover Wilson's tour there. The British government took pains to make journalists feel important, literally extending the royal welcome to them. E. M. Hood was among a group of American journalists who shook hands with the king and queen at Buckingham Palace, the first time the press had ever been so received there.[77] Indeed, the opportunity to encounter famous people might have been (might still be) journalists' most prestigious perk. Accommodations in England were, after all, not perfect.

> The heating system went on strike and the room was almost at the freezing point but we had a memorable dinner notwithstanding and I am only returned to my room trying to write on this strange machine, while half a dozen of the boys who live elsewhere have gathered in the room and are indulging in reminiscences [sic] and stories of the day and I wonder how and when I can get in to the pink satin covered bed which awaits me. The whole thing seems like a dream as I have said and I am always feeling that I have only to open my eyes and the whole thing will disappear. We have a program that promises to fill up every minute of our time for the four days we shall be in England, all the time in the hands of the govt.[78]

For Hood the social compensations of being a newspaper correspondent were amply rewarding. Here he talked with kings, hobnobbed with statesmen, enjoyed near-diplomatic status himself. He, too, was a celebrity, being wined and dined by other celebrities. In addition to Reuters officials with whom he was associated, Hood indulged in the confidence of Lords Bryce, Reading, and Cecil. He shared dinners and drinks and sometimes a quiet conversation. Hood also earned the distinction of being the American correspondent chosen to interview Lloyd George on behalf of a large group of journalists, "with the most satisfactory results—who would ever have thought of me in London interviewing the Premier, something the British reporters never dare attempt."[79] But even when he was not busy interviewing a source, Hood still savored the hullabaloo. Just before the new year he detailed his fast time in a letter to his wife, a letter breathless with delight:

Since my last to you I have gone from London up to Manchester in the heart of England and had some interesting experiences travelling as we did (we means the correspondents) on the Presidential trains and boats ever since we touched English soil. Of course we shared the reflected glory of his presence and you cannot imagine the enthusiasm with which the English people welcomed our President; honestly I believe he is more popular than their own king, who by the way, with his queen came to the station in London this morning to see us off. Our last night in London was a glorious finale as we (again the correspondents) were entertained at the Carlton at a banquet by Lord Mont. . . . I met a number of scions of the nobility who turned out to be the liveliest and nicest of men.[80]

Hood did not fail to view his meetings with important people with some measure of circumspection. "So much did they go out of their way to be good to us," he wrote, "that I suspect they are haunted by the fear that in this wave of democracy their own titles will not last long unless they can popularize themselves, and they know no other means as promising as the press."[81] Mainly, however, mingling with Britain's "scions" thrilled Hood, and his diary contains the same exuberance as the letters he wrote home. He remembered his time in England this way: "I'm in [the Savoy Hotel] in beautiful suite. . . . One round of banquets and receptions for several days. Including presentation to King & Queen in Buckingham Palace—fancy!!" He lists his encounters with notable gentlemen, then mentions "a wonderful presentation in the Guild Hall—Oh Boy!!"[82] This is as close as most middle-aged men come to sheer giddiness.

Hood was obviously overwhelmed by the pomp and pageantry that accompanied a presidential convoy, so much so that he admitted to having been changed by the experience, to becoming more adventuresome himself. When Associated Press chief Melville Stone urged Hood to see Rome and other cities if he wanted while in Italy, Hood told his wife matter-of-factly: "Of course I did (you can see how much I have changed in this short time, a few weeks ago I would have declined. Dick says I must be getting crazy, even trying to get up in airplanes) and I am now trying to get the Visa; if successful you may expect to hear from me next in Rome. All of which is much on my conscience when I reflect on your condition at home while I am seeing so much that you should share with me."[83] While in Italy Hood met the pope in a quiet, though still formal, meeting arranged by the Italian government.

Hood wrote home that the pontiff was "very human but you must strain your imagination to see me on my knees before him (true bill) and going through all the formality which marks the audience with the prelate. We were told that it was most unprecedented for him to greet any newspapermen at all much less to deliver an address to them."[84] These types of encounters were bound to make reporters feel a bit dizzy.

Swope, a pseudo-celebrity himself, relished the name-dropping and star-gazing, too. One souvenir he picked up in Paris and apparently treasured so much he brought it back to the United States was "a chewed-up pencil stub that he preserved forever in an envelope marked 'Lord Bryce's pencil.'"[85] Even Mark Sullivan, whose magazine normally effected a wary, skeptical attitude toward the president, seemed swept up in the momentum of Paris and the peace conference's mission. He pointed to a legal adviser whose sole duty was to ensure that America not give up any constitutional privileges in the new League of Nations, then explicitly reassured doubters like "Senator Reed or ex-Senator Beveridge" that they had little to worry about.[86] Like Sullivan, many journalists' early experiences colored their reporting for several months at a time, making that period between December and January stand out as the epitome of optimistic coverage. Certainly, the experiences exceeded in picturesqueness anything the correspondents had known before. Coming to Europe had indeed been an adventure for American correspondents, for many of them a glorious adventure, and with the start of the conference just around the corner a historic one as well.

LIFE IN PARIS

Paris during the conference was a cold, damp, sunless place. The temperature often dropped to between twenty and thirty degrees Fahrenheit, and occasionally there was snow. More often than not between December and January it rained, making everything seem "water-logged," one journalist said.[87] Because of the heavy precipitation, the Seine was high, resulting in frequent fog.[88] As a consequence of the season and the recent wartime shortages of fuel, the accommodations journalists held were usually frigid at night. Hood complained to his wife about the chilly conditions where he was lodging: "My hotel room has not had a bit of artificial heat for many weeks I think; I awake in the morning to watch the steam from my own breath rise in the air and shudder to think of rising."[89] Hood also described the agony of cold baths but conceded he was lucky in having such a facility in the first place at that time.[90] Not surprisingly, reporters frequently caught colds, nagging coughs, the flu, or worse, and the constant pressure of work made recovery from these ills slow. "No American at [Paris] felt well for long," one historian aptly put it.[91]

La vie chère, the high cost of living, was also a frequent source of complaint, journalists and others criticizing French shopkeepers for usurious prices. "Paris is Washington at the height of the war season, crowded, expensive, and irritable," A. D. Call wrote.[92] Clothes and cab fares ran high, but living accommodations and food were downright exorbitant. Du Bois paid ten francs a day for a room; Samuel Blythe paid seven.[93] Sam McClure wrote that "[h]otel rates are double what they were" before the war. "It is impossible to get a meal of the simplest sort . . . for less than a dollar on the average."[94] The scarcity of food, particularly good food, made journalists wax nostalgic in their personal letters home about "farm food."[95] Meat and vegetables they could find easily, but butter, milk, and sugar were very rare.[96] Exceptions caused waves of excitement throughout Paris. Arthur Krock tells of a journalistic convoy whose mission was locating a restaurant rumored to use real butter.[97] A bottle of wine could cost the equivalent of $10, for some journalists a week's wage.[98]

One of the most striking characteristics of Paris immediately after the war was the motley, cosmopolitan nature of the city. "Paris was not Paris, but a foreign city in France," William Allen White wrote, the "air filled with international horse-trading."[99] Between the signing of the armistice in November of 1918 and the end of the peace conference in June of 1919, leaders of the international community descended en masse to the site of the negotiations. Paris was "full of presidents, premiers, and princes of the blood in 'civies,'" Harry Hansen remembered, and their presence produced all kinds of unlikely social interaction:

> To-day in Paris ministers plenipotentiary and commissioners extraordinary mingle on the boulevards and in the cafes, sit beside bronzed doughboys in the "metro," haggle with tradesmen in the rue, run after elusive cabs and await their turn among the unnumbered hundreds for a room with bath at the few available hotels. At night in the music halls, theaters, and opera-houses of Paris one sees the men who have won the war with their fists and the men who are to secure peace of the world by their wits and mental power sitting side by side.[100]

Hansen reported that the eclectic visitors gathered in one casino included, among the "blue, khaki, red and gold" of innumerable soldiers, U.S. Secretary of State Robert Lansing, General Francis Wingate, and cartoonist Rube Goldberg.[101] Sometimes the huge volume of new pseudo-Parisians led to comical embarrassments for people who really were Parisians. On one occasion, French premier Georges Clemenceau was denied entrance to the Hôtel de Crillon by a policeman who asked to see identification. A nearby Y.M.C.A. man vouched for the premier, who promptly thanked his good Samaritan: "'Well, I am glad you recognized me.' 'Yes,' replied the latter. 'I have seen your head carved on a pipe.'"[102]

The world had come to Paris in 1919. There were armies of experts selected to advise their countries' delegations; approximately eight hundred journalists, publicists, lobbyists galore; and soldiers everywhere—a "preponderance of blue and khaki in the streets."[103] Americans abounded—"more Americans than French," it seemed,[104] and professionals of various stripes sauntered all about. Samuel G. Blythe noted that General Tasker Bliss brought a personal ethnologist, Colonel House a physiographer.[105] As both Blythe and Hansen had observed, the mix of diverse people was truly astonishing. Northern France was flooded with foreigners, and Parisian society had been dramatically shaken by the enormous influx of temporary residents and other transients. Foremost among the new denizens, it appeared, were Americans. "Paris seemed now almost an American city," Will Irwin thought.[106]

To those who had been to Paris before the war, the city looked strange. It had obviously suffered from bombardments and mobilizations—streets and sidewalks broken here and there, buildings torn or smoke-damaged, makeshift fortifications built for a city under siege. Paris was an urban battlefield, sections of which had been demolished, sections of which had survived. According to Alfred M. Brace, of the *New York Tribune,* the city was "still on a war basis": "Cafés and restaurants close sharply at 9:30 and empty their patrons out into the boulevards. At 10 o'clock streetcars and autobuses cease to run, and at 11:30 the trains of the subway system make their last trip, leaving belated theatergoers to walk home in the rain or to submit to browbeating taxicab drivers."[107] Police told Brace that the measures were necessary on account of the thousands of soldiers then living in Paris. The city, then, was part encampment, part battleground. It was filled with the refuse of war: armaments, stockpiles, debris. The Place de la Concorde, for example, was so festooned with some of the captured trophies of war—German guns and tanks mainly—that eventually it came to resemble a military salvage yard, "a gigantic junk-pile."[108] The weather-beaten army hardware stood, on the same square, in striking contrast to the simple garlands draped on the Strasbourg statue to commemorate the loss of Alsace-Lorraine. Most of all, Paris resembled a bandaged wound. "Everywhere are evidences of war—cannon, protected buildings, soldiers of all nations—but most of all the women clothed in silent black!"[109]

What Marguerite Harrison remembered most from her visit to the city in 1919 were the soldiers from all over the world, many of them simply "waiting," the ubiquitous disrepair, and sandbags.[110] Nighttime brought a different-looking Paris as well, a dark and largely invisible one, for during the war lamplights had been blackened out, painted over in dark blue or green to provide minimal visibility, or knocked out altogether. Even many automobiles still kept the old wartime dimmers in place.[111] After the war the situation took time to remedy, so correspondents out at night during the conference normally found themselves "groping" about in order to make their way to hotels and restaurants and private residences.[112]

The atmosphere in Paris was a peculiar one. Weary, broken, and hungry from the war, the city also showed an awkward and irritable but nonetheless emerging vitality, thanks in large part to the economic injection provided by thousands of new cash-carrying consumers. The high prices that caused American doughboys and journalists to grumble were lifting the city out of impoverishment and into something like a respectable self-sustenance. If prosperity were months or years away, it was closer because the peace conference was held within its limits. Coinciding with this gradual economic recovery was the rise in morale that had first buoyed spirits when the armistice was declared. By the spring of 1919, Paris had been turned into the world's international hub, with the heterogeneous consequences that entailed. At theaters, restaurants, and other public places, a quirky, off-beat mood oftentimes prevailed. Practical jokes and hoaxes abounded. Will Irwin tells of the petition he circulated advocating independence for California, which many press bureaus actually took seriously.[113] Every now and then, quirky behavior gave way to a circus-like surreality. Arthur Krock, of the *Louisville Courier-Journal*, described a freakish scene in which one of Teddy Roosevelt's nephews and a friend jokingly set up a stand in front of a large French bank and proceeded to auction it off![114] The profusion of mischievous journalists and discharged soldiers, who were not uncommonly drunk, contributed to the occasional wildness of life in Paris. Above all the city was pervaded by its visitors' sense of excitement. "You can hear any kind of story you want in Paris," Chester M. Wright of the *New York Tribune* practically exclaimed, "because men and women of all kinds and from every corner of the world are gathered here. In the fringe of the official show are those who have come here to offer their advice, those who have come because they want to see the performance, those who have come 'free lancing' it as writers, those who have come just because they can't keep away from what's doing as long as they can rake up the price of steamer fare."[115] France's capital was alive in 1919 with the boisterous sounds of reporters, soldiers, delegates, propagandists, and other guests, most of whom were quite elated to be there.

With the end of the war, and the end of the fear of German air attacks, in fact, Paris had suddenly grown loud again. On most main streets you could hear "the steady drumming noise of the big motor-busses that run from the Bastille to the Madeleine; . . . [the] maniacal tooting of motor-horns . . . [the] ringing laughter of a group of American doughboys on leave."[116] Paris was sounding like a large city again. Much of the noise emanated from traffic snarls that only a capital and a river city can know. Clunky military vehicles, of course, still clogged the streets. But the sounds of old Paris were coming back, too: the sounds of music (bands playing the omnipresent tune "Madelon"); celebration; the bustle of haggling shopkeepers; vigorous conversation. Naturally the presence of peacemakers from around the world stirred endless animated discussions about everything from Germany's financial resources to blueprints for the proposed League of Nations. Continual crises—the attempted assassination of Clemenceau, Wilson's summoning of his ship, the *George Washington,* in the middle of the conference—supplied a never-ending source of clamorous debate.

Recreation was limited for journalists on account of their intensive schedules. But when they did have time for activity other than work it was usually sightseeing, dining out, attending plays and concerts, and writing and receiving personal mail. For W. E. B. Du Bois, socializing in Paris was a profoundly pleasant experience, a source of great racial solace to a black man from America: "God! It was simply human decency and I had to be thankful for it because I am an American Negro. . . . Fellow blacks, we must join the democracy of Europe."[117] The possibilities of making new friends and acquaintances inevitably came, and particularly during the journalists' first two months in Europe.

Communication with family and friends in the States also provided entertaining diversion. Indeed, one of the most moving and meaningful experiences journalists enjoyed in Paris was reading letters from home. These letters were their lifeline to kith, kin, and the world outside the peace conference. Such correspondence connected them with their past and with home, as well as their identity in a far-away present. If certain letters made them cry or worried them, others would encourage and comfort them. Hattie McClure reassured her husband, Sam, that she was fine, and more concerned with the developments of his work overseas than with her welfare at home: "You—your well-being and satisfaction and your ability to do your work and carry out your plans—are my first thought, as you always are. I hope you are getting on well right now and doing all just according to your ideal."[118] Such letters were obviously important for bolstering journalists' morale when they felt homesick, for nothing tore their hearts more than to learn of or worry about any pain or sadness their absence was causing loved ones. Swope's wife, Margaret, suffered a nervous breakdown during his absence, which greatly upset him. When apprised of the crying spells at home of one correspondent's spouse, possibly Margaret Swope, E. M. Hood sharply commented to his own wife: "[L]et us hope that it was ill health on her own part and not mere selfishness that caused this, otherwise she would be no fit wife for a newspaperman."[119] But Hood could not leave it at that. Evidently his trip to Paris triggered occasional guilt that his wife was not there to share his exotic adventures:

> I know that you did not feel particularly happy over my departure but you were too good a sport to stand in the way of my advancement in my profession and too unselfish to grudge me so much of a good time as I could get out of the trip along with the work. For the latter has not been lacking you may believe me; here it is again the beginning of a seven day week of work as I have had from the beginning of the Conference and I feel that I am entitled to snatch what enjoyment I can out of the odd moments.[120]

Hood's frequent references to his arduous labor suggest that he regarded his work in Paris as a glamorous experience but did not want to flaunt his privileged opportunity too much before his wife, who might be making sacrifices at home during his absence.

Telegrams between the continents were notoriously slow but still faster than regular posted mail, which took about a week to travel between France and the United States. Although communication with family was never instantaneous, it could still be frequent. The dates affixed to the correspondence of some journalists showed they wrote home as often as every three or four days. They were quite detailed, too: some letters ran as long as two thousand words. These were writers, after all, men and women for whom putting pen to paper and sharing thoughts were second nature. The fact, though, that journalists often had to fight fatigue, busy schedules, and constant interruptions when they did write testifies to the personal importance mail held for them. And, of course, reading correspondence written by others must have been a special treat for individuals daily responsible for producing it themselves.

Sightseeing also provided occasional relief from the daily duties of conference routine. The French and Belgian governments believed that the more people who saw the battlefields and the sites of wanton German destruction, the more sympathy they could generate for their suffering during the war, and thus the fatter the indemnities the enemy would be forced to pay in compensation. They were particularly eager that American diplomats, especially Wilson, and all American journalists, be given ample opportunity to tour these sites, because it was feared that the United States would use its influence at the conference to "soften" the peace. In most Allied political circles, Wilson's Fourteen Points was regarded as a diplomatic package likely to produce a treaty merciful to Germany. Therefore, every effort was made after the war to show the Americans what unforgivable evils the enemy had perpetrated. By contrast, journalists were forbidden to travel to Germany after the war, where, it was believed, they might show pity for the plight of the vanquished.[121] Given journalists' need for restful and alternative activity while covering the conference, many eventually made at least one trip to the French or Belgian battlegrounds.

Wilson's departure for the United States in February provided some abatement of the intensive concentration journalists devoted to the conference, and many correspondents tried to arrange a few leisurely activities during that month. Hood, for example, wrote his wife that he would attempt to take advantage of the president's absence for some long-awaited rest. "[O]n the whole . . . feeling very well, which is surprising considering the fact that I have worked every day including Sundays for two months past and every night as well except for two nights at the theatres. So I am getting a little stale I think, but perhaps I will have a chance to go around and see some of the city and country after President Wilson goes off a week from tomorrow."[122] Journalists ventured out to opera houses and theaters for entertainment.

There they often found themselves rubbing elbows once more with the diplomats they trailed and hovered around during the day. Paris, it turned out, was a small world for the people making and reporting the peace. But there were others there as well, of course, most notably the soldiers whose presence no observer could miss. Every public performance of music, art, and theater became an opportunity for groups of boisterous *poilus* to lead audiences in tearful, throat-swelling singing. Indeed, the "variegated" nature of the crowds attracted the attention of many journalists. At a Paris casino Harry Hansen was struck by the many different foreigners gathered in the same place, laughing and drinking together, singing the same songs: "Throughout the hall men were joining in—Chasseurs Alpins wearing their tam-o'shanters, Scotchmen in plaids, Canadians and Tommies liberally sprinkled with brass insignia, and Americans with all sorts of odd devices on their sleeves."[123]

Work never ended altogether. Many reporters, in fact, were given temporary assignments that took them out of Paris or even France while the president was away. Switzerland was an important stop. According to Simeon Strunsky, "the interest of many of the professional correspondents and unattached observers about the Peace Conference shifted from Paris to Berne" for the International Socialist Conference.[124] The latter gave them the opportunity to compare assemblies and personnel, politics and ideologies. It also helped to make them, incidentally, more seasoned diplomatic correspondents.

As the end of the conference approached and attention turned toward Versailles, the French government provided tours for visiting journalists and diplomats, taking care to focus on selected points of interest depending on the company. The French were not flawless tour guides. A mishap one day greatly amused Patrick Gallagher, when a tour leader mistook a group of British visitors for Irishmen and proceeded to show them a painting of the Battle of Fontenoy, of 1745, in which Irish volunteers fighting for France defeated a British force. The delighted Gallagher could not contain himself: "I am afraid I scandalized the company by letting out a good Indian warwhoop. The Englishmen were frozen in their tracks."[125]

American journalists remembered these sojourns fondly. For many individuals such trips were heady adventure, replete with exotic sights and the exclusively shared camaraderie of foreign travel. A. D. Call described a trip to Belgium as though in a reverie: "At seven o'clock we were all on our way prosaically sliding along in a Hotchkiss limousine, trying as best we could to sense the things we had seen, the meaning of it all, just sliding happily along into Paris, thinking of the fun of telling our less fortunate friends all about it. But the note-maker of the party knows that the thing can't be told so what's the use?"[126] For Call, as for other reporters, these journeys were not presents given out of sheer generosity or hospitality, but given for a purpose—for propaganda aims not difficult to fathom. Still, these governmental efforts to garner favorable publicity by systematically courting the press were unprecedented for a major diplomatic summit. And the correspondents generally appreciated and made use of them, if for no other reason than to get out of a raucous and somewhat vengeful city that was beginning to indulge in its postwar right to grumble and criticize and occasionally even lash out.

POLITICS AND PROFESSIONALISM

The political climate in Paris made an indelible impression on American journalists covering the conference. Lucian Swift Kirtland believed that "every vibrant nerve, individual and national, is on edge."[127] Many soon doubted it was the wisest choice for a site where the fate of nations would be decided. As H. Wilson Harris pointed out, one needed to remember that in "the last months of the war, the months most recent in memory, shells had fallen day by day and bombs dropped night by night in her streets."[128] The mood of Paris—the collective emotions of the majority of the inhabitants—indeed resonated with the echoes of a wounded survivor. The result was an atmosphere of hatred toward the enemy and a quick indignation toward the expression of anything but ruthlessness. More than anything else, it seemed, Parisians clamored for revenge. At minimum, they insisted on a severe treaty that would exact the utmost from Germany. The enemy would pay for its crimes against France, and—make no mistake, they believed—this would be a thoroughly French treaty. "The city," Harris remembered, "was passionate in its nationalism."[129]

Part of that nationalism was, of course, the natural consequence of a war so recently ended. But another main factor was a French reaction to the presence of so many foreigners, above all Americans, in their capital. There were "too many Americans over here mussing things up, crowding people out of the hotels and pensions, and unsettling the foundations of things."[130] A. D. Call worried aloud about the growing animosity between the French and the Americans, calling it "disturbing" but saying it probably would not last long.[131]

H. Wilson Harris believed that the institution most responsible for trumpeting nationalism and which in essence "made the atmosphere of the Conference" was the French press. Most Parisian journals, and only to a lesser extent those in the provinces, identified the American diplomatic agenda as the one most in opposition to that of their own country. Right-wing and numerous centrist publications accordingly targeted President Wilson. Indeed, one of the ironies of the French press during the conference was its devout affinity for Republican Party politics in America. That was clear to one American peace delegate, George Bernard Noble. His thorough analysis of French journalism after the war, in many ways still the best work on the subject, detailed what amounted to a vociferous campaign against the president beginning in December. By contrast, Wilson's journalistic defenders within the French press corps proved quieter allies: "[O]nly the scantiest news favorable to Wilson appeared in the Left Wing press, for the press of the Left did not have correspondents in the United States and was, therefore, almost entirely at the mercy of the semi-official news agencies which carefully selected the news to be given out to the papers."[132]

The sympathy of French newspapers and journals for Wilson's Republican critics gave the voice of the American opposition party tremendous publicity and clout in France. The intensity of the criticism ensued from a concerted campaign by Parisian journalists and diplomats determined to forge the kind of peace treaty they believed in by mounting maximum pressure on President Wilson. Combined with the editorial style of French journalism, this campaign produced a shrill and narrow political wavelength which reverberated throughout the capital.[133] And from Wilson's standpoint it did not help matters that virtually everyone in Paris, American journalists and diplomats alike, regularly picked up and read the French newspapers, thereby constantly amplifying the official French view on all conference issues.

The French view, typically, challenged the American view, Wilson's ability to speak for it, and the pieties about the proposed society of nations. David Lawrence said that the American press was "surprised to find the French more often arrayed against us than alongside us."[134] But American journalists quickly sensed the winds of postbellum politics in France, eventually ascribing to it part of the blame for weaknesses in the treaty. If much of the problem was French politics, American journalists contended, then the French press had to be as guilty as Clemenceau or the other political leaders, for the two sectors were said to be insidiously intertwined. Many American correspondents blamed that situation on the supposedly antiquated nature of

French journalism. Harris and others noted in disgust the "subsidized" nature of the press in France, its unabashed partisanship and close relationship to political leaders. According to these American critics, the press in France was simply less developed, less mature, less *professional*. To what extent they themselves were professionals was an issue to be played out during the work of the conference.

One small but important change occurred in the testimony and reportage of many of the American correspondents gathered there—a subtle shift toward a more collective consciousness. In William Allen White's letters and memoirs, for example, his ego starts to recede a little from the pages. From an overweening focus on "I" and "me" (one out of every ten words in some writings),[135] the Kansan gradually starts referring more and more to "we" and "us." His perspective becomes less narcissistic, more collective, more communal. In February, he was writing his wife, Sallie, about a conversation with Colonel House in which White insisted that he "would go to Prinkipo [for a proposed conference with the Soviets] only if they let all the newspapermen go who wanted to go," perhaps no extraordinary sacrifice but yet remarkable for White.[136] On the subject of professionalism, White was never a journalist to push book learning, academic training, or bureaucratic expertise. And yet while he worked overseas, he did begin to appreciate the value of an organized front in the war for publicity, whatever the frustrations along the way. In other words, the presence of large numbers of American and foreign journalists seemed to have stirred White's sense of solidarity, his spirit of professionalism. If he was a hard nut to crack in this respect, the experience in Europe did seem to have softened him.

CONCLUSION TO PART THREE

In January 1919 several hundred American correspondents invaded Paris to report on the peace conference formally ending World War I. These journalists represented newspapers, magazines, and wire services; professed allegiance to all the major political parties; included both old and young, men and women; and possessed a variety of experience. All, however, regarded the opportunity as perhaps the greatest one of their career, and almost all eagerly hoped for some fulfillment of the promise of "open diplomacy." Indeed, their professional aspirations were closely tied into Wilson's postwar rhetoric, just as they were to Wilson's progressive approach to presidential activism. If the day of secret treaties and backstage deal-making was over, then negotiation would have to be publicized, and if negotiation was now to be publicized, then the press would at some point have to be involved, perhaps even gain a revolutionary new influence.

The correspondents' journey to Europe and the time they spent in some of the victorious countries did little to discourage their ambitions. For many reporters, in fact, the glamorous postwar hobnobbing had generously inflated those hopes. Though most recognized the divisions among the Allies and sensed the steadily growing political hostility to Wilson, they also observed the spellbinding effect their president had on the European masses, and with that kind of power—one inseparable from publicity, after all— anything seemed possible. Two years after a food riot in Petrograd upended czarist rule in Russia, public opinion was an entity politicians and the press took very seriously.

What journalists eagerly anticipated, therefore, was the extent to which they, and through them the people, would receive respect and accommodation once diplomatic talks started. With the Committee on Public Information soon to be entirely out of the picture, news correspondents awaited their chance to resume the dominant access to public opinion they had held before the war. The press had lost its near-monopoly in 1917. In 1919 it would seek to get it back. But dominance was not the same thing as professionalism, which stood mainly intact on the eve of the Paris Peace Conference. In reaffirming their professional status and political independence, American journalists found a useful foil in the French press. But they still had to deal with diplomats, including their own. How well they would fare in that encounter is the subject of the next section.

PART FOUR

CONFRONTATION AND STABILITY

The Role of the Press at the Paris Peace Conference

⁓ 7 ⁓

"THE AMERICAN NEWSPAPER MEN ... WENT BOLSHEVIK"

The Controversy over Press Access

America's news correspondents came to Europe in the winter of 1918–1919 filled with optimism and a high degree of purpose. As they embarked upon their postwar duties, many individuals looked upon the peace conference as a professional opportunity for the press to assert itself prominently in the diplomatic resolution of World War I, as a chance for journalists to make a difference not just in Paris but in the subsequent course of American foreign relations. At the outset, though, America's itinerant newsmen and -women first had to establish a framework within which they would operate. They had to understand and to try to shape that context. Establishing a routine, then, was their first order of business.

Past conferences failed to provide adequate guidance, however, for so much had changed since, for example, the Portsmouth Conference of 1905. Publicity was an important and compelling factor at the turn of the century but still in a relatively modest state of development. Then a world war, an even more astonishingly expanded executive branch, the growth of propaganda, Wilson's ideal of open diplomacy—all raised expectations of what the press was supposed to do and how it would fit in. More than expectations, though, the progressive publicity *practices* already established by everyone from presidents, cabinet secretaries, and members of Congress to corporations, lobbyists, unions, consumer groups, and muckrakers signaled a vast new opportunity for journalists supposedly attending "the greatest peace conference in all history," the dawn of a new era in diplomatic relations.[1]

American correspondents were thus prepared to accept challenging duties and responsibilities, or to fight for them if necessary. Regardless of journalists' exact contributions, however, publicity—not secrecy—would unmistakably distinguish this peace summit. Lloyd George recalled that the issue of publicity was one "which occupied a good deal of our time."[2] Members of the press helped make it so. Like all who worked in the public sphere during the progressive era, journalists favored orderly agitation through communication. But diplomats, too, whatever their level of discomfort, found agitation inevitable and publicity irresistible. What remained, then, was for both groups to agree to ground rules. These proved highly sensitive to professional and national differences alike.

On January 15, 1919, Ray Stannard Baker, America's official press agent in Paris, fingered the conference's first official communiqué as if he were handling spoiled fruit. Most people had expected the president to name George Creel as press liaison, but the now-"tarnished" CPI director rightly believed himself to be a public relations liability and said no, perhaps a mistake in retrospect, but staying on would have been politically difficult at the time.[3] In his place Wilson had chosen Baker, at the last moment, to assist in communicating the peace proceedings to the public from Paris, and this particular announcement was one that the head of the American Press Bureau did not relish delivering to his former colleagues. According to the statement, authorized communiqués would be the primary means, apparently the only means, for disseminating news to the world. Contrary to popular belief, at least among journalists, and ostensibly in defiance of the first of Wilson's Fourteen Points, the press would not be permitted to sit in to witness and record the making of the peace. Either the president had misled them or miscalculated, or perhaps they had misled themselves. Either way they felt disillusioned. Recalled Baker, "I shall never forget the disappointment, exasperation, disgust, when that first communiqué was put out."[4]

Nor did the correspondents gathered there. *Chicago Tribune* correspondent Arthur M. Evans reported that a "secrecy gag" had been placed on the conference.[5] Mark Sullivan called it "a step backward," a document whose words sounded rather "medieval."[6] "Secret Sessions of Peace Conference Are Decreed Over Americans' Protest," the *New York Tribune* announced.[7] Richard Oulahan of the *New York Times* accused the delegates of trying to "keep the people of the world in the dark."[8] The rest of the American press was equally startled and disappointed. And their British colleagues were no less disturbed.

The caption in the *London Times* hung like a shroud over the text of its article: "VEIL OVER THE CONFERENCE. OFFICIAL NEWS ONLY."[9]

An editorial the next day made clear the paper's mood. According to the writer, the conference had bungled the task of balancing the "right of the principals—that is to say, the people at home who read the newspapers—with the efficient discharge of the duties by the agents who are the delegates."[10] This was certainly no aristocratic view of diplomacy. It was, however, recognition that the older form of statesmanship was giving way only grudgingly to a newer, democratic version—a sad fact for journalists not just because it revealed an uncharitable stubbornness but also because it allegedly demonstrated a backward-thinking, unprogressive mentality. "Unfortunately," the editorialist declared, "the truth seems to be that the majority of the Delegates still do not understand the meaning of publicity and in their heart of hearts still regard the Press, without whose support the war could not have been won, as a dangerous and impertinent intruder into the diplomatic holy of holies."[11]

Richard Oulahan registered the same alarm for his paper, saying that "already a feeling of discouragement and indignation is displayed among newspaper representatives from allied countries."[12] The correspondent Mark Sullivan was even angrier, calling Wilson "conspicuously and disastrously the loser," a capitulator who squandered an opportunity for the press to be "in such a position as it has not occupied since the printing press was invented." Wilson, Sullivan charged, had "surrendered the best weapon he had—publicity."[13] Joseph Tumulty was so alarmed he rattled off an immediate telegram to Wilson's physician-confidante, Admiral Cary Grayson: "In my opinion, if President has consented to this, it will be fatal." Wilson responded later the same day, saying the worst rumors were false and that he would do his best.[14]

The clanging discrepancy between what democratic governments preached during the war and what they were officially telling the press now seemed to amount to simple hypocrisy. "In spite of condemnation while the war was on of the secret methods prevailing at the Congress of Vienna," Oulahan wrote, "the conclusion is being forced upon the observers here that this conference is the Congress of Vienna all over again."[15] It might be true, as British delegation member Harold Nicolson later wrote, that the press is subject to the allure of the picturesque, all the more so at large conferences where famous plenipotentiaries gather,[16] and being confined to "colorless" communiqués might indeed seem a harsh sentence to people who tell stories for a living. But if conference policy was undercutting the freedom and enjoyment many reporters savored in doing their jobs, they were also angry, perhaps most angry, because the announcement contradicted what they had been told to expect.

Many correspondents seemed to share the idealism of people like Oula-han, who subscribed ardently to Woodrow Wilson's vision of a world made orderly by international law and cooperation. If reporters met Wilson, or the other conferees, or the idea of a league of nations more than halfway, perhaps it was because they wanted very much for Wilson, the conference, and the league to succeed. As Oulahan testified, "In a journalistic experience covering many years I never knew a time when American newspapermen were so thoroughly filled with an unselfish and patriotic desire to help their country, and for that matter the entire world."[17] Oulahan believed both young and veteran journalists had come to Paris inspired or invigorated by Wilson's Fourteen Points. Most really expected an end to secret diplomacy and thought they were helping to establish a new version in which press and government combined as partners to represent the interests of the people. In this respect, the *London Times* and the *New York Times,* indeed, probably a majority of newspapers, stood united in challenging sharp divergence from this ideal. If Baker is right, public anticipation bordered on the theatrical:

> Whatever the complicated causes . . . it is a fact that by January 12, when [the Conferees] . . . met for the first time there in the already famous council room in the Quai d'Orsay, the public interest, anxiety, and expectation had grown to enormous proportions. The curtain was at last to rise. A new heaven and a new earth were to be revealed.
>
> And then the anticlimax! The curtain did not go up.[18]

January's limited-publicity announcement also alarmed reporters in the sense that it threatened professional morale, for the policy smacked of a reprimand, or, at worst, a repudiation of what journalists did for a living. Being snubbed, however, could be more than a personal blow to the ego (particularly if it was more than a perception); it also withheld from the press the prestige and professional influence that diplomatic access would have offered.

Baker verifies this surging self-consciousness among reporters in describing how the press reacted to the January communiqué. After a British press protest, an American contingent stormed into the French Foreign Office on January 15 "demanding that they be admitted to the first general session of the Peace Conference. They horrified the upholders of the old methods, they desperately offended the ancient conventions, they were as rough and direct as democracy itself."[19] "Their protest stopped all business of the Peace Conference until action was taken upon it."[20] Democracy and democratic rhetoric, obviously, could serve as a weapon for social advancement for members of the press who recognized its possibilities. What journalists wanted was access to the high and mighty, with whom by association, if nothing else, they, too, became important people, their duties an important profession, their profession a democratic calling. "At Paris these ambassadors of public opinion," as Baker fondly referred to members of the press, "at least those from America—had come, not begging, but demanding. They sat at every doorway, they looked over every shoulder, they wanted every resolution and report and wanted it immediately."[21] American journalists, Sullivan claimed, "had more or less a monopoly of the indignation."[22] They "blew up," William Allen White wrote, "went bolshevik and met in formal conference of protest."[23]

The American correspondents issued a personal petition to President Wilson, reminding him of his and the Allies' responsibility to uphold the Fourteen Points, since it was those principles on which, after all, the armistice had been drawn:

> [W]e vigorously protest . . . against what we have every reason to regard as gag-rule; and in common with the action of our British colleagues, who have laid their case before the Prime Minister, we appeal to you for relief from this intolerable condition.
>
> We stand where you stand: "Open covenants of peace, openly arrived at."[24]

Wilson already championed publicity, as did Lloyd George at this point, but initially Clemenceau had sided with Japan and Italy in opposing it, and their majority vote won the decision. Eventually, however, Wilson and Lloyd George swung Clemenceau to their side when he realized, and when they helped him realize, the potential damage of public disapproval. All during these first few weeks, the delegates spent a nearly exhaustive amount of time talking about how best to make arrangements with the press. Wilson continually pointed out the inevitability of leaks and disclosures, at one point even explaining to his colleagues one of journalists' tricks of the trade: "There was a well-known dodge in the American Press by which, after trying falsehood after falsehood and obtaining denial after denial, the seeker after information narrowed down the alternatives to the only possible residuum."[25] Insisting that "publicity could not be avoided," the president recommended that the press "be put on trial."[26] Perhaps because he was widely rumored to control a lion's share of the Paris press, Clemenceau eventually succumbed to the president's and the premier's appeal.

Meanwhile, the correspondents conferred with journalists from other nations. The French government hosted a meeting of press representatives at the foreign press club at 5 o'clock, Thursday, January 16, where journalists such as Baker and his British counterpart, Lord George Riddell, presented their case. The participants at this international journalism conference adopted several resolutions, the thrust of which, the *New York Times* noted in a headline, was "limited admission to [the] peace congress."[27] Six decisions were unanimous:

1. "It is essential to insure full publicity for the peace negotiations."
2. "The official communiqués should be as complete as possible."
3. "Informative 'background' material should be given to the press for 'guidance' and perspective."
4. "There should be no interference between the delegates and responsible journalists."
5. "Journalists should be permitted to attend the formal sessions of the conference."
6. "It is recommended that there be equal treatment of the allied press by the abolition of the censorship in all allied countries."

All but the French consented to allow press members to attend "sittings," or less formal meetings, and they also agreed on a specific number of journalists to attend from each nation—five.[28] English-speaking correspondents had been up in arms, then angry about conference developments and determined to change them for the better. They did.

In response to the press's demands, the delegates on January 17 discussed the issue of publicity. At that meeting the United States, Britain, France, Italy, and Japan all agreed to permit three (rather than five) journalists from each of the major powers to attend the peace talks in person, though only for formal, plenary sessions. They also drafted a statement to summarize their views on the role of both the press and public opinion, a document which André Tardieu referred to as a "marriage contract" between the press and the peacemakers. The contract discussed the importance of establishing limits on publicity and the need for avoiding controversy and misunderstanding: "The essence of democratic method is not that deliberations of a Government should be conducted in public, but that its conclusions should be subject to the consideration of a popular chamber and to free and open discussion on the platform and in the press."[29] It was, essentially, an apology for the restrictions, but not an altogether unfair prenuptial agreement. Indeed, the delegates stressed that they understood their accountability and the press's role in auditing them: "In calling attention to these necessary limitations on publicity the representatives of the Powers do not underrate the importance of carrying public opinion with them in the vast task by which they are confronted. They recognize that unless public opinion approves of the result of their labors they will be nugatory."[30]

It might be easy to dismiss these statements as simply empty lip-service, but viewed in light of the Western nations' extensive propaganda efforts during the war, it is more plausible that at least some of the delegates took public opinion extremely seriously and were prepared to make certain concessions to see that the press, and through it the public, was satisfied. In fact, because of some journalists' notoriously short memories of other conferences, the press as a whole seemed to downplay the significance of the compromise reached. Reporters grumbled, griped, and moped. But only a minority expressed any appreciation or awe of their obvious influence at that time. Diplomats, by contrast, showed more awareness. Most delegates who wrote about the press's involvement in Paris, in fact, seemed genuinely taken aback. In his memoirs, Lloyd George, for example, concluded that it would be necessary to avoid "peace by clamour" in the future.[31] In fact, he and a great many other observers—including some journalists, it should be noted—often referred to "the problem of publicity." Harold Nicolson blamed the presence of the press for the conference's constant "leaks."[32] American delegate Joseph Grew said he "knew from the start that the press would be the most dangerous element which we should have to handle."[33]

Whatever it meant to diplomats, the publicity confrontation had meant much to journalists. Two themes are striking from the press's involvement in the controversy.

First, Baker was right about the insistence with which the correspondents "demanded" their rights. They had been courteous, Ernest H. Abbott said, but not in a "tone of requesting a privilege."[34] They believed some measure of access was what was owed to them, and they would not be turned down quietly. Of course, the idea of "rights" itself is part of the lexicon of democratic rhetoric. These journalists were affirming their status as citizens in democracies; they were also proclaiming a special status as public representatives— "ambassadors," to use Baker's term—a concept they seemed wholeheartedly to embrace. "Had it not been for the activities of the Americans and the British the conference would have been closed to the public," Kentucky correspondent Arthur Krock wrote.[35] The other interesting element in this package is a subtly aristocratic plea, evident in the use of the word "responsible." Surely, the meaning of responsible journalism is a matter of some debate, the merits of specific practitioners likely hinging on political congeniality. As a *London Times* editorial pointed out, the conference could admit any and all journalists and keep busy punishing them afterward, or admit a few of the more responsible ones from the outset. "You can restrict the number of newspaper representatives to those who can be trusted to make a reasonably discreet and loyal use of their information."[36] Or, in other words, if you must discriminate, the editor seemed to be saying, pick on the other guy.

Inclination to compromise, however, should be viewed in light of the still-experimental relationship between diplomats and journalists in a democratic society. It should be viewed, moreover, in light of the war which preceded it. Baker describes this instability well:

> It is easy, of course, to criticize the publicity methods at Paris, but the failure, if it was failure, was highly complicated. It must not be forgotten that the war was still only halted by a truce, and that many little conflicts, which might easily have become greater, were going on all over Europe. War is secretive, and the fear and greed which lie behind war are secretive. The old diplomacy, with its tenacious traditions, was secretive, and the nations were entangled in a mesh of secret treaties. For more than four years the press had been strangled with a rigid censorship. It was a new thing for publics to be represented at such conferences at all; there were no standards, no technique. To ask complete frankness at that time was to ask that the world stop instantly being fearful, greedy, revengeful.
>
> The struggle for publicity was thus a part of the struggle out of war into peace, out of the traditions of the old diplomacy into new methods, out of the conception of international dealings as the concern of a few autocratic heads of State toward a new conception of international dealings as the business of people.[37]

Not even all journalists expected ample disclosure. An editorial in the *New York Tribune* said too much was made of the phrase "open diplomacy." "What the American people want is not a daily report of the bickerings and frictions in the council," but simply some idea of what Wilson's team of negotiators was asking on behalf of the United States.[38]

An unexpected result of the publicity controversy was a sense of professional affinity experienced between British and American journalists, as well as the alienation of the French journalists from the American press.[39] Reflecting on the episode, William Allen White recalled how American journalists felt a "righteous anger" about French support of government secrecy.[40] Baker noted, none too admiringly, that Clemenceau's government had originally entertained the idea of sequestering journalists "in the yard outside, near the gate, which they camouflaged with shrubs."[41] Hiding behind bushes was obviously not what American or British journalists had in mind at the time.

There had been tensions between the French and American press before January 1919, but after that date American observers detected not just hostility but a concerted campaign against them. George Bernard Noble, part of the American delegation at that time, made a careful study of the French press during 1918 and 1919 and noticed a sudden barrage of anti-Wilson, anti-American sentiment between December 15 and January 9, so much so that he was convinced it had been inspired.[42] American reporters had noticed, too, and they began complaining in their accounts of conference activity. In all, then, relations had begun to sour between the two countries. By February several French journals, in turn, were excoriating American correspondents for their "harmful" dispatches. They named the *New York World* and the *New York Times* as particularly offensive for suggesting France was delaying completion of the treaty.[43] American correspondents increasingly noted the differences between their own journalism and that of the French, Ernest H. Abbott pointing out French journalists' focus on editorial and opinion writing. "Paris would no more support an American newspaper except for American visitors," Abbott noted, "than it would patronize an American quick-lunch counter."[44]

American correspondents, on the whole, described the publicity outcome as a "partial" victory—"Open covenants but not openly arrived at," David Lawrence remarked.[45] Lawrence noted that press protest had "stirred up a hornet's nest here during the last few days" and that all "business of the peace council has been subordinated to the effort to satisfy the clamor of many hundreds of journalists." The *New York Tribune* declared the so-called gag rule "partly lifted," "diplomacy ajar but not open."[46] Yet the *Tribune's* correspondent in Paris, Frederick Moore, held a more positive outlook than his editors back home. First, he understood that on any issue news would eventually come out, "as it will always be in some nation's interest to divulge inside information." And second, like Lawrence, Moore shared in the pride and exhilaration of assertive action taken by the American press as a whole: "That the correspondents together form a formidable bond is demonstrated by the fact that they caused the five-power conference to reopen the question immediately."[47]

Within a week he was even more upbeat, and the headline accompanying his story reported that American journalists had "saved Wilson's first 'Point.'"[48]

Even for those allowed to attend the first plenary session of the Paris Peace Conference, the situation was not exactly ideal. When the session opened on January 18, 1919, the American correspondents found themselves in a troubling situation. Instead of observing the world's peacemakers from within the Hall of the Clock, journalists were forced to look on through archways from an adjacent gallery and thus not allowed the privilege of technically being in the same room. Many in the press were upset at the arrangements, and readers heard journalists' lament loudly:

> The world has no desire to watch the Peace Conference through "narrow archways," whether these orifices be architectural embrasures or the mouthpieces of an official "secretariat." We have a right to the clearest view, for we have been promised "open covenants, openly arrived at." A desire for the fullest possible publicity, of course, does not preclude our understanding of the necessity for secrecy in delicate preliminary business; nor does it imply any suspicion of the statesmen involved. It is only common sense. Moreover, it will automatically sterilize the indiscretion of too eager newspaper men who have hitherto had to base their dispatches largely on gossip and rumor.[49]

The "most important gathering of influential men in one hundred years" got under way while just off-stage the eyes and ears of the world—the reporters there to cover the event—were struggling mightily to see and hear.

> The room was already filled with men, and most of them, standing on chairs and tables, were trying to look through three doorways into the room beyond, a hazardous feat not at all easy, and which led to much jostling and many expressions of disappointment and disgust. These men represented the world outside the PC; these doorways were the windows through which they were to be permitted to view the august personages in session, and through which they were to be allowed to hear, if they could, the discourses that fell from the lips of the rulers.[50]

Their location in the Ministry of Foreign Affairs thus put reporters in an awkward and less-than-exalted position: covering the conference as vigorously as they could, while being kept at arm's length from the proceedings. In 1919 the press still possessed a most nebulous status among diplomats and statesmen. Journalists were there to attend the peace process, even though many of the peacemakers were decidedly uncomfortable in their presence.

And yet, despite the perceived indignity of being sequestered in an adjacent room, the fact that the press was there at all was something of an achievement. In peace conferences past, journalists enjoyed no such official inclusion. Typically, they were barred at the door of the building. A representative example from that era is the Portsmouth Conference, the New Hampshire peace talks held in 1905 to end the Russo-Japanese War. At that conference reporters eventually stopped hanging outside the Portsmouth Navy Yard (that they went there in the first place, though, suggests they hoped for access they did not get) and took up residence in the lobby of the nearby Hotel Wentworth, where they lounged and gossiped while waiting for the daily phone call from a delegate who would speak to just one reporter, who in turn would pass on to others an official statement for the day. Frequently the delegate's communication referred to secret documents, and because "no one knew the content of the document on which they were working, this meant less than nothing and passed as a diplomatic joke."[51] Whether the delegates were deliberately or only inadvertently having fun at journalists' expense, the result was the same: a purposeful distance and utterly sharp demarcation between the two groups. Journalists at the Portsmouth Conference were unmistakable outsiders. And they were also, inevitably, bored. Will Irwin, for example, thought it "the most newsless event [he] ever covered."[52] The Portsmouth Conference thus symbolized an earlier epoch of relations between the press and diplomatic officialdom. "How simple and primitive the Portsmouth Peace Conference seemed to those journalistic survivors who attended the Conference of Versailles!" Irwin wrote.[53] *New York World* managing editor Charles Lincoln, at hand for the Paris Peace Conference, also compared it favorably with the Portsmouth Conference: "The results thus far have far exceeded those attained at the last conference of this nature, that at Portsmouth."[54]

In Paris in 1919 reporters not only found themselves in the same building as the diplomats, they were practically in the same room. The problem was not their proximity, in other words. It was the cacophony of a crowded room. So journalists' advantage had definitely improved by the end of the First World War.[55] And some correspondents, like the representative of the *Advocate of Peace,* were still considerably impressed with the current surroundings: "We were allowed to view the whole proceeding from the room adjoining, also beautifully adorned, a thing which was perfectly possible, because there are three large archways leading directly into the 'Clock Room.'"[56] Enthusiastic observers like Charles Lincoln even claimed that the press had "won out."[57] Despite the shaky start, journalists were positively thrilled to be in attendance at the first plenary session. As David Lawrence remembered it, "Some of them have desks, but most of them stand. They do not mind this inconvenience, but are glad to be there after the struggle of a week for admission."[58] Associated Press correspondent E. M. Hood was upbeat as well: "It was a memorable occasion and one that I never shall forget."[59]

Simeon Strunsky's view was also affirmative. He acknowledged that "[c]ynical opinion" was not especially impressed with "the victory of the American newspapermen on the issue of publicity," that "our ultra-pessimists here look upon the plenary sessions as a device of stage-management." If so, he said, then the stage-management was "perfect." Besides, the American press had forced concessions. While other nations' correspondents only asked that a single representative be admitted, American correspondents demanded five and wound up with three. "We imposed our will on the Conference," Strunsky said. "To the extent of obtaining admission for three representatives from the press delegations of the five Powers and three for the rest of the newspaper world. Having fought hard to keep us down to three, the Conference, as I see it, smiled quietly to itself, and gave order to admit the whole mob of us."[60]

Another distinction of the Paris Peace Conference was its heavy use of published material. Indeed, the conference nourished a vast cottage industry in Paris for printed documents. Typesetters cranked out paper after paper, report after report. Within two hours of the first plenary session, journalists had access to a printed stenographic record, a massive package of more than 100,000 words.[61] In 1919 the conference assigned to end World War I became, like most other organizations during the war years, a publicizer both directly and indirectly. This was not the Congress of Vienna. In fact, in terms of the explosive generation of information then, Paris would turn out to be more like Vesuvius than Vienna.

Even when information was not made public, it was generated in gargantuan quantities. A frenzy for facts, for expert information, rumbled through the city. The ambition by all governments to "know the most" at the conference was thought essential for steering through the endless and complex negotiations. While diplomatic preparation was not exactly novel then, the armies of experts brought along to Paris were. These delegates would be expected to compose masterly documents and master those composed by others. Wilson led the way. "The President is a quaint bird," Lord George Riddell wrote. "This afternoon he came from the Conference Room and gave instructions for someone to telephone for his typewriter. He conjured up visions of a beautiful American stenographer, but in a short time a messenger appeared, bringing with him a battered typewriter on a tray. . . . The typewriter was placed in a corner of the Conference Room with Hughes."[62] Perhaps it ought not surprise us that a magazine editor approached Tumulty in March 1919 with a $40,000 offer for Wilson to write ten articles about his presidency.[63] With typewriting plenipotentiaries, there would be no shortage of information and little chance to keep secrets for very long, as journalists soon found out on their own.

8

ROUTINES

Having gotten off to an unsettling and controversial start, the conference placed immediate demands on the press. The first challenge was the business of simply getting information, either the news or the "color stuff" (depending upon the correspondent's specialty),[1] not a simple affair given the conference's early firestorm over publicity. After preparing stories and reports, journalists then faced the equally complicated task of getting them out. Correspondents were allotted a circumscribed amount of words, time, and expense with which to transmit the news of the day. Since only eight of seventeen cables were functioning at the time, CPI member Walter S. Rogers helped arrange the use of a Lyons wireless station, which allowed "American newsmen to have 9,000 words transmitted daily free of cost."[2] But this facility was granted only for "non-interpretative news," and there was always a long line of reporters waiting to use this service. Most of the time the organizations paid for transmissions. And there was plenty of expense involved. Typically the correspondents were responsible for daily leads, plus a weekly summary, analysis, or occasional "forecast."[3] At a cost of some ten to fifty cents a word, they transmitted their four hundred-word dispatches RTP (receiver to pay) to home offices in America.[4] The cables were "overworked, the wireless . . . decidedly limited," one correspondent complained; the former usually took eighteen to thirty-six hours for transmission, the latter, about half the time.[5]

Before they could do that, however, journalists first had to submit their cables to a French censor located in the Bourse Building, an individual who was not normally disposed to generosity or liberality in his attitude toward the press. To no one's surprise, the censorship in France was selective and political. "It was like having someone over your shoulder all the time," David Lawrence wrote.[6] French censors were naturally sensitive to criticism aimed directly or indirectly at their nation's leaders, and American journalists keenly sensed the imposition:

> The trouble about reporting the Paris Peace Conference was that many people there thought the war was still on, and that war conditions should continue to prevail with respect to public expression. Many correspondents felt intimidated by the situation. Others found themselves called to book by the French in various ways whenever they endeavored to speak in criticism of French proposals. Altogether, there was none of the freedom which newspapermen would have felt had the Conference been held in a neutral country.[7]

American journalists believed members of the French press were less "professional," less independent, than they, because their government still seemed to operate according to old authoritarian rules.

Some appalling incidents did occur, including one Orwellian mishap whereby a *New York Tribune* dispatch that mentioned rumors that Wilson might leave the conference if not given his way was plucked by the French censor and wound up in Clemenceau's hands. According to Mark Sullivan, Clemenceau kept that report for about a week, confronted Wilson with its contents (which the president denied), then read it before the Chamber of Deputies. All the while, of course, the would-be article had never appeared in the *New York Tribune*. But since it was being discussed openly now, other correspondents were mentioning the *Tribune* article in their dispatches. Before long the Committee on Public Information released a statement on January 16 that insisted that "President Wilson categorically denies making the statement attributed to him in the telegram in the *New York Tribune* that he threatened to withdraw American troops from France unless the conference agreed with his views."[8] The *Tribune* wryly reported the confounding incident in the terse headline, "Wilson Denied Cable Tribune Did Not Have."[9] It was times like these, Sullivan said, when "you just threw up your hands and wondered if you were living in the twentieth century or whether you had gone back to Louis XIV."[10] It was, as Gerald Stanley Lee described a few months later of the peace conference generally, "comic opera."[11]

The bane of censorship, of course, often lies in the fact that victims are not always sure of its application. A note at the bottom of one of A. D. Call's dispatches to the *Advocate of Peace,* for example, contained this somber message: "From a personal letter. Defective postal service and, possibly, censorship are interfering with this correspondence."[12] Journalists usually discovered the delays, whether they were notified by a telegram official in Paris ("the censor was much too busy to let you know he had thrown your dispatch in the wastebasket") or, more typically, by their home office. For example, in February Mark Sullivan experienced the latter scenario, the source of terrific consternation for the *Collier's* correspondent, who made it the subject of one of his dispatches:

> Upon being moved to investigate by your prolonged failure to receive my manuscript, I have succeeded in finding that one manuscript, which was mailed by me on January 7, was taken out of the mails without my knowledge and was sent to the American General Headquarters at Chaumont. It was held there for eight days. I am informed by General Headquarters that they put it back in the mails, addressed to Collier's, New York, on January 15. As to the other two manuscripts which I put in the mails in December, two or more weeks preceding this one, I have been unable to get any information, but I am compelled to assume that something of the same kind happened to them.[13]

Sullivan went on to say that great damage would be done to the administration's credibility with the American people if Wilson permitted such egregious carelessness to recur.

In addition to dealing with censors, American journalists faced long hours of work. Charles Lincoln pointed out that most reporters were at it all day long, attending the different delegations' regularly scheduled briefings, two a day at the Hôtel de Crillon alone. The fact that the delegations were housed at sites all over the city meant it was "no uncommon thing for an American newspaperman to travel twenty miles or more about the city in 'cleaning up' on his work."[14] "It is safe to say," Lincoln concluded, "that the correspondents will return satisfied that they have done the hardest work of their lives." For many, doing their duty involved putting in sixteen- to eighteen-hour days. The conference was like a living organism from which a conscientious reporter could not just walk away in the middle of the day. Covering the sessions, describing the scenes and the players in it, relating the discussions, disputes, daily briefings (by Colonel House or French foreign minister Ste-

phen Pichon), the formal decisions, requesting and conducting interviews—
all went on at ceaseless pace for two-thirds of every day. Committee meetings
were always taking place, and there was rarely a lull: "The work has been almost continuous and of such a nature that it has not been possible to divide
it up between night and day forces; the result has been that rising at seven I
have been obliged to keep at it until nearly midnight and sometimes beyond
that hour most of the nights of the week."[15] Ironically, the fact that much
conference business went on confidentially in chambers made journalists
have to work twice as hard, in tracking down delegates who could fill them
in, explain what was going on, outline the basic issues at stake.

It was not uncommon for journalists to forego time off in a six- or seven-
day workweek. They essentially lived in a cocoon whose geographic center
was the Place de la Concorde. "As a matter of fact," E. M. Hood told his
family, "I have not been more than a half mile from this place except on one
or two occasions and those were at night in the subway."[16] Depending upon
their changing mood, reporters regarded the cluster of buildings, streets, and
walkways they inhabited there in Paris as alternatively magnet or manacle. A
second home for most correspondents was the posh international press club,
inside the Maison Dufayel, where they often wrote their stories, conferred
with colleagues, or just stopped to exchange the latest gossip. American reporters also spent a lot of time in one room of the Hôtel de Coislin, near the
American Post Office, where "they came to get official statements, to read notices posted about upcoming events, to receive passes for official gatherings,
to use typewriters in emergency, and, if they wish, to file their copy."[17]

Despite the frequent difficulties and taxing burdens, American journalists
did occasionally find ways to alleviate the workload. Arthur Krock and Herbert Bayard Swope developed an informal partnership, whereby Krock did
much of the routine "legwork" while Swope cultivated inside sources. The
two reporters also pooled their allotment of four hundred-word dispatches,
giving them twice as much space with which to write and more room to engage in speculation, analysis, or simple description. Word of the collaboration eventually spread and produced grumbling from other correspondents.
Swope was a flamboyant scofflaw. In May he ignored the pre-arranged selection of eight journalists to witness the delivery of the peace treaty to Germany and attended in defiance of the rules. News of his actions sparked a
formal protest by *New York Times* correspondent Charles Selden, who was so

angry that someone might elude the limitations that he wrote up a petition and tacked it to the wall in the press room. Upon seeing the petition, Swope coyly added his own name! No one else signed.

Krock and Swope continued to work together, but not without occasionally withholding information from each other in the spirit of competitive rivalry. When he learned that Swope had surreptitiously cheated him on one scoop, for example, Krock cheated him in return on another. "Next day, very early for Swope, he was on the telephone reproaching me for the betrayal (he had read *Le Matin*) until I cited the several of his that provoked it. There were no similar acts of treachery on either part."[18]

The teamwork of Krock and Swope underscores one of the main duties journalists in Paris bore: maintaining and developing contacts with sources of information. There were, historian Reginald Coggeshall concluded, about half a dozen sources for conference news: official conference communiqués, individual delegates' statements and conferences, delegation press bureau releases and comments, overt lobbyist propaganda, and private sources.[19] Three more ought to be added to this list: extraneous personnel (most notably Wilson's physician, Admiral Grayson), other correspondents, and the French press. All were essential parts of the peace conference supply line, and most reporters dutifully tapped as many of them as possible. Journalists also had to play off sources against one another, check the papers, make inferences, take educated guesses, challenge delegates with information they pretended to have, test and corroborate information in whatever way they could. Mark Sullivan described how a correspondent did it: "He gets a clue from an Italian delegate whom he may happen to know, adds a hint from a Frenchman, puts the combined rumor up to an American for verification and makes deductions from the manner of the one who denies or confirms it."[20]

Krock's and Swope's personal networking was an especially crucial facet of acquiring news for publication, especially in so secretly and aristocratically structured a world as diplomacy. Being a successful journalist at that time perforce meant the ability to hobnob, to mingle with the mighty. Swope was a natural at doing just that, and so brazen a socializer, in fact, that he could seemingly do the work of two journalists. The relatively unknown Krock could only marvel at his colleague's bravado at any gathering. "Disposing as usual of my presence by muttering the preposterous statement, 'Of course, you all know Arthur Krock,'" Swope was determined that his friend "should know 'the important people.'"[21]

Encountering "the important people" was unavoidable for journalists in Paris, but actually gaining an audience for meaningful conversation, and ideally an interview, was somewhat more intimidating. News gathering therefore necessitated initiative—and hustle. At some sessions journalists were not above stepping atop furniture to collar prospective sources. While in London a few weeks before the start of the conference, sixty-one-year-old E. M. Hood resolved to speak with Lord Bryce at a public affair, and to do so he "violat[ed] all rules and proprieties, as the assemblage was dispersing. . . ." Hood continued: "I climbed over the chairs and rails up to the stage only to receive from him the warmest kind of welcome."[22]

To advance in the news business one could not afford to be lazy. And since many conferees would insist on anonymity, a reporter had to secure more interviews in order to weigh the credibility of what was said.[23] "Speaking generally," H. Wilson Harris wrote, "all the news that was worth getting was obtained by individual journalists through personal investigation and enquiry [sic]."[24] It thus paid to ask favors, impose on friendships, call on acquaintances. When E. M. Hood met General Pershing in Paris, he was sure to mention the name of a mutual friend, and Pershing said "he remembered him well."[25] The name of the game was—and still is—personal access to news sources. And acquiring access meant greasing the wheels of social intercourse.

Due to his oversaturated schedule, Woodrow Wilson was not an easy person to arrange conversations with in Paris, but some journalists did manage to meet with the president individually. Arthur Krock was one. His success in meeting with Wilson resulted from his friendship with Wilson's physician, Admiral Cary Grayson. Thanks to Grayson, Krock saw Wilson personally on two occasions during the peace conference and twice more with all the other correspondents, in February and in late June.[26] Krock also obtained an interview with Bernard Baruch, the august New York financier who had come to Paris as an economic adviser to the American mission. Krock's meeting with Baruch was itself a picturesque encounter. Escorted and introduced by Swope, Krock recalled a magisterial presence:

[T]he Babylonian king sank back into his reclining chair and the minions resumed their operations: a pretty girl manicured his nails, a barber shaved his face and trimmed his hair, a chasseur shined his boots, while over him hovered his valet, Lacy, to perform any final touches to Baruch's toilet that might be indicated. "Have you any message for the American people," I asked, having been prompted by Swope to frame this question, "now that they have saved democracy in Europe and the world?" "Yes," replied Baruch through a mask of scented lather, "they must work and save."[27]

Men like Baruch were clearly individuals whom not just anyone, not just any journalist, could meet in private. Without contacts like Swope and Grayson, Krock would probably never have been able to interview Wilson or Baruch.

Samuel McClure, who had come to Europe with a variety of professional ambitions, never hesitated to accept obligations in return for favors. A brief excerpt from one of his letters home in the spring of 1919 suggests just how important personal references were:

> Sunday forenoon I took the train to Brussels, passing through Malines, where Cardinal Mercier lives. Sunday afternoon I called on the American Minister, Brand Whitlock. He promised me letters to Monsignor Rutter, the most intimate friend of the Cardinal's; also to Capt. Jackson of the Belgian Relief Commission, who also provides means for visiting journalists to see Belgium, and also to the great banker, Mr. Farquin. I got the letters Monday afternoon, and immediately called on Father Rutter, who was very cordial, and at once telegraphed to Cardinal Mercier. That was Monday evening.[28]

A week later McClure was exchanging courtesies with the Queen of Rumania, pledging to mention Rumania in his lectures and to be her "American representative" in return for unspecified access in the future. It always paid to make friends—the sooner the better, the mightier the better. Many correspondents had nurtured contacts long before the peace talks. Hood, for example, wrote in 1917 that he was *"making some good and useful friends,* such as Sir Cecil Spring-Rice, British Ambassador, DeJean, French Councelor & others."[29]

No one, however, was more a master in the barter for letters of introduction than William Allen White. Reading his personal correspondence between 1918 and 1919, one gets the impression that for him, and perhaps for many Americans at the time, a written recommendation was one of the currencies of power. White constantly wrote letters commending individuals to friends and acquaintances. He was also quick to mention mutual friends to persons from whom he wanted favors. Much of this networking surfaced in his intensive effort to go overseas in 1918, but undoubtedly he applied it while in Europe as well.[30] What today we might derisively call "schmoozing" was then simply how one got around and ahead. In so social an enterprise as journalism, nurturing contacts was an essential part of the job. And letters of introduction were both calling card and memorandum. They were formalized instances of networking, which conveyed a recognition of the social pecking order and employed the language of deference, obligation, and elitism.

Yet journalists' access to diplomats at the peace conference was greater than is often recognized today, which is to say that there was another facet of networking that in Paris both benefited and concerned journalists. This dimension involved the motives, initiatives, and demands made by government representatives—the flip side, if you will, of conventional journalist-diplomat interaction. On these occasions, energy proceeded from the other direction in the relationship: from delegates or their "friends." These were situations in which diplomats did the pursuing. Many such contacts originated from a bulletin posted on a board at the press club with the announcement that

> Monsieur or Signor or Mister or Pasha or Rabbi or Cadif or Sheik or Chieftain Somebody or Other will be pleased to meet the English-speaking press at such and such an hour. This generally means the expounding of some claim for territory or recognition of some sort. There is the unwinding of what the claim is in a prepared speech and then follow questions. And the questions which the "hardboils" of the press can ask these days are posers. Many is the propagandist who has rued the day when he became so intrepid as to ask for queries.[31]

Delegates also simply passed information to reporters, either by telling them or handing them documents directly, or at times in going through charades of unintentional disclosures. Colonel House, for example, arranged to place "accidentally" for Herbert Swope a secret document "containing the [League Covenant] text on a corner of his desk and left the room, giving him time to take complete notes."[32]

Journalists at the peace conference dealt daily not only with diplomats but also with courtiers, petitioners, "advance agents," and spies. Putting up with propagandists' appeals was the trade-off journalists accepted in order to get information that would constitute the stuff of a news story. In the same breath with which journalists bragged about encountering royalty, they also recognized why foreign delegations sought their company—to further their causes through publicity. Krock's introduction to his "first king," the Emir Faisal, was arranged by Lawrence of Arabia: "Lawrence and the eventual King of Iraq made their propaganda pitch," and though Krock does not say whether they persuaded him of the justice of their cause, he did walk away rather bewitched by Lawrence's charisma.[33]

Propaganda, Will Irwin wrote, "was a weapon of statesmanship too useful to abandon in time of peace," and so the "larger nations had transformed their departments of war propaganda into departments of peace propaganda. Before the delegates ran a line of skirmishers—agents of superpublicity, eminent directing journalists who showered flattering attentions on the representatives of the foreign press, humbler figures with engaging personalities. These expounders of national aims took the reporters ostentatiously into their confidence in both daily conferences and private meetings, and they put forth a deluge of mimeographed matter."[34] During the war Irwin himself had been an "unpaid publicity agent" for Belgian relief in the winter of 1915, and an occasional contributor of stories intentionally designed via the CPI to advance Allied interests, neither of which he apparently believed compromised his work as a journalist.

Still, the concentration of propagandists in Paris in 1919 was unprecedented, enough so that it stirred comment from virtually all the reporters. William Allen White recalled the persons "assembled from the uttermost parts of the earth from 'every kind and every tribe on this terrestial [sic] ball,' first the accredited delegates of the tribe or kindred to the conference, second those who disputed the right of the delegates to represent the tribe."[35] *Chicago Daily News* special correspondent H. Wilson Harris marveled at the bombardment of solicitations which "poured in from every side on the Allied journalists and anyone else whose influence on the public was of any account."[36] Harry Hansen was also struck by the glut of agents at the conference, with the "hangers-on . . . a fringe [that] would be called the lobby"[37] in the United States. Du Bois thought "not a single great, serious movement or idea in Government, Politics, Philanthropy or Industry in the civilized world has omitted to send and keep in Paris its Eyes and Ears and Fingers!"[38] Dr. E. J. Dillon wrote for the *Philadelphia Public Ledger* that many "distinguished members of the legal and other word-weaving professions" were playing a "large part" in behind-the-scene conference discussion.[39] According to Ivy Lee, the "men have perfect reams of publicity material thrown at them."[40] Lucian Swift Kirtland, of *Leslie's,* was at first determined to save and eventually go through all that material, so he converted his hotel room into a library for its perusal. "This 'library' of mine occupies every chair, every table, every drawer, and every corner," he wrote, and the collection grew so out of control it became his "Frankenstein, [which] I have not yet had the courage to destroy."[41]

Delegations wined and dined journalists during the conference, courted and wooed them. America's correspondents were not the only journalists so treated, but their large numbers and aggressive demeanor made them seem the special focus of such efforts. In any case, American journalists recognized and enjoyed the treatment. An Associated Press dispatch from March marveled, for example, at the "social" invitations journalists received:

> Newspaper correspondents accredited to the peace conference are more popular than beautiful debutantes in their first season.
>
> Queens, counts, princes, lords, ladies, ambassadors, ministers, premiers, presidents, would-be presidents, peace delegates and plain citizens who are unique in being mere messieurs shower the correspondents with invitations to teas, tiffins, dinners and occasionally to audiences which have no serial disguise.[42]

This ongoing flirtation included everything from granting exclusive personal interviews to extending dinner invitations and "propaganda luncheons,"[43] from sponsoring club meetings and tributes to organizing large-scale field trips. The trips were popular with journalists, both because of the diverting change of scenery they provided and also because many offered genuine newsgathering possibilities. What with transportation and passport difficulties, Lucian Swift Kirtland reflected, they were a welcome opportunity. The fact that on some trips governments spent as much as $5,000 per guest was a matter of both embarrassment and flattery for journalists.[44]

Hood tells of one such expedition in February that he could not join on account of illness: "About forty of the correspondents went last night on a special train as guests of the French government to the battlefronts at Arras and Lens and elsewhere."[45] Why France wanted foreign journalists to go there was understood and accepted. The British government, in particular, showed the keenest appreciation for public relations, helping, hosting, and honoring the American correspondents whenever possible. If the motive for their efforts was not entirely invisible, they still won what they were after—gratitude and sympathy by journalists. Hood gave them credit: "The British are really very clever in getting next to the American pressmen (that's what they call men of our calling over here) and have succeeded in making warm friends of all of us, which we are perfectly well aware is what they wanted to do."[46] Of course, biting the hand that feeds one is never easy, and Kirtland admitted that a reporter had to struggle to "criticize one's hosts and hospitality" after receiving special favors.[47]

In addition to more-or-less direct publicity agents, there also existed in Paris the professional spy, and of these everyone was much more apprehensive. Indeed, the line between journalism and espionage has always been a very hazy one, which is why spies so frequently pose as journalists. Both are, after all, in pursuit of a common quest: useful information. And war always further complicates the distinction. As Will Irwin learned both firsthand and secondhand, "a war correspondent captured by the enemy ranked as an officer-prisoner. But if he found himself in enemy terrain and did not at once unfold himself was in the status of a spy."[48]

During the war Irwin himself was arrested numerous times and once almost executed by the Germans. Later the Allies also questioned his patriotism and blacklisted him as a suspected agent.[49] No doubt by 1919 most reporters put full trust in colleagues only after observation and experience, and took far less seriously the organizations certain journalists supposedly represented. Correspondents like Irwin, McClure, and White sometimes wore many hats, and how could you really *know* what an individual was up to in Paris?

One of the most remarkable stories of World War I is the personal saga of Marguerite Elton Harrison. Harrison was a former society princess from Maryland who, after her husband's early death, slowly worked her way up the ranks of the *Baltimore Sun* to become a political reporter, then went to Europe as a correspondent during the peace conference, all the while working undercover for the State Department. "I was convinced that I could be of material assistance . . . and at the same time satisfy the constant craving to know the truth about Germany," she explained.[50] Determined to help the Allied cause, Harrison traveled mainly in Germany, reporting on events there, as well as on reaction to the developments in Paris. Hers was a most unusual, unique, and dangerous perspective on the making of peace, but during and after the war intelligence operatives were roaming all over Europe. Switzerland, for example, was "an international spy-nest."[51] And according to Harrison, Berlin was "the meeting place for all the international plotters and intriguers who had grievances, real or imaginary, against the Entente Powers," a category that included many Russians, for example.[52] The chameleon nature of so many personalities during and immediately after the war struck Harrison full-force one day in Berlin when she discovered that the British roommate with whom she was living temporarily, Mrs. Stan Harding, was herself a German spy.

It is highly likely that special agents were spying on a variety of journalists at Paris. A secret intelligence memo in January 1919 asked all officers to report to the American Expeditionary Forces Headquarters any movement by W. E. B. Du Bois, representing the *Crisis,* so it seems plausible that the agents of various governments would target other correspondents as well, particularly those with radical affiliations.[53] And of course keeping tabs on correspondents was in some ways helpful for monitoring, perhaps affecting, public opinion in the nations they represented. Whether it was a carryover from wartime paranoia about security or fully justified fears, governments spied on governments. So-called "friendly" governments were not immune. Arthur Krock observed Colonel John Carty, of AT&T, keeping close tabs on intra-Paris cables on behalf of the American mission. Carty explained why: "'The constant attempts of our loving allies to tap these lines.'"[54]

The result of this routine mixture of diplomats, spies, propagandists, and journalists made Europe, and Paris in particular, an international clearinghouse of information. But it was more than a clearinghouse; it was really a kind of crucible, too, for information was traded, analyzed, and interpreted in literary constructions, much of which was destined for public consumption and even official consideration. However mundane the tasks or tedious the chores, journalists covering the peace conference understood the political significance of the work they did and were aware of how the people and events they reported on came alive and grew meaningful through the words and imagery they used in their correspondence. Journalists appreciated their own role, even if others did not formally acknowledge it.

REACTION

W hat did American correspondents think of the work they were doing in Paris? How did they like it? Perhaps their strongest emotional reaction to their experience in Paris was a feeling of pride in
doing important work and doing that work around important people. These
feelings and experiences, especially early on, would have a profound impact on journalists' sense of professionalism. The "destinies of mankind center there," Du Bois wrote, grateful that his newspaper credentials had given
him the opportunity to promote his views on racial equality.[1] "We got, in
fact, the ear of the civilized world."[2] Even the opening conference session, at
which journalists were looking on from several yards away, filled many in the
press with a sense of excitement that they were witnessing a historic moment.
Few spared superlatives: It was . . . after all the "greatest deliberative body
in the world," the "greatest peace conference in all history."[3] A. D. Call felt
"the eyes of the world . . . upon us there," an exhilaration heightened by the
statesmen in attendance: "The silent gathering that I saw there in that ancient
palace, men from all nations aligned against Germany, the living idealisms
personified there, the future bending as if to listen, the fate of the generations
yet unborn hanging there as if by a thread. I was thrilled there at that place.
It seemed so stupendous, resistless, uncertain but fateful."[4]

The continual parade before them of internationally renowned leaders
(some of whom, like Clemenceau and Pichon, had actually been journalists)[5]
reinforced correspondents' belief that they enjoyed an exceptional opportunity. "It has been a great privilege to meet so many of the world's great men at
close hand," E. M. Hood thought. In his diary Hood made an entry that no

doubt spoke for many correspondents attending the conference: "Altogether more work than I had done in many years but it was so exceedingly interesting and important I was glad to do it."[6] Indeed, Hood's personal correspondence during the peace conference was apparently so infused with starstruck wonder that his letters inspired his daughter at home to dream that her father had snubbed her. Hood wrote back to reassure her that this would never happen: "Certainly I find it hard to visualize to myself your old father putting on airs from his association with notables; for never for a moment do I forget that whatever considerations I receive from such persons may be credited to the A. P. and not at all to my insignificant personality."[7]

Their French hosts certainly encouraged the temptation for American journalists to feel privileged by giving them plush working accommodations in the ritzy Dufayel estate. Selected French speakers like André Tardieu reminded them that they were the best of the best.[8] And if they still needed reminding, several correspondents were treated to large, full-scale advertisements in newspaper and trade magazines marqueeing their glamorous assignments and important credentials.[9] Not a few correspondents, naturally enough, became caught up in and entranced by the glittering diplomatic atmosphere.

Even more superficially, Americans' paradoxical fascination with royalty made itself felt in Paris. Edward Bellamy Partridge, with his customary satire, comically captured the correspondents' changing tastes:

> We were toasted and hosted by practically all the uncrowned nobility of Great Britain. We got so accustomed to mingling with the peerage that we had no time for commoners at all.
>
> "Is he a Lord?" we would ask whenever it was proposed to introduce us to anybody.
>
> "No," the answer was likely to be; "but he is the greatest—"
>
> "Never mind, old top. If he isn't a member of the peerage I don't believe I'll bother."[10]

Paul Scott Mowrer, correspondent for the *Chicago Daily News,* admitted his democratic discomfort in such kingly surroundings while trying to describe Wilson's Paris headquarters: "I realized then that I was a mere plebeian with uncreased trousers and awkward literary manners, and that it would take an aristocratic journalist to describe an aristocratic mansion."[11] Lucian Swift Kirtland described his own sense of self-worth as a motorcade carrying him and other correspondents made its way to the Versailles Palace: "We were waved on with a deference which flatteringly chloroformed our last sense of democracy. We were of the elect."[12] Clearly many journalists were impressed with what they saw and experienced in France.

But it was more than just the trappings of power, too. American reporters were also enthusiastic about the possibility of political and diplomatic reform. Hamilton Holt, a dedicated league advocate and editor/correspondent for *The Independent,* was deeply moved by the completion of the covenant for the League of Nations in February. "The dreams of poets, prophets and philosophers have at last come true," he wrote.[13] "I am sure there was not one American present who was not thrilled with pride in his country's spokesman." Holt was also exhilarated at his fortune to be among those in attendance, one of the "few representatives of the press who squeezed themselves into the ante-room."

Above all, American reporters developed a strong sense of solidarity with their colleagues. "Possibly for the first time in newspaper history unity . . . was displayed by the correspondents at the Peace Conference," Frederick Palmer wrote. Palmer was referring to the publicity controversy, when he thought the members of both the American and British press had distinguished themselves for their proud professionalism.[14] But he was also looking ahead, too. Not only would journalists partially determine the future of the League of Nations, but the peace conference "is showing that the power of the future is in the press."[15] Magazines and newspapers at the time buzzed with excitement about prospective international press societies.[16] And journalists had good reason to feel optimistic about their prospects. As Arthur Walworth describes their attitudes, "Young men who were at the beginning of distinguished careers, unwed by the tradition that had held an earlier generation at arm's length from public policy in the making, were asserting a quasi-professional prerogative to enter into the confidence of the peace delegates."[17]

Inextricably linked to journalists' appreciation for the grandeur and import of the work was their sense of pressure—both from their home offices and from the situation at hand. Home offices' investment in their transportation, accommodations, food, cable fare, and other expenses—not to mention the showy advertisements many took out—certainly underscored their own competitive sense of the significance of their assignments, and no doubt that sense was impressed upon the journalists in Paris. Newspapers wasted no opportunity to boast about their scoops and other accomplishments. On the front page of the *Chicago Daily News*'s February 10 issue was the following list of journalistic coups:

> Paul Scott Mowrer cabled from Paris to the Daily News last Saturday the FIRST outline of the probable constitution of the league of nations as made public by a French member of the commission. . . .
>
> John Bass cabled the FIRST outline of the American plan for a league of nations.
>
> David Lawrence made the FIRST announcement of a complete agreement for the establishment of the league.
>
> Paul Scott Mowrer sent the FIRST statement of what is to be done with the German colonies.
>
> Harry Hansen reported the FIRST interview with the Prince of the Hedjaz, sketching the territorial hopes of the Arabs.[18]

Though they may not have read directly those promotional plugs back home, American journalists no doubt heard plenty from their employers, who wanted to beat the competition and then brag about their results when they did. Consequently, especially conscientious correspondents like Hood dared not miss an important news announcement or fail to mine sources for possible scoops. The high expectations placed on their work may have come primarily from themselves, but that was pressure enough. As Harry Hansen pointed out, a good many people were depending on the press to tell them about the conference:

> Presently the door would open to these men and to the world. That, at least, was my thought, for these were newspaper men and they were here to see and hear for the American public. They must be, I judged, men who had reached the pinnacle of their profession. What they wrote in the morning was carried by the cables to the American people at noon, and soon after the printing presses would be grinding out their stories and the newsboys would be hawking them in the streets.[19]

Krock and Swope, two men who liked each other well enough to form a "reportorial team" (also because they could double their dispatches that way), occasionally succumbed to the temptation of scooping the other. Journalists sometimes, but not commonly, broke confidences for such opportunities.[20] As ever in the news business, getting the story first could make a career. Not getting it first could end one.

Added to journalists' stress was the frustration of being unable to touch the fruit of their labor. "The correspondents are handicapped by not 'seeing their stuff,'" Charles Lincoln wrote. "Every newspaperman knows what a stimulant it is for a correspondent to visualize his matter and to 'see what was done with it.' The men in Paris are shooting in the dark, largely. They are, of course, kept informed as to how things are going, but they do not have the great satisfaction of actually seeing their dispatches until three or four weeks after they are filed."[21] Reporters in Paris therefore worked in a kind of limbo, kept officially at bay from the people and events it was their job to describe, and never quite sure what was becoming of their descriptions. They had to rely on their imperfect communication with their colleagues and supervisors in the United States.

Correspondents drove themselves harder when prompted by their editors at home, or when, as frequently happened, a coworker became sick. Hood's Associated Press colleague Dick Probert was long plagued by illness in Paris, and that gave Hood added responsibility and a heavy workload. In February he remarked calmly to his wife that "all the others insist that I am indispensable, which is very flattering but uncomfortable now."[22] A few days later his tone had become noticeably strained: "I have not been able to do what [Probert] said I should when ordered to Paris—simply sit around and act as advisor, on the contrary I have been writing my darned head off."[23] One consequence of stress, of course, is an increased likelihood of both fatigue and susceptibility to sickness, so journalists who toiled fiercely often broke down themselves, or else carried nagging minor ailments like colds for months at a time. *Saturday Evening Post* writer Herbert Corey, who was only intermittently in Paris but in Europe all during the war and through 1919, abruptly concluded a letter home to his mother in this way: "There is plenty to tell, I suppose, but I must stop. I am tired and I have more salaried writing to do today."[24] Not long before the peace conference got underway, in fact, Corey had already appeared virtually at wit's end: "This is a duty letter, for if I ever did feel like not writing, it is today. Not sick—just tired, infinitely tired of the war and all things connected with it. . . . I do not feel that I can stand much more of it. . . . I am tired, very, very tired, and I want to go home. Maybe I can before long. Meanwhile, until my next letter, don't forget that I love you."[25] Corey was not touring England with other American journalists freshly disembarked in Europe. He had fulfilled a lengthy reporter's tour of duty.

But even for those correspondents who had only been in Europe for a few months, the demands of work and the symptoms of stress eventually made themselves felt and bubbled to the surface in the personal mail they sent home. In his letters to his family, E. M. Hood routinely peppered his optimism and excitement with frequent references to the "pressure" he said he felt. He admitted that his work schedule was "in large part . . . self-imposed," that he could occasionally delegate responsibility, "pass some part of my work off to another or let it go altogether, but cannot find myself willing to do so; it is my old habit of seeing the job done as well as it should be done."[26] In the emerging star system of American journalism, the individual reporter had to make a name for himself to advance. As the famous war correspondent Richard Harding Davis once advised a reporter, one sells the news by selling himself, by standing out, by being noticed.[27] Delegating work divided up the potential glory for every given story, so it was a trade-off not lightly accepted. Correspondents old and young wanted to make a name for themselves; they wanted home offices to recognize their efforts and sacrifices.[28]

Many American journalists attending the peace conference experienced terrible bouts of homesickness. The correspondents who usually suffered most were those who had been in Europe all throughout the war, men like Herbert Corey or Berton Braley. Granted a brief reprieve in December 1918, Braley expressed his joy in corning home in a poem, its last lines capturing the longing of those kept away:

> And I'm gripped by a spell and a thrall;
> There's a catch in my throat, and my eyes
> Blur at the picture, and then
> A jubilant voice in me cries,
> "I'm coming home. I'm coming home again!"[29]

But even those who often appeared to be enjoying themselves royally did on occasion express heart-wrenching emotion at being separated from loved ones, an anguish that grew deeper as time passed: "I have been very lonesome for you and for the farm," Samuel McClure wrote his wife in January. In May he penned the following words: "I miss you more than I can say. After all those dear months together I find it hard to work without you."[30] In mid-February Hood wrote to his wife that the demands and curiosities of work helped preoccupy his thoughts only during the day. "This spirit keeps me up pretty well during the working hours but in the nights I get homesick and want to see and be with you, and I get up at night at times and look at your picture, and that is not a little thing considering that the room is as cold as all outdoors."[31] Gerald Stanley Lee, more bitter than most, and surely atypical in his utter dejection, spoke of being so isolated, so lonely, so entombed in the "blood-less," rarefied atmosphere of places like the Crillon and the French Foreign Ministry that his "first wild impulse is to rush outdoors, run up the street to the first man I meet—any warm, natural fellow human being will do—and grab him by the hand and wring his hand silently, to get the current of life once more, to reassure myself that I am in with real folks in a real world."[32]

Since no one could say how long the formal peace process would take in Paris, it was impossible for journalists to know how long they would be in Europe. This uncertainty made journalists' homesickness more frustrating. Oftentimes they wrote their families back home that they anticipated leaving in a few weeks' time, only to have their hopes suspended indefinitely. Herbert Corey's note to his mother that his "future plans are quite in the air" accurately described the position of most correspondents in Europe at that time; they simply could not predict their whereabouts for more than a couple of days at a time.[33] The fact that they weren't prophets did not stop them from trying, however. Hood, for example, kept trying to guess when he might be dispensable: "It does not follow of necessity that I shall have to stay to the end; it is possible that after the big thing—the Society of Nations—is put out of the way and a provisional treaty of Peace has been signed the news value of the Conference will so diminish that it will not be necessary to keep the big force that we now have here. In that case I shall try to get away as soon as possible."[34] A month later he was still speculating about the prospect of departure: "In fact I am not sure that I could not get away even before Wilson goes but I do not feel that unless my health weakens I should try to shirk my job after having made what I myself feel is a creditable record over here. It must depend on my own and Mr. [S]tone's estimate of the importance of the work to be done here."[35] On more than one occasion Hood was sure the end of the conference was imminent or sufficiently in sight for him to be "spared."[36] Perhaps correspondents' homesickness and uncertainty were what made them so impatient with conference delays and impasses. Perhaps, too, those emotions predisposed them toward rooting for a quick victory and booing at complicated wrangles.

Possibly the most enduring memory American journalists shared was of how difficult the work was at the peace conference, "never a more difficult assignment in the history of journalism," Arthur Krock wrote.[37] But mixed with the sweat, the frustrations, and the anxieties, the work had been inspiring and important. According to Krock, "men like [Herbert] Swope, [Larry] Hills, [Richard] Oulahan, [Dick] Probert, [Robert] Bender, [John] Nevin and Mark Sullivan have done work that should make all American newspaper men proud to include them. They are the best that have ever worked anywhere and deserve a parade and a memorial arch of their own when they come home."[38]

Despite the relentless work schedule, the pressure, the homesickness, and the inhospitable weather, though, most American correspondents did genuinely enjoy their assignment and considered it a significant benchmark of accomplishment. The pride they took in what they were doing, their camaraderie and sense of self-worth, the many exotic experiences they felt fortunate to go through—all these things gave them tremendous satisfaction. A large number of journalists even admitted to having the time of their lives in Paris.[39] Both for themselves personally and for their colleagues as a whole, they believed they were making professional headway, and January's controversy over press access provided one conspicuous test case.

But that dramatic early confrontation should not at all be regarded as a conclusive settlement of the matter. At the time, it was viewed as a compromise, but one which in practice was prone to continual renegotiation. Diplomats could not set specific working boundaries, after all, without expecting journalists to push at, reinterpret, and even elude those restrictions. Equally important, diplomats often dropped the constraints themselves when doing so suited them politically. Between confrontation and stability, in other words, lay a balancing act, for in Paris diplomats and journalists alike faced daily choices affecting various allegiances: personal, professional, national, political, ideological, international. In some ways, the arrival of the American press in France was as much an encounter between America and the rest of the world as it was between journalism and diplomacy. It is no wonder that the interplay between the latter two caused such strains and such emotions.

≈ 10 ≈

RELATIONSHIPS

The role of the American press at the Paris Peace Conference was shaped to a large extent by what Woodrow Wilson and the U.S. delegation did or did not do in the way of publicity. But that role was not altogether determined by American diplomats, nor would it have been fundamentally changed if it were so determined. For no less than other delegations, American peacemakers hoped for good "public relations" and favorable press coverage during their stay in France. The difference between the Yankee contingent and its European counterparts, rather, was the former's leaderless news management. While Wilson appeared extremely sensitive to press criticism and ridicule in Paris, that is, he did relatively little about it.

Other nations' commissioners proved less reluctant. If they generally abstained from grand pronouncements on open diplomacy, they practiced a subtler daily version, seeking out special correspondents on occasion when it suited their needs and retaining regular reporters as confidants and allies. In this chapter I make the case that those relationships were an important facet of the Paris Peace Conference, one which has been obscured by an overweening attention on Wilson and the all-too-easy practice of juxtaposing his soaring Fourteen Points rhetoric with journalists' free-falling disappointment. Neither focus accurately conveys what was distinctive about this conference or about diplomacy in progressivism's twilight years. Contrary to conventional historical wisdom, journalists then were indeed involved in the making of peace after World War I. Involvement, it should be noted, hardly signifies a professional accomplishment. In fact, it can suggest more the opposite: an abandonment of the ideals of political independence, detachment, and objectivity. Yet in the context of progressive publicity both before and during the war, as well as of the appeal of the "new diplomacy," the quest for participation in foreign affairs by the press does seem at least a partial gambit for prestige, status, and influence—all of which are important components of the professional spirit. From routines carved out in December and January, journalists strove to expand their opportunities and access, to strengthen their contributions toward the making of peace.

The correspondents' circle of friends, acquaintances, and professional contacts was probably their most consistent social reward in Paris. But it was also a real lifeline, too. As discussed earlier, letters of introduction were a primary means for journalists to obtain mobility and access. After some among the Allies came to suspect Will Irwin's patriotism for his association with Lord Northcliffe and a series of devastating articles about the lack of British military preparedness, Irwin carried around in his coat pocket a letter of support from French ambassador Jules Jusserand. It was, he said, "for two years my most useful possession."[1] More typical in 1919 were letters like that of *Chicago Daily News* foreign bureau chief Edward Price Bell to the American ambassador in London, John William Davis. In it Bell made no secret of his desire to develop a close working relationship with Davis:

> Throughout the late Dr. Page's service in London as American Ambassador, I had the honor of an intimate relationship with him. I should esteem it a great privilege to have a similar connection with yourself. Of course, I realize how careful you must be in selecting your friends—especially, I fancy, your journalistic friends—and therefore I venture to send the inclosed [*sic*] documents for your consideration. It seems to me they will introduce me fairly well. If you will be so kind as to return the documents at your convenience, I shall be immensely obliged.[2]

Bell's letter clearly demonstrates the value journalists placed on "useful" friendships. It also reveals the inherent compromises they accepted—trustworthiness and personal obligation, for example—in exchange for authoritative information.

Other letters written by Bell during the peace conference attest to the same ongoing solicitation. About a week after his letter to Ambassador Davis, Bell wrote to Philip Henry Kerr, editor of the political review *The Round Table* and Lloyd George's private secretary, to introduce him to the *Daily News*'s man in Paris, Charles H. Dennis. "I have been trying to bring him

[Dennis] into fruitful relationship with the British mission," Bell wrote, adding that Dennis would provide a good "link between Britain and America" on account of his numerous readers in the United States.[3] This letter followed up one Bell had sent to Winston Churchill in early January about a possible interview and the chance to strengthen Anglo-American relations.[4]

Journalists had good reason to pursue contacts aggressively in Paris. Except for six formal plenary sessions, authorized briefings and communiqués, and the opening and closing ceremonies, there were no full-fledged public events at the conference. "All its real work was done behind rigidly closed doors," H. Wilson Harris said, angered by the delegates' seeming preference for secrecy at a time when, as a colleague of his had said, "little important business is transacted without the presence of stenographers."[5] For him and other correspondents that meant intensifying their efforts—by getting more information from delegation liaisons, for example, through briefings by commission members (such as House), or from the formal and informal interviews they themselves arranged privately.[6]

The reality of covering the conference was that journalists had to confront the reflexive diplomatic tendency to proceed, at least officially, with secrecy and caution. "A whispering gallery," Richard Washburn Child called the peace talks.[7] It did not matter what combination of plenipotentiaries was conferring— the Council of Ten, the Big Four, the Big Five—most statesmen preferred not to have reporters in attendance. In fact, the fewer the peacemakers, the more secret the conversations became: "The Four hid their deeds behind a veil ever more opaque than had concealed the endeavours of the Ten."[8] Patrick Gallagher was even less charitable about the "Ossified Four": "The term . . . was the one most popular among the newspaper writers, particularly after an exasperating hour torn from a grueling, busy day, and wasted upon unsuccessful efforts to extract anything like news from the four excellent gentlemen supposed to be cooperating with the President in the conduct of our business in Paris."[9] When diplomats did grant journalists interviews, they often put sufficient conditions on the information to make publication impossible. In March, Hood complained to his wife of having interviews with four men in one day—Secretary of State Robert Lansing, advisor Colonel Edward House, delegate Charles Crane, and French Foreign Minister Stephen Pichon—but not having much to show for it afterward. "I . . . am able to use only a small portion of the ideas which I have gotten from them," he said.[10]

Despite the efforts of diplomats, however—indeed, oftentimes *through* the efforts of diplomats—the information journalists sought almost always surfaced. "It turned out later that even the leaders were unable to keep the world in ignorance," Harry Hansen wrote, but he might have used the word "unwilling" rather than "unable," for many officials were eager to talk: "Delegates with a grievance were only too glad to give interviews and information anonymously in order to influence public opinion in their behalf, so that despite the alleged precaution and the reports of secrecy, everything the conference did sooner or later saw the light of day."[11] Wilson himself personally released information on two occasions: a rumor just before the drafting of the league covenant in early February that the conference might have to be relocated, and the news that he was summoning his ship to take him home in April. In the first case, Edward H. Talley of the *New York Herald,* one of many reporters privy to the rumor, blew his cover and the ploy backfired. In the second case, Wilson told only *New York Times* correspondent Richard Oulahan and got just what he wanted—a reprieve from some of the obstinate diplomatic stonewalling and some of the vitriolic press abuse he encountered in the spring. Contrary to the statement of one historian, therefore, that "the President's relations with the press, after three months of secret sessions, made it impossible for him to enlist their aid," it was not and never was out of the question.[12] Wilson simply had to ask. The most cynical, least cooperative correspondent at the conference would not have turned down a scoop if the president had offered one. Yet with just a few exceptions, he chose not to do so. Compared to other nations' delegates, Wilson was a wallflower in Paris.

Traditional news sources actually helped journalists do their work, in some cases almost working as journalists. Frederic Howe, New York Commissioner of Immigration, in Paris before the opening of the first plenary session, shared with Inquiry member James T. Shotwell his secret for gaining access. As Shotwell recalled: Howe "explained that he represented some mythical magazine at moments like this."[13] Another more substantive such case was the arrangement between Admiral William S. Sims and the *Chicago Daily News.* According to Bell, Sims had agreed "to get some naval news for us," but apparently did not do a satisfactory job. "As a matter of fact," Bell wrote Charles Dennis, "I think they do not fancy the idea of being enlisted as reporters."[14] However atypical, this incident does reveal the popular compulsion toward publicity, a compulsion felt even by normally tight-lipped military officials. Another situation, touched on earlier, was when diplomats and delegates resorted to direct publicity themselves. Georges Clemenceau authorized printed messages to the United States during the middle of the conference, just as Wilson and various officials from Britain and Japan had done during and after the war.[15] These efforts to speak directly to the public underscore progressives' pervasive influence on diplomacy at the time: it was not enough merely to take a position; one had to campaign for it.

Journalists understood diplomats' occasional need to "get out" news, then, and they embraced it, whatever the motive. But that cultural obsession with publicity also drove them all the harder to find information. Arthur Balfour commented at the outset of the peace talks—in part coquettishly, no doubt—that if "we had any secrets, the journalists would guess them; when we have no secrets, the journalists surmise them."[16] Balfour's ingratiating remark might have been intended simply to salve reporters' egos, but it also spoke to a truth in the news business: a correspondent delivered a story because that was how he or she made a living. British ambassador to the United States Lord Reading made a similar point, saying that "[o]fficially it is announced that there is nothing to divulge, but we are able to read a full account of what happened written by an American correspondent."[17] Since writers would insist on writing something on a particular subject or issue, delegates knew that to get positive publicity it would be wiser to give the press a bit of information than to have it guess wrongly or damagingly to its interests.

That reality thus widened the playing field in Paris. Simeon Strunsky said the conference was "as big as Paris and its hotels, and it is pretty nearly coextensive with the Parisian press, and through that, with the public opinion of the world," meaning that what took place inevitably got out and about. Richard Washburn Child made the same argument in quoting an anonymous diplomat, who admitted that the "truth always came out unofficially"; it was the timing of that release that was always problematic.[18] News leaks, in fact, were a notorious "problem" at the conference—a problem if yours was not the newspaper or magazine who first published the leaked news, or if you were not the country which benefited from the slip. Information "was given out by the agents of the conferees and the rest leaked through those who were clamoring at the doors of the Conference," Walter Lippmann wrote.[19] Journalists could eventually get what they wanted, Gallagher insisted: "At no time did I experience any difficulty in securing sufficiently exact information regarding anything that I wanted to know. The only difficulty was how far one could go in utilizing information without endangering the work of the conference and American interests or getting an official friend into hot water."[20]

Of course, many reporters and diplomats, emphasizing their disappointment rather than their delight, harped on the news and access that did not materialize in Paris and complained that "leaks" were not quite the same thing as the openness promised in "open diplomacy." British delegation member Sir Harold Nicolson expressed the conference's orientation to publicity in characteristically pessimistic fashion: "There are only two ways of dealing with a democratic Press. The best way is to tell them everything; that bores them stiff. The second best way is to tell them nothing, which at least provides them with the glory of a 'secrecy' stunt, which provides a highly pleasurable form of news value. The worst method is to tell them half-truths in the form of conciliatory leakages. It was this flabby method which was adopted by the Conference of Paris."[21] But Nicolson's cynicism is misleading. First of all, the fact that after profound disillusionment he could still call complete disclosure the "best" method says something about his original subscription to the idea. Second, Nicolson continued to maintain that diplomats needed to take a few correspondents into their confidence. Indeed, his preference was for "more obscure" individuals, as "less obscure correspondents will tend to reject that acquaintance."[22]

Even as bitter an analyst of the Paris Peace Conference as the author of an article called "The Blur That Is Paris," a writer who complained about the lack of news, conceded in spite of himself that communication positively abounded there:

[T]alk there has been, of course, much talk. The Cercle Francais de la Press Étrangère, gorgeously housed in the palace of a merchant prince on the Champs Élysées, has been and is a hive of gossip. There is the Hôtel de Crillon, headquarters of the American delegation, the American Press Bureau in the same building, the various press delegations at the hotels of the other leading commissioners, all with their many writers, most of whom are also talkers, generous talkers. There are around-the-table talkers, over-the-glass talkers, with-the-coffee talkers, smokers and talkers, street-corner talkers, some of them whispering talkers. There are the officials, communicative, non-communicative, lightsome, heavy-browed, all kinds. There are the diplomats and the semi-diplomats at the dinners, the drawing rooms, the "functions," who sometimes talk. There are the four-page newspapers, some fifty of them in Paris, some with remarkably large circulations. There are the editors in their offices. There are the crowded but efficient subways, the sidewalk restaurants and theaters with their sociable "entre actes." There are the homes, high and lowly. There are the "experts," sometimes off but usually strictly on guard. There are the students, the waiters, the bar-maids, the secretaries of the various delegations, and "representatives" of all hues. There are the soldiers, Red Cross workers, steel magnates, social workers, church, museum, and art gatherings. There are plenary sessions of the Peace Conference and other lectures. There are the oceans of books and pamphlets and communication. Looking back across a winter of all this, the net impression is of a babel; if not of a Donnybrook Fair, of a jumble, a blur of political turmoil, greed, and hatreds, a mess.[23]

In what is probably the richest single passage of American journalism relevant to the Paris Peace Conference, the writer seems without realizing it to be complaining not of a lack of information but of too much information, not of stinting communication but of overwhelming communication. Though much of it may have taken place in informal settings and less-than-official forums, discourse at the conference absolutely flourished. "So far," Lucian Swift Kirtland wrote from Paris, "no representative from any nation having a 'claim' to go before the Conference committees has resisted publicity."[24]

This is not the way most scholars portray the Paris peace talks, of course. It is usually described as a desert of dialogue, as utterly devoid of democratic participation, a result, perhaps, of the historical sources used.[25] But as this author and other correspondents revealed, dialogue actually proliferated in Paris. Everyone was talking about the conference, and journalists themselves were often at the heart of such intercourse. David Lawrence said that "it was literally impossible to keep a secret long at the Paris peace conference. There were too many reporters present, too many eyes watching."[26] Lawrence proceeded to explain in more detail how those reporters did get their information:

> No rule forbidding discussion of the various points of view expressed within the Council of Ten could be effective so long as it was to the interest of some delegate or some delegations to make such view-points public. Nobody professed to know how the news-paper men got hold of inside "secrets" on such occasions, and not infrequently the members of the Council of Ten would look accusingly at one another as they resumed their sessions with big head-lines staring them in the face telling the world exactly what had been discussed in the morning or on the night before.

Old-fashioned diplomacy was impossible in such an atmosphere. Even gentlemen's agreements to withhold certain questions from the press could not be observed, however willing or anxious may have been the principals to do so. Secrets could not be kept with so many people acquainted with them and with no censorship to restrain their despatch [*sic*] on the cables or telegraph. Too many individuals knew these "secrets." Every mission at Paris had a personnel of several hundred. The correspondents of the several countries knew these men intimately. Some one remarked in Paris recently that the easiest way to get something printed in a hurry was to mark it "secret and confidential" and distribute it through the different delegations at the peace conference. Thus the principals discussed peace with a consciousness that they were being watched.[27]

Though both diplomats and journalists might have expected "open diplomacy" to look like something else, there was on many levels an abundance of openness, a willingness not just to answer questions but actually to approach members of the press to convey information and commentary. To some extent, this might have been anticipated, considering the wartime devotion to propaganda and other forms of executive publicity. "[W]here there are people gathered together," Chester Wright wrote, "there can be found some one who will talk. And not only are there those in Paris who are willing to talk, but there are those whose business it is to talk."[28]

More than simply "using" journalists, however, diplomats at some level struck partnerships with them, for they knew that reliable, confidential friends in the press were a necessity when trying to time the release of official statements or unauthorized leaks. One April evening outside a theater Wilson's physician and intermediary, Admiral Cary Grayson, joined a party of reporters with whom he was friendly and offered to give them a lift in the president's limousine to the restaurant at which they were planning to have dinner. Seated alone with Richard Oulahan in the front seat of the car, Grayson quietly told the correspondent of the *New York Times* that the president was considering leaving Paris and actually summoning his ship to France unless his fellow conferees began to show more willingness to compromise. Grayson had asked Wilson if he could give Oulahan "for publication the news that the George Washington was to be sent for and why." Oulahan explained the deal:

> Admiral Grayson said that the President had assented, but wished me to withhold cabling the news until the next day, as the instructions would not

be sent to the Navy Department until then and he thought it better that the Department should be informed before any newspaper publication.

You may be sure that I was up betimes the next morning and after writing my dispatch about the George Washington's recall. I hurried to the Bourse cable office and filed it.[29]

Oulahan's story was one of the biggest scoops of the peace conference, of inestimable value both to Oulahan's own reputation and to that of Wilson's. Each understood the other's position and what was gained by the temporary alliance. The correspondents were not stupid. They were only too happy to trade a bit of confidentiality for closer access, for hotter news, for an exclusive scoop, and they knew their editors back home would applaud their gamesmanship. Information was a priority that outranked every other consideration, including a principled independence, which at the time was in a state of murky development. Correspondents wanted newsworthy information before all else. And even the delegates appreciated that fact, sometimes sympathized with it, and often tried to use it to their own advantage.

To help slake the thirst of the journalists gathered there, as well as to facilitate the efficiency of the peace process itself, moreover, most governments appointed intermediaries to coordinate the relationship between their respective delegations and the press. Indeed, according to one account, "the American custom of press conferences gained considerable momentum . . . among the delegations from other Allied countries."[30] Apparently, delegation leaders liked them, too. Soon after the controversy over press access, former Associated Press Washington correspondent George Peet resigned and was named liaison between the French government and American correspondents. The French had evidently heard journalists' complaints and were troubled by them, E. M. Hood said: The French "have become alarmed at the growing dissatisfaction of the latter apparently and think Peet can help, which no doubt he can as I think the whole situation is the result of a complete misunderstanding of the relative needs and abilities of each side."[31]

The British delegation won high marks for its courteous assistance to journalists: "Nothing could have been finer than the way in which the British officials, without exception, opened their minds and their hearts to the American correspondents. They held no aces up their sleeves. They wanted to play with us, not against us."[32] The American press happily met with British conferees for the information they provided and worked with them when it suited them both.

Journalists' main dissatisfaction ironically resulted from the operations of the American mission, from whom the press expected the most cooperation but whose publicity program appeared most confused. U.S. peacemakers were not well organized and, from all accounts, little disposed toward communicating with reporters. "The Americans have the reputation of being the hardest of all to pry loose from information," Chester M. Wright griped.[33] Charles Dennis reported only one main American perspective available in Paris: the echoes of disapproving Republican senators whose comments were generously printed in French journals. "These wonders of international acoustics deserve more attention from the American peace delegation than they have received thus far. The delegation has chosen to make itself inarticulate."[34]

In practice, the American mission did regularly communicate with correspondents. But lacking strong leadership at the top, many delegates spoke without complete confidence or full information and certainly without any overall orchestration. As early as January, the predicament was not lost on Tumulty back in the United States: "I wished we could have better cooperation on matters of publicity."[35] Wilson had issued no special instructions, outlined no general strategy. Unlike the French and British delegations, the Americans came with no blueprint for the society of nations—at least none that the correspondents could detect in January.[36]

Worse, the American delegates had not agreed on any standard procedure for regular counsel and for policy design or implementation. Members of the American team simply tackled it all on the spot, extemporaneously. Little coordination existed, and some frictions—between Secretary of State Robert Lansing and the president—actually developed into a kind of casual sabotage.[37] Patrick Gallagher angrily declared that the president was to blame: "It was Mr. Wilson's fault that the organization of our peace mission in France was so lamentably weak and inefficient that at no time while I was in Paris was there intelligence, cooperation, or precision in the conduct of the American people's business."[38] Some correspondents thought that the American mission, including House but Lansing in particular, were personally predisposed toward secrecy and were not infrequently clumsy. Chester Wright, of the *New York Tribune,* gave House more credit for helping the press, not that he didn't impose sufficient conditions:

> Every nation has its spokesman who can be "induced" to talk at the right time. Colonel House is generally conceded to be the great moulder of public opinion in the American mission. He talks little for quotation, but he "indicates"

and "lets it be known," and so on. He thinks this would be well or that would be inadvisable. In his fatherly Texas way he does a great deal of which the man on Rural Route No. 9, Somewhere in America, never suspects him. If it's not in the communiqué, ask Colonel House. He may tell you who can tell you.[39]

In fact, most journalists appreciated House, giving him more praise than they did any other American delegate for his overall helpfulness and accessibility. As for the slight discrepancy between his reputation for being useful and his penchant for being manipulative, the answer is that he was both. House was smart enough to know that the American mission needed to maintain good terms with the press, and usually smooth enough (however self-serving) to make reasonable attempts in that direction. Before the conference started, he had worked quickly to try to eliminate French censorship of American reporters. During the conference he made himself more available to the press than most other delegates, paid careful attention to what correspondents were saying, and recommended that Wilson give interviews as much as possible.[40]

Practically no correspondent found Lansing helpful. Years later, Ray Stannard Baker accused the secretary of hypocrisy, saying that "no one of the Commissioners, in practice, had been more hostile to any real publicity than he. He had been too long disciplined in the school of diplomatic timidity."[41] Most journalists simply felt that foreign delegations were more experienced and consistently better prepared than America's untested team. On House, Gallagher said, "all along the line it seemed to be his misfortune to put his foot into every hole in an undoubtedly dark and dangerous road that demanded much knowledge and experience in order to avoid pitfalls."[42] John F. Bass also questioned the American delegates' competence: The "delegations of other nations were better informed and surer in the details of their proposals."[43]

American correspondents were probably most disappointed by Wilson's disinclination to meet with them, even if in strictest confidence. After following a few of Tumulty's cabled suggestions in December, Wilson turned his back on press relations for most of the conference.[44] "He likes publicity in the abstract," Baker wrote in his diary, "but shrinks from the specific application."[45] The president who had helped create a multimedia behemoth at home now mysteriously retreated from communication channels altogether. It was as if the newly established rules of presidential public relations suddenly did not apply overseas. When aides advised him to answer the French press, which was busy shredding his reputation, Wilson demurred: "If I were to do that it would immediately break up the peace conference—we cannot risk it yet."[46]

Perhaps because of the strain, the onset of illness, or the disassembly of the CPI, Wilson simply cut off most of his ties to the outside world. This decision helped neither the press nor his diplomatic team. By staying away from reporters Wilson ensured that his fellow commissioners would be able to offer journalists little. "The absence of the president from these conferences left the other commissioners more or less tongue-tied. They could not answer questions as to the American policy in the conference."[47] Under Wilson's orders, Colonel House met with reporters each evening at six to supplement the work of the American press liaison: "a counter-attraction."[48] Talking in "airy generalities," Gallagher recalled, House "often made statements that were, unintentionally, of course, misleading. He was always quite sincere. Colonel House is a very charming gentleman who tries to do the very best that he can. Sometime he tried to do too much. He tried to settle the Irish question. He tried to settle the Shantung question. He made a horrible mess of both."[49] The colonel was often glib and casually arrogant. Asked by a reporter about the Shantung dispute, House responded, "Oh, there won't be any trouble about that. I can settle it in ten minutes."[50] According to Arthur Krock, House routinely bullied Lansing and saw to it that the secretary of state would be an irrelevant presence in Paris.[51] Still, it was better than nothing, and at least House was communicative.

Journalists generally disapproved of the performance of America's diplomats, but they did not, however, usually fault the American Peace Commission's liaison, Ray Baker, "the most consistent source of news for the reporters."[52] Woodrow Wilson chose Baker to help smooth out the difficulties between the American press and the American delegation, a position he did not entirely welcome. He had not anticipated the role either, making the assignment which was thrust into his lap all the thornier. But most correspondents personally liked Baker, and most appreciated his difficult situation. Hansen, for example, thought that Baker had provided "a really notable service for the Peace Conference and for the American people by the conscientious and intelligent manner in which he performed his duties."[53] Gallagher said Baker "sympathized heartily with our sometimes hectic efforts to pry loose the news from the masters of mankind."[54]

Edward Bellamy Partridge lampooned the American delegation's disinclination to talk substantively. He quoted Ambassador White as saying he felt sorry for the correspondents assigned to cover peace conferences because nothing usually happens at them. "They just talk—and you can't make a story out of talk." Feigning enthusiasm, Partridge tells another correspondent of his "scoop": "Well, don't give this away—but I got an exclusive story from Mr. White . . . it's about the trials and tribulations of a correspondent who is sent to cover a peace conference."[55] Three congressmen who met with Wilson briefly after touring battlefields were spoken of enviously as being on the "inside."[56] The press obviously felt less fortunate. Yet some of the hand-wringing seems to have been exaggerated, because by their own accounts correspondents regularly obtained information, and along various paths.

The way journalists went about arranging private interviews, for example, varied from individual to individual, but usually they set them up in one of four ways—through their own initiative and approach, with the help of a friend, through the offices of an official liaison, or by chance or design in the foreign press club. David Lawrence, who had known Woodrow Wilson in his Princeton days, simply approached the president at the conclusion of the first plenary session and began asking questions. Lawrence did not, however, believe he ever received special favors from Wilson: "I saw him no more than did the other correspondents," and "the truth is I saw him alone much less than did some other men in the newspaper business and I never received from him in private conversation any stories which could be used in the newspapers at the time."[57] Isaac F. Marcosson, who wrote often about the art of interviewing and of interviewing important people in Paris, admitted that personal influence was always helpful, "but when you write for a publication that reaches millions of people every week half the labor of approach is accomplished automatically."[58] Marcosson found delegates quite talkative in Paris.

W. E. B. Du Bois's method was more formal but equally straightforward. He simply wrote Clemenceau when he wanted to talk to him, asking for just "fifteen minutes to explain just what we want to do and say."[59] Du Bois's situation was complicated, given his political agenda—the Pan-African Congress —but he, too, found diplomats less prominent than Clemenceau willing to discuss topics and provide information. Edward Price Bell's requests—like Du Bois's in writing—also demonstrate the direct approach. Bell, however, applied more flattery and subtle solicitation, and he also enclosed formal "documents" testifying to his trustworthiness. Clearly he wanted a strong, mutually beneficial relationship with that particular diplomat. Both Du Bois's and Bell's letters, especially the latter's, played on the value inherent in letters of introduction and personally written recommendations.

An unnamed correspondent lauded the usefulness of the Maison Dufayel, the French club for the foreign press, for eliciting conversations and interviews. With its roughly 2,200 members, 150 of them American, the "establishing of this club," the correspondent wrote, "did more than provide a working place. It made possible the free intercourse of hundreds of journalists with literally thousands of men officially connected with the Peace conference, thus promoting in an unusual degree the contact necessary to keep abreast of the real news of the conference day by day."[60] Its array of banquets, music programs, and speakers also made the club an ideal place to combine diversion with investigation, social intercourse with information gathering.

From buttonholing delegates on their way to and from meetings, to quietly sharing "a cup of fragrant tea and a pleasant chat" in a diplomat's private office, journalists arranged access as best they could.[61] The erratic nature of such a process made cultivating a few productive relationships as well as working with official liaisons the most efficient combination for gathering news. What surprised them most was an ironic series of discoveries: coming to Paris expecting access and openness yet finding little of it officially, then in practice getting the news, though not without confronting stubborn resistance from, of all quarters, the American mission. In reality, as many journalists testified, there were actually plenty of people in Paris who wanted to talk, plenty of people who needed an audience and therefore regularly required journalists to listen and, occasionally, to help.

Relations between journalists and diplomats were, of course, not always marked by official business. Sometimes the two groups simply asked and did favors for one another. E. M. Hood congratulated himself in his diary one day during the war that he had "succeeded in getting President Wilson to make an executive order placing Norma in the Treasury Department—in her husband's Dept, in fact."[62] Hood also received requests from diplomats and other international figures, such as Elihu Root, who wrote the busy Associated Press correspondent in January to recommend a friend for a job in journalism.[63]

An anecdote from Krock's memoirs also demonstrates the occasionally fraternal relationship between journalists and diplomats. While accompanying Wilson on a pre-conference tour of Italy, Krock enjoyed a moment of friendly "bonding" with the president. The site was Turin: "When our party arrived there, was in the room with Wilson in the ducal palace, and a mob was gathered outside, cheering him and demanding his appearance. Turning to me he asked, 'How do you say "Long live Italy?" I said, 'I think you say "Eviva Italia."' 'I hope that's right,' he said, and went onto the balcony, raised his hand, and took the chance."[64] Patrick Gallagher also went beyond the call of duty in his support of certain diplomats. At the outset of the peace conference he loaned the use of his apartment in America to a Chinese delegate and his wife. The delegate soon joined his countrymen in Paris.[65]

American correspondents generally enjoyed the challenge of working with diplomats—smart, educated, or at least cultivated or charming persons with exalted titles and connections. The periodic fêtes a government sponsored on their behalf must have been welcome temptations, too. The journalists sent to Paris would hardly have been human not to delight in the attention, flattery, and conveniences showered upon them. Whatever their own interpretation on the courtship taking place, journalists certainly did not resent it, and, in fact, probably felt the way Will Irwin described his reaction to a bribe tendered to him early in his career: "I felt as a debutante must feel when she gets, from a man whom she doesn't much like, her first proposal. She's going to turn him down, of course. But oh, the compliment of it!"[66] The difference, though, is that in many cases journalists did like and often admired the diplomats they worked with in Paris, and "turning down" solicitors was not necessary since diplomatic friends were useful contacts and the obligations incurred were a small sacrifice for obtaining information.

United Press correspondent Henry Wood spoke for many American correspondents in exulting over journalists' newfound contacts. But these relationships were more than contacts; they were alliances, even friendships:

> The intimacy between world rulers and the press, to my mind, is one of the most beneficial developments of the war. It is serving to open new avenues of cooperation in every country, which has never before been known. The diplomats and the newspaper representatives become personally acquainted and gain confidence in one another. The future benefits seem inconceivable. . . .
>
> The correspondents who participated feel that they can now go to any part of the world at any time and meet their old Paris diplomatic friends in their home countries. Knowing and respecting one another, they can talk over world affairs in a way that has never before been known.[67]

At no other time in American history have journalists talked that way about statesmen. A bond had been formed, obviously, one that contained tensions and frictions, to be sure, but one that in many cases was also deep, complex, and symbiotic. Sentimental, too: When Germany signed the treaty in June, journalists and diplomats alike scoured the Versailles Palace, pocketing whatever souvenirs they could find, "from inkwells to the tabs from the camera film packs."[68] Both groups also signed autographs for one another. They wanted to remember these relationships.

~ 11 ~

PARTICIPATION

Participation is a fuzzy, subjective concept. If we define it, as the dictionary does, as joining in or sharing in something, then we are still left with the question: Did journalists join in or share in the experience of making peace? The answer is complicated because while journalists may have regarded themselves as participants, diplomats may not have accorded them the same distinction, and so the next question becomes, whose perspective is correct—journalists or diplomats? Arriving at the truth must therefore address both perspectives.

Journalists attending the peace conference invariably expressed the belief at one time or another that they were participating in the proceedings. E. M. Hood repeatedly stated his exhilaration at being involved in the process:

—The work has been so interesting and I feel that I am really playing such a part in the game that I do not mind the long hours so much. [February 9]
—I am bound to say that I do find a good deal of compensation in the exceedingly interesting and important nature of the work. . . . [February 13]
—As I have often written the work is so interesting, taken with the feeling that I really am playing a small part in it . . . [February 23][1]

The monotony of this testimony suggests something more than egocentrism. It indicates journalists' belief that the work of the conference involved large-scale collaboration requiring a part to be played by journalists and diplomats alike. What was this "part" that Hood frequently referred to? It is not easy to say because he did not elaborate further on the point. But we can infer from what he did say, as well as from the testimony of other journalists, that Hood and his colleagues gradually came to realize that, however humbly, they were integral to the peace process. If he himself might have occasionally wished to be dispensable in order to go home and be with his family, Hood would not have thought the same thing about the correspondents as a group. Nor would have his peers.

Journalists believed their ongoing presence was essential for ensuring maximum publicity. This belief was grounded primarily in occupational pride. But the correspondents from America also regarded their presence as important for reminding diplomats of the promises and requirements of the Fourteen Points and pointing out inconsistencies between those principles and subsequent developments. Finally, American journalists believed they were fulfilling a benign international role, and an ideological one, in fact, in assuming the status of ambassadors-at-large, supposedly representing the people of the world, though Americans in particular.

Diplomats, too, were aware that the press was knocking at the door, that public opinion was attempting to make its presence felt. And most delegates did usually express sympathy toward the principle, sometimes giving indications of how they worked with journalists, though they may not have phrased it in just that way. Charles Haskins and Robert Lord, members of the American delegation, wrote in 1920 that outside information and outside contacts were never lacking in Paris: "Information the conference had in huge quantities, literally by the ton. It came in every day in scores of foreign newspapers, in masses of pamphlets, in piles of diplomatic reports and despatches [*sic*]. Every special interest was on hand."[2] Journalists, too, were part of that unceasing demand, yet not wholly on the "outside" as were other sources of opinion and pressure. Because they struck daily agreements throughout 1919 the correspondents and the diplomats at times occupied the same plane.

As a rule, diplomats and journalists did not spend time talking in their memoirs about how they viewed one another as partners, and though journalists often used the word "participate" to describe the role of the press, diplomats seldom did. Indeed, it is not always easy in diplomats' accounts to find basic references to meetings between the two groups, even when we know, or can be reasonably sure, that one took place on a certain day. There are three reasons why diplomats may have kept silent: first, because they may not have considered them important enough to mention; second, because they may have had so many such meetings it would have seemed too tedious to record each and every encounter; third, because they wanted to conceal their publicity enterprise during the peace talks—perhaps because it was still considered undignified or self-indulgent for statesmen to court press attention. No doubt, the reasons vary according to the individual diplomat involved. Colonel House, for example, often omitted reference to his journalistic contacts, yet we know that he met constantly with reporters during the conference. In his case, then, his motives appear to be a combination of the second and third explanations.

As a result, it is necessary to piece together journalists' involvement by often reading between the lines in their and others' accounts of peace conference life. Most journalists did believe they were helping in the process of making peace, and using their descriptions and anecdotes as a starting point, we can document three ways in which they did so participate: cooperatively, prominently, and systemically.

COOPERATIVE

Evidence of this kind of involvement can be seen, first of all, in the letters of introduction and the expressions of friendship that passed between diplomats and journalists. In a letter by the *Chicago Daily News*'s Edward Price Bell to the American ambassador in London, John William Davis, for example, he emphasizes the reciprocal nature of both enterprises and implies that theirs is a common pursuit: "In my opinion, there are junctures in international relations offering a fruitful opportunity for the cooperation of diplomacy and journalism, and I, as European Director of the Foreign Service of the CDN and its Associated Newspapers, desire to avail myself of any such opportunity."[3] Bell was talking about more than a theoretical aspiration. He was speaking of a teamwork that regularly took place in practice. So established was this convention of advisement, in fact, that Harold Nicolson sardonically referred to the influence of the Fourth Estate in this manner. "The term 'blunder' is employed these days to signify those actions on the part of statesmen regarding which they have failed previously to consult one or another of our Press Lords."[4] This cooperative style of participation was quiet, ancillary support, whose facets were normally advisory, fraternal, and informal. Journalists who tendered this service either operated as intelligence gatherers, confidants, or congenial go-betweens. Occasionally, as with Patrick Gallagher and to some extent Frazier Hunt, they became independent advocates seeking to effect some change important to them or to right what they considered to be a wrong. But in most cases these journalists acted less autonomously, less conspicuously.

Frazier Hunt, for example, who spent much of his time in 1919 in Russia, was summoned briefly while in Paris by Colonel House. House told him that he would like Hunt to speak with both President Wilson and Herbert Hoover about conditions in Russia. Hunt gladly complied because, having seen severe food shortages in that country, he was passionately in favor of sending immediate humanitarian aid and equally convinced that there should be no Allied military intervention. Eventually, "the blockade was lifted, and two years later Hoover's men were feeding hundreds of thousands of starving Russian children and their hungry parents. Maybe I didn't have anything to do with it. . . . And yet maybe I did."[5] Hunt's role in this affair can be described as volunteer fact-finder working for the State Department, even though he was not at all affiliated with the American government.

A more basic service provided by journalists was passing on information to delegates that the delegates probably should have had in the first place—official decisions and resolutions, for example. Bass noted that delegates skipping sessions frequently went first to journalists to catch up on what they had missed. Evidently competition among reporters sometimes made them more devoted peacemakers than the diplomats officially sent to do such work. If Bass is correct about delegate absenteeism, it might be that journalists physically participated in the making of the peace more often and more diligently than their diplomatic counterparts.[6]

The press listened to and sometimes helped conference officials come to decisions—not that they always succeeded in persuading their associates. While Hunt was in Paris he also served as a confidant to William Bullitt. When Bullitt read to Hunt his letter of resignation to the American Peace Commission, Hunt tried to persuade Bullitt to remain: "I still had some little faith in Wilson, and I advised Bullitt not to present his resignation. Wilson, I argued, was having more than his share of trouble with the wily Lloyd George, the demanding Orlando, and the domineering old Frenchman."[7] Hunt's failure to dissuade Bullitt from resigning is less significant than their close relationship: Bullitt trusted Hunt well enough that he treated the correspondent as a sounding-board and friendly editor.

A frequent diplomatic duty American journalists were asked to carry out in Paris was the unpleasant task of breaking bad news to foreign missions. In most cases, it seems, they fulfilled such assignments, but occasionally they declined. In late April when conference leaders decided to give the Japanese effective control over the Shantung Province, the American mission sought a correspondent friendly to China to be the one to tell its delegates. "Earlier in the evening," Gallagher wrote, "Mr. Baker had requested me to break the news to the Chinese, but I told him that I thought he had better do it himself."[8] John Bass, too, accepted the responsibility of bearing bad tidings—and an apology. After a newspaper reported an upcoming annexation deal between Greece and Italy, an "expert" working for the Italian delegation phoned an American "expert" denying the deal. Later, when the deal actually took place, and the Italian "learned that his country had sold out he did not care to face the American" that he had inadvertently misinformed, so he asked Bass "to explain the situation to him."[9] The American mission also authorized Bass to deny French-fed rumors about an American general's actions.[10] Situations like this one gave journalists the pleasant double duty of publishing an exclusive report and, at the same time, performing a patriotic service.

Gallagher went beyond the usual role of friendly listener or advisor, however, and aggressively pushed for his own ideas at the conference. He sympathized with the vulnerabilities of both Japan and China, and, in fact, was one of the few true friends the Orient had in Paris. In January, for example, he fought for admission of Chinese representatives, and he urged Secretary of State Lansing to demand that Wilson support their place in the first League of Nations meeting. Either Wilson ignored the advice or Lansing failed to relay it.[11] Gallagher also respected the pressing political needs of the fifth member of the Alliance, Japan: "Again and again, I begged all the Americans whom I knew in Paris to take a serious and forcefully sympathetic attitude toward Japan's plea for racial and national equality."[12] He also resumed this campaign in the spring when the issue resurfaced.

Finally, when the Shantung decision was reached Gallagher refused to let the matter rest. Here, too, his compassion toward the Chinese exceeded the bounds of mere sympathizer. Discussing the decision with Wellington Koo, China's minister to Washington, Gallagher was able to offer more than consolation:

"What will you do now?" I asked him.

"As soon as we get the formal decision," he told me; "we shall, of course, enter a firm protest."

"I think you will find," I said, "that there will be protests a-plenty within the American delegation. I am going over to the Crillon now, and I am going to ask some of our people to make a vigorous protest to the President."[13]

Before the conference ended Gallagher also found himself fighting for China's admission to the signing of the Treaty at Versailles.[14] From dignified rabble-rouser to indignant advocate, Gallagher performed a number of assertive quasi-diplomatic roles at the peace conference. The fact that not once in his four-hundred-plus-page book does he address the possibility that his several functions constituted a conflict of interest suggests that at the time no firm line was drawn between the cause of political publicity and the business of journalism. They could be one and the same thing. And for a few journalists in Europe who kept a foot on both sides of the occupational fence, their participation was fully diplomatic.

PROMINENT

Where it did not altogether disappear, a thin did line existed between Gallagher's usual brand of advocacy and outright, conspicuous involvement in the peace proceedings. Of the latter, there were obvious examples of journalist-diplomats—men like Du Bois and White, for example—who tried to perform both functions at once. W. E. B. Du Bois served as correspondent for his own publication, *The Crisis*. He also went to Paris as the secretary of the Pan-African Congress, an advocate for racial equality and the rights of black people everywhere.[15] As discussed earlier, Du Bois's purpose in Europe as in America was less strictly journalistic than political; Du Bois was a man with a cause that fully defined his life's work. His methods were secondary. He was the new type of publicist, the agent for a particular cause.

Lincoln Steffens was a journalist chosen to perform diplomatic service, one of a group of "ambassadors errant appointed without constitutional warrant or responsibility," sent to Russia to initiate dialogue with the Bolshevist leadership.[16] Steffens went to Russia with William Ruffin: a journalist and a former journalist. Perhaps prejudiced by Steffens's politics, the critic quoted above complained that Steffens was not going to report but to agitate. He "goes nowhere to learn the dreary truth. He is, happily, beyond that. He knows drearier truth already. He goes to advise, to exhort, and to pontificate."[17]

But Steffens was not a diehard communist, and though he had radical political leanings he wanted to go to Russia to write about events, not get lost in them. Few if any specific political causes so animated William White. A moderate and very pragmatic Republican, he was driven by a love of journalism in general—for finding news and writing about the big changes taking place in the world. Going to Paris as both a journalist and a diplomat was a way for White to ensure that he would be where the action was. His wife recognized his interest in diplomatic involvement: "This thing that he is engaged in means more to him, I think, than anything that has ever come into his life before; means so much, because he is so absorbingly interested in the Russian thing and has been, as you know, from the revolution."[18] But nowhere in White's voluminous personal correspondence before the conference is there mention of a specific desire to go to Russia. In fact, in all of his letters asking friends to help him go overseas White emphasizes his willingness to serve in any capacity—and presumably, on any matter. Clearly, Russia interested him, but so, too, did a great many other things. White's objective was to travel and to be part of the peacemaking process. It is telling that he solicited both diplomats and politicians for a foreign post and editors and publishers for a journalistic assignment. White wanted to go where there was news, and the aftermath of the "greatest war in all history," the peace conference, was the biggest news story of 1918–1919.

Will Irwin was another correspondent who wore two hats in Paris. Irwin was the correspondent for the *Saturday Evening Post* and the energetic foreign-propaganda chief of the Committee on Public Information. Though he sported a "correspondent's uniform" and brassard in Europe, Irwin shared accommodations not with another journalist but instead lived with his old Stanford pal Herbert Hoover "in a house leased . . . in Étoile quarter."[19] Irwin had two employers during the conference, and two main objectives as well: to produce newsworthy copy for his magazine and to further the cause of American foreign policy.

At the end of the conference *Chicago Daily News* correspondent John Bass was named a member of a mission selected to go to Poland to "investigate economic, political and military conditions." Bass accepted, went to Eastern Europe, and saw firsthand the inter-Allied propaganda battles then underway in the new states created by the peacemakers. The French "by insidious propaganda sought to undermine our influence with the Poles." Numerous stories were circulated by the French delegation—and the British delegation had been given a free hand to assist the French—"to make the Poles believe we were against their welfare."[20]

There were many precedents for journalists pulling diplomatic duty. David Lawrence had performed diplomatic work during his career. In his account of Woodrow Wilson and the peace Lawrence admitted carrying out "delicate missions" on behalf of the president. One dealt with Wilson's wrangling with the Carranza regime in Mexico during the summer of 1915, when Wilson sent Lawrence, along with William Bayard Hale, south of the border to propose to General Carranza the possibility of a peace conference for all disputing Mexican chieftains.[21] Of course, Walter Hines Page, the ambassador to England, was a famous former magazine editor, and Norman Hapgood, a frequent magazine contributor, was named by Wilson in March of 1919 to become his country's ambassador to Norway.

Why would journalists want to participate directly in the peace process? As discussed in Chapter 3, Americans of all sorts were eager, almost desperate, to pitch in for and help in the war effort. Arthur Krock's description of Robert Bingham's procurement of the *Louisville Courier-Journal* exemplifies this ardor for service. Krock encountered Bingham one night in the library of a Louisville country club, the latter appearing to be in a state of utter dejection.

> "You seem troubled," I said.
>
> "I have been rejected for military service," he replied, "and abstention from it in wartime is alien to the tradition of my family. Also, I don't know of anything useful to my country in its need that is available to me to do."
>
> "Wouldn't you be performing a great public service as the owner and publisher of the Courier Journal and Times?" I asked.[22]

Like many of his countrymen, Bingham could hardly bear the idea of being an ordinary civilian while the rest of the nation went to war. Humanitarian organizations like the Red Cross and the YMCA were two means by which individuals disqualified from military service or disinclined because of pacific beliefs could participate in the prosecution of the war. Journalism was another means, and Bingham snapped at the chance to aid his country through the power of the press. Journalism also allowed individuals passionate about a cause to fill two functions at once, or one function in different ways. For Du Bois the publication he represented was but another front for his personal political activism. And like Du Bois, Marguerite Harrison used different means (journalism and espionage, in her case) for the same goal. Similarly, businessmen sometimes volunteered to travel abroad as "diplomatic scouts."[23] These individuals responded primarily to one call, but actively experimented with the means they used to pursue it.

People like Irwin or White, on the other hand, were interested in more than one agenda, and, indeed, interested at heart in more than even many agendas. They were interested in agency itself. For these Americans what mattered was doing, acting, participating—undergoing the experience of war—becoming a citizen-soldier. Irwin, for example, had gone to Europe in 1914 first as a stretcher bearer, before turning to publicity as a fighting venue—a freelancer in methods as well as subjects. And Spearman Lewis, who worked with Irwin in Europe, became a journalist only after the military rejected him. But the key to understanding the wartime role of Irwin and others is their willing pursuit of duty. While the military had its conscription system, other sectors of society during the war relied and thrived on the vitality of volunteers. Irwin complimented the staff of workers in Hoover's Food Administration for their patriotic duty in a way which might apply equally to members of the Red Cross, the YMCA, or the news business: "The American has a special talent for voluntary work in an unofficial organization."[24] Most Americans did not want to experience the war merely vicariously but to understand it firsthand. These voluntary organizations allowed them that opportunity.

Journalists, in particular, felt that desire. Shortly before America's entrance into the war, Marguerite Harrison noticed the growing curiosity among reporters at the *Baltimore Sun* in what was going on "over there." But it was more than curiosity, and much more than a delight in spectacle. It was zeal: "Nowhere was there more excitement or more feverish activity at that time than in newspaper offices. We watched the course of events with breathless attention, knowing that when the time came for action we would have an important part to play in the great drama."[25]

As with the war, journalists at the conference wanted something beyond good spectator seats; they persistently sought to become actual insiders. In fact, the image of being inside is an apt metaphor, considering the furor raised in January over the issue of press access. But journalists did not necessarily want to take the place of diplomats, though as we have seen they did sometimes perform minor diplomatic tasks. What they wanted was involvement, engagement. They frequently thought of themselves, after all, as "representatives," and representatives in a democracy are entitled to input, to influence, to a voice. American correspondents, it seems, were not content to be merely the medium for someone else. They invariably sought, as did Patrick Gallagher, for example, to make known their own observations and judgments. Theirs was an array of assertive individual voices.

SYSTEMIC

There was a larger, subtler, and extremely pervasive role journalists played at Paris, an involvement more difficult to describe but perhaps most influential of all. This form of participation relates to the ways in which the press shaped the climate of the conference by conveying commentary likely interpreted as popular opinion. Newspapers and magazines housed a kind of public register for various perspectives about the peace, including specific language, areas of interest, and ranges of expectations, thus giving diplomats a basis of reference, or menu, from which to make decisions. This aspect of journalistic influence supplied a forum for ongoing "dialogue" between the press and the peacemakers—provided feedback, in a word. And as a practical matter much of it was directly dependent on the French press. Most of the major statesmen in Paris, in fact, were to a significant extent the "servants of a public opinion formed by editors, politicians and 'practical' business men."[26] By their presence alone in Paris, American journalists constituted, so they insisted, "the people's representatives"—diplomats at large for all the publics of the world.

The first of these functions related to the atmosphere of popular fears, hopes, and expectations toward which the correspondents and their editors at home contributed. Hood felt proud about this contribution: "I . . . feel some pardonable pride in the belief that in a very small way we American newspaper correspondents have had some influence for good upon the Conference by reason of effect that our writings have had upon the entente nations as represented here through their own newspapers."[27] Simeon Strunsky explained it this way:

> The question of publicity and the Conference, as it has reached you through the cables, is really but one side of the problem. The world has been concerned with what the Conference would do to publicity. It has rather left out of account what publicity can do to the Conference. The fact is, of course, that from every side a feverish activity is being brought to bear on the proceedings at the Quai d'Orsay. It is propaganda, for the most part legitimately and openly carried on. The British delegation is living up to the reputation established by British talent for publicity during the war. Lord Robert Cecil, for example, with his passionate interest in the League of Nations, has kept in constant touch with our American and other Allied newspapermen. In London and repeatedly here in Paris he has conducted conferences with the re-

porters from which our men have come back tremendously influenced by the frankness, the sincerity, and the thorough likableness of this British aristocrat. . . . Altogether I am far from convinced that the Conference will be allowed to carry out its programme without the help of the newspapers, or without their knowledge.[28]

Later, Strunsky altered his optimism slightly, saying "we can still keep our faith," but clearly in the preceding paragraph he had identified a vital relationship between the reporters and the delegates. Even the language journalists used made an impact on political and diplomatic leaders. Secretary of State Lansing worried constantly in late 1918 about the popular mantra that "national self-determination" (a phrase "simply loaded with dynamite") had become and the dangerously loose and wild way it was bandied about in the press.[29]

This broader participation involves journalism's dialogic role—in providing a kind of ongoing but indirect conversation with diplomats and others assigned to make peace. An example from the French press during the conference will also help make concrete this "talking" back and forth. When Wilson returned to Paris in March of 1919, after a brief sojourn home, he discovered that the other plenipotentiaries had taken advantage of his absence by trying to squeeze the League of Nations out of the preliminary treaty. Wilson was furious. He made a public statement ("the greatest moment of the Conference")[30] confirming the intent of the delegates to incorporate a league covenant into the treaty, reminding everyone that the Allies had previously accepted that clause of the Fourteen Points. Soon, however, the rest of the Big Five began stepping up the pressure, France demanding the Saar basin, Italy clamoring for Fiume, the French press escalating its heated criticism of the president. The stress and hostility mounted until Wilson had finally had enough. On April 7, he summoned his ship, the *George Washington,* whose approach signaled his impatience with conference obstruction; the president was going to leave. The next day in the French papers a quiet statement announced that rumors of disagreement had been exaggerated, and that things were fine. The fiery storm directed at Wilson abated.

This example is a simple demonstration of conversation taking place between diplomats and the press. Here, the French press, with its obvious connections to the government, responded to Wilson's boldness with a note amounting to a retraction and an apology. The statement communicated to the American mission and to American journalists a change of tone in Clemenceau's diplomacy, a moderating of anti-league, and anti-Wilson, expression.

The president had been so angry with the French press that his gesture to quit the conference forced French journalists (and diplomats) to take a step back. Their temporary penitence was evidently clear enough in that single news item to reassure American journalists and diplomats that the president's gambit had succeeded. As Ray Baker described it, "On April 8th appeared one of those extraordinary little items in Le Temps which everyone recognized at once as inspired from above, as a kind of final decision upon a great policy."[31]

Newspapers' political ties were of course not new then, but the extent to which American journalists and diplomats so closely followed and relied upon the French press for unmistakable signals probably was. And in the midst of an international peace summit, moreover, the fact that crucial dénouements were being conducted through the press must certainly have represented a novel state of affairs in foreign relations. The press and publicity exerted an impact on the deliberations of peace, as surely as did domestic politics and international rivalries.

Secretary of State Robert Lansing reveals in his memoirs several occasions when the weight of press opinion forced its way through conference doors and altered diplomats' actions, and he also singled out the preceding example. At that time "the common opinion was that the drafting of the Covenant had delayed the restoration of peace, an opinion which was endorsed in the press of many countries. The belief became so general and aroused so much popular condemnation that Mr. Wilson considered it necessary to make a public denial."[32] Lansing does, incidentally, complain in his book on the peace talks about the secrecy and the "whispering diplomats," but most of what he seems to be referring to was the secrecy of information kept from him, or in other words his personal estrangement from Wilson and his jealousy of the president's confidant, Colonel House.[33] David Hunter Miller noted Wilson's bruising in January at the hands of the French press, an assault so painful the president mentioned it before the Council of Ten and threatened to release a statement to combat the negative publicity directed at *him*. Miller also describes encounters between Lord Cecil and Wilson, when the former would ask the latter what to tell the press, how to term for the public the events of the day. And the French were also concerned with the various impressions news releases would make on the public.[34]

Indeed, in reviewing the transcripts of meetings between the conferees, one is struck with how often the subject of the press came up then, how frequently Lloyd George, Wilson, or Clemenceau complained about the newspapers, at times bitterly. A typical exchange:

WILSON: Are we ready on reparations?

LLOYD GEORGE: I think we should make haste. The press is agitated at home as well as in France, and our newspapers are exaggerating the concessions that they think they foresee. If they should continue, it would result in difficulties of all kinds.[35]

Lloyd George later recalled how the "question of publicity to be given from day to day to our deliberations occupied a great many sittings. There were swarms of newspaper correspondents from every part of the world clamouring for copy."[36] Delegates made routine reference to what "the people" or public opinion would allow.[37] At times, in fact, their conversations were saturated with such concerns. Far from not mattering, journalists drew a terrific amount of attention from the delegates.

For journalists and diplomats alike, the problem was to steer a comprehensible course through a hailstorm of information. Said British diplomat Harold Nicolson: "The trouble about the Paris Conference was not that there was too little information, but there was far too much. The fault was not lack of preparation, but lack of co-ordination."[38] Trying to digest that information and relay it to reporters was thus an extremely difficult task. The intensely nationalist presses in Britain and France, Nicolson said, also made matters worse with their constant traffic in the old wartime mentality. "The cumulative effect of all this shouting outside the very doors of the conference produced a nervous and as such unwholesome effect. Our breakfast tables became a succession of intemperate yells."[39] Diplomats loudly heard journalists and other opinion leaders, then.

And journalists and diplomats did, indeed, pay attention to each other. Mark Sullivan reported that the American delegation took careful note of what the press back home said, concerned that certain comments betrayed confusion or misinformation.[40] All the delegates could not escape comment and action abroad, which is why so many observers at the time thought of the peace talks as an enterprise taking place in a much grander arena than the mere confines of a single district in Paris. "There is a larger peace conference going on to-day than the allied representatives in Paris appear to realize," one editor wrote. "Theoretically, Germany is excluded from the discussion. The program is said to be to summon Germany's representatives to Versailles there to receive and accept without question the terms to be imposed. In point of fact, Germany is to-day participating actually in the debate. She may not be expressing her views across a table, but she is expressing them across the Rhine. And that amounts to pretty much the same thing."[41]

"[E]xpressing her views . . . across the Rhine": how was this possible without the popular press? For every announcement issued by the peace delegates in Paris, a quick reaction automatically came forth from members of the German assembly, the new Cabinet, this or that official from Berlin. And the situation was, of course, equally true with respect to members of the U.S. Congress, British Laborites, etc. *Thanks to the press, one did not have to be physically in Paris to make known one's views to the peacemakers there assembled.* For the purpose of distributing information, for communicating, mass media like the wire services, the national magazines, and influential newspapers rendered transportation all but obsolete. Views traveled quickly back and forth across Europe or the Atlantic. And it was journalists who performed this function. But journalists affected the peace talks even more directly than in serving as a transmission system.

Ex-President William Howard Taft wrote angrily that the peace conference was "under bombardment by cocksure critics who are correspondents in Paris and by editors resident in distant lands."[42] Everybody, it seemed, had an opinion and wanted that opinion registered at the peace table. Reporters and editors in and out of France wanted to influence the proceedings in Paris. One journalist who had been there told Edward Price Bell in London that "[c]ertain correspondents are trying to smoke out the big four, particularly Mr. Wilson. They are concocting yarns designed to force an official clearing up of the whole situation."[43] Bell's informer told him that these journalists had different motives but most wanted honest revelations, even if they had to resort to dishonesty in provoking them. Then he explained to Bell why: "Unfortunately, in Paris, there is something like a feud between journalism and secretive statesmanship. Journalism, feeling itself scorned, perhaps does not always examine very meticulously its means of retaliation. These considerations should be borne in mind by anyone trying to understand the situation at the peace conference."[44] News of the confrontation between Wilson and Orlando in April seemed to confirm this perspective. The Italian premier was trying then to secure concessions on the Dalmatian coast (namely, the city of Fiume). Wilson kept saying no, and after renewed attempts by Orlando, the president finally lost his patience and on April 23 issued a public statement to the press explaining the disagreement. Orlando immediately issued a public reply, upon which he and the Italian foreign minister returned to Rome. The *Chicago Daily News* put Paul Scott Mowrer's correspondence in the following happy headline: "Adriatic Question 'Smokes Out' Envoys."[45]

A certain prominent element of British journalism was notoriously trying to shape the peace talks. According to one journalist: "The Northcliffe press . . . was hammering the conference, to make it impossible for Lloyd George to soften the hard terms that had been agreed on for Germany, as well as to help France in her effort for a greater degree of security. That was the immediate objective. I doubt if Lord Northcliffe's heart was in it, for it involved shooting around President Wilson's feet more than he could have liked."[46] Newspapers and magazines with a political agenda definitely made no bones about the pressure they tried to exert onto the diplomats in Paris. Was that pressure felt? The answer has often depended upon the perspective of the observer, whether of that time or this. But it seems fair to conclude that journalists had made a palpable impact on the making of peace between 1918 and 1919. As one writer noted, by "sedulously cultivating a revolutionary mood," journalists created a powerful wave of public expectation too large for statesmen to ignore: "It is true that in Paris one found official France resenting this diplomatic revolution, but not publicly resisting, and great masses were accepting, passively it may be, but still accepting, the Wilsonian policy."[47]

What type of revolution? Publicity, in a word. The very fact that statesmen were not reserving communication for private venues but often quite deliberately courting public opinion through the pages of the press—authoring "messages" and "statements" and "addresses" to one another and to certain public audiences[48]—demonstrated the change wrought on diplomacy in the progressive era. Journalists might joke sarcastically about "a report, rising almost to the authority of a statement,"[49] but what the press seemed most aggravated by was not the lack of information but the lack of *attributable* information. And even here times were clearly changing. The most prominent example during the conference was probably the public appeals made by both President Wilson and Premier Orlando, both of whom had grown frustrated with one another and felt compelled to apply leverage of a different kind. In Orlando's "reply" to Wilson, the Italian Premier noted the changed times: "The step of making a direct appeal to the different peoples certainly is an innovation in international intercourse."[50] *The New Republic* called it "open diplomacy at last."[51]

Indeed, one of the conference's most trenchant critics, Gerald Stanley Lee, found much about foreign relations that had changed. "The new diplomacy," he wrote, "seeks to pick out something concrete, dramatic and revealing for a nation to do to other nations, something revealing for a nation to say to other nations, which the other nations will like better from day to day and from year to year and will be gladder of the longer they have had it." He continued:

> People did not use to conduct diplomatic negotiations with reference to the fact that thousands of people were sitting in windows looking down on the top of what they were doing. They have to now. Diplomacy to-day is exposed to crowds, to crowds of people looking down from above on the roofs where they plot. We must arrange for airplane diplomacy now. Little innocent facades for people merely to look across to have gone by. Facades of diplomacy from now on must be built with six exposures to them so that what men do shall be looked down upon, shall be looked up at, and shall be looked at across from four sides—exposed to the four winds of heaven.
>
> Statesmanship after this is going to be carried on in glass houses, with the people of all the earth flocking by in the streets. The people are going to stand in crowds when they want to, looking in at the windows as they are looking at the shutters of the Peace Conference now.[52]

Lee was emphasizing the heightened presence of the public, journalists in particular, at the Paris Peace Conference. But Isaac Marcosson and others were probably closer to the truth in their description of the ways in which *diplomats,* and government leaders generally, had changed. "Statesmen who looked with horror upon personal exploitation in 1914 now regard it as an essential like meat and drink," Marcosson explained. "Just as the war smashed all traditions so did it give interviewing a whole rebirth of distinction."[53] And he was right. Government no longer saw itself as a helpless observer in the face of public communication, no longer understood its function to be that of mere censor. Leaders increasingly embraced the role of communicator.

The second of these systemic influences, the idea of public representation, was a concept widely shared by many of the American journalists attending the conference. The correspondents refused to be "just middle men in the transfer of information from officials to the public."[54] They fought for full-fledged recognition. "The newspapers are a great and definite power," Frederick Palmer exclaimed. "They stand between the people and sources of news, and what they select for publication has a powerful effect upon the sentiments, the opinions and the judgments of their constituents."[55] David Lawrence stated flatly that the correspondents were the people's representatives in Paris,[56] while Patrick Gallagher put it more dramatically: "The American people will never know their debt to the men and the women who were their best representatives."[57] When representatives of the American press met in mid-January to discuss the publicity crisis, they all expressed their sense of themselves as "trustees obligated to inform public opinion."[58]

In a sense, the presence and role of American journalists at the conference mirrored those of the American mission, which sought no apparent material concessions for the United States. The American press went to Europe unencumbered by the pressure of specific, parochial concerns. Indeed, the only overarching objective for Wilson, in reality, was simply attaching his name to a treaty that Congress would sign. There was more pressure to it than that, of course. The Fourteen Points were a basis for peace and certainly an idealistic guide for the postwar international community, but most of the issues to be argued in Paris were not intrinsically ones that could undermine Wilson's presidency. His political fate at home would turn only on a very vague effectiveness abroad. In any case, he and the rest of the American mission had no specific "trophies" they needed to bring home.

The American press enjoyed a similar advantage. Unlike the reporters of other nations, the American correspondents there did not feel the pressing weight of urgent national requirements. They could be more flexible in concentrating on whatever perspectives they thought best. For most the obvious agenda was therefore the Fourteen Points. And just as French reporters might ask American sources their views on reparations and postwar alliances, American reporters could devote attention to such matters as open diplomacy, the League of Nations, and President Wilson himself. To some degree, American journalists were auxiliary members of the American Peace Mission, because they inevitably asked questions arising out of an American context— they routinely asked about the Fourteen Points, for example—and because they often sympathized with the American delegates charged with seeing those ideals realized. Better coordination between the American delegation and the American press might thus have improved Wilson's advantage at the conference and put the heat on his adversaries more often than it was put on him. At any rate, it would have helped him politically in the United States, and that context, it turned out, overshadowed what he did in the Place de la Concorde. If Wilson had cooperated more fully with America's journalistic "ambassadors" in Paris, therefore, he would have done himself a double service—pleased the press and the congressmen who depended upon the authority of that information.

But correspondents in Paris believed that regardless of the outcome of the peace talks—regardless of how fair or just or wise the eventual treaty would be—they rendered a crucial and integral service by simply being there and transmitting the developments as soon as they could. Gerald Stanley Lee exclaimed that the "only way in getting at the truth in expressing the relations between governments is to have a crowd at the keyhole when the teacup is thrown. If we are going to have a League of Nations, America will have to provide through its newspapers an enormous safe-guaranteed equipment and machinery for having crowds at keyholes."[59] Lee was a curious critic of the conference. It seems that no matter how hard he tried to disparage its publicity lapses, he always came around to an optimistic appraisal of journalism's future role in diplomacy. He sensed, apparently, that the press had tried hard—and with some success—to report the peace talks, to employ the "spotlight," as he liked to say. By the end of a gloomily titled article, he was waxing visionary about the time already "at hand when nations will arrange to have moving-picture treaties, treaties proposed to the peoples by moving pictures, discussed by the people in moving pictures, voted on by moving pictures, and enforced in detail—following every man up—by moving pictures."[60]

Finally, the very fact that American journalists were transmitting the results of the treaty as fast, as accurately, and as intelligently annotated as they did indicates another way in which they participated in the making of the peace. As one writer put it, "The old idea of diplomacy was to send an ambassador to live near some court from which he could transmit what gossip he gathered in secret messages to his government. The new idea is to send a journalist to explain to the people what his nation thinks, wants and means to do."[61] American journalists did so. By delivering the treaty to the world, the correspondents who labored in France did their utmost to ensure that the American public back home knew what Wilson had agreed to and what the U.S. Senate, and the American people, would have to approve. As with so many other aspects of the press's role in Paris, perhaps the most impressive thing was not so much journalists' level of participation but the detailed organization, speed, and technology with which they were expected by diplomats to participate—not so much the qualitative as the quantitative publicity surrounding conference work:

> The plan proposed on behalf of the United States is for the American delegates to cable, for simultaneous distribution on the American continents, first, a 250-word official summary of the treaty; second, a 5,000-word official summary, and, third, the text of the treaty.
>
> The two summaries would be given to the American press at about the same time and the treaty a day or two later, the text possibly to be distributed by installments as it was received.[62]

Not surprisingly, publication of just the five thousand-word treaty summary constituted the longest telegraph cable release in history up to that point, a testament to at least one measure of the conference's openness.[63] One month later, Floyd Gibbons's replacement in Paris for the *Chicago Tribune,* Frazier Hunt, did not hesitate to smuggle a copy of the German-approved treaty out of the country and into the United States, a contrast with the release of the earlier version but still a measure of journalists' determination to share publicly the work of the conference.[64] Within days of its appearance in the newspapers and upon Senator Borah's specific recommendation, the treaty was forthwith published in the *Congressional Record.*

Most historians, when they mention it at all, have consistently portrayed the press's role in Paris as minuscule or virtually nonexistent. Like Margaret Macmillan, in her beautifully written account of the conference, these scholars dwell on journalists' hurt feelings in January and seldom return to the subject.[65] Yet it is simply not true that journalists got "little" or no information at the conference.[66] A few, such as James D. Startt, do speak of "partnership," but fail to give much credit to reporters' degree of participation.[67] Startt is right that Wilson missed an important opportunity at Paris, that journalists were severely disappointed with their actual level of participation, and that that level was far less than they had been led to expect. But he misses a larger point: Wilson and the other diplomats in Paris did make frequent efforts to accommodate journalists, efforts that were unprecedented and rather extraordinary. At times, it seems, they bent over backward to conciliate the press, to reassure or console correspondents when things turned out badly. And the routine manner with which delegates constantly used and cooperated with the press, a reality which journalists were aware of, sympathized with, and often proudly initiated (cooperation was usually how they got news), also testifies to the close relationship between both groups. These gestures indicate a revolutionary change in the attitude of diplomats toward members of the press, and that intellectual shift represents a large-scale ideological transformation: an acceptance of the influence of public opinion on statecraft, as well as the growing recognition that journalists shaped, spoke for, or actually represented that opinion.

Thomas Leonard, in an important work on American political news, says that progressivism, "and especially its journalism, undermined the ritual of political participation" because the spirit of that time was essentially elitist.[68] That may be true, but however much they may have embraced popular political participation, and they certainly paid homage often enough to the idea, there is no doubt that the American journalists in Paris believed themselves to be the *instrument* for that ritual, the means for public participation. And that is really the point. Publics had historically been denied timely, accurate information about ongoing peacemaking. Journalists could hardly undermine a ritual that had never been there to start. Quite the contrary, they seemed to be trying to inaugurate a new ritual. And, finally, journalism at the time was so porous an occupation that an extraordinary number of people could and did get involved in publicizing the peace process—not just full-time journalists or, interestingly, full-time diplomats, but persons who fit into neither category, or, occasionally, who fit into both.

Michael Schudson gives conflicting answers. In the single-most-cited work of journalism history during the last twenty-five years, *Discovering the News,* Schudson writes that the peace conference "symbolized the modern relationship between government and press. It undercut the self-image of the press as a key actor in decision making at exactly the moment the press was most enchanted with its own powers."[69] Actually, the governments gathered to make peace in Paris generally validated journalism's role in peacemaking through all sorts of means, large and small. They did so in just the manner that Schudson mentions, if briefly—through "publicity." "From beginning to end, publicity was a political issue of the first importance," he writes. But in even subtler ways publicity was not just a significant political issue at the Paris Peace Conference. Publicity was the very process itself. By the end of World War I it had become so.

Despite Robert Hilderbrand's dour conclusion that progressive presidents generally ignored public opinion as a consideration in making foreign policy,[70] it seems patently the case that Wilson was exceptionally conscious of it and even initiated a couple of prominent fights on its behalf. And even he was in many respects less aggressive on this front than other plenipotentiaries. Hilderbrand himself mentions elsewhere in his book some of the unprecedented steps the president and other conferees took to benefit publicity and the press.[71] Public opinion had indeed become a critical factor at the Paris Peace Conference. While government representatives sometimes resisted the idea in principle, in practice they almost instinctively embraced it. If officials did not elevate journalists onto a conspicuous plane of partnership, they did routinely involve correspondents in their work. They did so because publicity, and therefore public opinion, was always of paramount concern.

CONCLUSION TO PART FOUR

Journalists' faith in mass communication as an instrument for diplomatic reform was uniformly strong at the beginning of 1919. In January, the *Chicago Daily News* transmitted news concerning a quintessentially progressive bit of new diplomacy: "The allied and associated powers to-day agreed to send a wireless message throughout the world warning all concerned that parties using armed force to gain possession of territory the claim to which the peace conference would be asked to determine, would 'seriously prejudice' the claims of those who used such force."[72] Mass media, the implication went, might still come to the aid of new diplomats. And a few months later, the paper was quoting Melville Stone, of the Associated Press, who upon returning to the United States predicted that a league of nations would avert war precisely through mass communication, "the development of intercommunication," as he put it.[73]

That faith was not gone in July 1919, but it had been, and was still further to be, substantially reinterpreted. Correspondents' comments in the second half of 1919 reveal a dejected detachment as they struggled to understand what they had experienced. In retrospect, some journalists thought they may have tried too hard, taken themselves too seriously in Paris.[74] Their anguish and exasperation after the peace talks certainly stand in sharp contrast to the bubbly enthusiasm of late 1918, but there was nonetheless a sense of responsibility, of proud accomplishment, of service performed and duty rendered.[75] Journalists' immersion in, and their own contribution to, talk of the new diplomacy throughout 1918 had conditioned their responses to the peace conference in 1919. Their expectations had been too high.

The correspondents' emotional flirtation with the idea of democratic diplomacy prejudiced their perception of the actual diplomacy in which they themselves had participated. Disappointment and disillusionment are, in fact, such well-known elements in the writing of journalists who covered the conference that that gloomy assessment has for more than three generations colored the judgment of historians interested in the twentieth-century American press. Certainly nothing had prepared journalists for the onslaught both the Fourteen Points and Wilson himself were to undergo in Paris, nor were they quite ready for the political bloodbath the treaty and the league faced in the United States once the conference was over. But both in Europe and in America governments had come to appreciate fully the importance of publicity, and so much so that they now routinely strove to conduct public relations themselves. Journalists were still a critical part of that process, but in America as elsewhere national governments no longer left public opinion to chance.

Journalists can be said to have participated in peacemaking in 1919, but that story has been obscured by the fact that peacemaking administrations were now themselves fully engaged in public communication. When progressive journalists and progressive diplomats met in Paris, then, they were both eclipsed by the new reality that publicists were the people who made peace, and publicists were not so much individuals from a particular profession (not even press agentry) as members of governments, the press, or specific political causes who reflexively turned to the media to advance their interests. The peace conference of 1919, in short, was replete with information. Publicity thus dominated the conference, only not the kind of publicity American journalists were expecting, for what came through loudest that winter and spring were not Wilson's messages but those of the French press and the French government.

One of the two biggest shocks in Paris, it turned out, was that a superlative communicator had lost his voice when he most needed it. The other surprise was that journalists resented Wilson's negligent leadership of public opinion, his apparent unwillingness to try to manage them. Rather than fill the void, they seemed simply bewildered by the vacuum. The American press became frustrated by the president's apparent disinterest in publicity at a time when most other leaders were consumed by it. For that seven-month period, his strategy (or lack of it) represented almost a throwback to that of presidents before McKinley, and journalists were disappointed that a near-Rooseveltian leader would, for a crucial stretch of time, act more like William Howard Taft. A modern, professional press needed a stronger, progressive president.

PART FIVE

THE DEMOCRATIC DIN OF PUBLIC OPINION

The Treaty Fight

❧ 12 ❧

ANTI-TREATY OPPOSITION

The war is over in France, but it is raging in Washington.
Leslie's, August 2, 1919

For the most part, the close-up encounter between American reporters and diplomats in Paris ended once the Germans signed the treaty
in June. That result was mainly circumstantial. Some correspondents
stayed on in European posts or prepared to cover the developing organization
of the League of Nations, but most came home for a well-earned rest. The experiment in peace via publicity did not turn out the way anyone had planned,
but all through the conference and afterward the press remained constantly
involved. In fact, publicity proved far more enduring than peace. Back in the
United States, the fate of the treaty would once again pass through the crucible of mass communication—journalists dealing with senators instead of
diplomats, for peacemaking at this juncture now required the services of rati-
fying legislators, not negotiating delegates. In any case, domestic statesmen
resumed or intensified information battles. Woodrow Wilson rediscovered
the publicity campaign, senators took to the press, political organizations
agitated and advertised, some journalists and some diplomats even became
directly involved themselves. Virtually all the major players resorted to forays
into the mass media. The question few if any historians have asked, curiously,
is *why.*[1] If ratification was simply a matter of politicians working out a compromise among themselves, why bother with public statements, press blitzes,
speaking tours, guest editorials, and essays? Why talk with anyone other than
senators? The answer appears to be both the importance of public opinion
and the reflexive progressive preference for publicity. Progressives could not
campaign without "printed materials."[2] By the second decade of the twentieth century, political methodology depended upon management of public

forums, upon newspapers and magazines especially. It had in Paris during the conference, and it did so again in Washington and throughout the nation during the ratification debates.

This time, however, the strong professional momentum achieved by the press in Paris appeared absent. Journalists were more consumed with the dynamic debates then flooding the forums they provided and less concerned with that other dimension of progressive publicity, the focus on expert information. The authority of facts certainly did not vanish from the scene, but its presence was obscured by the divisive controversy over ratification and the power struggle over the new presidency.[3] What one notices, then, in the writings of journalists during and after the summer of 1919 is not so much their professional orientation as their political and ideological sensibilities. Professionalism may have mattered less to them then perhaps because its usefulness was provisional. If that possibility makes Paris seem all the more extraordinary as a professional opportunity, it also makes the treaty fight in the United States appear all the more remarkable as a vigorous democratic exercise, one contemporaries thought might well have been the greatest in half a century.[4] At both venues of statecraft, though, public opinion was the target and publicity the means. Progressive peacemaking's tribunal function was always present.

With but one exception it also inhabited each of the factors that killed the campaign to get the Versailles Treaty adopted by the U.S. Senate: Wilson's abandonment of public relations while in Paris (discussed in the previous chapter); the effective propaganda sponsored by anti-treaty forces; the weak and disorganized pro-treaty publicity campaign in the United States; and the president's illness and intransigence in the fall of 1919. To this list, I would add one more: the New York printers' strike of October 1919—a dispute which removed a central, influential forum at a critical time. Most of these factors directly involved the medium of the press, which means that, however conscious of their influence, journalists continued to play a critical part in the American conclusion of peace. These chapters examine how they did so, and why that was necessary.

BEFORE PARIS

Republican opposition to the treaty was early, strong, and sustained. The campaign against the peace terms had its roots in the fall of 1918, as political foes winced at Wilson's pursuit of a negotiated or "covenanted" peace. They exploited the opportunity by positioning themselves as warriors who championed the enemy's unconditional surrender. "No peace that satisfies Germany in any degree . . . can ever satisfy us," Senator Henry Cabot Lodge proclaimed before Congress. "It must be a dictated peace."[5] Anxiety increased as notes were exchanged between Wilson and Prince Maximilian in the fall. Would the president cede too much in order to end the war? A paper representative of hawkish sentiment, the *Boston Transcript,* thought so: "Discussion is desertion of our defenders at the front, the living and the dead."[6]

Attacking the league idea, as well as Wilson's Fourteen Points, followed naturally from the hubbub surrounding October's peace parleys. Was charity toward an enemy really preferable to cold justice? Did a negotiated peace reward aggressors and, more important, could it even last? These and other questions arose in discussions about how the war ought to end as well as the future of conventional diplomacy, subjects seldom and lightly touched upon during the war but all-important as formal peace talks were at hand.

From September 1918 on, Wilson's vaunted peace principles began to receive exacting scrutiny and frequent Republican dismissal. *Current Opinion* addressed the new, politically charged atmosphere: "[T]he basis formulated by President Wilson as a sort of beginning of peace negotiations has come under shell-fire and become the subject of heated partizan [*sic*] discussion. It is an ominous beginning, showing what possibilities of debate and dissension lie in the program before the peace delegates."[7] It was a prescient observation. The writer went on to note that Wilson's famous speech had been complacently absorbed in January, "at the time received with apparent acquiescence in this country. . . . [T]here was no political campaign on then." Now, however, something had changed. "In the recent campaign Mr. Roosevelt, ex-Secretary Shaw, Chairman Hay and other Republican leaders attacked these Fourteen Points from various directions."[8] That "recent campaign," begun in the last few months of the war, ran unabated until the treaty's rejection and consistently drowned out positive commentary about the league idea.

Early criticism of the president or his administration usually came when triggered by tense moments or confusing circumstances. More concerted, however, were the deliberative strikes launched against the White House from that time forward, between roughly September 1918 and November 1919. In that time the president's political foes took the gloves off and began swinging fiercely.

Senator Lodge's congressional address on August 23 formally inaugurated the Republican campaign against Wilson. In it the Republican leader in Congress asserted his version of what America's war aims ought to be: namely,

Germany's complete destruction and unconditional surrender—an imposed peace or no peace. His speech stirred anxiety among numerous editors worried about Wilson's diplomatic trigger finger. "The country is against a negotiated peace," declared *The Outlook*. But not everyone took the Massachusetts senator so literally. *The New Republic,* for one, pronounced Lodge's address a simple political ploy by an "extremely shrewd politician" whose "only hope for party success is the advocacy of war and more war."[9] Indeed, the war aims were less "war aims for the Allies" than "Republican party war aims for the United States."[10] A *Current Opinion* writer boiled down Lodge's remarks in the same way, saying that the speech "is accepted throughout the country as a Republican key-note" and noting liberal opposition to it.[11] Lodge had done an about-face in 1917 on the issue of the league, and second only to Wilson was probably the most complex political personality involved in the 1919 treaty fight. His priorities were the Senate and the Republican Party, and his outstanding objective appeared to be simply "preventing Wilson from emerging as 'the maker of peace,' and reaping the enormous electoral benefits that would surely follow from this," historian David Mervin writes.[12] What he would do in the struggle for ratification was never clear. The conflict, at any rate, was on between the president and the Senate, with the press very closely in step.

SPRING 1919

Oppositionist fulmination had an effect. In the United States, Senate criticism went seemingly unanswered. Though ordinarily in the logic of journalistic priority, a president "trumps" a senator, Wilson's absence from the United States effectively created a domestic vacuum of political leadership in the press at home. The president's actions abroad perforce commanded high-profile headlines, but a prominent senator's address concerning the peace or the president himself could, too. By not committing resources to generate positive news about the conference, Wilson ceded a tremendous opportunity to hostile Republicans. And make no mistake—Wilson's enemies knew where to turn. In March 1919 William Borah wrote to a friend that "[o]nly by organizing public opinion can we succeed."[13] Borah followed through, too. Later that year he would join Senators Hiram Johnson of California and Medill McCormick of Illinois to shadow Wilson's speaking tour out west and to make speeches further criticizing the treaty. Yet already in the spring of 1919 the senator from Idaho had embarked on a publicity tour of his own against the league.[14] Along with Senator James A. Reed, of Missouri, and Senator Johnson, Borah was one of the most vigorous anti-league campaigners. All three "spoke frequently in the Senate, took to the stump again and again, usually had immediate comments on the latest breaking news stories, and were active in considerations of strategy."[15]

The president's foes embraced a vigorous propaganda campaign, one that yielded benefits in a variety of publications, whether political or not and whether friendly or not. A January editorial in *The Independent,* a reliable supporter of the president and the league concept, for example, took pains to rebut Senate criticism—but not before generously allotting half the space of its message to the content of that criticism.[16] Lodge, Borah, Senator Philander C. Knox, of Pennsylvania, and their allies took continual advantage of that opportunity, sniping at the president's decisions and at conference results (usually failing conveniently to distinguish the two). Republicans accordingly expressed outrage at armistice details[17]; the arrangements for publicity at the conference; the delays Wilson's League of Nations was said to cause ("Blessed are the peacemakers who actually succeed in making peace")[18]; the president's gambit in summoning the *George Washington* in April; his public rebuke of the Italians; his concession to the Japanese concerning Shantung[19]; and finally, his handling of the release of the treaty's first draft in May. The resulting vituperation inevitably found its way, and daily, into the press, causing more than one observer to note in the spring of 1919 that Wilson received more abuse at home than he did abroad.[20] Observers noted the relationship between the president and the Senate going "steadily from bad to worse" during those spring months.[21]

The Republican "round robin," which was orchestrated by Lodge and Knox to coincide with the president's temporary return to the United States in February, represented the party leadership's undisguised opposition to Wilson's peace aims. In it thirty-seven senators signed a statement on March 3 that the League of Nations as constructed in Paris would be unacceptable to them, a majority sufficient to kill American ratification.[22] "In the Senate it's the league of fulminations," quipped the *Newark News.*[23] Most of the press, friendly or not to the president, was quite serious and acutely alarmed by the course of events, though. The *Chicago Daily News* complained that "the world is in a fair way to get together and abolish war, if the United States does not stop it." Some of the more insulting political cartoons directed at the U.S. Senate appeared at this time, painting Republican members as babies, dainty old ladies, or effete old men. The *Springfield Republican* angrily accused Senate opponents of "attempting to wreck the peace of the world,"[24] while the *Greenville Piedmont* wondered aloud whether the "senate's chief objection to the League idea is that Wilson is a Democrat."[25] But the damage had been done. "President Wilson's plan is dead," declared the *New York Sun* in commenting on the Republican maneuver.[26] The *New York Tribune* pronounced it the end of the covenant, and time for the president to recollect himself and try again. "But his first victory must be over himself, must spring from his own perception of his own errors, must represent a turning away from everything savoring of arrogant self-will."[27] Senate critics had scored a major triumph.

Anti-league sentiment sometimes coalesced around a powerful tide of sentiment personally directed against the White House: "Wilsonphobia," one writer dubbed it, a widespread neurosis with terrible consequences. "It is within the bounds of possibility that the hostility to one individual on the face of the globe may defeat the plan to end war adopted unanimously by the official representatives of thirty-two nations."[28] Diehard critics of the president like magazine editor Colonel George Harvey made vitriolic speeches condemning the covenant and its dark implications for American sovereignty. The rumbling hostility toward Wilson was scarcely hidden: "[A]bout half of Washington is not standing behind the President, except for the purpose of kicking him,"[29] one writer said. Animus against Wilson in the United States was further stimulated by the palpable disenchantment Europe itself had exhibited toward the president. Though some American writers challenged the authenticity of that disappointment, there was no mistaking the fact that many in the U.S. press were beginning to describe in colorful fashion the way Wilson had "forfeited the hearts of the European masses, denied their hopes, darkened their faith."[30]

Opposition also stemmed from genuine suspicion of international entanglements and distrust of league obligations. Henry Watterson, having recently resigned from the *Louisville Courier-Journal* on account of his aversion to the league idea, helped found a league of his own: the League for the Preservation of American Independence, organized in March 1919. Politicians and journalists alike constantly raised the specter of faraway Europeans—or worse, Asians, Africans, or Islanders—dictating internal domestic policy to the United States of America. Whatever its particular bogeymen, the anti-league movement inspired virtuoso performances of publicity from politicians and the most expressive political exuberance from publishers, editors, and reporters.

Senators demonstrated their gifts as publicists between the end of the war and the remainder of the treaty fight, authoring innumerable treatises detailing the reasons for their criticism, concern, or distrust, and stepping up anti-league activities in the spring of 1919. They contributed guest columns and wrote frequent letters to editors in order to ensure that their anxieties were kept constantly before the public. In March former Indiana senator Albert J. Beveridge enumerated the drawbacks of the league idea in the *North American Review*,[31] while Connecticut senator Frank B. Brandegee wrote a blistering indictment in the *New York Sun*. In June Senator Lawrence Y. Sherman of Illinois provided *Leslie's* with his argument against the covenant, entitled "Why I Oppose the League."[32] (In the same issue, George Creel discussed the advantages of America's participation in the league and stated confidently his belief that the United States would eventually join, because Senate obstruction would be political "suicide."[33]) A few months later, Senator Hiram Johnson, a Roosevelt-style progressive from California, arranged to write a regular column for *Sunset*, a magazine editorially in favor of the league and the treaty. More demagogue than statesman, Johnson was known as a riveting rabble-rouser. Along with Brandegee, Knox, Miles Poindexter of Washington, and Reed, he helped stir up considerable doubt about the league and the treaty through a steady stream of negative publicity. By the summer, American sentiment "seemed to be shifting from what had once been a largely uncritical acceptance of the idea of a league to a more skeptical attitude toward the actual League Covenant."[34]

The fact that anti-league activists were adopting the state-of-the-art tools of progressive publicity no doubt had something to do with those shifts in attitude. Borah, for example, held daily press conferences, sought out correspondents for personal conversations, and took reporters' phone calls to his home at almost any hour.[35] The League for the Preservation of American Independence, moreover, virtually imitated the CPI in its methods, style, and energy:

> Subdivided into eight district units with many state and city chapters, the Independence League functioned as a nationwide publicity organ for the opponents of the League of Nations. . . . Its chief importance to the irreconcilables was in helping finance their speaking tours, arranging for newspaper advertisements, renting halls, and in general preparing the scene for effective

performances. Speeches and articles were also reprinted and mailed out by the tens of thousands, form letters were written so that local citizens could petition their senators, and phonograph records were even made of some of the senators' speeches so that they could be replayed in outlying hamlets which were denied the presence of the orators themselves.[36]

George Creel could not have organized such efforts better if he had done it himself.

As in Paris when statesmen and journalists sometimes exchanged roles, in the United States that fluidity was present, too. Not only were Watterson and Harvey involved to the teeth politically, but Wilson's staunch wartime critic, New Hampshire newspaper publisher George H. Moses, was elected to the Senate in 1918 and soon became a committed Irreconcilable. This was a time, after all, when politicians still frequently rose from the journalistic ranks.[37] Other prominent publishers joined the fight as well—William Randolph Hearst and Frank Munsey gave considerable support, counsel, speeches, and press coverage that were hostile toward the president. Munsey, for one, "had excellent contacts with the 'bitter-enders.'"[38] Most successful politicians had to keep up close contacts of that sort to be effective. If leaders like Taft and Roosevelt were unusual in writing regular columns after their presidencies— "the great syndicated patriot of America, Brother Taft," Senator Reed sarcastically put it—they were typical (even Taft) in having intimate press allies.[39] The uproarious political controversy caused by league debate in the United States seems to have thawed many journalists' cooler professional detachment in Paris and even ignited embers of the old partisan patronage.

Opponents of the treaty took advantage of methods old and new. The publication of personal letters probably represented an older tradition, though the frequency, timing, and explosiveness of their release often suggested a more modern sensibility. Elihu Root's letters to Republican chief Will Hays (March 29, 1919) and to Senator Lodge (June 21, 1919), William Howard Taft's letter to Will Hays (July 1919), and Sir Edward Grey's famous *Times* letter (January 31, 1920) all caused a tremendous sensation when they were published. The onset of a whole library full of memoirs, studies, and monographs would soon begin trickling out toward the end of the year, too—Ray Stannard Baker's and John Maynard Keynes's among the most famous of these early book-length pamphlets.[40]

Other instruments of publicity—the speaking tour, in particular—were also a traditional means to drum up support. As a political method, stumping represented a throwback to nineteenth-century campaigning. But the lofty emphasis on public education was pure progressivism. So were the sophisticated planning and coordination that accompanied these tours. Once more, the Irreconcilables led the way. Hitting the road were such senators as Borah, Johnson, McCormick, Poindexter, Reed, Sherman, and Colorado senator Charles Thomas. Like Wilson's autumn efforts, these peripatetic campaigns focused on midwestern and western states, where populations were less politically predictable than, say, the South. According to what is still the best scholarly work on the subject, Borah, Poindexter, and Reed gave the most speeches against the treaty, Borah delivering sixteen in half a dozen states between March 6 and April 10.[41]

The senators touring the country to offer counter-treaty speeches met with unexpected enthusiasm along the way.[42] In Chicago, Senator Borah warned an audience that America might soon have to send a hundred thousand troops to Constantinople, and, perhaps to some embarrassment, elicited a thunderous anti-administration reaction from the crowd, with cries of "Impeach him!" to be heard throughout the auditorium.[43] A later assembly in Chicago, in September, sparked similar passions. Hiram Johnson was ecstatic about the reception there. The meeting, he told his sons, "paralyzed everybody. No such demonstration had been seen there since Roosevelt['s] time. *We made the news.*"[44] The back-and-forth between the two foreign policy positions, between the two branches of government, raised the stakes and lent considerable zest to the political atmosphere of the time. As one New York journalist put it: "So far the peace is almost as exciting as the war."[45]

SUMMER 1919

Amid the rising clamor of treaty debate in 1919, the Republicans made another decisive assault against the treaty in June. This time it was Senator Knox who delivered the blow. In a resolution condemning the myriad entanglements lurking within the treaty, Knox urged his countrymen to arrange formal peace terms separately with Germany and to reserve talk of an international association until later. Knox's resolution was hardly likely to be accepted, but it was threatening nonetheless: "[I]t is regarded by the friends of the League of Nations as the most dangerous move yet against the League. In the first place it is a flank attack. Its supporters can still claim to be favorable to a League of Nations and to be asking simply for a fuller discussion of its terms. In the second place, a support by even one-third of the members of the Senate will create a serious situation for the Peace Conference at Paris, as one-third of the Senate can defeat the ratification of the treaty."[46] Press support of the Knox resolution was, at best, light and "half-hearted"—the *New York Tribune,* the Hearst press, and a few of the other usual oppositionist journals expressing solidarity with the Republican dissidents. Elsewhere, though, there was considerable criticism of Knox, and much of it quite ferocious. Most papers scored the senator for the timing of his resolution, but they also let him have it for his transparent motives. The *New York Times,* for example, said that "the astonishing and dangerous resolution of instruction and menace to the Peace Conference" was "flagrantly improper and impertinent" and designed simply to hamper American representatives in doing their work overseas. The *New York World* decried Republicans' "irresponsible" and "peculiarly offensive sort of politics."[47] Undeterred, Knox renewed his stance the following month in even stronger language.

But the criticism seemed to be taking its toll. Despite the fact that Wilson had incorporated critics' recommendations into the league covenant, the president's foes acted as though he had done nothing.[48] In May Lodge declared the covenant no better than the draft he had seen in February. And some magazines were beginning to reconsider the league's overall merits. Delay almost surely played a factor in producing the "growing criticism" prevalent at the end of the conference.[49] A British observer noticed that by mid-June in America the "most significant aspect of the situation is the 'line-up' of the Liberal weeklies with the Republican Senators. Most influential in this respect is the *New Republic.*"[50] Another observer commented in July that liberals and progressives were demonstrating more "dissatisfaction" with the treaty than were even conservatives like Lodge.[51] Even as traditionally sympathetic an organ to Wilson as the *Advocate of Peace* had greatly tempered its support of the treaty. By June the president could no longer count on its pages for editorial support. In July the magazine set forth the treaty's perceived weaknesses and urged thorough amendment and revision, saying that America's "hope . . . lies with the Senate."[52] France, a third editorial said, had "a keener sense of reality than we. In private conversation they reveal their grave doubts of the practicability of the League of Nations. That doubt is now a matter of world knowledge."[53] In subsequent editorials in the same July issue, the *Advocate of Peace* called the president's July 10 speech "a disappointment," then settled into a discussion of how Senate revision of the treaty would suffice, being "all that we can get for the present, for it is the only thing concretely before the nations. . . . We must get something."[54] *The World's Work* also echoed this sentiment of impending trouble: "The discussion of the covenant of the League has already disclosed so many defects that even its most enthusiastic advocates are beginning to lose faith in its value as a bringer of universal peace and international good will."[55]

The intellectual maelstrom caused by this divisive foreign policy debate made the nation's capital a confusing place, where answers seemed elusive, where doubt and contradiction ruled. "The man who goes to Washington to take his seat in Congress to-day must be a man of iron," one writer said, "because he will encounter the greatest enemy of statesmanship—public opinion. It is a monstrous menace just now, in the confused state of world affairs, divided as it is between ideal expectations and better realities."[56] What did the people want? "What will the people endorse?" It was a question that troubled both journalists and politicians.[57] The public, or at any rate the press, seemed in a surly mood in August. "The world is now in a somewhat depressed and critical period," a writer for *The World's Work* wrote.[58]

Things were complicated in the Senate. A poll taken by the *Chicago Tribune* during the summer showed that forty-three members favored the covenant without reservation, forty favored it with reservations, eight opposed it regardless of reservations, while five were unsure.[59] These remarkable numbers highlighted two facts: the overwhelming majority of congressmen (over eighty) wanted some kind of league, but most of them opposed the current league then under consideration. Not surprisingly, most observers interpreted this to mean that an amended league would probably pass. But determined senators bent on upending the treaty were not prepared to surrender so easily. And their antagonism coincided with a number of skeptical voices, all of whom thickened around a sticky resistance that to the end took many supporters by surprise. "Perhaps the remarkable thing," one editor noted, "is that so much opposition has developed to this treaty which, despite its internal weaknesses, is well designed to win popular approval."[60]

The Senate Foreign Relations Committee took the politically savvy step of announcing its intention of opening its normally closed doors to the press during the summer. As the historian Ralph Stone points out, open hearings surely resonated with progressives like Borah, Johnson, and others.[61] But they were also a public relations coup and put the president in a less favorable light. "President Wilson was unable to force European diplomats to swallow this pill of 'pitiless publicity,' but the Senate has determined that the full light of public discussion shall pervade the atmosphere during its discussions of the treaty with Germany."[62] Months before, Senator Lodge had expressed outrage in May that "every shopkeeper in Germany . . . was reading the treaty as made public at Berlin, yet the Senate was provided only with a 'worthless' official abstract."[63] The U.S. Senate now looked as though it was going to put Wilson's "open diplomacy" into practice in America. It certainly looked that way, but the Senate did not quite deliver on the publicity it promised. A month later, journalists were denied entrance to a meeting between the Senate committee and the president, and instead compelled to pay $25 an hour for a commercial secretary's typed account; the reporters "literally were 'shouting at the key-holes,' in their demands for uncensored stenographic reports of the exchanges."[64] An editorial in *Editor & Publisher* bitterly complained of the press's less-than-aggressive response to this insult. Reporters were accepting "official communiqués" all over again.[65]

But on the whole the press was more critical of the administration than the U.S. Senate, some bitterly contending that complete secrecy would be preferable to the State Department's "aggravating" partial publicity, which was then gradually releasing bits and pieces of supplementary peace treaty documents.[66] And yet the German peace treaty was taken up in open session by the Senate, "the first great document of its kind to be discussed" there "in the full light of publicity."[67] Open diplomacy had at least altered an established tradition in the upper chamber of the U.S. Congress.

≈ 13 ≈

THE PRO-TREATY CAMPAIGN

Intemperate criticism has diligently sought to find fault with the covenant which has been devised and underwritten by the deputies of the great powers. The criticism has been animated and voluble, but it has been singularly futile on the whole. At the same time the spokesmen of this covenant show a singular lack of assurance; they speak in a tone of doubtful hope rather than enthusiastic conviction.

The Dial, May 17, 1919

Animated discussion of an international league was lacking throughout most of the war, all the belligerents focusing on the fighting at hand rather than the negotiation somewhere down the road. Discussion that did seep out before the armistice was necessarily sketchy. As victory loomed for the Allies, however, articles began to appear more frequently, then to proliferate. But most suffered from an inescapable imprecision, the president, for one, not talking much himself about the League of Nations until his Fourth Liberty Loan address on September 27, 1918. The result was a kind of vague endorsement by the nation's press as the league concept was "smothered with praise."[1] Indeed, most journalists who favored a league of nations and first supported the treaty were characterized more by overconfidence and complacency than by vigilant campaigning. William Allen White, who was sure the league would come about, told his fellow Republicans at the time of the armistice that if they did not provide responsible service in the treaty discussion the Democrats would "come into power for a generation as the liberal party of this nation."[2]

The public relations machinery utilized by the League to Enforce Peace, organized in 1915 by the journalist Hamilton Holt and others, had benefited the general idea of a league throughout the war. In fact, by one estimate, "public acceptance . . . owed more to the L.E.P. than to Wilson."[3] The League to Enforce Peace attracted an impressive array of support, most notably ex-President William Howard Taft and former cabinet members—but also such "diplomatists" as James Angell, Oscar S. Straus, Theodore Marburg, and Andrew White; university presidents; politicians; and prominent editors like Holt, Frank Crane (Associated Newspapers), William Allen White (*Emporia Gazette*), Victor Rosewater (*Omaha Bee*), Albert Shaw (*American Review of Reviews*), and Anton Weiss (*Duluth Herald*). The organization was influential. At one point before the armistice, the group placed so much pressure on Senator Reed (an Irreconcilable Democrat from Missouri) and Senator Lodge (the Massachusetts Republican) that they were forced to tread carefully in their home states.[4]

The League to Enforce Peace had begun gathering a striking momentum during the winter of 1918–1919. With its New York base, the organization began spreading out in February, hosting congresses in Boston, Chicago, Minneapolis, Portland, San Francisco, Salt Lake City, St. Louis, and Atlanta in that one month alone. The meetings drew speakers and interesting debate, its purpose being to "stimulate and consolidate American public opinion behind the League of Nations."[5] Taft, chosen president of the organization, actually found his public reputation substantially rehabilitated by his persistence in promoting the league concept.[6] In terms of publicity, the Republican was more a "new president" while head of the L.E.P. than he was while in the White House. Taft wrote regular short columns defending the league's benefits and fencing with critics who attacked it.[7] Interestingly, though, many of Taft's columns on the league were placed quietly on the editorial page, while Theodore Roosevelt's more skeptical views, until his death in January anyway, normally occupied one of the news pages.

All through the treaty debate, pro-treaty advocates beseeched their journalistic contacts for maximum publicity and favorable coverage. Taft made extensive use of his favorite Ohio correspondent, Gus Karger (apparently, the only reporter he had liked and trusted while president). Taft's half-brother owned the newspaper Karger wrote for, the *Cincinnati Times-Star.* Another Ohio institution, James E. Scripps, was deputized by Democratic National Committee chairman Vance McCormick "to put his chain of five . . . newspapers at the service of the party," although support from the Scripps empire ebbed all year long.[8]

Taft and other members intensified their publicity campaign that spring. The result was a series of two dozen articles called collectively "The Covenanter" and printed daily in the press from May 21 through July 7. Organizers knew what they were doing: "'The Covenanter' letters were sent to about eighty selected papers, were printed in full in about thirty of them, and in part or in summary in at least thirty more. An official summary was sent to a thousand smaller journals. . . . The New York office made a survey of the editorials of the nation's press for the week ending June 3, 1919, and found that out of approximately 1,200 editorials, 1,100 favored its adoption and 100 opposed."[9] It was an impressive publicity campaign, reminiscent of the CPI in its thoroughness and energy. "In all," John Milton Cooper Jr. writes, "the L.E.P. enrolled around 300,000 members, sponsored over 36,000 speakers, and distributed some of its publications in runs of 500,000 copies."[10] Like the efforts by its nemesis—the League to Preserve American Independence, not to mention those by individual Irreconcilables—the League to Enforce Peace waged an all-out war of information. There appears an implicit disagreement about which side in the treaty debate exerted more effort regarding publicity—Stone maintaining the Irreconcilables worked harder than anyone, Cooper citing the L.E.P.'s superiority.[11] It seems, though, that much of the discrepancy can be resolved as a simple matter of timing: by midsummer, 1919, anti-treaty activity was fast overtaking pro-treaty activity.

In fact, the L.E.P. had started to founder in the middle of the year. While it was going full blast on behalf of the covenant and the treaty during and immediately after the Peace Conference (reaching its peak, perhaps, in June 1919),[12] internal divisions were threatening its effectiveness. Taft seemingly "lost his way" with a couple of embarrassing missteps, including a letter he wrote Will Hays about the treaty's need for amendments, a letter the Republican party chairman promptly published in the papers.[13]

And all the while, the organization never did secure the endorsement of the president. Indeed, Wilson released a statement from Paris in December saying that he had never specifically approved its program.[14] Trying to keep his options open, believing his flexibility paramount, President Wilson always maintained distance from this group. Thus a strong base of political support went totally unexploited. And with the L.E.P.'s internal problems, Wilson's indifference to it significantly impeded pro-league momentum.[15] Worse, the disassociation must have greatly confused supporters. Wilson appeared with Taft at a Metropolitan Opera House meeting on March 4, where both men warmly endorsed the league of nations principle. Yet once more the president remained cool toward the L.E.P.

The organization's members nonetheless soldiered on. Harvard University president Abbott Lawrence Lowell, a member of the L.E.P., debated Senator Lodge in Boston on March 19, 1919. "In spite of stormy weather," one writer said, "the hall was packed to its utmost capacity," the city fixated on the meeting as though "it were a great athletic contest."[16] As many commentators noted, the "debaters were not far apart when they began," and overall the encounter seemed to give league advocates great hope for eventual consensus.[17] But an opponent of the White House could easily interpret the proximity of Lodge's and Lowell's views from the other perspective, as did a *New York Tribune* headline: "Both Lodge and Lowell in World League Debate Say Pact Needs Changes."[18] At the end of March, Senator Gilbert Hitchcock (D-Nebraska) spoke of the league's growing popularity and of Wilson's desire to meet Senate critics halfway.[19] Still, modest cheers like Hitchcock's were drowned out by the rancorous diatribes delivered by wrathful senators.

In December 1918 the League of Free Nations Association sponsored advertisements in newspapers like the *New York Times* and the *Philadelphia Public Ledger* in order to "crystallize public sentiment" in favor of the idea of an international association. A January ad in *Survey* asked "Which Shall It Be?" then presented the following choices: "Wilson or Clemenceau, Smuts or Lodge, Cecil or Reed, Economic Freedom or Rival Armaments, League of Nations or Balance of Power."[20] Norman Hapgood formed the L.F.N.A. in November 1918 to offer a more idealistic alternative to the more tough-sounding and "imperialistic" L.E.P., to appeal to more Democrats and liberals, and to ensure that President Wilson's vision of the postwar world stood a better chance of realization.[21] Nevertheless, the efforts of both groups tended to coalesce around a common cause.[22]

Individuals and organizations favoring a treaty with some version of the league were either too ambivalent or too shrill to make much impact in the press. Editorials backing the president almost always sounded either overly confident or else rather desperate. The *New York Times* insisted that the Senate "must ratify the Treaty of Peace for the same reasons that constrain and compel the Germans to sign the instrument."[23] In April *The Independent* fairly begged readers that "all may be lost in a moment if those who believe in what he stands for do not stand by him."[24] A month later the magazine reminded Republicans that the president had actually incorporated the concrete suggestions made by "Taft, Lodge, Hughes and Root, easily their most influential and competent men,"[25] but it also reminded Wilson that "the new

Congress has come more recently from the people than he."[26] In May the *Chicago Daily News* reported that Democrats might urge the president to run for a third term if the Senate failed to ratify the treaty containing a league of nations.[27]

By June Hamilton Holt, *The Independent*'s editor, attacked Senate Republicans by pointing to the discrepancy between their opposition to the league covenant and indications of popular support.[28] Within days he seemed near panic: "There are those in Washington who count the League of Nations already lost. Admittedly the morale of Senators supporting the League is at its lowest ebb."[29] *The Independent* pointed to the "almost pathetic faith" with which league supporters looked to Wilson and Taft. Clearly something was missing from pro-league, pro-treaty forces. It may have been the punctured enthusiasm some writers thought seemed widespread as the interminable peace talks finally came to a grinding halt.[30] Would-be league architects like William Howard Taft also may have stymied their cause unwittingly by urging changes in the treaty at untimely moments.[31]

Republican senator Frederick M. Davenport of New York wrote an essay for *The Outlook* arguing that while amendments would be in order, the Senate should do the "responsible" thing and ratify the treaty.[32] Herbert Hoover made similar appeals.[33] Most Americans, Davenport said, wanted the wartime atmosphere officially ended and desired some form of an association of nations.

By mid-July *The Independent* and other magazines found their confidence restored by Wilson's jubilant return to America.[34] After meeting with the president on July 10 for forty minutes, some prominent Democrats did, too. Senator Gilbert Hitchcock told reporters he did not now think reservations would be necessary.[35] Senator Claude A. Swanson, of the Foreign Relations Committee, gave the treaty a hearty thumbs-up, but it was one of the few enthusiastic endorsements the treaty got, and compared with those of opponents of the treaty an extremely tardy one.[36] In August Senator Davenport, having toured Minnesota, Montana, Wyoming, North and South Dakota, Oregon, and Washington, found public sentiment strongly in favor of a league and in favor of ratification, though with reservations.[37] By September Hitchcock changed his mind on the likelihood of reservations, but both he and *The Independent* were certain that the treaty "cannot by any possible combination be defeated in the Senate."[38] The press spoke of America's moral duty to ratify the treaty.[39]

Many journalists pressed Wilson to keep up the campaign, to lobby hard for the treaty and the covenant, to continue the fight to get them adopted. A few gave him practical advice, such as loosening up and getting personal with the senators, taking them into his confidence with blunt candor. "If the President Would Only 'Be Natural,'" it was said, he might win over more legislators.[40] Others just wanted him to be franker. "Mr. Wilson is like a man trying to sell the Senate a second-hand automobile," *The New Republic* said. "He admits it has its faults. But instead of discussing those faults in order to determine whether they are vital or trivial, he brandishes the original advertisements showing what a splendid car the unused machine was."[41] Tumulty hoped that Wilson's old presidential flair would reappear when he got back to the United States: "Your return, presence, and leadership will be of great psychological value to us. We must have a definite programme, with aggressiveness written all over it. Our enemies have been able to say everything in derogation of you and your programme."[42]

An influential segment of the liberal press (*The Nation* and *The New Republic*) blasted the treaty's harsh terms, but liberals in general overwhelmingly supported the principle behind the League of Nations, and even a preponderant majority still favored adoption of the treaty. While some believed in the need for amendments or reservations, they still wanted to see the Senate eventually give its blessing. Many liberals, in fact, were so confident of long-term ratification that they still demonstrated a striking complacency. One writer expressed his concern with such foolish passivity by describing liberals as "hypnotized into thinking that everything will come out all right anyway."[43] Even when such never-gushing skeptics like Harold Stearns discussed the proposed league, they detected strong support for the idea. "Public opinion," Stearns wrote, "is being gradually swung around into warm favor of it."[44] *The Crisis* offered a representative defense of the treaty's league covenant: "The colored folk want the League of Nations. The proposed League is not the best conceivable—indeed, in some respects it is the worst. But the worst Internation is better than the present anarchy in international relations," W. E. B. Du Bois wrote. "No opponent of the League offers anything better that has the slightest chance of adoption. Most opponents want no League at all. They want a swashbuckling anarchy, with a Jingo United States yelling in chorus with Jingoes of all Europe."[45] Du Bois was still pleading for the league in the spring of 1920, saying that eventually "it must succeed, for civilization needs it; and this, despite the present champions and enemies."[46]

Like their rhetoric, it turned out that most of the pro-league forces' successes were hollow at best. Take the Lowell-Lodge debate of March 19. It became evident, one observer noted, that there was little substantial disagreement; it was scarcely a debate, both men advocating the need for amendments.[47] Other pro-league measures fizzled as well. In August the League to Enforce Peace made available $100,000 in funds to distribute propaganda on the league's behalf, but news of the deep-pocketed campaign reeked too much of the wartime CPI, and the effort never seemed to catch on. Worse, Senator Reed Smoot's discovery that the Bureau of Education and the Department of the Navy were churning out literature promoting the league—the public actually footing the bill for both—blew up in the faces of league advocates, even though hardly anyone was aware of it at the time. "Propaganda of this sort ought not to be paid out of the public Treasury," the *New York Tribune* grumbled.[48]

Wilson's international friends were not able to offer much assistance. Viscount Grey arrived in the United States in September as special ambassador both to push British objectives and to win American acceptance. But Britain's view on the subject of Senate reservations, for example, was not at all clear at the time, and, worse, Grey attracted abuse from Americans opposed to English naval supremacy, sympathetic to Irish national aims, or suspicious of Britain's extra league votes on account of its status as an empire. The last straw was Grey's publicity gambit in February 1920, a letter to the *New York Times* (dated January 31 but delayed) expressing kindly understanding of the Senate's, and America's, need for reservations. "Grey's letter was aimed at breaking the American impasse by encouraging Lodge to go as far as he could with the Republican mild reservationists in reaching a compromise," George Egerton has explained. But Grey's letter only made matters worse in the pro-treaty camp because it outraged President Wilson, who still refused any compromise and who thought the action meddlesome, untimely, and "officially inspired."[49] When he came to the United States in the summer of 1919, Irish nationalist Eamon De Valera thought better of things and kept a low profile.[50]

Prudent silence may arguably have helped the cause of foreign nationals, but it scarcely helped treaty supporters in the pages of the press or the halls of Congress. Individuals committed to getting the treaty ratified in the United States needed to conduct their campaign much more aggressively, and that meant soliciting many more proponents to stand up and speak in its favor, to do so on a daily basis or at least as often as Senate foes were standing up to denounce it, and to capitalize quickly on opposition weaknesses and divisions. As it was, administration-friendly writers and senators strutted coolly and confidently and quietly toward a vote they thought would result effortlessly in ratification. Neither the Irreconcilable camp nor President Wilson, however, was ready to make things quite so easy.

Wilson's erratic combination of an ambitious speaking tour and his sulking, taciturn stubbornness might have been the clearest political sign that the president was not well. At times during 1919 he displayed the worst publicity tactics and personality traits of both of his immediate predecessors. There is no question that his collapse in September contributed to the eventual rejection of the treaty. But the president's impotent publicity campaign, coupled with an obsession with his executive prerogatives, seems more consequential. In fact, it is hard to say which was more telling: the fact that, as Thomas Knock puts it, "Wilson had done less than Roosevelt—which was not much—to cultivate public opinion on the question of an international league," or that Wilson had done less than the legendarily indolent Taft.[51]

During the summer of 1919 President Wilson dedicated himself to informing Congress of his work overseas. He briefed Senate and House committees on the details of the treaty, trying to quell concerns about the proposed agreement. When Senate Republicans gave the president an icy reception, Wilson decided to tour the country to generate enthusiasm and to stir up popular pressure on Congress. The announcement of his tour commanded respect, even from unfriendly critics, who had to admit that Wilson was a powerful orator. "In our time no one has approached him as a platform speaker," an editorial writer acknowledged.[52] Some in his cabinet thought the president might do better to stay in Washington, or perhaps to make just one or two detailed defenses in places like New York, whose press would give him all the publicity he desired.[53] And some journalists already seemed to be warming to his attempts at rapprochement with Congress.[54]

Against their advice, Wilson opted to go. For the president it was a sensible choice, perhaps one of the few open to him, considering the deep rift that existed between senators like Lodge and himself. The president also believed delay might cool tensions in the Senate and increase the chances for a looser ratification.[55] And, finally, a speaking tour did give some credence to the notion that diplomacy had changed since the end of the war, for here was a statesman come home to defend before his constituents the merits of a treaty he wanted them to support. That was the angle used by *Current Opinion* in its laudatory October article "President Wilson Carries the Treaty to the People." "Ever before," the writer explained, "foreign relations have been synonymous with secrecy. The making of treaties has been left to a few. The secrets of treaties have belonged to a few. If territories were bartered away, if mortgages were put upon the prosperity and the happiness of the people, if schemes were laid, the full fruition of which would send millions into carnage, the people were kept in ignorance. But now all this is changed, and today a treaty, the most important ever negotiated, is under consideration."[56] The people were now "arbiters." It was a glowing interpretation. But there was some justification for the praise. The president's train was truly a "combination White House and newspaper office on wheels," with "eighteen newspapermen, three motion picture camera-men and a staff of stenographers" on board—a regular propaganda locomotive.[57] Rhetoric aside, Wilson was indeed taking the treaty to the people and defending it before them.

The *Rochester Times-Union* also applauded the president's decision and anticipated favorable results. Surely, the editorial writer said, Wilson would "arouse public opinion to such a pitch that the petty-politics-playing, prejudiced Senators will not dare longer to obstruct the nation's progress."[58] The Democratic *Indianapolis Times* shared the same view, complimenting the president on his choice of "battle-ground" and "weapons." Wilson's "tour of the United States will be very disconcerting to the Republican brethren who will sit idle in Washington and listen to the echoing cheers."[59]

Others expressed skepticism or in some cases disdain. Would it not have been better for Wilson and the Senate to work their disagreements out in Washington? Was a propaganda tour replete with "glittering generalities" really the best way to find a bipartisan compromise?[60] But most journals believed that a speaking tour probably could not hurt much and might help at least a little.

By two measures, it did help. Members of the press who accompanied him were growing increasingly sympathetic to the president's cause. They admired his stamina, his dedication, even his cordiality toward them. Despite a tragic automobile accident that killed one correspondent in Portland, the speaking tour was, like the Paris Peace Conference, a positive experience that contributed to their sense of solidarity with one another and with Wilson.[61] The president therefore benefited from his personal relationships with the press while the journey continued. Though his rhetoric was becoming more aggressive, more defiant, his rapport with journalists temporarily softened and improved. Out of sight of hostile critics, Wilson fought on resolutely. He also succeeded in making the League of Nations, and the treaty as substantially written, the most important national issue separating the two parties.

But Wilson also aggravated the differences between Congress and the White House. During the trip his language grew tougher, more politically volatile. The *Chicago Daily News* noted that "his addresses on the covenant and the peace treaty become more militant and more dramatic."[62] They were more "effective," the writer conceded, but he also pointed out that Wilson's militancy was not quite "relevant," considering that only a handful of senators were "irreconcilables," while a substantial majority would be content with modest changes. Despite some hedging in mid-September, the president was thus talking past the possibility of compromise.[63] He continued to widen the division in Wyoming and Colorado, sounding as uncompromising as he had ever been in public. In Cheyenne he showed his determination to raise the stakes by threatening to withdraw the treaty if the Senate imposed too many reservations on it. Unfortunately for the treaty's supporters, however, Wilson's health failed him at a critical time. In Pueblo he suffered a stroke, which definitively ended the western tour.

In the meantime Senate Republicans had not been letting up. Indeed, "while the President has been on tour the reservation forces in the Senate have grown stronger," one journalist noted.[64] And another writer, a loyal league supporter, came to believe that however much the president might have won over ordinary Americans, the speeches he had been making were "widening the breach" with the Senate.[65] The *New York Tribune* observed that since the president began moving east from California his rhetoric became more suddenly hostile toward the idea of reservations. "A Strange Reversal," it concluded.[66] With hindsight, then, Wilson's stridency may have hurt his campaign on behalf of the league. Speeches reassuring the public of his intent to work with Congress in order to win ratification might have proved more useful to treaty proponents in retrospect. Even at the time, Senator Hitchcock was said to be telling Wilson to "tone down" his rhetoric on Article X, a controversial provision guaranteeing member nations their political autonomy.[67] As it was, Wilson's cancellation of the tour so soon after expressing such fierce, irreconcilable differences left the playing field in a suspended state of heightened antagonism, a state the controversy never seemed to move beyond. As one writer put it, the president had given "the debate a stimulus too strong to allow . . . any actual truce between contending factions."[68]

He had drawn a line in the sand, then vacated his own spot. Wilson's illness could not have come at a worse time, then—not just "at an hour in which the need for his clear vision and gifts of logic and eloquence was never more urgent,"[69] but at a time when the movement toward rapprochement would have left the atmosphere amicable. Instead, Wilson's side of the debate ended on a tense and acrimonious note. The Senate assumed an equally defiant mood, while communication between the president and Republican opponents all but disappeared. For people concerned about the treaty's fate it was a miserable accident.

Wilson's collapse in September also served to divert attention away from the treaty and the league. It did so both because of the president's prolonged condition and because of the fitfully slow way journalists came to realize the severity of that condition. Suddenly the advantages and disadvantages of, say, the Shantung compromise paled before the questions of whether the president would be able to continue in office and who exactly was in charge of the federal government. One editorial writer complained that Wilson's choice of a "third-rate cabinet" now made his serious illness doubly troubling. Tumulty, the writer made clear, ought not to be conducting negotiations on the president's behalf.[70] And journalists rankled, too, at having to correct earlier wrong impressions. In one week, the *Chicago Daily News* displayed headlines in this confusing order: "feeling slightly better"; "better rested"; "refreshed"; "President Is Worse," "must postpone work"; "Wilson's Daughters Rush to Bedside; Condition Is Grave"—non sequiturs which could not have given them confidence in the news they were feeding the public.[71]

Of course, Wilson's illness did generate some measure of sympathy for him. All magazines and newspapers dutifully registered their concern for his condition and hope for a speedy recovery. But many also interpreted the president's physical condition as one of the reasons for the treaty's defects—in other words, it was the product of a tired and sickly soul.[72] As much as anything, though, the fact that an administrator who preferred one-man rule was now dangerously bedridden could not bode well.[73] In fact, it was difficult to say to what extent the president's adamantine position was the product of illness or the result of his particular understanding of executive authority.[74] Wilson's maddening confidence that "the Senate is going to ratify the treaty" perhaps supports both contentions.[75]

A year after publicly throwing down the political gauntlet, and a month after appealing over the heads of dissident senators by taking his case directly to the people, Wilson became incapacitated, and his personal campaign to enlist popular support sputtered and died. Henceforth, when they moved at all, pro-treaty forces stumbled forward in headless, disorganized fashion, though mostly they seemed curiously quiescent. By contrast, Wilson's foes made their views heard loudly and often. At times between September and November they actually appeared to be the *only* voices that were audible. The president's friends naturally evinced more concern about his health than they did about his treaty, confident perhaps that both the people and the press would continue the fight. As it turned out, it was the press that faltered.

≈ 14 ≈

THE PRINTERS' STRIKE AND
OTHER DISTRACTIONS

As winter begins to be a little restive on the lap of spring, some people are getting
more interested in the National League than in the League of Nations.

Columbia [S.C.] State, quoted in *Literary Digest,* February 8, 1919

In addition to an active campaign seeking to dispute the league's supposed virtues, discredit the president, and vilify the treaty, the coalition
of forces led by Lodge also benefited indirectly from all publicity un-
related to the issues at hand. In other words, any diversion away from talk
about internationalism and the new diplomacy made selling the league, and
thus the treaty, that much more difficult. And 1919 was a year full of distractions, particularly in the five months following Wilson's return to America.
Trouble with Mexico reappeared, the "difficulty . . . never quite so pressing as
it is at this present moment," one writer brooded.[1] Prohibition and women's
suffrage, nationwide campaigns that would eventually constitute the Eigh-
teenth and Nineteenth Amendments, were being actively discussed in 1919,
the former ratified in January, the latter proposed and passed by Congress in
June. Race riots erupted in Washington and Chicago in late July. The high
cost of living was another ubiquitous concern. The *Chicago Daily News,* for
example, ran articles and cartoons nearly every day on the subject, often simply mentioning the familiar sobriquet "H.C.L"—not to be confused with
Henry Cabot Lodge.[2]

Without question, though, industrial unrest produced the strongest
anxiety. Recurring labor strikes—by one estimate several thousand[3]—made
magazine and newspaper editors anxious for the president to settle down to
business, national business. In 1919, steel workers went on strike, as did coal
miners, longshoremen, policemen, printers, even actors. So many unions decided to force their employers' hand that a South Carolina newspaper came

up with a new adage for the times: "Strike and the world strikes with you, work and you work alone."[4] The president called a labor conference for October, amid the ominous signs that the country was "drift[ing] toward an open break."[5] One such stoppage in particular undermined the president and pro-treaty forces—a printers' strike.

Regular readers must have been surprised not to receive the October 8, 1919, issue of *The Outlook.* Subscribers would, in fact, have to wait three more weeks for their magazine before learning the details. There had been a strike, the result of a disagreement between labor factions, and five thousand press-men and typesetters "in 250 of the biggest job printing plants in the city" had demanded a forty-four-hour week as well as higher wages.[6] A year earlier the magazine had been late with one issue because the press feeders had walked off the job. This time the strike was bigger, longer, more disruptive. According to *Printers' Ink,* about "150 magazines and 300 business papers in New York were . . . held up,"[7] including *Printers' Ink* and some of the most popular, influential periodicals in America, such as *Century, Collier's, Cosmopolitan, Everybody's, Good Housekeeping, Harper's Bazar, Harper's Magazine, McCall's, McClure's, Munsey's,* and *Scribner's.* And it was impossible to say when the printers would return.

So editors of *The Outlook* were understandably angry, then, in the issue that finally appeared on October 29:

> After a month's suspension of publication this issue of The Outlook for October 29 reaches our readers a little delayed and without the usual cover. Its publication is possible, not because there has been any yielding to the revolutionary and outlawed pressmen's unions of New York City, whose leaders have rebelled against the authority and explicit instructions of their National organization, but because it is manufactured by trade-union workmen who are loyal to their contracts and agreements and who have the authority and approval of their National body.[8]

The Outlook was not the only publication to devote its first page to news of the "revolutionary and outlawed pressmen." In a city where most magazines had been forced to suspend printing, or else relocate upstate, in New England, in Maryland, even across country, many editors were ready to comment when finally afforded the chance.[9] The *Literary Digest* did—at two separate occasions, the first on September 20, the second on October 18. The magazine issued a shorter, adless version of its September 20 issue because of the escalating labor feud, while its October 18 issue was actually produced without any typesetting whatsoever.[10] *The New Republic* used a web press, run by union printers.[11] *The Survey* explained its complicated composition measures by saying that the combination of an unusual 'justifying' machine and unconventional offset presses produced an issue "which has no counterpart in the history of magazine making."[12] *The World Tomorrow* thanked "the kindness of the Co-operative Press in making room for us," but its October issue was held up until the end of the year.[13]

The *Literary Digest* showed more restraint than *The Outlook* in denigrating the strikers. "[O]ur compositors and the compositors employed in many other offices in New York are taking a 'vacation,' in direct defiance of the orders of their own union chiefs to return to work," its explanation in October began.[14] *Collier's* summed it up this way: "New York City magazine typesetters have taken a so-called 'vacation' (walk-out), while two local pressmen's unions, having made exorbitant demands, have repeatedly refused to submit these demands to arbitration."[15] Like *Collier's,* most other magazines sternly blamed the "radical element" among the unions for delaying their publication. A few showed the sense of humor that W. E. B. Du Bois's *The Crisis* did on his magazine's ninth anniversary: "Forgive us, while we hide our diminished head. We had contracted for a new, large suit of clothes on our Ninth Birthday, and behold us, in short clothes. Forgive us, it is the Printers' Strike."[16] *The Independent* chortled that the "stereotyped phrase 'as we go to press' turned into a question for the publishers of periodicals in New York during the last two weeks of September."[17] The magazine ended on a more serious note: "Incidentally it may mean that the presses won't print your next week's Independent. We had some anxious moments wondering if you'd get this one." Eventually, issues were missed, and in late November the magazine celebrated the failure of the "radical elements" to continue their "contract-breaking."[18]

Editor & Publisher ran a series of patronizing rhetorical questions, designed to remind the printers of the common interests and responsibilities which they shared with the publishers. "Whatever your grievances, fancied or real, your prosperity is linked with that of the newspapers. You stand or fall with them."[19] *Chicago Daily News* editor Frank Crane applauded the move by several publishers to pick up and relocate their printing facilities elsewhere.[20] But virtually no periodical spoke out to defend the strikers.[21] Indeed, most editors seized on the crisis as an example of the general chaos said to plague the times. "Labor must realize that when it makes a contract it must fulfill that contract just as it expects the employer to fulfill it," the *Sioux City Journal* of Iowa pronounced.[22]

The New York printers' strike in October 1919 impaired the efforts by treaty supporters to get the peace agreement ratified—not necessarily because pro-treaty magazines were forced to stop printing (though, of course, that happened in some cases, just as the strike so affected anti-treaty publications), but because the printers' strike presented a monumental distraction for all journalists—*newspaper editors included.* In fact, the four dailies examined for this study (the *Chicago Daily News,* the *Chicago Tribune,* the *New York Times,* and the *New York Tribune)* all dramatically lowered the percentage of coverage devoted to the league and the treaty, while "the labor problem" began pushing those topics out of the front-page headlines. The strike simply shut down a substantial portion of public discussion about the treaty, instead diverting editors to talk anxiously about labor strife, industrial problems, and the dangers of radicalism, particularly foreign-born radicalism transplanted to American shores. The printers' strike brought home to journalists the challenges awaiting postwar America and crystallized, more powerfully than anything else might have, the country's economic challenges. In a year already filled with strikes, uprisings, and bombs—"All's riot with the world," quipped the *Chicago Tribune*[23]—editors and publishers in the United States suddenly began exhibiting signs of xenophobia and a general fatigue with international responsibilities. America's own turbulent problems seemed to outweigh arcane territorial disputes in central Europe. The result was a tendency by American journalists to concentrate on domestic news and to downplay the significance of foreign news. "The shutdown which paralyzed the periodical publishing trade of New York City during October and November was one of the most significant episodes in contemporary industrial history."[24] Discussions of foreign relations, then, sharply began to dwindle during October and immediately afterward.

For treaty supporters, it was an unnerving development. Here, with the vote on ratification little less than a month away, those periodicals still in operation were consumed with labor issues, not diplomatic ones. Debate on the treaty was pushed aside, even by those most vocal in its support. It was telling that in the midst of the printers' strike, Wilson's staunchest journalistic supporter, *The Independent,* for example, did not even report the November vote. Instead, it seemed preoccupied with strikes and the threat of Bolshevism. In an ironic twist, then, the most heralded feature of modernism and the hope of American progressives for two decades—the mechanics of mass communication—had broken down and been unable to deliver liberal reform to the diplomatic arena.

The fight to get the treaty accepted, therefore, suffered most visibly in the fall of 1919, when both the president and the press nearly fell silent in October. Diehard friends of the treaty continued to speak out then, and newspapers never totally stopped their publicity on the subject, but for a few critical weeks preceding the vote in the Senate, many American journalists had their minds on something else. It might be argued that the editorial loss of magazine support was even more crucial than a comparable loss of newspaper support would have been, for forensically their respective opinions are packaged so differently. Regardless of the differing influence, however, certainly the drop in overall press attention at that time lowered the political risks for senators uninterested in compromise.

❧ 15 ❧

THE PRESS AND THE SENATE

In one paper we read there's a great wave of public sentiment for the League sweeping over the land, and in another that an equal wave is setting in against it. Mr. Wilson's trip is expected to settle the problem what are the wild waves saying.

Philadelphia North American,
quoted in *Literary Digest,* September 20, 1919

The majority of newspaper correspondents covering the ratification battle in the Senate were not, as a rule, the same journalists who had been to Paris to cover the treaty's formulation. Robert B. Smith of the *Chicago Tribune,* Carter Field and Edmund Taylor of the *New York Tribune,* and John B. Pratt of the *New York Times,* for example, had been in Washington for most of 1918–1919. There was more continuity among magazine correspondents. Some, like Mark Sullivan of *Collier's* or Hamilton Holt of the *Independent,* actively followed congressional events upon their return from Europe. Yet many magazine writers pulling stints in France drifted on to other subjects or assignments, and contributors of course changed markedly from issue to issue. So there was a sharp disjuncture between the press that covered the treaty's fate in Paris and the press that covered its fate in Washington. Did it make a difference? It appears so.

Numerous observers often remarked on the feverish glow apparent on so many dispatches sent from the peace conference. It was not that many journalists didn't have their doubts, worries, or disappointments in Paris. They certainly did. And it was also not the case that correspondents didn't occasionally express their disapproval of or outrage at certain events, for those accounts carried an emotional intensity hard to miss. But in conference reportage and commentary, taken as a whole, that emotional intensity also conveyed excitement, anticipation, and, often, an underlying compassion for

President Wilson even when the writer seemed overtly critical. Correspondents covering the treaty question in the United States generally wrote without the same fervor or empathy. Despite open admiration for Borah, Johnson, or Lodge by members of the congressional press gallery, most journalists, on balance, supported the league and the treaty.

Based on my own and other surveys of the press, as well as contemporary canvassing done by the *Literary Digest, Current Opinion,* and the *New York Tribune,* it seems that the bulk of American editorial opinion supported passage of the Versailles Treaty in 1919, most news organizations favoring ratification with reservations.[1] The South and the West gave the president backing he could count on. The Midwest was more mixed, and the Northeast was not only split sharply in two but in New York City alone constituted, at once, "the bulwark of his support as well as the core of his resistance."[2] Just as most journalists had supported the covenant in February and March, most in the press favored ratification of the treaty between June and December.

And not surprisingly, most journalists were confident that the treaty would be passed, even if with some revision.[3] The Senate could, for example, amend the treaty, which would entail changing its text. It could also express "reservations" by recommending how the treaty should be interpreted or applied. Regardless, after the year-long frictions between the president and the Senate, few journalists doubted that Republicans would now leave their fingerprints all over the document. The treaty, Leroy T. Vernon of the *Chicago Daily News* announced from Washington, "will eventually be ratified with reservations."[4] The monthly *Sunset* concluded in September that with Wilson "touring the country to crystallize public sentiment in favor of the Treaty and the League, the Senate probably will be compelled sooner or later to approve of the document practically as it stands."[5] The magazine estimated that a majority—60 percent—of westerners supported the treaty. Even on the eve of the vote, *Sunset* expressed steadfast confidence: "It seems practically certain, as these lines are written, that the Treaty will be ratified by the Senate without amendments but with certain comparatively mild reservations." "Reservations Seem to Suit All Parties."[6] There was certainly throughout the year a rapidly growing inclination by members of the press to accept reservations, which by the fall formed a consensus closely mirroring that of Congress.

Indeed, throughout 1919 American journalists joined fully in the congressional controversy, with whole newspapers taking on the appearance of party organs and even resembling certain troublesome U.S. senators. "The *New*

York Sun," it was pointed out at the time, "has joined the *Tribune* as one of the implacables, and every change in the covenant but makes it all the worse to the *Sun*."[7] These journalistic "implacables" became as important to the anti-treaty and anti-Wilson campaigns as any senatorial "irreconcilable," perhaps more important as readers might expect the press to demonstrate more impartiality than would a Lodge or a Borah.[8] The *New York Tribune, Times,* and *World* all traded accusations of partisanship.[9] The *Tribune,* with some justification perhaps, boasted that it had "endeavored, within the limits of human frailty, to be non-partisan."[10] The *Literary Digest* noted in July that staunch opponents of the league draft had not been "converted," that a "countrywide survey of the press still shows many discordant voices."[11] Paralleling Senate discussion, writers of various political persuasion also battled contentiously. Walter Lippmann, a league supporter but treaty critic, was unhappy with Article X, he announced in a series of articles for the *Chicago Daily News*. Victor Yarros promptly delivered a rebuttal of Lippmann's position, defending Article X and explaining its uses.[12] Writers used the press as their own Senate floor, and depending on the publication probably reached a larger audience.

It also did not help that some periodicals spent time questioning the credibility of others, whether they supported or opposed the treaty, for public relations momentum undoubtedly slows when people take the time to examine one another's motives. *The Dial,* for instance, accused *Outlook* of pushing Germany's vanquishment too hard and thus "defending the Covenant under a complete misconception of its spirit and purpose."[13] Supporters, then, were not particularly unified or even organized, and that was as true of the U.S. Senate as it was of the American press.

On the whole, however, a tremendous reservoir of editorial support for the treaty and the league existed in the American press in 1919. Criticisms, constructive and otherwise, abounded, too, though. It remained for Wilson and his allies to act on or defuse these criticisms, but mainly they kept quiet. Editorial writers seemed to show considerably more boldness than senators in explaining the virtues of the league or the benefits within the treaty. The problem, however, was that in American journalism the editorial's influence had waned markedly by the turn of the century. It was not editorials but news that shaped public opinion and public policy, not the editor but the correspondent who was the star.[14] And for the second half of 1919 it was Republican critics of the treaty, not the Wilson administration, that dominated or most colorfully occupied press forums. American editorial opinion mattered, and it helped promote and defend the cause of both the treaty and the League of Nations. But in a country with pressing domestic concerns and engaging distractions, active journalistic support for a new internationalism was lost amid cultural, economic, and political turmoil.

Also lost, apparently, has been an understanding of how journalists were engaged in the process. Robert Barry, a correspondent for the *Philadelphia Public Ledger,* dropped hints in an end-of-the-year article about the Senate treaty debate. In it, he speaks of "daily conferences, many of them confidential, with Senator Lodge . . . and Senator Hitchcock . . . and frequent chats with various other leaders in the fight."[15] Much of this consultation appears to be briefings conducted to inform the press, but Barry also elsewhere suggests that journalists gave some measure of feedback and even influenced discussion, too. As in Paris, it appears that American correspondents at home participated informally in the peacemaking process. Their networks of contacts ensured that they would exert some influence, even as they ceded the limelight to legislators preparing for the outcome on Capitol Hill. When members of the Senate Foreign Relations Committee tried to get Walter Lippmann to testify before them, he begged off but recommended the thoroughly discontented William Bullitt instead.[16]

Journalists themselves may have helped clinch Senate opposition. Barry counted a few more league critics among the Senate press gallery than among the Senators. Indeed, according to Donald Ritchie, that group of journalists "betrayed their attitude in August 1919, when they joined in cheering Senator Lodge's attack on the Treaty."[17] Washington correspondents, as a rule, did not have the sweeter memories of Paris to flavor their understanding of the treaty debate in the United States. Ritchie tells a revealing story about the difference: "When . . . Northcliffe, an old friend of Oulahan's, visited Washington in 1921, he attended a luncheon of American 'Overseas Writers' who had covered the Paris negotiations, and then visited the Senate press gallery. 'You have just been the guest of the men who make treaties,' said the chairman of the Standing Committee of Correspondents; 'let me present those who unmake treaties.'"[18] No doubt, Oulahan exaggerated—both on the difference and on journalists' influence. Yet there is enough substance of the truth in that quote to carry weight: Washington correspondents were less sympathetic to Wilson and to the treaty than were the foreign correspondents, and these journalistic landlubbers did often consult with senators. Barry noted, somewhat mysteriously, journalists' influence in conversations with congressmen: "It is entirely unlikely that the extent of the influence of certain correspondents upon the final shaping of the Lodge program of reservation ever will be stated, since it involves a great amount of confidential discussion with Senate leaders that must remain inviolate."[19] Apparently, these anti-treaty reporters helped fine-tune or confirm their views.

Journalists believed that, ratification or no ratification, they had played an important part in the domestic debate over the treaty. Senate reporters recorded their faith that through their services, the people, then the Senate, had spoken: "[I]t was the task of the Senate correspondents to pry into the mail of the Senators to discover the trend of public sentiment. Senators were doing the same, but they were shaping their courses on what the public would believe was proper, while the press gallery was setting out to instruct and guide the people. It was in this respect that the correspondents performed their greatest historical service. They created sentiment for the Senators to follow."[20]

On a more perfunctory level, then, journalists performed the same service in Washington that they had in Paris: they constituted an important forum through which the public at large—including Congress—got much of its information. Those correspondents able to remain neutral embraced journalism's dialogic function in promoting accord—the "newspaper model of conflict resolution."[21] A Senate Foreign Relations Committee meeting, at which Wilson was present, involved a dispute over which draft of Article X the American people were to pass judgment on. There the participants compared versions, one of which hinged on one magazine's release:

> SENATOR LODGE—Then there was a previous draft in addition to the one you have sent to us. You spoke of a redraft. That was submitted to the committee.
>
> THE PRESIDENT—No, that was privately my own.
>
> SENATOR LODGE—Was it before our commission?
>
> THE PRESIDENT—No; it was not before our commission.
>
> SENATOR LODGE—The one that was sent to us was a redraft of that?
>
> THE PRESIDENT—Yes, I was reading some of the discussion before the committee, and some one, I think Senator Borah, if I remember correctly, quoted an early version of Article X.

SENATOR BORAH—That was Senator Johnson.

SENATOR JOHNSON—I took it from The Independent.

THE PRESIDENT—I do not know how that was obtained, but that was part of the draft which preceded the draft which I sent to you.

SENATOR JOHNSON—It was first published by Mr. Hamilton Holt in The Independent; it was again subsequently in the New Republic, and from one of the publications I read it when examining, I think, the Secretary of State.

THE PRESIDENT—I read it with the greatest interest, because I had forgotten it, to tell the truth, but I recognized it as soon as I read it.

SENATOR JOHNSON—It was the original plan?

THE PRESIDENT—It was the original form of Article X, yes.[22]

Clearly, the U.S. Senate depended on information from the press to carry out its peacemaking duties. But the press, used to the government's wartime management of publicity, could only marvel at the impasse created by the administration's frail leadership in 1919. The White House proved itself utterly disorganized concerning publicity, perhaps tilting "the balance of press attention back in favor of Congress."[23] The Senate battle, more than anything, revealed to journalists the centrifugal power of public opinion and their own cloudy but influential relationship to it.

CONCLUSION TO PART FIVE

Much of the treaty fight centered conspicuously on one crucial principle: publicity. And, as publicity inevitably involved journalists, it seems fair to say that, except for the month he toured out West with reporters, Wilson lost the treaty fight because he destroyed his relationship with the press. No one knows what might have happened if the White House had carefully cultivated such contacts all along, but Wilson clearly retreated from the management of public opinion, if, indeed, he had ever been as fully and directly engaged as Creel and other progressives in his administration. With the exception of Ray Stannard Baker, David Lawrence, and perhaps one or two others, no peace conference correspondent afterward campaigned publicly and vigorously on the president's behalf. A few weeks of intimacy traveling with reporters in September, two months before the vote, and with congressional opposition hostile, adamant, and entrenched, was not going to alter things much. Wilson waited far too long to court public opinion, and then at a moment when it seemed nearly beside the point. More than any political leader with the possible exception of Theodore Roosevelt, Wilson should have known better. He was well aware, and had frequently written, that the leadership of public opinion was the modern statesman's paramount duty. And yet he scorned public relations in the United States in late 1918, then essentially suspended it for nine months. As one commentator wrote at the end of the year, "The Peace Treaty was the supreme salesmanship opportunity of the age. . . . Its miserable failure at least so far as the people of the United States are concerned, may be called 'truly a superb fiasco of selling.'"[24] After the November defeat, and amid cries to hurry and ratify the treaty, Wilson's energy seemed to flag considerably. Even his commitment appeared in question as journalists noted his increasing willingness to walk away from the fight.[25] Generating support for the treaty demanded more careful, regular, and systematic manipulation than that. Wilson thought he might get away with foregoing that manipulation. He was wrong.

The administration's near-monolithic effort to control public opinion during the war was deferred in 1919 in favor of decentralized drift. Whereas the president had heretofore directed publicity himself personally or else centrally through the Committee on Public Information, the White House seemed to lose focus immediately after the armistice, when Wilson's disorganized campaign to found a league of nations dissolved amid a babel of public expression. Advocates of the treaty there certainly were in abundance— indeed, probably more so in July 1919 than in December 1919. But by that point the distracting welter of competing events, coupled with the more vociferous and concerted campaign to defeat the treaty, had drowned out Wilson's feeble forces.

The campaign against the treaty and the league included loud and prominent members of the press, much of which felt disillusioned after Paris, and the absence of that discouragement might well have made the difference in the treaty fight. In the long run, it also seems to have made a difference professionally. The press's participation in the treaty fight in the United States resembled its involvement in France. But while the process was little different, journalists' attitudes about their work were sharply revised. Abroad, American journalists were so united by their demanding duties as well as familiar ties to English-speaking comrades that they were able to maintain a coherent sense of professional self-identity. This changed in America, where a largely different set of Washington correspondents followed the treaty's fate in the New World and frequently concluded that public opinion was too complicated and unpredictable. These individuals worked closely with lawmakers, too, but in the midst of declining certainties about what "the people" wanted, their professional confidence appeared fast-fading. One heard less of their vaunted solidarity. In the wake of a printers' strike, moreover, when even the machinery of mass communication had broken down, their authority and very livelihoods appeared precarious.

What happened to journalists' quest for professional status? It appears to have been deflated by unrealistic expectations and a negative assessment of their recent experience in Europe, then disoriented by noisy confusion over the treaty dispute. Having lost the lion's share of influence over public opinion to the government during the war years, and having undergone an anomalous relationship with government leaders in Paris, the American press took an increasingly personal approach to the treaty question after the spring and summer of 1919. In the United States, journalists found themselves with more contacts and personal influence, but so, too, did Congress, and now its members took to the pages of newspapers and magazines to air their appeals directly. The result was a confusing cacophony of political expression in America, the relative obfuscation of support for the treaty, and the diminishment of journalists' interest in professionalization. Considering the "chaotic state of public opinion," as Frank Cobb put it in December of 1919, it was no surprise that journalists' faith in their own expertise began to crumble.[26]

CONCLUSION

Peacemaking, 1919, and the Role of Journalism

D espite their many disappointments, journalists helped to "make" the peace in 1918–1919 almost as much as statesmen did. Their part was different in kind but not in degree, for the press of all belligerent countries prepared the way for the cessation of hostilities by its particular espousal of peace demands, pressured the delegates to take certain stances at the conference, and affirmed or assailed various decisions concluded there. Contrary to the prevailing contention of some scholars that journalists were "controlled" at the Paris Peace Conference,[1] it seems more the case that it was primarily Woodrow Wilson who was controlled—manipulated by other conferees and by the foreign press. The lesson of the conference had been that the U.S. government neither managed the news, nor even worked very effectively with the press.

Wilson might have won ratification through an early popular referendum. But in light of a Republican-dominated Congress neglected during the war and almost embarrassingly ignored during the making of peace, the treaty's passage was far from guaranteed. Compromise was necessary to secure its passages. But compromise with the Senate, Wilson would not do. He was a man of rigid principle, convinced that the League of Nations was the only worthy provision in an otherwise shabby treaty, and he would not hear of vitiating the league's strength after leaving Europe. He had compromised then when he felt he had to, and he often had to in the face of excruciating choices. Now at home he expected affirmation in a more serene environment—affirmation from the American people if not their elected representatives. When his campaign to mobilize public support slowly started to crumble and it was obvious that Congress would make no major concessions, he was left with just one or two driving sentiments: bitter disdain for those elected representatives and the vague notion that the people—democracy, too, perhaps—had let him down. Others believed that the two parties had neutralized each other, muddled popular enthusiasm for both sides, and ended up with a stalemate from which the president would not compromise.[2]

THE PRESS, THE PRESIDENT, AND THE NEW DIPLOMACY

But it is important not to view the treaty battle in the United States simply as a straightforward political or even ideological dispute. Any glance at the writings on international affairs by Henry Cabot Lodge before 1918–1919 will clearly indicate his interest in the league idea. The contest between Congress and the administration had rather more to do with a struggle over interpretations of the new presidency and the new diplomacy. Like the conflict between the president and the press, what Wilson and the Senate actually fought over was the control of public opinion. Politics naturally infused the struggle, but the expansion of presidential power since 1917 fueled a desire among legislators to rein in the executive and reassert their own influence, and at the end of the progressive era such a confrontation involved competing for publicity. Members of Congress would not be outdone by the president's propaganda. And they weren't. Indeed, the bitter-enders wound up dominating the publicity battles. Thus the Senate refused to be led by the president after the war's end and instead strove to exert its own stamp on public treaty-making. In the context of a movement for "open diplomacy," the American Congress was taking pains to publicize every aspect of the domestic debate, even if that meant embarrassing the president (and for some foes, especially if it meant embarrassing the president).

Yet despite all the gloom and ill-will that Wilson wrought overseas and at home, and the suspicion brought down upon diplomacy generally, the legacy of the Paris Peace Conference is, surprisingly, that "open diplomacy" was *not* just an empty phrase, that the progressive impulse which had affected so many areas of social enterprise had also touched the hoary realm of diplomacy, that journalists *had* made a difference in the peace process. Something had changed: publicity. Publicity became perhaps the most important and visible tool for government leaders, statesmen, agencies, and organizations. Even before the peace conference took place, vigorous communication existed between the nations:

As a matter of fact peace discussion between the belligerents have been going on ever since the war began, both openly and secretly, both officially and thru newspapers, periodicals and books, thru parliamentary debates, thru the resolutions of commercial and political bodies, thru the researches of scholarly organizations, thru the programs of labor parties, thru the intermediary of the Pope and neutral Powers, thru the declarations of opposing chancellories, thru the exchange of notes like the present and thru innumerable private channels by authorized and unauthorized individuals.[3]

Propaganda, of course, is not the same thing as openness, yet neither is it incompatible with it. In fact, diplomacy had become more open in part *because of* propaganda, and this is an important aspect missing from most accounts of the era. Diplomacy became more responsive, more active, more publicity-oriented, as its every move was increasingly scrutinized by a press corps ready to transmit developments instantaneously. It became more open as leaders in Paris and in Washington recognized that public opinion mattered. The people did exert influence on treaty-making, a writer observed after the peace conference; "new precedents were created in the case of the Versailles Treaty"; and Wilson's battered old rhetoric actually portended something real.[4]

As the president told the world in the conference's first plenary session, "We are not here alone as representatives of governments but as representatives of peoples, and in the settlements we make we need to satisfy, not the opinion of governments, but the opinion of mankind."[5] Was this merely lip service? It was high-blown rhetoric, to be sure, but to dismiss it as insincere politicking seems unfair. Rather, this type of rhetoric was so often employed because of its serviceable vagueness. But the frequency with which statesmen and journalists alike resorted to it testifies at least to some general feeling of democratic accountability.

Everyone actively engaged in public relations, in "diplomacy *à l'americaine*," which at some point meant involving the press of the nation.[6] At the conclusion of the Paris Peace Conference, Lucian Swift Kirtland reflected how diplomacy had changed by the end of the decade. "Under the old system of diplomacy, it was much more important to influence the individuals connected with a foreign office (or State department) than to go behind them to influence public opinion." The new role for diplomats was not of course necessarily easy or simple. As Japanese ambassador Kijura Shidehara pointed out in a tart essay a few years after the war, the "position of the diplomat who appears in print is always one of delicacy."[7] Shidehara confessed the awkwardness of trying to be "a special pleader" and yet not immediately dismissed as a government stooge. Those conditions continued after the war, too. "For the first time in the history of international relations," observed *Editor & Publisher* on Mexican-American relations in late 1919, "the press of one nation has appealed to the press of another and neighboring nation to exert its influence upon its Government and people to prevent war."[8] By the mid-twentieth century, George Kennan could write that public opinion and politics were nearly insurmountable conditions for average diplomats.[9]

Diplomats were hardly better loved after the war. In the United States, with the possible exception of the presidency, diplomacy suffered more criticism than any other institution from the fallout of the peace conference and the American debate over ratification. The fact that Yankee statesmen had brought home a much-maligned treaty, coupled with the fact that European statesmen had made a peace treaty necessary to begin with, did not increase confidence in diplomacy. Indeed, some Americans returned to their antebellum affection for un-international diplomats. "I am of the opinion," one writer said, "that nationality has no great affection for diplomatic training. . . . [A man] knows, if he can read, that diplomacy is an art with all the tendencies of trick and illusion that belongs to the arts."[10] Statesmen were still inflicted, probably always would be, by the reflex toward secrecy; theirs was still a "backward profession."[11]

Or was it? Writers, sometimes even within the same articles, gave contradictory conclusions. An editor for *The World's Work* could make a gloomy assessment, then assert the following paradox: "In spirit we may have a new and better diplomacy. But we have not yet developed a new and better diplomacy in effectiveness."[12] Many writers, while they criticized or ridiculed diplomats, also stressed the need for effective, practical changes in the American system. Walter Lippmann, for one, had soured on diplomacy but thought that the remedy was not a less engaged, less professional diplomatic crew but a State Department that shrewdly cultivated international intelligence, and in a systematic manner.[13] Most writers could at least agree on professional reforms—merit-based promotions, for example. "Give the Nation Real Diplomats," a newspaper headline insisted.[14]

Ironically, it turned out, Wilson's distance from the State Department had to some extent insulated it from criticism and kept its hopes for further professionalization alive. During the immediate aftermath of World War I there was more public interest in merging America's diplomatic service with its consular service and in democratizing the both of them, but while the Rogers Act of 1924 temporarily sacrificed American diplomacy's independence from its sister branch, it also strengthened entrance requirements, rationalized the criteria for promotion and tenure, and in general improved the path of a diplomatic career. Within a decade, the diplomatic service would regain even its independence.[15]

THE FUTURE OF JOURNALISM AND FOREIGN RELATIONS

American journalists may have developed a jaundiced view of their experiences at the Paris Peace Conference, but their attitude toward their future in foreign relations was hardly pessimistic at all. In fact, many expressed optimism. An essay by war correspondent William G. Shepherd in 1919, for example, underscored that belief. Shepherd was writing from Geneva, the place chosen for the League of Nations. At that site, "it occurred to me that a new branch of journalism had been born and that the world is soon to see a new kind of newspaperman."[16] That new newspaperman would still have to fight the old brand of diplomacy, but at least now he would be joined by advocates for the new diplomacy, too, for "new-time publicity and open covenants." Shepherd was convinced that the press would enjoy a prominence even beyond what it achieved in Paris: "Here at Geneva, if the League of Nations is to be seated here, newspapermen of hitherto unknown power and influence will rise to heights of great importance and distinction and usefulness. There will be some newspapermen who will become known to the statesmen of the world, who will have more influence, in many lands, than many statesmen."[17]

Other writers also believed that the nascent league would by necessity involve more publicity, with its benefits.[18] And in the main, confidence in the role journalism could play in diplomacy still abounded. Technological breakthroughs—in bringing about both more sophisticated media like the wireless or astounding modes of transport like the airplane—promised hope . . . and peace. "The better the means of communication between the peoples, the less danger there is of misunderstanding," one editorial writer declared.[19] Melville Stone, Associated Press general manager, strongly equated "the growing interchange of news" and peaceful, orderly relations between nations.[20] And to other journalists that connection seemed eminently plausible, the international-communication version of Norman Angell's economic theory about why it was not in most governments' best interests to go to war in the modern age.

Lord George Riddell, a newspaper proprietor who had served with the British delegation in Paris, believed a new era was in progress. He represented his colleagues in sixteen international conferences between 1918 and 1933, and thought diplomacy changed forever—not so much by what statesmen were forced to do as by what they could not themselves resist. Members of the press had their fingerprints all over the disarmament conference held in Washington in 1921, for example, sometimes with a hundred correspondents attending the meetings: "One marked feature of this Conference is the attention paid to the Press. Hughes sees the reporters daily, and all the other delegations give similar facilities. The Chinese and Japanese have the most elaborate publicity arrangements."[21] Open diplomacy was alive and well, and there was no turning back.[22]

Long afterward, too, journalists covering foreign relations would exert a strong influence on diplomats, the latter believing—correctly or not—that the press could directly and indirectly disturb the peace, affect negotiations, and determine the ratification of treaties.[23] The number of correspondents covering international affairs, and the amount of newsprint devoted to their work, rose dramatically in the 1930s, 1940s, and 1950s.[24] Their influence rose, too. Drew Pearson and Walter Lippmann became recognized authorities, Lippmann serving as unofficial adviser to numerous presidents. Most students of history now accept as a commonplace the notion that TV news anchor Walter Cronkite helped amplify American frustration with, and then opposition to, the Vietnam War following the Tet Offensive in early 1968.[25] Even on a less glamorous level, publicity proves its usefulness to statesmen on a daily basis. "When Washington and Paris get into an awkward argument over policy and consultation, Secretary Kissinger can either call a press conference and denounce the French, or both sides can 'inspire' articles that make their points clear, and still leave room for maneuver."[26] By the end of the century, some journalists would exert as much influence on policy making as would the highest-ranking diplomats.[27] Finally, the advent of certain technological tools, such as fax and Internet communication, has transformed the interaction of publicity and diplomacy once more. In an era of laptop broadcasting and "digital diplomacy," democratic communication between nations is not something to dismiss lightly.[28]

In a sense, then, subsequent events proved Shepherd and Stone right, even if not precisely in the fashion they predicted. Journalists did become more powerful, and more of an international force, not least in a commercial sense. World War I had "accelerated" that process, demonstrating more clearly than ever before publicity's natural proclivities toward business as much as politics.[29] Just as diplomats found themselves grouped with consuls after 1918–1919, journalists got lumped together with press agents, syndicators, and propagandists for hire—and sometimes by choice. David Lawrence formed David Lawrence, Inc., a syndication service that almost immediately found sixty-eight subscribers.[30] Rather than routinely going through the organization of a newspaper or magazine, or a middleman like S. S. McClure, writers were establishing their own organizations. So, too, were publicists for various programs. "Everybody is syndicating causes," one editorial exclaimed. But the war-tested techniques that Edward Bernays promoted in his writings were naturally highly prized by businesses large and small, and privately sponsored propaganda loomed as no less a menace than before, certainly no less common. Indeed, all types of organized publicity appeared to be something of an obsession in the United States, with "as many kinds of press-agents as there are enterprises and interests in this little world."[31] In 1921 a Belgian journalist familiar with the United States described the phenomenon:

> It is by means of the newspaper that one reaches the public, creates reputations, gets goods sold, petitions signed, a district voted wet or dry, the subscriptions filled up for a drive. That shows why there is no reason to be astonished at seeing, for example, such an organization as the Red Cross including in its personnel "publicity directors," all of whom are former editors or reporters. I mention the Red Cross proposal because its eminently philanthropic character is above all suspicions and its accounts are open to the light of day.[32]

The commercial "obsession" with publicity, combined with the progressive quest for orderly political reform and the practical need for peace, all merged to give Americans hope that journalism and diplomacy might have a future together. If progressive writers could not count on government officials or diplomats to bring about the sort of political change they desired, they could at least count on their own commercial potential in a new writing market. The world might still depend on journalists after all.[33]

What remained was simply to improve further the means of communication. Toward that end, weary writers called for "less propaganda," and bristled at what they called "organized lying."[34] People urged the press to do better. More "honest" journalism and closer professional ties were two of the most common prescriptions for reporters and editors. Ironically, the new challenge was in *withstanding* information. Critics pleaded with reporters to render an impartial service of information-clearing, -sorting, and -interpreting for their fellow citizens.[35] Whereas pre-war criticism of journalism had hinged on the basic progressive critique of unrestrained commerce, post-war criticism of journalism now fully recognized the dangers obviously posed by governments, which some writers said had taken an "autocratic assumption of the responsibility for public opinion."[36] Two years of censorship and the CPI had convinced journalists of that fact.

Some journalists routinely noted encouraging signs.[37] And they praised the old stand-bys, namely specialized training and education, as well as self-policing and accreditation practices.[38] A central disagreement arose briefly over the question of paid editorial advertising. Some trade journals like *Editor & Publisher* opposed its acceptance in newspapers because it was felt such matter diminished journalists' editorial integrity, while others supported it because it underscored the press's role as a vehicle of political information, as a liaison between government and the people.[39] By World War II, *Editor & Publisher* had itself begun "including public relations as a regular department," so the press as a whole had recognized the overlapping functions it shared with political and commercial publicists.[40]

A fallout from the peace process was for many journalists a more jaded view of public opinion. "Public opinion is what the majority think they think," said a writer in *The Independent,* a magazine sharply disillusioned by the apparent political impasse over the treaty's fate in America.[41] Walter Lippmann declared it "vain to suppose that our problems can be dealt with by rallying the people to some crusade that can be expressed in a symbol, a phrase, a set of principles or program."[42] Open diplomacy, the Fourteen Points, a new era: all these things had simply bewitched popular support without real fulfillment, Lippmann complained. Others were more philosophical, concluding that in the long run "public opinion can never be final. . . . Yet the very inconstancy of public opinion is its brightest feature."[43] A consensus seemed to be developing, nonetheless, that the United States needed to continue tinkering with how the public came to know what it knew. "The reconstruction of our organs of opinion is now declared one of the pressing needs of the hour," the *Literary Digest* observed in 1920.[44] This loss of confidence in public opinion left journalists unsure of their own heralded expertise as "public ambassadors." That ebbing faith meant that they could no longer simply assume journalistic objectivity, an ideal that had partly inspired the progressive quest for professionalization of the press as well as other fields.[45]

Journalism in the 1920s was similar to that of the war era in the sense that the press was "used" more than ever and courted more aggressively than ever; only now journalists no longer held a monopoly on publicity. Sometimes they were carriers, sometimes competitors, sometimes accomplices. But at all times they had to contend with the fact that they were surrounded by other publicizers. At the moment in which the forces of professionalization reached their peak in American journalism, then, the press simultaneously witnessed the relative dilution of its influence. Journalists' authority had actually increased after the war, but the context for that power had changed drastically. The progressive-era incubation of commercial press-agentry and government propaganda gave the *process* of journalism unprecedented value but placed its practitioners along a crowded spectrum of public relations peopled by many other actors. The fact that cabinet officials or diplomatic leaders, for example, now routinely issued press releases meant that when journalists surrendered their preponderant control over public opinion at the outset of the war, they did not win it back afterward. Clearly for journalists as for most Americans, the peace process had left a scar on the national psyche. The Senate's failure to ratify a treaty brought home by a president who appeared not to have consulted its members, the press, or anyone else along the way—such striking dissonance between expectation and actuality—produced a widespread eagerness to put the Paris Peace Conference in the past.

NOTES

INTRODUCTION

1. Delos F. Wilcox, "The American Newspaper: A Study in Social Psychology," *Annals of the American Academy of Political and Social Science* 16 (July 1900): 56.

2. Much the same confusion abounds today, though social scientists have taken pains during the last thirty years to employ somewhat more precision. In this study, while I fully recognize that public opinion and press opinion are not identical, I will assume that the former encompasses the latter. For more on this issue, see Melvin Small, "Historians Look at Public Opinion," in *Public Opinion and Historians: Interdisciplinary Perspectives,* ed. Melvin Small (Detroit: Wayne State Univ. Press, 1970), 13–22. Small downplays the influence of editorials but says that they may be more important during crises. He also notes that many political and diplomatic leaders instinctively equate these types of opinion, which would seem to be an argument for continued attention to news content.

The influence of public opinion itself on foreign policy carries an irresistible pull for historians. According to Small, "No studies *prove* this traditional piece of folklore. On the other hand, few historians or political scientists challenge it, either on empirical or intuitive grounds" (ibid., 14). Also, see Melvin Small, "Public Opinion," in *Explaining the History of American Foreign Relations,* ed. Michael J. Hogan and Thomas G. Paterson (Cambridge: Cambridge Univ. Press, 1991), 168.

3. Thomas. J. Knock, *To End All Wars: Woodrow Wilson and the Quest for a New World Order* (New York: Oxford Univ. Press, 1992), 246–270.

4. Robert C. Hilderbrand and George Juergens fall into the latter category. Of the two, Hilderbrand comes closer to conceding journalists a victory in publicizing the conference. Robert C. Hilderbrand, *Power and the People: Executive Management of Public Opinion in Foreign Affairs, 1897–1921* (Chapel Hill: Univ. of North Carolina Press, 1981), 166–196; George Juergens, *News from the White House: The Presidential-Press Relationship in the Progressive Era* (Chicago: Univ. of Chicago Press, 1981), 226–245.

5. The period is proving to be elastic, though. Daniel Rodgers, for example, describes a sixty-year period by including European patterns in his analysis. Daniel T. Rodgers, *Atlantic*

Crossings: Social Politics in a Progressive Age (Cambridge, Mass.: Belknap Press of Harvard Univ. Press, 1998).

6. Peter Filene's skepticism about whether the progressive era existed at all is a provocative stance but offers an argument more obscurantist than constructive. Peter Filene, "An Obituary for 'The Progressive Movement,'" *American Quarterly* 22 (1970): 20–34.

7. This seems especially true of the intellectual cross-currents described by Rodgers, *Atlantic Crossings*, 5–6, 21–25, 62, 276. But other historians have also pointed to or suggested the important role of communication during the progressive era. See, for example, Charles Forcey, *The Crossroads of Liberalism: Croly, Weyl, Lippmman, and the Progressive Era, 1900–1925* (New York: Oxford Univ. Press, 1961), xxii; David M. Kennedy, *Over Here: The First World War and American Society* (New York: Oxford Univ. Press, 1980), 45–92; David Paul Nord, *Newspapers and New Politics: Midwestern Municipal Reform, 1890–1900* (Ann Arbor: UMI Research Press, 1981); John Durham Peters, "Satan and Savior: Mass Communication in Progressive Thought," *Critical Studies in Mass Communication* 6 (1989): 247–263; James W. Carey, "Commentary: Communication and the Progressives," in *Critical Studies in Mass Communication* 6 (1989): 264–281.

8. My view on this issue generally follows that of David P. Thelen, *The New Citizenship: Origins of Progressivism in Wisconsin, 1885–1900* (Columbia: Univ. of Missouri Press, 1972), 1–3. On participation by the working classes, however, see John D. Buenker, *Urban Liberalism and Progressive Reform* (New York: Charles Scribner's Sons, 1973).

9. Woodrow Wilson, "Democracy and Efficiency," *Atlantic Monthly* 87 (March 1901): 289–290.

10. Rodgers, *Atlantic Crossings*, 3–7.

11. Thelen, *The New Citizenship*, 84.

12. Richard Hofstadter, *The Age of Reform: From Bryan to F.D.R.* (New York: Vintage Books, 1955), 135, 148–162; Robert H. Wiebe, *The Search for Order, 1877–1920* (New York: Hill and Wang, 1967), 111–166

13. JoAnne Brown, "Mental Measurements and the Rhetorical Force of Numbers," in *The Estate of Social Knowledge*, ed. JoAnne Brown and David D. van Keuren (Baltimore: Johns Hopkins Univ. Press, 1991), 134–153; Theodore M. Porter, *The Rise of Statistical Thinking, 1820–1900* (Princeton: Princeton Univ. Press, 1986). Interestingly, however, physicists were experiencing doubts in objectivity at the turn of the century (Theodore M. Porter, "The Death of the Object: *Fin De Siècle* Philosophy of Physics," in *Modernist Impulses in the Human Sciences, 1870–1930,* ed. Dorothy Ross [Baltimore: Johns Hopkins Univ. Press, 1994], 128–151).

14. Theodore M. Porter, *Trust in Numbers: The Pursuit of Objectivity in Science and Public Life* (Princeton: Princeton Univ. Press, 1995)

15. Dorothy Ross, "American Social Science and the Idea of Progress," in *The Authority of Experts: Studies in History and Theory,* ed. Thomas L. Haskell (Bloomington: Indiana Univ. Press, 1984), 157–179.

16. Richard L. McCormick, "The Discovery That Business Corrupts Politics: A Reappraisal of the Origins of Progressivism," *American Historical Review* 86 (April 1981): 258.

17. Ibid., 252.

18. Melvin I. Urofsky, "State Courts and Protective Legislation during the Progressive Era: A Reevaluation," *Journal of American History* 72 (June 1985): 64

19. Paul Boyer, *Urban Masses and Moral Order in America, 1820–1920* (Cambridge, Mass.:

Harvard Univ. Press, 1978), 261–276. Other historians who emphasize progressivism's moral basis, and on whose work I draw, include Jon C. Teaford, *City and Suburb: The Political Fragmentation of Metropolitan America, 1850–1979* (Baltimore: Johns Hopkins Univ. Press, 1979); *The Unheralded Triumph: City Government in America, 1870–1900* (Baltimore: John Hopkins University Press, 1984); and Robert M. Crunden, *Ministers of Reform: The Progressives' Achievement in American Civilization, 1889–1920* (New York: Basic Books, 1982).

20. Whatever the disagreements among them, many students of the subject do recognize the frequent serendipity of American public policy. On reforms affecting women's lives, for example, female activists understood that they could seldom count on men, on traditional forms of protest, or on seemingly obvious policy precedents for social change. See Theda Skocpol, *Protecting Soldiers and Mothers: The Political Origins of Social Policy in the United States* (Cambridge, Mass.: Belknap Press of Harvard University Press, 1992); Ulla Wikander, Alice Kessler-Harris, and Jane Lewis, eds., *Protecting Women: Labor Legislation in Europe, the United States, and Australia, 1880–1920* (Urbana: Univ. of Illinois Press, 1995); Kathryn Kish Sklar, *Florence Kelley and the Nation's Work: The Rise of Women's Political Culture, 1830–1900* (New Haven, Conn.: Yale Univ. Press, 1995).

21. Crunden, *Ministers of Reform,* 163.

22. Hofstadter, *The Age of Reform,* 186.

23. Crunden, *Ministers of Reform,* 182, 197.

24. Herman Hagedorn, "You Are the Hope of the World," *Red Cross Magazine* (April 1918): 1.

25. Daniel T. Rodgers, "In Search of Progressivism," *Reviews in American History* 10 (December 1982): 114. Rodgers, an accomplished sleuth of intellectual history, has also explored some of the controversies surrounding eighteenth-century republicanism.

26. Ronald Steel, *Walter Lippmann and the American Century* (New York: Vintage Books, 1980), 36; McCormick, "The Discovery That Business Corrupts Politics," 259.

27. Steel, *Walter Lippmann and the American Century,* 36.

28. Michael Schudson, *Discovering the News: A Social History of American Newspapers* (New York: Basic Books, 1978), 7–9. See also Schudson's chapter on journalism in Nathan O. Hatch, ed., *The Professions in American History* (Notre Dame, Ind.: Univ. of Notre Dame Press, 1988); and Schudson's books *Origins of the Ideal of Objectivity in the Professions: Studies in the History of American Journalism and American Law, 1830–1940* (New York: Garland, 1990), and *The Good Citizen: A History of American Civic Life* (New York: Free Press, 1998).

29. David T. Z. Mindich, *Just the Facts: How "Objectivity" Came to Define American Journalism* (New York: New York Univ. Press, 1998), 10; David Paul Nord, *Communities of Journalism: A History of American Newspapers and Their Readers* (Urbana: Univ. of Illinois Press, 2001), 4–5.

30. Marion Tuttle Marzolf, *Civilizing Voices: American Press Criticism, 1880–1950* (New York, Longman, 1991), 3–5, 50–59.

31. Christopher P. Wilson, *The Labor of Words: Literary Professionalism in the Progressive Era* (Athens: Univ. of Georgia Press, 1985), 12–13, 31.

32. George Creel, *The War, the World and Wilson* (New York: Harper and Brothers, 1920), 23. I use the term "publicist" in the way Americans in the early twentieth century used it—as a word mainly synonymous with "writer" but vaguely suggesting something more. That is because the term had not yet assumed its later, intimate association with press agentry and public relations, even though these occupations were already developing rapidly in the first years of the century.

The *Oxford English Dictionary* lists three definitions for the term, along with the earliest date of usage:

(a) "one who is learned in 'public' or international law; a writer on the law of nations" [1792];

(b) "a writer on current public topics; a journalist who makes political matters his specialty" [1833];

(c) "a press or publicity agent" [1930]

From my reading, it seems obvious that (b) was the usage most in vogue.

The *Reader's Guide to Periodical Literature* first lists "publicist" as a term in the volume covering 1915–1918 (vol. 4).

33. Walter Lippmann, "The Basic Problem of Democracy," *Atlantic Monthly* (November 1919): 622.

34. Don S. Kirschner, "'Publicity Properly Applied': The Selling of Expertise in America, 1900–1929," *American Studies* 19 (spring 1978): 65–78.

35. 'Lysis,' "German Corruption of the Foreign Press," *Atlantic Monthly* (June 1918): 815, 825.

36. Lloyd Ambrosius, *Woodrow Wilson and the American Diplomatic Tradition: The Treaty Fight in Perspective* (New York: Cambridge Univ. Press, 1987), 9, 14. See also Warren Frederick Ilchman, *Professional Diplomacy in the United States, 1779–1939: A Study in Administrative History* (Chicago: Univ. of Chicago Press, 1961), 11–81.

37. Samuel G. Blythe, "The Peace Machine," *Saturday Evening Post* (February 15, 1919): 3.

38. For arresting explorations of these themes, see, for example, Emily S. Rosenberg, *Financial Missionaries to the World: The Politics and Culture of Dollar Diplomacy, 1900–1930* (Cambridge, Mass.: Harvard Univ. Press, 1999); and Frederick S. Calhoun, *Power and Principle: Armed Intervention in Wilsonian Foreign Policy* (Kent, Ohio: Kent State Univ. Press, 1986).

39. Tantalizing hints, references, and anecdotes suggesting a connection between diplomacy and the power of public opinion, or influence of the press, appear in such diverse works as John Milton Cooper Jr., *Breaking the Heart of the World: Woodrow Wilson and the Fight for the League of Nations* (Cambridge: Cambridge Univ. Press, 2001); Arthur Walworth, *Wilson and His Peacemakers: American Diplomacy at the Paris Peace Conference, 1919* (New York: Norton, 1986); Robert L. Beisner, *From the Old Diplomacy to the New, 1865–1900* (New York: Thomas Y. Crowell; reprint, Arlington Heights, Ill.: Harlan Davidson, 1986); Sidney Bell, *Righteous Conquest: Woodrow Wilson and the Evolution of the New Diplomacy, 1917–1918* (Port Washington, N.Y.: Kennikat Press, 1972); Arthur S. Link, *Wilson the Diplomatist: A Look at His Major Foreign Policies* (Baltimore: Johns Hopkins Press, 1957); and George F. Kennan, *American Diplomacy, 1900–1950* (Chicago: Univ. of Chicago Press, 1951).

Historians who have called more attention to the subject include Lawrence E. Gelfand, "Where Ideals Confront Self-Interest: Wilsonian Foreign Policy," *Diplomatic History* 18 (1994): 128; Robert Hilderbrand, *Power and the People*; Michael Leigh, *Mobilizing Consent: Public Opinion and American Foreign Policy, 1937–1947* (Westport, Conn.: Greenwood Press, 1976); Melvin Small, "Public Opinion," in *Explaining the History of American Foreign Relations,* ed. Hogan and Paterson; James N. Rosenau, *Public Opinion and Foreign Policy: An Operational Formulation* (New York: Random House, 1961); Henry Wriston, *Diplomacy in a Democracy* (New York: Harper, 1956); Thomas Bailey, *The Man in the Street: The Impact of American Public Opinion on Foreign Policy* (New York: Macmillan, 1948).

CHAPTER 1. FEDERAL POWER AND PUBLICITY

1. Louis J. Alber, "Making Up America's Mind," *The Independent* (June 9, 1917): 475. "There is a cry for enlightened leadership of the masses," in Arthur Hunt Chute, "Brain Sweat versus Brawn Sweat," *Leslie's* (May 3, 1919): 682.

2. Arthur E. Bestor, "Mobilizing the Mind of America," *The Independent* (August 31, 1918): 290.

3. Editorial, "The Press Agents' War," *New York Times* (September 9, 1914): 8.

4. See Stephen L. Vaughn, *Holding Fast the Inner Lines: Democracy, Nationalism, and the Committee on Public Information* (Chapel Hill: Univ. of North Carolina Press, 1980), xii–39.

5. "Can't All the Races Get Together," *The Forum* (November 1918): 635.

6. Paul L. Murphy, *World War I and the Origin of Civil Liberties in the United States* (New York: Norton, 1979), chapters 3 and 4. Arthur S. Link sharply criticized Murphy's thesis: "The most important reality of 1917–1918 was the fact that the United States was engaged in a total war, and it seems a bit much to expect the government to tolerate any significant opposition to or obstruction of the war effort. Murphy avoids this problem by ignoring it. Actually, compared to the civil-rights policies of the governments of European belligerents during World War I, those of the United States seem almost tolerant" (Arthur S. Link, review of *World War I and the Origin of Civil Liberties in the United States,* by Paul L. Murphy, in *Journal of American History* 68 [June 1981]: 165). My objective, however, is neither to refute nor diminish Murphy's conclusions, only to broaden his frame of reference.

7. Woodrow Wilson, *Constitutional Government in the United States* (New York: Columbia Univ. Press, 1908; reprint, 1961), 68–72.

8. Walter Lippmann, *Drift and Mastery: An Attempt to Diagnose the Current Unrest* (New York: Kennerley, 1914; reprint, Madison: Univ. of Wisconsin Press, 1985), 96.

9. Kennedy, *Over Here,* 47.

10. See, for example, Stephen Ponder, "Federal News Management in the Progressive Era: Gifford Pinchot and the Conservation Crusade," *Journalism History* 13 (summer 1986): 44; Kirchner, "'Publicity Properly Applied,'" 69.

11. For a partial list of executive efforts in publicity, see Stephen Ponder, *Managing the Press: Origins of the Media Presidency, 1897–1933* (New York: St. Martin's Press, 1998), 86.

12. James R. Mock and Cedric Larson, *Words That Won the War: The Story of the Committee on Public Information, 1917–1919* (Princeton: Princeton Univ. Press, 1939), 68.

13. "Government Appreciation of Advertising," *Printers' Ink* (October 10, 1918): 123. The trade magazine also quotes at length the October 5 edition of *Collier's.*

14. Frank Luther Mott, *American Journalism, A History: 1690–1960,* 3rd ed. (New York: Macmillan, 1941; reprint, 1962), 627.

15. Ibid, 623. Bernard Weisberger also concludes that "the American people had more information on world affairs at their disposal than ever before," but he qualifies this by questioning how much of that information they understood. He also paints a dispiriting picture of war correspondents, depressed by the censorship—a characteristic I have not generally found to be the case in my research. Bernard A. Weisberger, *The American Newspaperman* (Chicago: Univ. of Chicago Press, 1961), 163.

16. See, for example, Robert Bruère, "The New Nationalism and Business," *Harper's Magazine* (March 1919): 511–518. For a discussion of whether and to what degree progressives fought or accommodated business, see Richard L. McCormick, "The Discovery That Business Cor-

rupts Politics," 247. McCormick underscores Americans' ambivalence but emphasizes that antibusiness sentiment was real, sincere, and prevalent.

17. The 1890s "marked the triumph of a new system based upon, characterized by, and controlled by the corporation and similar large and highly organized groups throughout American society" (William Appleman Williams, *The Tragedy of American Diplomacy* [New York: Dell, 1959; reprint, 1972], 29).

18. O. A. Hilton, "Public Opinion and Civil Liberties in Wartime, 1917–1919," *Southwestern Social Science Quarterly* 28 (December 1947): 201.

19. "Publicity Will Cure Inefficiency," *Sunset* (July 1918): 7.

20. Bruce Bliven, "Uncle Sam's Megaphone," *Printers' Ink* (October 24, 1918): 3.

21. Robert H. Ferrell, *Woodrow Wilson and World War I, 1917–1921* (New York: Harper and Row, 1985), 203.

22. Mock and Larson, *Words That Won the War,* 48. "It is indicative of the impromptu organization and development of the Committee that no one can draw a definitive outline of its work" (ibid., 65).

23. "Uncle Sam a Voluminous but Little-Read Publisher," *Literary Digest* (May 3, 1919): 80.

24. Will Irwin, *Propaganda and the News; or What Makes You Think So?* (New York: Whittlesey House, McGraw-Hill, 1936), 185.

25. John Jay Chapman, "The Bright Side of War," *Atlantic Monthly* (January 1918): 139.

26. "Government Call for Typewriters and Stenographers," *Literary Digest* (May 25, 1918): 95.

27. Arthur Hunt Chute, "Brain Sweat versus Brawn Sweat," *Leslie's* (May 3, 1919): 657, 680.

28. I am not, of course, arguing that other nations underwent a "progressive era" in the sense that the United States did. But various progressive elements—and certainly the growing influence of publicity in political life—could hardly be kept confined to a single country. As Daniel Rodgers and Robert Crunden have convincingly shown, American reformers learned a lot from their European counterparts, Imperial Germany included. For more on these transoceanic connections, see Daniel Rodgers, *Atlantic Crossings: Social Politics in a Progressive Age* (Cambridge, Mass.: Belknap Press of Harvard Univ. Press, 1998); and Robert M. Crunden, *American Salons: Encounters with European Modernism, 1885–1917* (New York: Oxford Univ. Press, 1993). See also Charles Forcey's perceptive discussion of Walter Weyl, "a German-American Francophile," in *The Crossroads of Liberalism: Croly, Weyl, and Lippmann, and the Progressive Era, 1900–1925* (New York: Oxford Univ. Press, 1961), 56–61. There is no question that the pre-war link between liberals in Britain, for example, and the United States was unusually solid.

29. "WANTED—Team Work," *McClure's* (March 1918): 8.

30. Gertrude Atherton, "When All Women Are Workers," *Cosmopolitan* (December 1918): 90. "That this war began in a 'battle of the books,' that it was begun by books, and won by books, and will have its full fruits reaped by books, that long before troops marched athwart the freedom of little estates, words, in orderly array, marched first—the children with the sword" (Donald Wilhelm, "The Failure of the Fourth Estate," *The Independent* [December 28, 1918]: 444).

31. Arthur Bullard, *The Diplomacy of the Great War* (New York: Macmillan, 1917), 150.

32. Some nations were slow to perceive the new force of international public opinion. "For months after the outbreak of war the foreign correspondent was a persona non grata in Germany. Then the German government awoke to the harm it was doing itself by letting the Allies monopolize the front page, and the newspaper correspondents were welcomed. Nevertheless, they were not wholly trusted, and a close watch was kept on them at the front or in the

cities by the authorities, and their reports were closely censored" (Adele N. Phillips and Russell Phillips, "The Decline of the Berliner," *Atlantic Monthly* [January 1918]: 14).

33. *The Dial* (March 22, 1919): 309.

34. Heber Blankenhorn, "The War of Morale: How America 'Shelled' the German Lines with Paper," *Harper's Magazine* (September 1919): 510.

35. Guy Stanton Ford, "America's Fight for Public Opinion," *Minnesota History* 3 (February 1919): 3, 4.

36. Ibid., 26. The first figure is roughly the equivalent of $382 million in 2008, expressed as a relative share of the nation's GDP. For an argument questioning the CPI's effectiveness, see Dale E. Zacher, *The Scripps Newspapers Go to War, 1914–1918* (Urbana: University of Illinois Press, 2008), 127–28, 183–86. Zacher gently raises a couple of fair objections to the conventional wisdom on the CPI, but his overall case, tangential though it is in the book, is thin and unpersuasive.

37. Frank I. Cobb, "The Press and Public Opinion," *New Republic* (December 31, 1919): 144.

38. Allen F. Davis, "Welfare, Reform and World War I," *American Quarterly* 19 (1967): 517; Knock, *To End All Wars,* 93–94; Vaughn, *Holding Fast the Inner Lines,* 35; John A. Thompson, "American Progressive Publicists and the First World War, 1914–1917," *Journal of American History* 58 (September 1971): 380; Charles Hirschfeld, "Nationalist Progressivism and World War I," *Mid-America* 45 (July 1963): 139.

39. Will Irwin made this claim in *The Making of a Reporter* (New York: G. P. Putnam's Sons, 1942), 354. According to another writer, though Creel "was not a cabinet member, he exercised far more influence and power than many members of the Cabinet" (quoted in "Creel, Who Headed Our Propaganda," *Leslie's* [April 5, 1919]: 486).

40. William Graebner, *The Engineering of Consent: Democracy and Authority in Twentieth-Century America* (Madison: Univ. of Wisconsin Press, 1987), 44.

41. Woodrow Wilson, *Constitutional Government in the United States,* 68.

42. Hilderbrand, *Power and the People,* 163–164.

43. Vaughn, *Holding Fast the Inner Lines,* chapters 1–3, passim; Kennedy, *Over Here,* 60–75. See also Murphy, *World War I and the Origin of Civil Liberties in the United States,* 112.

44. Graebner, *The Engineering of Consent,* 44. For an almost equally cynical portrait of public opinion manipulation, see Benjamin Ginsburg, *The Captive Public: How Mass Opinion Promotes State Power* (New York: Basic Books, 1986).

45. George Creel, "The Measure of a Permanent Peace," *Advocate of Peace* (October 1918): 271.

46. For this phrase I am indebted to George Kennan's analysis of Open Door policy and his criticism of the empty idealism of pretty slogans. Kennan, *American Diplomacy,* 440–445. Also see K. Shide Kara [*sic*], "The Platitude in Diplomacy," *The Forum* (March 1921): 249–253 [Shide-hara's name was misprinted in this article].

Logology often simply became logophilia at that time, as evident in the following excerpt from an article on French and American journalism: "The Word, the creative mandate, the substance everlasting, retains its pristine power when spoken by one having Authority. . . . The Word is man's most precious inheritance. It is the scepter of dominion. It is the minister of authority. It is now, as in the beginning, the creative force. It is substance. It is life" (Henri-Martin Barzun, "Better Understanding Dawning between French and American Press," *Editor & Publisher* [May 22, 1919]: 66).

47. Many of the tributes paid to Creel at his retirement party—a party at which many reporters seemed conspicuously absent—centered on just such an emphasis on publicity ("Tributes Paid to George Creel on Retirement," *Editor & Publisher* [December 7, 1918]: 34).

48. "The newspapers, at all times, were their own and only censor. . . . With the nation in arms, the need of America was not so much to keep the newspapers from doing the hurtful things as to get them to do the helpful things. It was not servants we wanted but associates" (George Creel, "The American Newspaper: What It Is and What It Isn't," *Everybody's Magazine* [April 1919]: 40).

49. "The business manger [of *The Masses*] took one of the issues adduced by the prosecution to George Creel, who was then supposed to be the national censor, in order to make sure that there was nothing unlawful in it. Creel himself testified that he understood this to be the purport of the visit, and that he had said it contained nothing in violation of the law, so far as he knew" (quoted in "The Masses Case," *The Liberator* [June 1918]: 4).

50. Robert Lansing, Newton D. Baker, and Josephus Daniels to Woodrow Wilson, quoted in Kennedy, *Over Here,* 160.

51. "There is only one point of contact between the present and the future: and that is the schoolroom" (quoted in S. W. Straus, "When Peace Comes This Will Come," *Ladies' Home Journal* [January 1918]: 1).

52. "The March of Events," *The World's Work* (July 1918): 232.

53. Creel, *The War, The World, and Wilson,* 35.

54. Meredith Nicholson, "The Standard of Americanism," *Cosmopolitan* (August 1919): 27.

55. Ibid., 15.

56. Copies of this and the following two posters are included in Stephen Vaughn's *Holding Fast the Inner Lines,* 80, 231, 169. Also see, for example, *Good Housekeeping* (July 1918): 140.

57. "I Am Public Opinion!" advertisement, *Leslie's* (September 21, 1918): 370.

58. James E. Pollard, *The Presidents and the Press* (New York: Macmillan, 1947; reprint, New York: Octagon Books, 1973), 665.

59. Juergens, *News from the White House,* 196; Murphy, *World War I and the Origin of Civil Liberties in the United States,* 81, 119.

60. Timothy W. Gleason, "Historians and Freedom of the Press since 1880," *American Journalism* 5 (1988): 242.

61. Richard Barry, "'Freedom' of the Press," *North American Review* (November 1918): 708.

62. Quoted in Donald Johnson, "Wilson, Burleson, and Censorship in the First World War," *Journal of Southern History* 28 (February 1962): 50.

63. Barry, "'Freedom' of the Press," 708.

64. Theodore Roosevelt, "Lincoln and Free Speech," *Metropolitan Magazine* (May 1918): 7.

65. Zechariah Chafee Jr., *Freedom of Speech* (New York: Harcourt, Brace and Howe, 1920), Appendix II, 387. Chafee's appendices provide historians with an invaluable record of U.S. prosecutions, as well as a thorough compendium of relevant state statutes.

66. Ferrell, *Woodrow Wilson and World War I,* 208.

67. The *Literary Digest's* survey of March 1917 showed widespread approval, complacency, or at least silence by the press on the issue. In addition, Murphy relates vividly how oppressive local defense committees and citizens' councils all across the country were in silencing the dissenting, converting the uncertain, and mobilizing the willing. He cites a bizarre but chilling example in Montana, "where the state council ordered the public schools to cease using a textbook on ancient history written by Professor Willis Mason West because he gave too favorable a treat-

ment of the Teutonic tribes prior to A.D. 812. At the time West was an active member of Creel's Committee on Public Information." Council of National Defense Papers, May 1918, in Murphy, *World War I and the Origins of Civil Liberties in the United States,* 119.

68. "1,178 Publications Quit in 1918," *Editor & Publisher* (January 11, 1919): 39.

69. Lindsay Rogers, *The Contemporary Review,* reprinted in "Freedom of the Press in the United States," *The Living Age* (September 28, 1918): 770–771.

70. The Espionage and Trading with the Enemy Acts were, to one Briton, "not very drastic; they did not go so far as the English Defense of the Realm Regulations . . ." (ibid., 769). For additional information on Britain's Defense of the Realm Act, see Deian Hopkin, "Domestic Censorship in the First World War," *Journal of Contemporary History* 5 (1970): 156.

71. "Freedom of Language," *The Independent* (May 11, 1918): 238–239.

72. Theodore Roosevelt, "No Half Measures," *Metropolitan Magazine* (August 1918): 6. Roosevelt, however, scorned the banning of German and the mistreatment of "loyal" American citizens of foreign birth.

73. "What of the Future?" *The World Tomorrow* (December 1918): 291.

74. Quoted in "Tributes Paid to George Creel on Retirement," *Editor & Publisher* (December 7, 1918): 34. Chillingly, Karger's remarks in *Editor & Publisher* lie alongside a two-paragraph bulletin announcing the indictment of three editors under the Espionage Act.

75. "Our Headline Policy," *Columbia War Papers,* Series 1, No. 4, New York, 1917; reprinted in "The Press in Wartime," *The Annals of America,* ed. William Benton (Chicago: Encyclopedia Britannica, 1968), 115.

76. Ida Tarbell, *All in the Day's Work: An Autobiography* (New York: Macmillan, 1939), 331.

77. Quoted in Melville Stone, *Fifty Years a Journalist* (Garden City, N.Y.: Doubleday, Page, 1921), 325.

78. "The Censorship," *New York Times* (May 24, 1917): 12.

79. Some acted as regular couriers and intellectual liaisons between units. "Floyd Gibbons Describes Conditions Under Which U.S. War Correspondents Work," *Editor & Publisher* (September 7, 1918): 5. Phillip Knightley compares the clothing worn by British and American correspondents in *The First Casualty, From the Crimea to Vietnam: The War Correspondent as Hero, Propagandist, and Myth Maker* (New York: Harcourt Brace Jovanovich, 1975), 96, 124.

80. Randolph Bourne, "War as the Health of the State," in *Untimely Papers,* ed. James Oppenheim (New York: Huebsch, 1919); reprinted, *The Annals of America,* ed. William Benton (Chicago: Encyclopedia Britannica, 1968), 137.

CHAPTER 2. THE NEW PRESIDENCY

1. The list of scholars who pay no heed to progressive publicity, other than making the obligatory nod toward muckraking, could probably fill a monograph. More and more historians and political scientists, however, do seem to be acknowledging the role of information during those years, but they tend to include it as one factor among many and not the most important. There is also an unfortunate pattern to conflate the CPI and censorship, so that the emphasis is on how the Wilson administration "stifled" information, squelched discourse, and robbed the public of untainted news. See, e.g., Ponder, *Managing the Press,* 91; Leigh, *Mobilizing Consent,* 56.

2. Ginsburg, *The Captive Public,* 9. "Propaganda," Michael Schudson writes, "has an ironically democratic feature—it appears when elites feel obliged to address the public" (Schudson, *The Good Citizen,* 201).

3. Douglass Cater, *The Fourth Branch of Government* (New York: Vintage Books, 1959), 25. See also Stephen Ponder's introduction in *Managing the Press,* x–xvi.

4. *The Independent* (November 23, 1918): 242.

5. Wilson, quoted in Link, *Wilson the Diplomatist,* 10.

6. Lewis L. Gould, "Theodore Roosevelt, Woodrow Wilson, and the Emergence of the Modern Presidency: An Introductory Essay," *Presidential Studies Quarterly* 19 (winter 1989): 41.

7. Fabian Franklin, "The President and Public Opinion," *North American Review* (April 1918): 539 (italics added). Wilson also became the target of envy by a number of Republican leaders, not least of them a former safari hunter. Often and poignantly, Theodore Roosevelt impressed on friends that he wanted more desperately to be in the White House since the war's outbreak than he had in 1912 or even 1904 (Oscar King Davis, *Released for Publication: Some Inside Political History of Theodore Roosevelt and His Times, 1898–1918* [Boston: Houghton Mifflin, 1925], 436). For more on this peculiar rivalry, see John Milton Cooper Jr., *The Warrior and the Priest: Woodrow Wilson and Theodore Roosevelt* (Cambridge, Mass.: Belknap Press of Harvard Univ. Press, 1983), 303–323.

8. "New Power for the President," *The Outlook* (May 29, 1918): 176.

9. McCormick, "The Discovery That Business Corrupts Politics," 268.

10. *Des Moines Register,* quoted in "How President Wilson Is Waging the War," *Literary Digest* (February 9, 1918): 15.

11. "Give the President Plenty of Power," *The World's Work* (May 1918): 17.

12. "The Call for a War-Lord," *Literary Digest* (January 26, 1918): 10. See also Herbert Kaufman, "Beneficent Autocracy," *Cosmopolitan* (August 1918): 25.

13. "Give the President a Free Hand," *The Independent* (February 16, 1918): 257.

14. Norman Hapgood, "The President and Congress," *Leslie's* (May 18, 1918): 684.

15. Nelson W. Polsby, "Studying Congress Through Time: A Comment on Joseph Cooper and David Brady," *American Political Science Review* 75 (1975): 1010. See also Samuel Kernell and Gary C. Jacobson, "Congress and the Presidency as News in the Nineteenth Century," *Journal of Politics* 49 (1987): 1016.

16. Hilderbrand, *Power and the People,* 5.

17. Walter Lippmann, *The Stakes of Diplomacy* (New York: Holt, 1915), 26.

18. Elmer E. Cornwell Jr., *Presidential Leadership of Public Opinion* (Bloomington: Indiana Univ. Press, 1965), 3.

19. J. D. Bourchier, "The Peace Congress and the Balkans," *Atlantic Monthly* (March 1919): 410.

20. Cornwell, *Presidential Leadership of Public Opinion,* 5–6.

21. Press Conference, March 22, 1913. Robert C. Hilderbrand, ed., "The Complete Press Conferences, 1913," in *Papers of Woodrow Wilson,* edited by Arthur S. Link, vol. 50 (Princeton: Princeton Univ. Press, 1985), 3.

22. Woodrow Wilson, quoted in Kendrick A. Clements, *Woodrow Wilson: World Statesman* (Boston: Twayne Publishers, 1987), 63.

23. France also regarded him as such and honored the president for his literary accomplishments by admitting him to membership in the French Academy. See "President in Wilson," *The Outlook* (December 25, 1918): 644.

24. One writer, possibly David Lawrence, described Wilson's literary style this way: "dignified, measured, and unmistakable in its original grouping of words musically marching to their climax . . . more effective than the oratory of any spellbinder, for its eloquence reaches thousands of miles beyond the confines of any hall" (quoted in "President Wilson," *The Outlook* [April 23, 1919]: 695).

25. Quoted in David Mitchell, "Woodrow Wilson as 'World Saviour,'" *History Today* 26 (1976): 5.

26. Wiebe, *The Search for Order,* 160.

27. Juergens, *News from the White House,* 154–157.

28. Robert C. Hilderbrand, "Introduction: The Complete Press Conferences," in "The Complete Press Conferences, 1913," in *Papers of Woodrow Wilson,* edited by Arthur S. Link, vol. 50 (Princeton: Princeton Univ. Press, 1985), ix. See also Hilderbrand, *Power and the People,* 93–104; and Juergens, *News from the White House,* 140–152.

29. Hilderbrand, "Introduction: The Complete Press Conferences," x.

30. See, for example, Senator Lee Slater Overman, "President Wilson as World Leader," *The Forum* (December 1918): 643. "And who among living statesmen today can speak so well for others as Woodrow Wilson?"

31. Dr. Theodore S. Woolsey, "Peace Terms; American and British," *Leslie's* (January 26, 1918): 117.

32. "In these expressions of war aims are part of a great diplomatic battle with Germany on the one hand, and part of a necessary process of freshly integrating the forces of public opinion at home on the other hand, the President appears certainly in the role of the master artist" (*Chicago Tribune,* quoted in "Smashing Our Historic Policy of Non-Intervention in Europe," *Current Opinion* [February 1918]: 80).

33. Wilson "has made our cause moral, and by making it moral he has made it victorious." In Norman Hapgood, "The President as I Know Him," *Leslie's* (June 22, 1918): 868.

34. "Woodrow Wilson," *The Independent* (January 19, 1918): 89. See also "The President Voices the World's Desire," *The Independent* (October 12, 1918): 39.

35. Joseph H. Odell, "Interpreting the People to the President," *The Outlook* (March 6, 1918): 372.

36. "The Two Battles," *The Independent* (February 23, 1918): 299; James Davenport Whelpley, *The Fortnightly Review,* quoted in "America's Weapon for Peace," *The Living Age* (March 9, 1918): 579.

37. Senator Lee Slater Overman, "President Wilson as World Leader," *The Forum* (December 1918): 643.

38. James W. Ceaser, Glen E. Thurow Jeffery K. Tulis, and Joseph M. Bessette, "The Rise of the Rhetorical Presidency," *Presidential Studies Quarterly* 11 (1981): 158–171; Jeffrey K. Tulis, *The Rhetorical Presidency* (Princeton: Princeton Univ. Press, 1987), 182.

39. Ponder, *Managing the Press,* xvi.

40. Ibid., xv.

41. *Chicago Daily News* (December 2, 1918): 1.

CHAPTER 3. THE NEW DIPLOMACY

1. *The New Republic* (February 2, 1918): 2.

2. "Let any one seriously ask himself what he understands by diplomacy and why it is that such disparagement hangs about it, and he will see what is meant" (John Dewey, "The League of Nations and the New Diplomacy," *The Dial* [November 16, 1918]: 402).

3. J. A. R. Marriott, *The Quarterly Review,* quoted in "Modern Diplomacy," *The Living Age* (March 16, 1918): 665.

4. Joseph C. Grew, *Turbulent Era: A Diplomatic Record of Forty Years, 1904–1945,* vol. 1, ed. Walter Johnson (Boston: Houghton Mifflin, 1952), 112–114.

5. For some examples, see chapter 11.

6. Quoted in John M. Blum, *Joe Tumulty and the Wilson Era* (Boston: Houghton Mifflin, 1951), 162.

7. Gregg Wolper, "Wilsonian Public Diplomacy: The Committee on Public Information in Spain," *Diplomatic History* 17 (winter 1993): 17.

8. Bullard, *The Diplomacy of the Great War,* 3–4.

9. Ibid., 99.

10. Arthur Bullard, "Democracy and Diplomacy," *Atlantic Monthly* (April 1917): 491.

11. Bullard, *The Diplomacy of the Great War,* 270. There seems to be a recurring historical connection between new technology, faith in mass communication, and diplomatic reform. Advances in electronic communication in the 1980s, for example, fanned hope for increased political participation. Steven V. Roberts, "New Diplomacy by Fax Americana: Technology Can Win Friends and Influence People," *U.S. News and World Report* (June 19, 1989): 32.

12. Bullard, *The Diplomacy of the Great War,* 207. Bismarck also made the caustic remark that "no diplomat expected to be believed and that the best way to deceive was to tell the truth" (paraphrased by Frederic Austin Ogg in "The Campaign Against Secret Diplomacy," *Munsey's Magazine* [September 1918]: 700).

13. Kennan, *American Diplomacy,* 55–73. For the classic rejoinder to Kennan's classic thesis, see Arthur S. Link, *Woodrow Wilson: Revolution, War, and Peace* (Arlington Heights, Ill.: AHM Publishing, 1979), 58–68. The quote comes from John A. Thompson, "Woodrow Wilson and World War I: A Reappraisal," *Journal of American Studies* 19 (1985): 328.

For scholars who push Link's rebuttal a good deal further and say Wilson was all too realistic, see John W. Coogan, *The End of Neutrality: The United States, Britain, and Maritime Rights, 1899–1915* (Ithaca, N.Y.: Cornell Univ. Press, 1981); Ferrell, *Woodrow Wilson and World War I;* Edward B. Parsons, *Wilsonian Diplomacy: Allied-American Rivalries in War and Peace* (St. Louis, Mo.: Forum Press, 1978). Lloyd E. Ambrosius gives a more nuanced account, but he might also be considered part of the realist school as well (Ambrosius, *Woodrow Wilson and the American Diplomatic Tradition*).

Most historians now generally acknowledge a whole host of considerations influencing Wilson's diplomatic approach, not the least of them economic, but also political, personal, and health-related factors. See, for example, Calhoun, *Power and Principle,* and Cooper, *Breaking the Heart of the World.*

14. Klaus Schwabe, *Woodrow Wilson, Revolutionary Germany, and Peacemaking, 1918–1919: Missionary Diplomacy and the Realities of Power,* trans. Rita and Robert Kimber (Chapel Hill: Univ. of North Carolina Press, 1985), 179.

15. Tony Smith, "Making the World Safe for Democracy in the American Century," *Diplomatic History* 23 (spring 1999): 176.

16. As an example of the unpredictability in diplomacy, immediately following the war, General Pershing and his staff without State Department or even presidential approval actually started negotiations with German officials on their own (Lloyd E. Ambrosius, "Secret German-American Negotiations during the Paris Peace Conference," *Amerikastudien* 24 (1979): 288.

17. David Steigerwald, "The Synthetic Politics of Woodrow Wilson," *Journal of the History of Ideas* 50 (1989): 484.

18. Link, *Wilson the Diplomatist,* 6.

19. "What Kind of Peace?" *The New World* (February 1918): 25.

20. John Foster Bass, *The Peace Tangle* (New York: Macmillan, 1920), 12. See also "The Revelations of the Secret Treaties," *The Independent* (January 12, 1918): 53. "Of these so-called 'secret treaties' it may be said that most of them are neither treaties nor secret. They reveal little but what was commonly suspected." Oswald F. Schuette confirmed this knowledge. "We who had the difficult task of writing for American newspapers as European correspondents during the war knew all about these treaties in 1917, and some of us whose work was most closely censored had incriminating details away back in 1916. . . . Everybody except President Wilson and Mr. Lansing seems to have known all about the secret treaties before these envoys went to Versailles" (Oswald F. Schuette, "On Guard at Washington," *Leslie's* [September 19, 1919]: 424). Secretary of State Lansing also testified before Congress in 1919 that he had made available to the White House the text of the treaties, after they were released by the Bolshevists, and, as *The New Republic* pointed out, the *New York Sun, Times,* and *Evening Post* all contained summaries between December 1917 and January 1918 ("Mr. Wilson Testifies," *The New Republic* [September 3, 1919]: 135). See also "The Nemesis of Secret Diplomacy," *The New World* (March 1918): 49.

21. Quoted in Bass, *The Peace Tangle,* 13.

22. For an explanation of the failure of this mediation offer, see John Milton Cooper Jr., "The British Response to the House-Grey Memorandum: New Evidence and New Questions," *Journal of American History* 59 (March 1973): 958.

23. Ambrosius, *Woodrow Wilson and the American Diplomatic Tradition,* 22. As Lord Robert Cecil complained to Lloyd George at the end of 1918, Wilson was getting international credit for the league of nations concept: "[W]e have let that eloquent pedagogue 'patent' this question" (quoted ibid., 55).

24. "Reaping the Whirlwind," *The New World* (April 1918): 75.

25. *Advocate of Peace* (January 1918): 4.

26. "League, Not Alliance," *North American Review* (November 1918): 653.

27. "The Nemesis of Secret Diplomacy," *The New World* (March 1918): 52.

28. J. L. Hammond, "The War and the Mind of Great Britain," *Atlantic Monthly* (March 1919): 356. Half a year after the armistice, the normally skeptical publication *The Dial* was still confident in the people's unalterable demand for an end to the old diplomacy (*The Dial* [April 5, 1919]: 363).

29. Bullard, *The Diplomacy of the Great War,* 215–216.

30. Arno J. Mayer, *Political Origins of the New Diplomacy, 1917–1918* (New Haven, Conn.: Yale Univ. Press, 1959), viii, 45, 53–58; Forcey, *The Crossroads of Liberalism,* 264.

31. Charles Seymour, ed., *The Intimate Papers of Colonel House* (Boston: Houghton Mifflin, 1926–1928), 4:141–148.

32. Robert L. Beisner, *From the Old Diplomacy to the New,* 84.

33. "Germany's Ultimate Offense," *The New Republic* (July 6, 1918): 277.

34. "Blue Pencil Wanted," *Collier's* (October 4, 1919): 17.

35. "The League of Nations," *The Liberator* (December 1918): 5.

CHAPTER 4. THE PROFESSIONALIZATION OF JOURNALISM

1. The classic authorities are Mott, *American Journalism,* 604–605; Weisberger, *The American Newspaperman,* 159–160; and Schudson, *Discovering the News,* 122, 152. Recently, however, some historians have distanced themselves from this view and instead stressed the gradual nature of

professionalization. See, for example, Stephen A. Banning, "The Professionalization of Journalism: A Nineteenth-Century Beginning," *Journalism History* 24 (winter 1998/1999): 157.

2. Penn Kimball, "Journalism: Art, Craft or Profession?" in *The Professions in America*, ed. Kenneth S. Lynn (Boston: Houghton Mifflin, 1965), 256.

3. See Weisberger, *The American Newspaperman*, 88–155; Will Irwin, "The American Newspaper, Part I.—The Power of the Press," *Collier's* (January 21, 1911): 15; Daniel J. Czitrom, *Media and the American Mind: From Morse to McLuhan* (Chapel Hill: Univ. of North Carolina Press, 1982), 91–93; Mott, *American Journalism*, 495–501.

4. For a different view of journalism's "power," see Francis E. Leupp, "The Waning Power of the Press," *Atlantic Monthly* (February 1910): 144. Leupp's thesis was mainly that amid all the flashy technology, the keen competition, and the general noise of democracy, the voice of the press was hard to hear.

5. Andrew Abbott, *The System of Professions: An Essay on the Division of Expert Labor* (Chicago: Univ. of Chicago Press, 1988), 215.

6. Douglas Birkhead, "The Power in the Image: Professionalism and the 'Communications Revolution,'" *American Journalism* 1 (winter 1984): 4.

7. Ibid.

8. Thomas C. Leonard, *The Power of the Press: The Birth of American Political Reporting* (New York: Oxford Univ. Press, 1986), 196, 198, 213–215, 223.

9. Wilson, *The Labor of Words*, 114.

10. Donald A. Ritchie, "'The Loyalty of the Senate': Washington Correspondents in the Progressive Era," *The Historian* 51 (August 1989): 589.

11. Edwin A. Ross, "The Suppression of Important News," *Atlantic Monthly* (March 1910), reprinted in Harvey Swados, ed., *Years of Conscience: The Muckrakers* (Cleveland: World Publishing, Meridian Books, 1962), 396; Will Irwin, "The American Newspaper, Part I.—The Power of the Press," *Collier's* (January 21, 1911). Also see Upton Sinclair, *The Brass Check: A Study of American Journalism* (Pasadena, Calif.: Upton Sinclair, 1919).

12. Rollo Ogden, "Some Aspects of Journalism," *Atlantic Monthly* (July 1906): 12.

13. Aaron Hardy Ulm, "Card-Indexing Your Politics: The Great Political Campaigns of Today Are Scientifically Planned," *The Forum* (October 1918): 416.

14. "Disillusioning the German People," *Munsey's Magazine* (October 1918): 56.

15. Carey, "Commentary: Communication and the Progressives," 266.

16. Editorial, *The Dial* (May 9, 1918): 458.

17. Schudson, *Discovering the News*, 129.

18. Edward S. Babcox, "The Printing Press and Victory," *Leslie's* (February 16, 1918): 219.

19. Harold Stearns, "The American Press since the Armistice," *The Dial* (February 8, 1919): 132.

20. "How to Study This Number," *The Independent* (June 7, 1919): 384; J. Madison Gathany, "Weekly Outline Study of Current History," *The Outlook* (December 18, 1918): n.p.; Daniel C. Knowlton, "Readers' Guide and Study Outline," *Leslie's* (March 29, 1919): 466; "Our Interest in World Politics," *The World's Work* (September 1918): 447.

21. "Lessons of the War," *Red Cross Magazine* (February 1918): 3.

22. Mott, *American Journalism*, 620.

23. Charles Audrey Eaton, "Let the People Judge," *Leslie's* (December 27, 1919): 865.

24. Von Ferdinand Tonnies, quoted in Edward Bernays, *Crystallizing Public Opinion* (New York: Boni and Liveright, 1923). 217.

25. Bernays, *Crystallizing Public Opinion*, 34.

26. Michael Schudson, "The Profession of Journalism in the United States," in *The Professions in American History,* ed. Nathan O. Hatch (Notre Dame, Ind.: Univ. of Notre Dame Press, 1988), 151. See also Schudson, *Origins of the Ideal of Objectivity in the Professions.*

27. "For Better Mail Service," *Editor & Publisher* (February 8, 1919): 32.

28. Ponder, *Managing the Press,* xvi, 81

29. "Specialists Who Win," *Chicago Daily News* (September 12, 1919): 8.

30. Christopher Lasch, *The New Radicalism in America, 1889–1963: The Intellectual as a Social Type* (New York: Norton, 1965), 165.

31. Brian Hooker, "An Opinion of Opinions," *Harper's Magazine* (September 1919): 602.

32. "Never in the history of the sciences have so many departments of research been so crowded with quacks and the incompetents as now . . ." ("Survival of the Unlit among Scientists," *Current Opinion* [July 1918]: 33).

33. Walter Lippmann, "Liberty and the News," *Atlantic Monthly* (December 1919): 781.

34. Hatch, ed., *The Professions in American History,* 7. See also Burton Bledstein, *The Culture of Professionalism: The Middle Class and the Development of Higher Education in America* (New York: Norton, 1976); Thomas Haskell, *The Emergence of Professional Social Science: The American Social Science Association and the Nineteenth-Century Crisis of Authority* (Urbana: Univ. of Illinois Press, 1977); Magali Sarfatti Larson, *The Rise of Professionalism: A Sociological Analysis* (Berkeley: Univ. of California Press, 1977).

35. Lieutenant Coningsby Dawson, "America's Compassion," *Good Housekeeping* (July 1918): 25.

36. See, for example, Edward Purinton, "The New Profession of Office Engineering," *The Independent* (August 16, 1919): 225.

37. Even at the opening of the century, some women sought to elevate working at home to a higher plane, "home economics," in order to satisfy the "sisterhood of brainworkers." Mrs. Burton Harrison, "Home Life as a Profession," *Harper's Bazar* (May 19, 1900): 148.

38. Schudson, *Discovering the News,* 10. Although most scholars see a connection between the importance of science and the rise of professionalization, not everyone agrees. See, for example, Bruce A. Kimball, *The "True Professional Ideal" in America: A History* (Cambridge. Mass.: Blackwell, 1992), 202–203. For more on this debate, see Sheldon Rothblatt, "How 'Professional' Are the Professions? A Review Article," *Comparative Studies in Society and History* 37 (January 1995): 202.

39. Mindich, *Just the Facts,* 113–115; Schudson, *Discovering the News,* 3, 11, 121–134.

40. Journalism historians generally agree that the press freed itself from party control by the turn of the century, yet their confidence in that belief seems lately to be more qualified. Richard L. Kaplan, for example, notes that "newspapers were not removed from the contentious arena of public debate" (Richard L. Kaplan, *Politics and the American Press: The Rise of Objectivity, 1865–1920* [Cambridge: Cambridge Univ. Press, 2002], 7–16). For the view that the press became less political but more corrupt by the twentieth century, see Gerald Baldasty, *The Commercialization of News in the Nineteenth Century* (Madison: Univ. of Wisconsin Press, 1992).

41. On progressive professionalism, see Wiebe, *The Search for Order*; Samuel P. Hays, "The Politics of Reform in Municipal Government in the Progressive Era," *Pacific Northwest Quarterly* 55 (October 1964): 157–169; Wayne K. Hobson, "Professionals, Progressives and Bureaucratization: A Reassessment," *The Historian* 39 (1977): 639.

42. "[W]omen reporters swarmed in every newspaper office," Gertrude Atherton recalled (Atherton, "When All Women Are Workers," *Cosmopolitan* [December 1918]: 59).

43. Marzolf, *Civilizing Voices,* 50.

44. Andrew Abbott, "The Order of Professionalization: An Empirical Analysis," *Work and Occupations* 18 (November 1991): 356.

45. Dorothy Ross, *The Origins of American Social Science* (Cambridge: Cambridge Univ. Press, 1991), 158–162.

46. Edwin Emery and Henry Ladd Smith, *The Press and America* (New York: Prentice-Hall, 1954), 736–737.

47. Quoted in "Gives Northcliffe Chief Rank as Real Ruler of England," *Editor & Publisher* (January 4, 1919): 9.

48. Mott, *American Journalism,* 405–406; 488–489.

49. Charles Moreau Harger, "Journalism as a Career," *Atlantic Monthly* (February 1911): 219.

50. Resistance to college-educated reporters certainly did not end at the time of World War I. And many people still noticed a large degree of "cynicism" directed toward graduates of journalism schools. See, for example, the editorial in *The Dial* (September 20, 1919): 258.

51. "'Journalism Is Not a Restful Profession,' But—" *Literary Digest* (July 31, 1920): 55.

52. "The Difference between 'Professions' and 'Trades,'" *Literary Digest* (May 17, 1919): 127.

53. Charles Moreau Harger, "Journalism as a Career," *Atlantic Monthly* (February 1911): 221. Scholars over the last two decades have begun emphasizing the monetary incentives behind professionalization. See, for example, Frank Stricker, "American Professors in the Progressive Era: Incomes, Aspirations, and Professionalism," *Journal of Interdisciplinary History* 19 (autumn 1988): 231.

54. Wilson, *The Labor of Words,* 31.

55. The development of these organizations in this way is the implication of Donald A. Ritchie, *Press Gallery: Congress and the Washington Correspondents* (Cambridge, Mass.: Harvard Univ. Press, 1991), 113–114, 126, 127–130, 143.

56. Mott, *American Journalism,* 604.

57. American attendance there was modest but "regular." Ulf Jonas Bjork, "The First International Journalism Organization Debates News Copyright, 1894–1898," *Journalism History* 22 (summer 1996): 57.

58. "Decide on Congress of World's Press," *Editor & Publisher* (January 4, 1919): 20. The meeting never took place, however.

59. See, for example, "Newspapers of Britain and United States Stand Together for Press Freedom," *Editor & Publisher* (January 25, 1919): 7.

60. "Should Reporters Be Licensed?" *Editor & Publisher* (October 16, 1915): 476.

61. "Licenses for Journalists," *Literary Digest* (April 7, 1917): 1022.

62. "Press Galleries Ban Publicity Men," *Editor & Publisher* (November 27, 1919): 8. Will Irwin thought the campaign by respectable publishers to counter their influence was sure to succeed (Irwin, "The Press Agent, His Rise and Decline," *Collier's* [December 2, 1911]: 24).

63. "News Pirating Forbidden by Highest Court," *New York Tribune* (December 24, 1918): 1. See also Mott, *American Journalism,* 711.

64. Victor S. Yarros, "A Neglected Opportunity and Duty in Journalism," *American Journal of Sociology* 22 (September 1916): 205, 206, 211.

65. "A Free Press and Freer Pressmen," *Advocate of Peace* (August 1919): 243.

66. Marzolf, *Civilizing Voices,* 72.

67. Press Conference, March 22, 1913. Robert C. Hilderbrand, ed., "The Complete Press

Conferences, 1913," in *Papers of Woodrow Wilson,* edited by Arthur S. Link, vol. 50 (Princeton: Princeton Univ. Press, 1985), 5.

68. Ponder, *Managing the Press,* 83. My treatment of the connection between the conferences and journalists' professional ambitions builds upon Ponder's.

69. Oswald Garrison Villard, "Press Tendencies and Dangers," *Atlantic Monthly* (January 1918): 66.

70. Walter Lippmann, "Liberty and the News," *Atlantic Monthly* (December 1919): 781–784.

CHAPTER 5. WOODROW WILSON AND THE PRESS

1. "With all due deference to Mr. Wilson we must affirm that neither he nor anyone else in America has yet attempted to set forth a definite program showing what has to be accomplished before the world is fit to live in again" (Editorial, "Coming Out of the Clouds," *Metropolitan Magazine* [December 1917]: 3).

2. See sample of criticisms in "Resentment Over the Treatment of General Leonard Wood," *Current Opinion* (July 1918): 3–4.

3. See, for example, "Unpardonable Unpreparedness," *Leslie's* (January 5, 1918): 5; Theodore Roosevelt, "Speed Up the War," *Leslie's* (February 2, 1918): 156; C. W. Gilbert, "Washington's Dismal Failure," *Leslie's* (February 2, 1918): 160; "Begin at the Top, Mr. President," *Metropolitan Magazine* (February 1918): 3. The last editorial complained that "[w]ithin nine months Mr. Baker has not put a single American division on the firing line," without pointing out the fact that American troops had to cross the Atlantic Ocean first.

4. "President Wilson has assumed a grave responsibility in attempting to prevent investigations by the Senate Committee on Military Affairs of the activities of the War Department in relation to aircraft and ordnance production and the Quartermaster General's supplies" (quoted in "The People's Right to Know," *The Independent* [May 25, 1918]: 310). Thomas F. Logan, "Watching the Nation's Business," *Leslie's* (February 9, 1918): 207.

5. Weisberger, *The American Newspaperman,* 163. See also Seward W. Livermore, *Politics Is Adjourned: Woodrow Wilson and the War Congress, 1916–1918* (Middletown, Conn.: Wesleyan Univ. Press, 1966); Ralph Stone, *The Irreconcilables: The Fight Against the League of Nations* (Lexington: Univ. of Kentucky Press, 1970); William C. Widenor, *Henry Cabot Lodge and the Search for an American Foreign Policy* (Berkeley: Univ. of California Press, 1980).

6. "Congress and the press must be free to criticize the Government without being charged with lack of patriotism" ("Constructive Criticism," *Leslie's* [May 4, 1918]: 606).

7. Horace C. Peterson and Gilbert C. Fite, *Opponents of War, 1917–1918* (Madison: Univ. of Wisconsin Press, 1957), 94.

8. Charlton Bates Strayer, "Making a Fatal Mistake," *Leslie's* (June 29, 1918): 917.

9. Among liberal journals, the *Chicago Tribune* had a reputation for being "reactionary and incurably nationalistic" (*The Dial* [February 8, 1919]: 130).

10. "His greatest mistake has been in the selection of his advisers" ("We Must Win the War," *Leslie's* [February 9, 1918]: 186). "With what joy could the country now regard the removal of Mr. Baker to a quieter and more contemplative sphere" (Editorial, "Begin at the Top, Mr. President," *Metropolitan Magazine* [February 1918]: 3).

11. "At Last!" *Leslie's* (April 37, 1918): 570.

12. "For God's Sake Hurry Up!" *Leslie's* (May 11, 1918): 641.

13. "No Peace Talk at Washington," *Collier's* (March 30, 1918): 10.

14. "The War-Making President," *Collier's* (October 19, 1918): 16.

15. The *Collier's* correspondent heard the quoted phrase from a group of British journalists who seemed particularly impressed with the American president. This disparity between Wilson's foreign admirers and domestic detractors proved frustrating for many of the president's supporters. One observer wondered, for instance: "Why should all that is generous and statesmanlike come from the other side of the ocean . . . , and all that is pettifogging come from ours?" (quoted in *Advocate of Peace* [May 1918]: 141).

16. "Blasting Germany's Hopes for Secret Diplomacy," *Current Opinion* (January 1918): 4.

17. "With Sane Vision and Patriotic Purpose Newspaper Makers Greet New Era," *Editor & Publisher* (November 16, 1918): 6.

18. John A. Sleicher, "Put Business Push Behind the President," *Leslie's* (February 26, 1918): 250.

19. "With Such a Spirit," *McClure's* (March 1918): 5.

20. See *Brooklyn Eagle* cartoon of "Pessimism" in "Internment Camp for Traitors," printed in *Literary Digest* (June 29, 1918): 19. An example of the general approval Wilson received can be seen in the following excerpt from a *Sunset* editorial: "We believe that, considering the magnitude of the operations, the mistakes in carrying out the various activities of the government have been relatively few in number and insignificant in consequences" ("Prying the War Lid Off," *Sunset* [February 1918]: 5).

21. "Stevenson," *The World Tomorrow* (August 1918): 185.

22. Indicative of reporters' esteem, they bestowed that ultimate of journalistic honors, "a bit of doggerel all his own," printed in 1920 in "The Honorable Joseph Tumulty, Human Buffer for the President," *Literary Digest* (January 17, 1920): 71.

> Who's got to listen to the bores
> Who ooze in through the White House doors,
> And hear all of the kicks and roars?
> Tumulty.
> Who's got to open all the mail
> And answer letters without fail,
> And send regrets out by the bale?
> Tumulty.
> Who's always got to be polite
> From early morn till late at night,
> And never lose his temper quite?
> Tumulty.
> Who's got to read the proofs on all
> Of Woodrow's speeches, great and small,
> And bear the brunt of every squall?
> Tumulty.

23. Hilderbrand, *Power and the People*, 104.

24. Ibid., 72.

25. Quoted in "Joe Tumulty Pulls the Strings," *Current Opinion* (April 1913): n.p.

26. Tumulty was often the only person in the entire administration to be charitably treated by Republican or otherwise-critical magazines and newspapers. "With the exception of Mr. Tumulty, [Wilson] seems to have no one in his confidence who will give him advice that is at once intel-

ligent and candid" ("The Plight of the Democratic Party—and Its Causes," *Collier's* [December 7, 1918]: 16).

27. Creel, *The War, the World and Wilson,* 29.

28. Ibid., 35–36.

29. "Are We to Have a 'Reptile Press'?" *North American Review* (January 1919): 11. This claim seems highly unlikely, but even if exaggerated it indicates the scarcity of Wilson's press meetings.

30. "Tributes Paid to George Creel on Retirement," *Editor & Publisher* (December 7, 1918): 34.

31. "Mr. George Creel Tells How Our Publicity Offensive Ended the War," *Literary Digest* (February 8, 1919): 58.

32. Will Durant, "The War within the War," *The Dial* (June 20, 1918): 7.

33. "The Right to Know," *The Liberator* (January 1919): 5. This, despite the fact that Creel had spoken in favor of the *Masses* issue that had supposedly violated the Espionage Act a year earlier.

34. Mock and Larson, *Words That Won the War,* 61; Murphy, *World War I and the Origin of Civil Liberties in the United States,* 112–113.

35. *The Nation* (April 18, 1918): 2.

36. See, for example, Donald Wilhelm, "Our Uncensorious Censor," *The Independent* (January 5, 1918): 20. Wilhelm quoted Creel's commitment to freedom of speech: "'We do not need less criticism in time of war, but more.'"

37. "Creel: An Announcement," *Everybody's Magazine* (January 1919): 25.

38. Irwin, *The Making of a Reporter,* 352.

39. See Mock and Larson, *Words That Won the War,* 60–62, and George Creel, "The 'Lash' of Public Opinion," *Collier's* (November 22, 1924): 20.

40. Robert Herrick, "The Paper War," *The Dial* (February 8, 1919): 114.

41. "Charge Plan to Censor News of Great Peace Conference," *Editor & Publisher* (November 23, 1918): 33.

42. *The New Republic* (June 22 1918): 217.

43. Norman Angell, "Shall We Fail Through Lack of Freedom?" *The World Tomorrow* (January 1919): 6.

44. Della Prescott, "A Useful Foreign Language Press," letter, *The New Republic* (May 4, 1918): 21.

45. "To Kill or Use OUT German Press?" *Literary Digest* (May 11, 1918): 12.

46. *The Nation* (January 3, 1918): 7.

47. Gompers, according to the essay, was "a salesman on a drummers rounds. . . . When Mr. Gompers drops the sample case and mounts the tripod . . . the public will get from him at his best merely the kind of information that a sturdy partisan drummer, traveling continually in an atmosphere of sheer bagmanism, is able to furnish; and with all that the public can do nothing" ("The One Thing Needful," *The Nation* [September 14, 1918]: 283).

48. "'The Nation' and the Post Office," *The Nation* (September 28, 1918): 336.

49. *The New Republic* (September 21, 1918): 210.

50. *The New Republic* (September 28, 1918): 240.

51. *The Nation* (May 11, 1918): 558.

52. Wythe Williams, the *New York Times* correspondent in Paris, made the same point in an article reprinted in syndication. The English, in particular, he said, were more intelligent, sophisticated, and sympathetic censors. They were "awake to the value of publicity," and gave the

reporters more credit for common sense and patriotism (Williams, "The Sins of the Censor: An Open Letter to Americans," *Collier's* [January 12, 1918]: 6).

53. Wythe Williams, "The Sins of the Censor: An Open Letter to Americans," *Collier's* (January 12, 1918): 6.

54. "Press Holds Peace League's Fate in Its Hands, Says Palmer," *Editor & Publisher* (March 1, 1919): 10.

55. George Creel, "The American Newspaper: What It Is and What It Isn't," *Everybody's Magazine* [April 1919]: 41–42.

56. Norman Hapgood, "Enlightened Conservatism," *Leslie's* (September 14, 1918): 348.

57. "Personality and Patriotism," *North American Review* (June 1919): 733.

58. Peterson and Fite, *Opponents of War,* 94.

59. Alexis J. Anderson, "The Formative Period of First Amendment Theory, 1870–1915," *American Journal of Legal History* 24 (January 1980): 58.

60. Murphy, *World War I and the Origin of Civil Liberties in the United States,* 70.

61. "We were a mixed group of professional men—lawyers, doctors, clergymen, journalists, and one eminent artist" (L. P. Jacks, "The Common Foe," *Atlantic Monthly* [July 1918]: 148).

62. "But in England 'press men,' as they are called, are patronized by their inferiors" (Charles Grasty, "British and American Newspapers." *Atlantic Monthly* [November 1919]: 579).

63. James Thomson, publisher of the *New Orleans Item,* declared that the "American press has never before attained such greatness in service and influence as has come to it in this war" (quoted in "With Sane Vision and Patriotic Purpose Newspaper Makers Greet New Era," *Editor & Publisher* [November 16, 1918]: 5). Journalism's influence was also touted in Great Britain; see, for example, Harold Cox, *The Edinburgh Review,* printed in *The Living Age* (July 13, 1918): 65.

64. "The Press an Essential Industry," *Leslie's* (October 5, 1918): 438.

65. "The role played by men of academic proclivities and of actual profession has been one of the minor surprises of the war . . ." (quoted in Gordon Hall Gerould, "The Professor and the Wide, Wide World," *Snibner's* [April 1919]: 465). See also Paul van Dyke, "The College Man in Action," *Scribner's* (May 1919): 560.

66. For a representative advocate of this philosophy, see Edward Earle Purinton, "Professions on a Business Basis," *The Independent* (January 19, 1918): 109.

67. Andrew Abbott, *The System of Professions,* 225.

CHAPTER 6. "THE GREAT ADVENTURE"

1. Page stepped down in January 1919 and died shortly thereafter. See tributes in *The World's Work* (February 1919): 372, 375.

2. E. J. Kahn Jr., *The World of Swope* (New York: Simon and Schuster, 1965), 215–216.

3. Forcey, *The Crossroads of Liberalism,* 288.

4. William Allen White to George Creel, November 13, 1918, William Allen White Papers (hereafter referred to as White Papers), Library of Congress, Washington, D.C.

5. White to Henry Cabot Lodge, 1918, White Papers.

6. Mark Sullivan to White, November 16, 1918, White Papers.

7. White to Sullivan, November 21, 1918, White Papers.

8. Cable to World, November 21, 1918, White Papers.

9. White to John S. Phillips, November 23, 1918, White Papers.

10. Medill McCormick to White, November 27, 1918, White Papers.

11. White to McCormick, December 2, 1918, White Papers.

12. One writer noted that "many correspondents were eager to go" and that there was "much speculation" as to who would be able to do so ("Creel Announces Abolition of News Censorship," *Editor & Publisher* [November 16, 1918]: 10).

13. Edna Ferber to White, 1918, White Papers.

14. Charles F. Lummis to McClure, October 1, 1918, Samuel S. McClure Papers (hereafter referred to as McClure Papers), Lilly Library, Bloomington, Indiana.

15. Edward Bellamy Partridge, "La Guerre est Finie!" *Sunset* (March 1919): 30.

16. "News Sends Stars to Conference," *Editor & Publisher* (December 28, 1918): 26.

17. "A Staff of Stars," advertisement, *Editor & Publisher* (January 18, 1919): 33.

18. "Who Is America's Greatest Reporter?" *Chicago Daily News* (December 26, 1919): 1.

19. Ishbel Ross, *Ladies of the Press: The Story of Women in Journalism by an Insider* (New York: Harper and Brothers, 1936), 449, 20. Birkhead was luckily on board the *Carpathia* in 1912 when it rescued survivors of the less-lucky *Titanic*.

20. George Creel, "Makers of Opinion," *Collier's* (May 15, 1920): 42.

21. "World's Correspondent Defied German War Orders," *Editor & Publisher* (October 23, 1919): 38.

22. "Frazier Hunt, Better Known as 'Spike,' Often Jumps But Is Never Pushed," *Editor & Publisher* (November 6, 1919): 7. Hunt traveled to Russia as a correspondent for *Red Cross Magazine*.

23. "News Sends Stars to Conference," *Editor & Publisher* (December 28, 1918): 26.

24. Atherton's film connection and philosophy were discussed further in "Mrs. Atherton and the Movies," *New York Tribune* (August 31, 1919): section VII, page 10.

25. W. E. B. Du Bois to Robert Lansing, November 27, 1918, W. E. B. Du Bois Papers (hereafter referred to as Du Bois Papers), Library of Congress, Washington, D.C.

26. The latest research attests to this interpretation. See the exchange between Mark Ellis, "'Closing Ranks' and 'Seeking Honors': W. E. B. Du Bois in World War I," *Journal of American History* 79 (June 1992): 96–124; and William Jordan, "'The Damnable Dilemma': African-American Accommodation and Protest during World War I," *Journal of American History* 81 (March 1995): 1562–1583.

27. *Advocate of Peace* (December 1918): 330.

28. "To Live in France," *Good Housekeeping* (August 1918): n.p.

29. "The Peace Table," *Leslie's* (November 30, 1918): 676.

30. Edward Price Bell to Charles Dennis, November 5, 1918, Edward Price Bell Papers ((hereafter referred to as Bell Papers), Newberry Library, Chicago, Illinois.

31. "President Again Assures of Unrestrained Conference News," *Editor & Publisher* (December 7, 1918): 11.

32. *Chicago Daily News* (December 5, 1918): 1.

33. "Wilson Peace Ship Now 450 Miles at Sea," *New York Tribune* (December 6, 1918): 1.

34. Simeon Strunsky, "Voyage Sentimentale," *Atlantic Monthly* (March 1919): 328.

35. McClure Diary, December 1, 1918, McClure Papers.

36. Simeon Strunsky, "Voyage Sentimentale," *Atlantic Monthly* (March 1919): 327.

37. A. D. Call, "Paris as Hostess," *Advocate of Peace* (March 1919): 71.

38. "Letter from Dr. Du Bois," written December 8, 1918, published in *The Crisis* (February 1919): 163.

39. Kahn, *The World of Swope,* 213.

40. *New York Tribune* (December 2, 1918): 2. The *Tribune* writer called the 350 "newspaper correspondents, photographers and motion picture men . . . only part of the host of writers who have obtained passports." See also *Advocate of Peace* (January 1919): 9; Mott, *American Journalism,* 699; and Juergens, *News from the White House,* 209.

41. The group included representatives from the following forty organizations: *Advocate of Peace,* Associated Press, *Baltimore Sun, Boston Post,* Central News of America, *Charleston Gazette* (W. Va.), *Charleston Mail* (W. Va.), *Chicago Tribune, Cincinnati Times-Star, The Crisis, Danville News* (Ill.), *The Day* (N.Y.), The Forum and Wildman News Service, Harris Ewing Photo News Service, *Hartford Courant,* International Film Service, *Jewish Daily Forward,* Kansas-Oklahoma Press Syndicate and *Guthrie Leader* (Okla.), *Leslie's Weekly,* McClure Newspaper Syndicate, *New York Age,* New York American Syndicate, *New York Call, New York Evening Post, New York Republican* and Cooperative News Syndicate*, New York Sun, New York Times, New York World, Norfolk Virginian Pilot, Ohio State Journal,* Pathe News, *Peoria Star* (Ill.), *Le Petit Parisien, Philadelphia Evening Ledger, La Prensa* (Buenos Aires), *St. Louis Times,* Underwood and Underwood Photo News Service, Universal News Service, *Washington Herald,* and the *Washington Star.* Listed in *Advocate of Peace* (January 1919): 9.

42. At least three journalists sailed on board the *George Washington*: Robert Bender of United Press, John E. Nevin of International News Service, and L. C. Probert of the Associated Press. "Newspaper Men Will Go Abroad on President Wilson's Own Ship," *Editor & Publisher* (November 30, 1918): 22.

43. A. D. Call, "The Paris Peace Conference," *Advocate of Peace* (February 1919): 40.

44. Simeon Strunsky, "Voyage Sentimentale," *Atlantic Monthly* (March 1919): 322.

45. Ibid., 323, 327.

46. A. D. Call, "The Paris Peace Conference," *Advocate of Peace* (February 1919): 9.

47. Simeon Strunsky, "Voyage Sentimentale," *Atlantic Monthly* (March 1919): 324.

48. "Letter from Dr. Du Bois," written December 8, 1918, published in *The Crisis* (February 1919): 163.

49. E. M. Hood to Sophie Hood, December 14, 1918, Edwin M. Hood Papers (hereafter referred to as Hood Papers), Library of Congress, Washington, D.C.

50. The last of which ended "in a 'battle royal' between six colored boys, which aroused great enthusiasm among some and, notwithstanding its sponsorship by the popular director of the Y. M. C. A., disgust among others" (A. D. Call, "The Paris Peace Conference," *Advocate of Peace* [February 1919]: 9).

51. E. M. Hood to Sophie Hood, December 3, 1918, Hood Papers.

52. Ibid. Du Bois was quite proud of his tutorial services: "There are fifty-two correspondents aboard, and both Moton and I have lectured them!" ("Letter from Dr. Du Bois," written December 8, 1918, published in *The Crisis* [February 1919]: 163). "The views of Professor Dubois [*sic*] relative to the laboring classes generally and to the African colonies in particular were so interesting that a summary of them appears elsewhere in the columns of the *Advocate of Peace*" (A. D. Call, "The Paris Peace Conference," *Advocate of Peace* [February 1919]: 10).

53. McClure Diary, December 8, 1918, McClure Papers.

54. Simeon Strunsky, "Voyage Sentimentale," *Atlantic Monthly* (March 1919): 323–324.

55. E. M. Hood to Sophie Hood, December 3, 1918, Hood Papers. Also see Hood Diary entry, June 20, 1919, a recap of the previous half-year in which he mentions the many "newspaper notables" he had met on the *Orizaba.*

56. A. D. Call, "The Paris Peace Conference," *Advocate of Peace* (February 1919): 9.

57. E. M. Hood to Sophie Hood, December 7, 1918, Hood Papers.

58. Howard Wheeler, *Everbody's Magazine* (March 1919): 58. Publication of Wheeler's correspondence came, according to the editor, three months after it was written.

59. Ibid.

60. Charles Hanson Towne, "Getting Us Over," *McClure's Magazine* (December 1918): 16, 46.

61. "Peace Reporters Ready for Big Story," *Editor & Publisher* (December 14, 1918): 30.

62. "We all left Brest with a feeling of obligation and gratitude for the many courtesies of the Army and Navy" (A. D. Call, "The Paris Peace Conference," *Advocate of Peace* [February 1919]: 40).

63. "Letter from Dr. Du Bois," written December 8, 1918, published in *The Crisis* (February 1919): 164.

64. Diary, n.d., Hood Papers.

65. "Letter from Dr. Du Bois," written December 8, 1918, published in *The Crisis* (February 1919): 164.

66. E. M. Hood to Sophie Hood, December 11, 1918, Hood Papers.

67. Ibid., December 12, 1918.

68. Ibid., December 9, 1918.

69. "And it is. It serves a real purpose. It is a fine place for an endless number of other official autographs when he reaches Paris" (A. D. Call, "Paris as Hostess," *Advocate of Peace* [March 1919]: 71).

70. Quoted in *Chicago Daily News* (January 24, 1919): 2.

71. Howard Wheeler, *Everbody's Magazine* (March 1919): 59.

72. Ibid.

73. Ibid.

74. "America in Europe," *New York Tribune* (December 14, 1918): 10.

75. Wythe Williams, "Welcome to Wilson Outglows Pomp of Napoleonic Days," *New York Tribune* (December 16, 1918): 2.

76. E. M. Hood to Sophie Hood, December 22, 1918, Hood Papers.

77. Ibid., December 26, 1918.

78. Ibid.

79. Ibid., December 28, 1918.

80. Ibid.

81. Ibid.

82. Diary, [1918], Hood Papers.

83. E. M. Hood to Sophie Hood, December 31, 1918, Hood Papers.

84. Ibid., January 7, 1919.

85. Kahn, *The World of Swope,* 217.

86. Mark Sullivan, "Crystallizing the League-of-Nations Idea," *Collier's* (February 1, 1919): 5.

87. A. D. Call, "The Paris Peace Conference," *Advocate of Peace* (February 1919): 40.

88. E. M. Hood to Sophie Hood, February 9, February 23, 1919, Hood Papers. Also see Harry Hansen, *The Adventures of the Fourteen Points* (New York: Century, 1919), 24.

89. E. M. Hood to Sophie Hood, February 9, 1919, Hood Papers.

90. Ibid.

91. Crunden, *Ministers of Reform,* 253. Rather less aptly, Crunden uses the word "Versailles" instead of Paris, even though from the people and illnesses he proceeds to describe he must mean the latter. Ibid., 253–254.

92. A. D. Call, "Paris as Hostess," *Advocate of Peace* (March 1919): 71.

93. "Letter from Dr. Du Bois," written December 8, 1918, published in *The Crisis* (February 1919): 14; Samuel G. Blythe, "The Peace Machine," *Saturday Evening Post* (February 15, 1919): 4.

94. S. S. McClure to Hattie McClure, January 9, 1919, McClure Papers. Also see Herbert Corey letter, December 25, 1918, Herbert Corey Papers (hereafter referred to as Corey Papers), Library of Congress, Washington, D.C.; and David Lawrence, *The True Story of Woodrow Wilson* (New York: Doran, 1924), 263.

95. S. S. McClure to Hattie McClure, January 11, 1919, McClure Papers. Tasty potables were not easy to come by either. "We drank some medicinal black liquid into which we were permitted to drop some little tablets called 'saccharine' but which tasted more like quinine, a liquid called here by the deceptive name of 'café' and which cost us one franc for a cup" (A. D. Call, "The Paris Peace Conference," *Advocate of Peace* [February 1919]: 40).

96. A. D. Call, "Paris as Hostess," *Advocate of Peace* (March 1919): 71.

97. Arthur B. Krock, *Memoirs* (New York: Popular Library, 1968), 51.

98. Ernest Hamlin Abbott, "Have the Germans Won the War?" *The Outlook* (January 15, 1919): 100.

99. William Allen White, "What Happened to Prinkipo," *Metropolitan Magazine* (December 1919): 67; William Allen White, *The Autobiography of William Allen White* (New York: Macmillan, 1946), 553.

100. Hansen, *The Adventures of the Fourteen Points*, 4, 183.

101. Harry Hansen, "World Reshaped by People, Not Princes," *Chicago Daily News* (January 11, 1919): 2.

102. Quoted by Harry Hansen, *Chicago Daily News* (January 24, 1919): 2.

103. M. K. Wisehart, "When Paris Is Paris," *Leslie's* (July 26,1919): 140. The estimation of journalists comes from "Publicity and the Peace Conference," *The New Statesman* (January 18, 1919): 315.

104. Edward Bellamy Partridge, "La Guerre est Finie!" *Sunset* (March 1919): 32.

105. Samuel G. Blythe, "The Peace Machine," *Saturday Evening Post* (February 15, 1919): 3.

106. Irwin, *The Making of a Reporter*, 364.

107. Alfred M. Brace, "'Seeing Paris,' With the Y.M.C.A.," *New York Tribune* (March 22, 1919): 12.

108. Hansen, *The Adventures of the Fourteen Points*, 20.

109. "Letter from Dr. Du Bois," written December 8, 1918, published in *The Crisis* (February 1919): 164. "Paris with its soul cut to the core, feverish, crowded, nervous, hurried; full of uniforms and mourning bands. . . . Paris has been dreaming a nightmare and though she awakes, the grim terror is upon her—it lies on the sandbags covering monuments, on the closed art treasures of the Louvre" (W. E. B. Du Bois, "In France 1918," *The Crisis* [March 1919]: 216).

110. Marguerite Harrison, *There's Always Tomorrow: The Story of a Checkered Life* (New York: Farrar and Rinehart, 1935), 102.

111. Edward Bellamy Partridge, "La Guerre est Finie!" *Sunset* (March 1919): 32.

112. Krock, *Memoirs*, 51.

113. Irwin, *The Making of a Reporter*, 384.

114. Krock, *Memoirs*, 55.

115. Chester M. Wright, "The Peace Show," *New York Tribune* (March 20, 1919): 12.

116. Hansen, *The Adventures of the Fourteen Points*, 137.

117. "For What?" *The Crisis* (April 1919): 268.

118. S. S. McClure to Hattie McClure, February 25, 1919, McClure Papers.

119. E. M. Hood to Sophie Hood, March 16, 1919, Hood Papers.

120. Ibid.

121. Irwin, *Propaganda and the News,* 206.

122. E. M. Hood to Sophie Hood, February 9, 1919, Hood Papers.

123. Hansen, *The Adventures of the Fourteen Points,* 181.

124. Simeon Strunsky, "Socialist and Bourgeois," *Atlantic Monthly* (May 1918): 705.

125. Patrick Gallagher, *America's Aims and Asia's Aspirations* (New York: Century, 1920), 105.

126. A. D. Call, "On the Wing Between Paris and Brussels," *Advocate of Peace* (May 1919): 144.

127. Lucian Swift Kirtland, "The Press and the Peace Conference," *Leslie's* (April 12, 1919): 522.

128. H. Wilson Harris, *The Peace in the Making* (New York: Dutton, 1920): 7.

129. Ibid.

130. A. D. Call, "Paris as Hostess," *Advocate of Peace* (March 1919): 71.

131. A. D. Call, "America and France," *Advocate of Peace* (April 1919): 107.

132. George Bernard Noble, *Policies and Opinions at Paris, 1919: Wilsonian Diplomacy, the Versailles Peace, and French Public Opinion* (New York: Macmillan, 1935), 84; Michel Launay, *Versailles, Une Paix Baclée? Le XXème Siècle Est Mal Parti* (Bruxelles: Editions Complexe, 1981), 85–86. Noble points out that right-wing French journals "suddenly" produced American correspondents out of thin air.

133. John Foster Bass, *The Peace Tangle* (New York: Macmillan, 1920), 131–132.

134. Lawrence, *The True Story of Woodrow Wilson,* 260.

135. White to John S. Phillips, November 23, 1918, White Papers.

136. White to Sallie Lindsay White, February 9, 1919, in *Selected Letters of William Allen White, 1899–1943* ed. Walter Johnson (New York: Holt, 1947), 197.

CHAPTER 7. "THE AMERICAN NEWSPAPER MEN . . . WENT BOLSHEVIK"

1. Lawrence, *The True Story of Woodrow Wilson,* 254.

2. David Lloyd George, *The Truth about the Peace Treaties* (London: Victor Gollancz, 1938), 215. Lloyd George's account was published the following year in America under the title *Memoirs of the Peace Conference* (2 vols., New Haven, Conn.: Yale Univ. Press, 1939).

3. "Surprised by Appointment of Ray Stannard Baker," *Editor & Publisher* (January 18, 1919): 6. Also see "Ray Stannard Baker as a Peace News Mentor, Not to Displace Creel," *New York Tribune* (January 16, 1919): 2; and Juergens, *News from the White House,* 220.

4. Ray Stannard Baker, *Woodrow Wilson and World Sentiment,* vol. 1 (Garden City, N.Y.: Doubleday, Page, 1922), 139.

5. Arthur M. Evans, "Secrecy Gag Put on All Peace Envoys," *Chicago Tribune* (January 16, 1919): 1.

6. Mark Sullivan, "Back to Truth," *Collier's* (April 26, 1919): 6.

7. *New York Tribune* (January 16, 1919): 1.

8. Richard Oulahan, "Adopt Secrecy for Peace Conclave," *New York Times* (January 16, 1919): 1.

9. *London Times* (January 16, 1919): 9.

10. Ibid. (January 17, 1919): 9.

11. Ibid.: 9–10.

12. Richard Oulahan, "Adopt Secrecy for Peace Conclave," *New York Times* (January 16, 1919): 1.

13. Mark Sullivan, "What Has Wilson Accomplished?" *Collier's* (March 1, 1919): 5.

14. Joseph Tumulty to Admiral Cary Grayson, January 16, 1919; Woodrow Wilson to Joseph Tumulty, January 16, 1919, in *The Papers of Woodrow Wilson,* ed. Arthur S. Link, vol. 54 (Princeton: Princeton Univ. Press, 1986), 105.

15. Ibid.

16. Harold Nicolson, *Peacemaking 1919* (Boston: Houghton Mifflin, 1933; reprint, New York: Grosset and Dunlap, The Universal Library, 1965), 3, 18.

17. Richard Oulahan, "Look to Wilson to End Secrecy," *New York Times* (January 17, 1919): 2.

18. Baker, *Woodrow Wilson and World Settlement,* 1:138.

19. Ibid., 1:116.

20. "Admit Press Representatives to Peace Conference," *Editor & Publisher* (January 25, 1919): 5.

21. Ibid.

22. Mark Sullivan, "Back to Truth," *Collier's* (April 26, 1919): 6. Henry Wood wrote that "reporters received a shock when they found that they could not have everything the way they anticipated" (quoted in "Close Intimacy of Press and World Rulers Planned by French Government," *Editor & Publisher* [March 15, 1919]: 8).

23. William Allen White, "Journalists' Revolt Helped Wilson Win," *Chicago Daily News* (March 8, 1919): 6.

24. Cited in Baker, *Woodrow Wilson and World Settlement,* 1:141.

25. Maurice Hankey's Meeting Notes, Council of Ten (January 15, 1919), in U.S. Department of State, *Papers Relating to the Foreign Relations of the United States, 1919,* vol. 3 (Washington, D.C.: U.S. Department of State, 1943), 552; ibid. (January 16, 1919), 580.

26. Ibid. (January 15, 1919), 563; (January 17, 1919), 597.

27. Richard Oulahan, "Press Demands Made on Council," *New York Times* (January 18, 1919): 1. See also "Newspapers of Britain and United States Stand Together for Press Freedom," *Editor & Publisher* (January 25, 1919): 7–9.

28. "Newspapers of Britain and United States Stand Together for Press Freedom," *Editor & Publisher* (January 25, 1919): 2.

29. "Statement of Peace Conference on Publicity, January 17, 1919," cited in Baker, *Woodrow Wilson and World Settlement,* 3:47. Tardieu's analogy was much bandied about by the press ("'Marriage Contract Between Journalists and the Peace Conference' at Paris," printed in *Editor & Publisher* [March 1, 1919]: 8).

30. "'Marriage Contract Between Journalists and the Peace Conference' at Paris," printed in *Editor & Publisher* (March 1, 1919): 8.

31. Lloyd George, *The Truth about the Peace Treaties,* 1:218–220.

32. Nicolson, *Peacemaking 1919,* 123.

33. Grew, *Turbulent Era,* 1:366.

34. Ernest Hamlin Abbott, "Peace and Publicity," *The Outlook* (March 12, 1919): 433.

35. Arthur B. Krock, "How U.S. Newspaper Men Lifted Pass Censorship," *Louisville Courier-Journal* (February 7, 1919), 4.

36. "Veil Over the Conference," *London Times* (January 17, 1919): 9.

37. Baker, *Woodrow Wilson and World Settlement,* 1:134–135.

38. "Open Diplomacy," *New York Tribune* (January 17, 1919): 12.

39. George A. Riddell, *Lord Riddell's Intimate Diary of the Peace Conference and After, 1918–1923* (New York: Reynal and Hitchcock, 1934), 21.

40. William Allen White, "Journalists' Revolt Helped Wilson Win," *Chicago Daily News* (March 8, 1919): 6.

41. Baker, *Woodrow Wilson and World Settlement*, 1:155.

42. Noble, *Policies and Opinions at Paris*, 82.

43. "Paris Press Attacks U.S. Papers," *Editor & Publisher* (February 22, 1919): 8.

44. Ernest Hamlin Abbott, "Golden Age or Fool's Paradise?" *The Outlook* (March 19, 1919): 474.

45. David Lawrence, "New Press Rule Is Attacked," *Chicago Daily News* (January 18, 1919): 2. Also see editorial, *The New Republic* (January 25, 1919): 353. Ernest Hamlin Abbott, in an article for *The Outlook*, wrote of his disappointment with Paris news during the first half of January, but by the time he finished describing the publicity controversy of the second half, his assessment seemed considerably more optimistic (Ernest Hamlin Abbott, "Peace and Publicity," *The Outlook* [March 12, 1919]: 433). Toward the end of his correspondence, moreover, Abbott ended on an unequivocally positive note, saying that publicity was won and "settled" before anything else.

46. Frederick Moore, "Wilson's Stand for Secrecy Is Deplored," *New York Tribune* (January 18, 1919): 1, 10.

47. Ibid., 1.

48. Frederick Moore, "U.S. Press Saved Wilson's First Point," *New York Tribune* (January 21, 1919): 1.

49. "Widen Those Archways!" *Collier's* (February 15, 1919): 15.

50. Hansen, *The Adventures of the Fourteen Points*, 36.

51. Irwin, *Propaganda and the News*, 203.

52. Irwin, *The Making of a Reporter*, 123.

53. Ibid., 205.

54. Quoted in "Peace Reporting Hardest Task Ever Before United States Press," *Editor & Publisher* (March 8, 1919): 30.

55. Speaking of conference communiqués and open plenary sessions, Robert Hilderbrand says that "it still seems noteworthy that the Big Four adopted such forms of publicity, which went far beyond those practiced at previous international conferences, only at the prodding of the much-maligned Wilson" (Hilderbrand, *Power and the People*, 177. Hilderbrand appears to be the only historian who notices this fact. An illustration of the conferees inside the Hall of the Clock can be found at http://memory.loc.gov/service/sgp/sgpwar/1919/191912/19191231/0494.pdf. I am indebted to Derik Shelor for bringing it to my attention.

56. A. D. Call, "The Paris Peace Conference," *Advocate of Peace* (February 1919): 40.

57. "Peace Reporting Hardest Task Ever Before United States Press," *Editor & Publisher* (March 8, 1919): 30.

58. Lawrence, *The True Story of Woodrow Wilson*, 254–255.

59. E. M. Hood to Sophie Hood, January 20, 1919, Hood Papers.

60. Simeon Strunsky, "The Peace-Makers," *Atlantic Monthly* (April 1919): 531–532.

61. "Some French Journalists Protest Against 'Favors' to Foreign Correspondents," *Editor & Publisher* (March 1, 1919): 8.

62. Riddell, *Lord Riddell's Intimate Diary of the Peace Conference and After*, 13–14.

63. Wilson declined: "[T]here is no present prospect that I shall be able to write any such sketch" (Wilson to Tumulty, March 3, 1919, in *The Papers of Woodrow Wilson*, ed. Arthur S. Link, vol. 55 (Princeton: Princeton Univ. Press, 1986), 392.

CHAPTER 8. ROUTINES

1. Lucian Swift Kirtland, "The Press and the Peace Conference," *Leslie's* (April 12, 1919): 552.

2. James D. Startt, "The Uneasy Partnership: Wilson and the Press at Paris," *Mid-America* 52 (January 1970): 63. See also Walter Rogers, "Memorandum on Wire and Radio Communication," February 12, 1919, in Baker, *Woodrow Wilson and World Settlement*, 3:427–442.

3. Diary, undated, Hood Papers.

4. E. M. Hood to Sophie Hood, March 16, 1919, Hood Papers; Frazier Hunt, *One American and His Attempt at Education* (New York: Simon and Schuster, 1938), 146.

5. Charles Lincoln, quoted in "Peace Reporting Hardest Task Ever Before United States Press," *Editor & Publisher* (March 8, 1919): 30.

6. Lawrence, *The True Story of Woodrow Wilson*, 264.

7. Ibid., 264–265.

8. Quoted in "Semi-Secret Diplomacy," *The Independent* (February 1, 1919): 140.

9. Frederick Moore, "Wilson's Stand for Secrecy is Deplored," *New York Tribune* (January 18, 1919): 1.

10. Mark Sullivan, "Back to Truth," *Collier's* (April 26, 1919): 6.

11. Gerald Stanley Lee, "Spineless Leagues and Faceless Nations," *Saturday Evening Post* (March 22, 1919): 150.

12. A. D. Call, "The Paris Peace Conference," *Advocate of Peace* (February 1919): 40.

13. Editorial, *Collier's* (February, 22, 1919): 14.

14. "Peace Reporting Hardest Task Ever Before United States Press," *Editor & Publisher* (March 8, 1919): 30.

15. E. M. Hood to Sophie Hood, February 13, 1919, Hood Papers. The work was extremely demanding for diplomats, too. See Harry Hansen, "No Gay Life for Peace Commissioners— Just Work," *Chicago Daily News* (March 17, 1919): 7.

16. E. M. Hood to Sophie Hood, February 13, 1919, Hood Papers.

17. Ernest Hamlin Abbott, "Peace and Publicity," *The Outlook* (March 12, 1919): 433.

18. Krock, *Memoirs*, 57. For more on Swope, see Kahn, *The World of Swope*, 226–228.

19. Reginald Coggeshall, "Paris Peace Conference Sources of News, 1919," *Journalism Quarterly* 17 (March 1940): 1. Based on the numerous personal interviews he conducted and the letters he exchanged with American correspondents who had been there, Coggeshall's account is an invaluable historical record for piecing together press life at the conference.

20. Mark Sullivan, "Back to Truth," *Collier's* (April 26, 1919): 6; also quoted in Coggeshall, "Paris Peace Conference Sources of News, 1919," 7–9.

21. Krock, *Memoirs*, 53, 54.

22. E. M. Hood to Sophie Hood, December 28, 1918, Hood Papers.

23. The higher up the delegate, the more typical, in fact, the confidentiality. In Paris it was a "well established rule that the President of the United States is not to be quoted at first hand by a newspaper correspondent" ("Europe's Ideas of Wilson the Man," *Current Opinion* [January 1919]: 19).

24. Harris, *The Peace in the Making*, 22.

25. E. M. Hood to Sophie Hood, February 9, 1919, Hood Papers.

26. Coggeshall, "Paris Peace Conference Sources of News, 1919," 3.

27. Krock, *Memoirs*, 53.

28. S. S. McClure to Hattie McClure, April 26, 1919, McClure Papers.

29. Emphasis added. Diary, January 1, 1917, Hood Papers.

30. Sally White, who ran her husband's newspaper in his absence, also exercised patronage and did so as often as, and sometimes in cooperation with, William. Her belief in such a system is obvious and best epitomized in a letter of recommendation she wrote to a New Yorker on behalf of a fellow Kansan: "He is filing his application with a letter each from Curtis and Copper, and expects to get one from Justice Johnston, but letters and applications, of course, will count for nothing unless there is some active and capable effort back of them" (Sally White to Colonel John S. Dean, April 4, 1919, White Papers). Both the Whites were like community parents, actively trying to pull strings for their extended family.

31. Lucian Swift Kirtland, "The Press and the Peace Conference," *Leslie's* (April 12, 1919): 553.

32. Coggeshall, "Paris Peace Conference Sources of News, 1919," 6.

33. Krock, *Memoirs,* 55–56.

34. Irwin, *Propaganda and the News,* 205, 206.

35. William Allen White, "What Happened to Prinkipo," *Metropolitan* (December 1919): 29.

36. Harris, *The Peace in the Making,* 13.

37. Hansen, *The Adventures of the Fourteen Points,* 101.

38. "My Mission," *The Crisis* (May 1919): 7.

39. Quoted in "Behind the Scenes with the Cast of the Great Peace Drama," *Literary Digest* (May 17, 1919): 47.

40. "Ivy Lee Discusses Some European Newspaper Conditions," *Editor & Publisher* (May 22, 1919): 146.

41. Lucian Swift Kirtland, "Queer Experiences in Propaganda," *Leslie's* (July 19, 1919): 100.

42. Associated Press, "Peace Parley News Writers Get Many Invitations to Tea," printed in *New York Tribune* (April 16, 1919): 7.

43. Lucian Swift Kirtland, "Queer Experiences in Propaganda," *Leslie's* (July 19, 1919): 100.

44. Ibid., 101.

45. E. M. Hood to Sophie Hood, February 23, 1919, Hood Papers.

46. E. M. Hood to Sophie Hood, January 14, 1919, December 22, 1918, Hood Papers.

47. Lucian Swift Kirtland, "Queer Experiences in Propaganda," *Leslie's* (July 19, 1919): 101.

48. Irwin, *The Making of a Reporter,* 215.

49. Irwin's fight to restore his patriotic credentials did not go quickly: "I had to work for three months on the British and French embassies at Washington before I won the privilege of returning to the war without danger of arrest as a spy!" (Irwin, *Propaganda and the News,* 136).

50. Harrison, *There's Always Tomorrow,* 90.

51. Irwin, *The Making of a Reporter,* 338.

52. Harrison, *There's Always Tomorrow,* 131.

53. Major F. P. Schoonmaker, Memo to Intelligence Officer, January 1, 1919. Du Bois mss., Library of Congress. See also W. E. B. Du Bois, "My Mission," *The Crisis* (May 1918): 8; and W. E. B. Du Bois, "Our Success and Failure," *The Crisis* (July 1919): 127–129.

54. Krock, *Memoirs,* 52–53.

CHAPTER 9. REACTION

1. W. E. B. Du Bois, "My Mission," *The Crisis* (May 1918): 7. Du Bois said he acted discretely before leaving the United States for precisely such an opportunity abroad: "I am not a fool. . . .

I knew perfectly well that any movement to bring the attention of the world to the Negro problem at this crisis would be stopped the moment the Great Powers heard of it."

2. Ibid., 9.

3. Hansen, *The Adventures of the Fourteen Points*, 276; Lawrence, *The True Story of Woodrow Wilson*, 254.

4. A. D. Call, "The Paris Peace Conference," *Advocate of Peace* (February 1919): 41.

5. "Journalism Made Pichon Power in French Politics," *Editor & Publisher* (March 29, 1919): 15.

6. Diary, undated, Hood Papers.

7. E. M. Hood to Gretchen Hood, February 18, 1919, Hood Papers.

8. "As you are—I can say this without flattery—the best journalists of your respective countries, it is impossible for you to declare yourselves satisfied" with the existing supply of news ("Peace Correspondents Dwell in Marble Halls of $2,500,000 Merchant's Palace," *Editor & Publisher* [March 1, 1919]: 7).

9. This list of correspondents included Montague Glass, William Allen White, Frank Simonds, Simeon Strunsky, David Lawrence, William P. Simms, Ed L. Keen, Frazier Hunt, Herbert Bayard Swope, Charles Lincoln, Louis Seibold, Lincoln Eyre, Cyril Brown, and Joseph Grigg.

10. Edward Bellamy Partridge, "On the King's Carpet," *Sunset* (June 1919): 33–34.

11. Paul Scott Mowrer, "Paris 'White House' As Aristocrat Sees It," *Chicago Daily News* (December 12, 1918): 2. Mowrer borrowed the description from *Le Gaulois*.

12. Lucian Swift Kirtland, "France's Great Day," *Leslie's* (August 2, 1919): 171.

13. Hamilton Holt, "The Birth of the League of Nations," *The Independent* (February 15, 1919): 217.

14. Quoted in "Press Holds Peace League's Fate in Its Hands, Says Palmer," *Editor & Publisher* (March 1, 1919): 10.

15. The "experiences of a reporter are the best preparation for any profession. . . . " And "the press . . . is the great centre of the world to-day." Ibid.

16. See, for example, "The Brotherhood for Which Humanity Yearns," and "Blumenfeld Urges Interchange of Men by British and American Papers," in *Editor & Publisher* (May 22, 1919): 6, 7.

17. Walworth, *Wilson and His Peacemakers*, 24.

18. "'Firsts' by The Daily News Peace Correspondence Bureau," *Chicago Daily News* (February 10, 1919): 1.

19. Hansen, *Adventures of the Fourteen Points*, 6.

20. Frazier Hunt, for example: Hunt, *One American and His Attempt at Education*, 126; also see following chapter.

21. "Peace Reporting Hardest Task Ever Before United States Press," *Editor & Publisher* (March 8, 1919): 30.

22. E. M. Hood to Sophie Hood, February 9, 1919, Hood Papers.

23. E. M. Hood to Sophie Hood, February 13, 1919, Hood Papers.

24. Herbert Corey to Mrs. Carrie Corey, [1918], Corey Papers.

25. Herbert Corey to Mrs. Carrie Corey, December 25, 1918, Corey Papers.

26. E. M. Hood to Sophie Hood, February 23, 1919, Hood Papers.

27. Cited by Will Irwin in *The Making of a Reporter*, 235.

28. "Fortunately the New York office knows what I am doing for we sign all of our copy and the signatures go forward too," in a letter from E. M. Hood to Sophie Hood, February 13, 1919, Hood Papers.

29. Berton Braley, "Home," *New York Tribune* (December 1, 1918): III, 3.

30. S. S. McClure to Hattie McClure, January 9, 1919, and May 14, 1919, McClure Papers.

31. E. M. Hood to Sophie Hood, February 13, 1919, Hood Papers.

32. Gerald Stanley Lee, "The Glass-House World," *Saturday Evening Post* (March 8, 1919): 4

33. Herbert Corey to Mrs. Carrie Corey, January 30, 1919, Corey Papers.

34. E. M. Hood to Sophie Hood, February 13, 1919, Hood Papers.

35. E. M. Hood to Sophie Hood, March 16, 1919, Hood Papers.

36. "I wonder how much longer I am to write this address? Somehow the feeling grows that I will soon be relieved and on my way home," ibid.

37. Arthur B. Krock, "Thinks President Should Have Conferred with Reporters," *Editor & Publisher* (April 26, 1919): 19. Based on its regular survey of press opinion, the *Literary Digest* came to the same conclusion ("Every Yankee Reporter in Paris Is a Diplomatic Storm-Center," *Literary Digest* [April 26, 1919]: 80).

38. Arthur B. Krock, "Thinks President Should Have Conferred with Reporters," *Editor & Publisher* (April 26, 1919): 19.

39. "Every Yankee Reporter in Paris Is a Diplomatic Storm-Center," *Literary Digest* (April 26, 1919): 80.

CHAPTER 10. RELATIONSHIPS

1. Irwin, *The Making of a Reporter*, 298.

2. Edward Price Bell to John William Davis, January 16, 1919, Edward Price Bell Papers (hereafter referred to as Bell Papers), Newberry Library, Chicago, Illinois.

3. Bell to Phillip Henry Kerr, January 21, 1919. Bell Papers.

4. Bell to Winston Churchill, January 10, 1919, Bell Papers.

5. Harris, *The Peace in the Making*, 22; Bass, *The Peace Tangle*, 46.

6. Harris, *The Peace in the Making*, 22.

7. Richard Washburn Child, "Under the Peace Table," *Collier's* (May 31, 1919): 6.

8. Ibid., 35.

9. Gallagher, *America's Aims and Asia's Aspirations*, 50.

10. E. M. Hood to Sophie Hood, March 16, 1919, Hood Papers.

11. Hansen, *The Adventures of the Fourteen Points*, 36.

12. George Goldberg, *The Peace to End Peace: The Paris Peace Conference of 1919* (New York: Harcourt, Brace and World, 1969), 157.

13. James T. Shotwell, *At the Paris Peace Conference* (New York: Macmillan, 1937), 126.

14. Bell to Charles Dennis, November 8, 1918, Bell Papers.

15. Georges Clemenceau, "The Appeal of France to the Heart of America," *Current Opinion* (March 1919): 150.

16. Quoted in "The Delusion of Secrecy at the Peace Conference," *Current Opinion* (January 1919): 10.

17. "Lord Reading Praises U.S. Reporters," *Editor & Publisher* (April 26, 1919): 17.

18. Richard Washburn Child, "Under the Peace Table," *Collier's* (May 31, 1919): 6.

19. Walter Lippmann, "The Basic Problem of Democracy," *Atlantic Monthly* (November 1919): 621. Lippmann's view, it should be noted, was manifestly skeptical, however.

20. Gallagher, *America's Aims and Asia's Aspirations*, 53.

21. Nicolson, *Peacemaking 1919*, 124.

22. Ibid., 138.

23. "The Blur That Is Paris," *Advocate of Peace* (May 1919): 135.

24. Lucian Swift Kirtland, "The Press and the Peace Conference," *Leslie's* (April 12, 1919): 552.

25. In this chapter as well as the preceding one, by contrast, I have focused on non-official sources: the records and writings left by journalists—whose nebulous status during the proceedings was often mirrored in the records and writings left by diplomats, who in turn have exerted far greater influence on historians.

26. David Lawrence, "Peace by Publicity," *Scribner's* (June 1919): 703.

27. Ibid., 706.

28. Chester M. Wright, "The Peace Show," *New York Tribune* (March 20, 1919): 12.

29. Richard V. Oulahan, "Capital Corps Praised for Diligence," *Editor & Publisher* (April 25, 1931): 32. The timing was still a little off: "There was delay in the receipt of the official cable at the Navy Department. The result was that my dispatch appeared in print before Franklin D. Roosevelt, Acting Secretary of the Navy, had read in plain decoded English the cabled order of the president. He denied that any such instructions had been received. Joseph P. Tumulty, the secretary to the president, emphasized the denial. But before the day was over the belated official dispatch reached the Navy Department and the denial was recalled." See also Grayson diary, April 7, 1919, cited in *Papers of Woodrow Wilson,* ed. Arthur S. Link, vol. 57 (Princeton: Princeton Univ. Press, 1987), 63.

30. David Lawrence, "Shop Talk at Thirty," *Editor & Publisher* (May 27, 1944): 60.

31. E. M. Hood to Sophie Hood, January 14, 1919, Hood Papers.

32. Gallagher, *America's Aims and Asia's Aspirations,* 221.

33. Chester M. Wright, "The Peace Show," *New York Tribune* (March 20, 1919): 12.

34. Charles Dennis, "U.S. Envoys Alone Do No Explaining," *Chicago Daily News* (February 3, 1919): 1.

35. Tumulty telegram to Wilson, January 14, 1919, in *Papers of Woodrow Wilson,* ed. Arthur S. Link, vol. 54 (Princeton: Princeton Univ. Press, 1987), 57.

36. Frederick Moore, "America Enters Without a League Plan," *New York Tribune* (January 17, 1919): 1.

37. On Lansing's disloyal behavior, see Dimitri D. Lazo, "A Question of Loyalty: Robert Lansing and the Treaty of Versailles," *Diplomatic History 9* (winter 1985): 36.

38. Ibid., 95.

39. Chester M. Wright, "The Peace Show," *New York Tribune* (March 20, 1919): 12.

40. Edward M. House telegrams to Lansing and Wilson, November 23, 1918, in *Papers of Woodrow Wilson,* ed. Arthur S. Link, vol. 53 (Princeton: Princeton Univ. Press, 1986): 180–181; House to Wilson, April 16, 1919, ibid., 57:390–391; Sir William Wiseman to the British Foreign Office, December 15, 1918, ibid., 54:395.

41. Ray Stannard Baker, *American Chronicle: The Autobiography of Ray Stannard Baker* (New York: Charles Scribner's Sons, 1945), 429.

42. Ibid., 196.

43. Bass, *The Peace Tangle,* 56, The correspondent for the *Brooklyn Eagle* also singled out the American mission for its reticence, compared to that of other delegations, like the British, who "speak right out, with quotation marks allowed whenever they have a definite statement to make" (quoted in "Our Delegates in Paris Specialize in Profound Silence," *Literary Digest* [May 10, 1919]: 85).

44. Tumulty's instructions were precise. In December he cabled the following recommendations to Grayson: "If the President visits hospitals have press representatives with him to get human interest story. Do not let his visits be perfunctory. Let him sit beside bed of common soldiers. Keep President in touch with [David] Lawrence, [Louis] Seibold. [Herbert Bayard] Swope, press associations, [Lawrence] Hills and [Clinton] Gilbert. Don't forget movie men" (quoted in Blum, *Joe Tumulty and the Wilson Era,* 171.

45. Baker diary, May 5, 1919, in *Papers of Woodrow Wilson,* ed. Arthur S. Link, vol. 58 (Princeton: Princeton Univ. Press, 1988), 459.

46. Quoted in Walworth, *Wilson and His Peacemakers,* 283.

47. William Allen White, "Journalists' Revolt Helped Wilson Win," *Chicago Daily News* (March 8, 1919): 6.

48. Gallagher, *America's Aims and Asia's Aspirations,* 54. See also "Ivy Lee Discusses Some European Newspaper Conditions," *Editor & Publisher* (May 22, 1919): 146.

49. Gallagher, *America's Aims and Asia's Aspirations,* 54.

50. Cited ibid.

51. Krock, *Memoirs,* 54.

52. Startt, "The Uneasy Partnership," 64.

53. Hansen, *The Adventures of the Fourteen Points,* 366.

54. Gallagher, *America's Aims and Asia's Aspirations,* 333.

55. Edward Bellamy Partridge, "Pressing Forward with the Press," *Sunset* (May 1919): 68.

56. *Chicago Daily News* (February 5, 1919): 1.

57. Lawrence, *The True Story of Woodrow Wilson,* 349.

58. Isaac F. Marcosson, "Adventures in Interviewing Lloyd George," *Saturday Evening Post* (May 31, 1919): 6.

59. Du Bois to Georges Clemenceau, 1919, Du Bois Papers.

60. "Peace Press Club a Great Success," *Editor & Publisher* (June 19, 1919): 28.

61. Hansen, *The Adventures of the Fourteen Points,* 84–85

62. Diary, Dec. [?] 1916, Hood Papers.

63. Elihu Root to Hood, January 14, 1919, Hood Papers.

64. Krock, *Memoirs,* 109.

65. Gallagher, *America's Aims and Asia's Aspirations,* 183.

66. Irwin, *The Making of a Reporter,* 167.

67. Henry Wood, quoted in "Close Intimacy of Press and World Rulers Planned by French Government," *Editor & Publisher* (March 15, 1919): 7.

68. Caption from a photograph by Helen Johns Kirtland, in Lucian Swift Kirtland, "The Greatest Moment in History," *Leslie's* (July 26, 1919): 142.

CHAPTER 11. PARTICIPATION

1. E. M. Hood to Sophie Hood, February 9, 13, 23, 1919, Hood Papers.

2. Charles Homer Haskins and Robert Howard Lord, *Some Problems of the Peace Conference* (Cambridge, Mass.: Harvard Univ. Press, 1920), 22.

3. Bell to John William Davis, January 16, 1919, Bell Papers.

4. Nicolson, *Peacemaking 1919,* 19.

5. Hunt, *One American and His Attempt at Education,* 167–168.

6. Bass, *The Peace Tangle,* 47–48

7. Ibid., 165.

8. Gallagher, *America's Aims and Asia's Aspirations,* 335.

9. Bass, *The Peace Tangle,* 92–93.

10. Ibid., 266.

11. Gallagher, *America's Aims and Asia's Aspirations,* 189.

12. Ibid., 213.

13. Ibid., 336.

14. According to Gallagher, the negligence of Colonel House was to blame for the oversight. "He was, it seems, asleep at the switch" (Gallagher, *America's Aims and Asia's Aspirations,* 346–347).

15. Du Bois had performed similar double duties in 1911 when he attended the "Races' Congress" in London as both a correspondent and a delegate to the conference. See "The Peace Conference," *The Crisis* (January 1919): 112.

16. "'Another Lincoln,'" *Collier's* (April 19, 1919): 16.

17. Ibid.

18. Sally White to Victor Murdock, February 11, 1919, White Papers.

19. Irwin, *The Making of a Reporter,* 365, 376, 379.

20. "John F. Bass Paints Bad Faith of Treaty," *Chicago Daily News* (December 12, 1919): 3.

21. Lawrence, *The True Story of Woodrow Wilson,* 350; Clements, *Woodrow Wilson: World Statesman,* 127.

22. Krock, *Memoirs,* 47.

23. Irwin, *The Making of a Reporter,* 210.

24. Ibid., 362.

25. Harrison, *There's Always Tomorrow,* 85.

26. "President Speaks for Mankind," *Sunset* (February 1919): 5.

27. E. M. Hood to Sophie Hood, February 13, 1919, Hood Papers.

28. Simeon Strunsky, "The Peace-Makers," *Atlantic Monthly* (April 1919): 533.

29. Robert Lansing, *The Peace Negotiations: A Personal Narrative* (Boston: Houghton Mifflin, 1921), 97.

30. Baker Diary, April 25, 1919, in *Papers of Woodrow Wilson,* ed. Arthur S. Link, vol. 58 (Princeton: Princeton Univ. Press, 1988), 142.

31. Ray Stannard Baker, *What Wilson Did at Paris* (Garden City, N.Y. Doubleday, Page, 1919), 66.

32. Lansing, *The Peace Negotiations,* 175.

33. Ibid., 217, 221.

34. David Hunter Miller, *The Drafting of the Covenant,* vol. 1 (New York: G. P. Putnam's Sons, 1928), 112, 135. On French sensitivity to public opinion, Miller quotes a French secretary's notes:

> Après un echange de vues sur cette question, au cours duquel M. Hymans et M. Vesnitch défendent le point de vue de l'adjonction de nouvelles Puissances, M. Bourgeois signale que le réfus d'admettre ces quatre nouveaux membres pourrait causer une impression morale regrettable, tandis que leur admission serait une solution liberale que serait favorablement admise par opinion publique sans qu'elle puisse rétarder sensiblement le travail de la Commission. [After an exchange of views on this question, in the heart of which M. Hymans and M. Vesnitch defended the point of view of the attachment of the new Powers, M. Bourgeois signaled that the refusal to admit these four new

members could cause a regrettable moral impression, while their admission could be a liberal solution that would be favorably accepted by public opinion, without which it could noticeably retard the work of the Commission.] (Quoted ibid., 149.)

35. Minutes, Council of Four Meeting, June 10, 1919, in *Papers of Woodrow Wilson,* ed. Arthur S. Link, vol. 60 (Princeton: Princeton Univ. Press, 1989), 344.

36. Lloyd George, *The Truth about the Peace Treaties,* 1:218.

37. Colonel House, for example, made these comments, both in the same entry: "The biggest concession made to public opinion at home was to set forth in unmistakable language the right of a nation to withdraw from the League. . . ." and "We know that public opinion demands an early peace" (Edward M. House diary, March 22, 1919, in *Papers of Woodrow Wilson,* ed. Arthur S. Link, vol. 56 [Princeton: Princeton Univ. Press, 1987], 284, 291). Lloyd George described how both he and Clemenceau were "specially anxious not to excite public opinion on the question of Reparations," though public opinion in their respective lands was often quite different (Lloyd George, *The Truth about the Peace Treaties,* 1:220).

38. Nicolson, *Peacemaking 1919,* 25.

39. Ibid., 58–60, 78.

40. Mark Sullivan, "Crystallizing the League-of-Nations Idea," *Collier's* (February 1, 1919): 5.

41. "The Larger Peace Conference," *Chicago Daily News* (April 3, 1919): 8.

42. William Howard Taft, quoted in "Let Critics Consider," *Chicago Daily News* (April 5, 1919): 8.

43. Edward Price Bell, "Foes of Secrecy Try to Smoke Out Wilson," *Chicago Daily News* (April 12, 1919): 2.

44. Ibid.

45. *Chicago Daily News* (May 1, 1919): 2.

46. Charles Grasty, "British and American Newspapers," *Atlantic Monthly* (November 1919): 581.

47. Norman Angell, "Quo Vadis?" *The Dial* (May 17, 1919): 488.

48. Walter Rathenau, *Vorwaerts,* reprinted in "Walther Rathenau to Colonel House: A Sentimental Appeal," *The Living Age* (February 8, 1919): 334.

49. "The Great Heritage," *New York Tribune* (April 20, 1919): 2.

50. Vittorio Orlando, "In Reply to Mr. Wilson," Italian Press Bureau, April 24, 1919, reprinted in *The Living Age* (May 31, 1919): 517.

51. "Open Diplomacy at Last," *The New Republic* (May 3, 1919): 4.

52. Gerald Stanley Lee, "The Glass House World," *Saturday Evening Post* (March 8, 1919): 76.

53. Marcosson, "Adventures in Interviewing Lloyd George," *Saturday Evening Post* (May 31, 1919): 6, 7.

54. Juergens, *News from the White House,* 270–271.

55. Quoted in "Press Holds Peace League's Fate in Its Hands, Says Palmer," *Editor & Publisher* (March 1, 1919): 10.

56. Lawrence, *The True Story of Woodrow Wilson,* 344.

57. Gallagher, *America's Aims and Asia's Aspirations,* 276.

58. "Secret Sessions of Peace Conference Are Decreed Over Americans' Protest," *New York Tribune* (January 16, 1919): 1.

59. Gerald Stanley Lee, "Spineless Leagues and Faceless Nations," *Saturday Evening Post* (March 22, 1919): 151.

60. Ibid.

61. "Plenipotentiaries to the People," *The Independent* (February 22, 1919): 243.

62. "Will 'Flash' Treaty to the World," *Editor & Publisher* (May 1, 1919): 37.

63. "Summary of Peace Treaty Longest Release by Telegraph or Cable in History," *Editor & Publisher* (May 15, 1919): 7.

64. See an account of Hunt's exploit in "A Newspaper Reporter Releases to America Text of the Allies' Terms of Peace," *Editor & Publisher* (June 12, 1919): 6.

65. Margaret Macmillan, *Paris, 1919: Six Months That Changed the World* (New York: Random House, 2001), 57.

66. Cornwell, *Presidential Leadership of Public Opinion*, 58. See also Blum, *Joe Tumulty and the Wilson Era*, 173.

67. Startt, "The Uneasy Partnership," 67.

68. Leonard, *The Power of the Press*, 198.

69. Schudson, *Discovering the News*, 164–165.

70. Hilderbrand, *Power and the People*, 202–203.

71. Ibid., 177.

72. "Warn World by Radio to Maintain Peace, Decision at Paris," *Chicago Daily News* (January 24, 1919): 1.

73. "Stone Sees Hope for League of Nations," *Chicago Daily News* (April 23, 1919): 6.

74. Kirtland, "The Press and the Peace Conference," 522.

75. Ibid., 553

CHAPTER 12. ANTI-TREATY OPPOSITION

1. Scholars usually pay a respectful nod to public opinion but without further explanation. Some of the better accounts thus far nonetheless include Ruhl J. Bartlett, *The League to Enforce Peace* (Chapel Hill: Univ. of North Carolina Press, 1944), 128, 130–132, 208; Stone, *The Irreconcilables*, 85, 100, 131; Ambrosius, *Woodrow Wilson and the American Diplomatic Tradition*, 168, 189, 209; Knock, *To End All Wars*, 239–243, 268; and Cooper, *Breaking the Heart of the World*, 80, 191, 302. Speaking of an address Wilson made before the League to Enforce Peace in 1916, Knock does say the appearance "demonstrated how closely yoked domestic politics and foreign policy had become" (Knock, *To End All Wars*, 75). This chapter is heavily indebted to all five works, but particularly to Stone's still-indispensable monograph.

2. I disagree, therefore, with Robert C. Hilderbrand's overall conclusion in *Power and the People*, 202. The phrase "printed materials" is used by Seward W. Livermore in discussing the change in campaign style from such things as May poles and parades to editorials and pamphlets (Livermore, *Politics Is Adjourned*, 186). See also Michael McGerr, *The Decline of Popular Politics: The American North, 1865–1928* (New York: Oxford Univ. Press, 1986).

3. Melvin Small, *Democracy and Diplomacy: The Impact of Domestic Politics in U.S. Foreign Policy, 1789–1994* (Baltimore: Johns Hopkins Univ. Press, 1996), 48.

4. "[League debate] is probably the most important and most ably conducted discussion the country has seen since the Lincoln and Douglas debates" (Mark Sullivan, "The Corning Issues in American Politics," *Collier's* [July 26, 1919]: 6, 28).

5. Quoted in "War Aims of the Republican Party," *Current Opinion* (October 1918): 208.

6. Quoted in "How the Press Viewed the President's Parleys," *Current Opinion* (November 1919): 278.

7. "Assailing President Wilson's Fourteen Conditions of Peace," *Current Opinion* (December 1918): 34

8. Ibid.

9. *The Outlook* (October 23, 1918): 282.

10. *The New Republic* (August 31, 1918): 122–123.

11. "War Aims of the Republican Party," *Current Opinion* (October 1918): 208.

12. David Mervin, "Henry Cabot Lodge and the League of Nations," *Journal of American Studies* 4 (February 1971): 203–209, 214. For more on Lodge's Republican commitments, see Widenor, *Henry Cabot Lodge and the Search for an American Foreign Policy,* 62.

13. Quoted in Stone, *The Irreconcilables,* 78.

14. "How the New Peace-League Plan Is Received," *Literary Digest* (April 26, 1919): 9.

15. Stone, *The Irreconcilables,* 85.

16. "Put the League of Nations First," *The Independent* (January 4, 1919): 3.

17. Among other things, Senator Lodge questioned the disposal of German ships (*Literary Digest* [January 4, 1919]: 53).

18. The same editorial nonetheless praised him for "admirable" service so far. "The President Abroad," *Leslie's* (January 25, 1919): 114.

19. The Paris settlement concerning the Chinese-Japanese dispute "has aroused opposition in the United States and has placed in jeopardy the already dubious outcome of the Senate's discussion of the peace treaty" (Kenneth Scott Latourette, "An Unpopular View of the Shantung Question," *Atlantic Monthly* [November 1919]: 711).

20. See, for example, Norman Hapgood, quoted in "The President Has Played His Cards Masterfully," *Current Opinion* (March 1919): 138.

21. "The President and the Senate Should Get Together," *The World's Work* (April 1919): 611.

22. The Senators were Borah (Id.), Brandegee (Conn.), Calder (N.Y.), Cummins (Iowa), Curtis (Kans.), Dillingham (Vt.), Fernald (Me.), France (Md.), Frelinghuysen (N.J.), Hale (Me.), Harding (Ohio), Johnson (Calif.), Jones (Wash.), Knox (Pa.), Lenroot (Wisc.), Lodge (Mass.), McLean (Conn.), Moses (N.H.), New (Ind.), Page (Vt.), Penrose (Penn.), Poindexter (Wash.), Sherman (Ill.), Smoot (Utah), Spencer (Mo.), Sterling (S.D.), Sutherland (W. Va.), Townsend (Mich.), Wadsworth (N.Y.), Warren (Wyo.), Watson (Ind.), Phipps (Colo.), McCormick (Ill.), Edge (N.J.), Keyes (N.H.), Newberry (Mich.), and Ball (Del.).

23. The second quote is from the *Manchester Union.* Both quotes are from "The Peace League Barrage," *Literary Digest* (March 15, 1919): 20.

24. Quoted in "Will the Senate Defeat the League of Nations?" *Literary Digest* (March 8, 1919): 11.

25. Quoted in "Topics in Brief," *Literary Digest* (March 22, 1919): 23.

26. Quoted in "Will the Peace League Prevent War?" *Literary Digest,* (March 15, 1919): 13.

27. "The Covenant's End," *New York Tribune* (March 5. 1919): 10.

28. "Is Wilsonphobia to Defeat the League of Nations?" *Current Opinion* (June 1919): 344.

29. Art Young, "All About It," *The Liberator* (September 1919): 20.

30. Simeon Strunsky, "The President's Homecoming," *Atlantic Monthly* (August 1919): 269.

31. Albert J. Beveridge, "Pitfalls of a 'League of Nations,'" *North American Review* (March 1919): 305.

32. Senator Lawrence Sherman, "Why I Oppose the League," *Leslie's* (June 21, 1919): 961.

33. George Creel, "The Hope of the World," *Leslie's* (June 21, 1919): 969.

34. Stone, *The Irreconcilables,* 85.

35. Ritchie, *Press Gallery,* 208.

36. Stone, *The Irreconcilables,* 80.

37. Some of the better-known holders of public office with journalistic resumés then were Senators Moses and McCormick, Kansas governor Arthur Capper, and cabinet members Josephus Daniels and Franklin Lane.

38. Stone, *The Irreconcilables,* 61.

39. Quoted in Cooper, *Breaking the Heart of the World,* 350. On the other side, Democratic senator Gilbert Hitchcock was said to have "*his* newspaper, the Omaha *World-Herald*" (Livermore, *Politics Is Adjourned,* 83 (italics mine).

40. Baker, *What Wilson Did at Paris*; John Maynard Keynes, *The Economic Consequences of the Peace* (London: Macmillan, 1919; reprint, New York: Harcourt, Brace, and Howe, 1920). On February 10, 1920, Borah "became the first senator to refer to Keynes's *Economic Consequences of the Peace* from the Senate floor" (Cooper, *Breaking the Heart of the World,* 331).

41. Stone, *The Irreconcilables,* 82.

42. Only Reed ran into trouble: An Oklahoma audience egged the Missouri Democrat (ibid., 133).

43. "Wild Scenes Mark Peace Plan Meeting," *Chicago Daily News* (September 11, 1919): 5.

44. Quoted in Cooper, *Breaking the Heart of the World,* 167–168. According to this scholar, "The senators did make news. Johnson found reporters traveling with him for the rest of his tour" (ibid., 168).

45. *Brooklyn Eagle,* quoted in "Topics in Brief," *Literary Digest* (March 29, 1919): 18.

46. "Senator Knox Attempts a Surgical Operation on the Treaty," *Current Opinion* (July 1919): 1.

47. Quoted ibid., 2–3.

48. Charlton Bates Strayer, "Shadows of the Peace Conference," *Leslie's* (April 19, 1919): 601. See also "How the New Peace-League Plan Is Received," *Literary Digest* (April 26, 1919): 9. Contrary to popular misconception, Wilson did not completely ignore the U.S. Senate. It was just that the timing of his request for input came relatively late (February through April), and was kept relatively quiet—not an effective job, in other words, of public relations. See Bartlett, *The League to Enforce Peace,* 125–126; and Knock, *To End All Wars,* 267.

49. "The March of Events," *The World's Work* (May 1919): 7.

50. Editorial, *The New Statesman* (June 21, 1919): 274.

51. "The Peace Treaty and Its Critics," *Sunset* (July 1919): 9.

52. "Our Duty to the Senate," *Advocate of Peace* (July 1919): 203; "Criticisms of the 'Covenant,'" *Advocate of Peace* (July 1919): 203.

53. "Practical-Minded France," *Advocate of Peace* (July 1919): 206.

54. "The President's Speech to the Senate," *Advocate of Peace* (July 1919): 207; "Compromise and Barter," *Advocate of Peace* (July 1919): 209–210.

55. "What Is Left of the League Covenant?" *The World's Work* (July 1919): 233.

56. "Listen to Congress!" *The Forum* (June 1919): 752–763.

57. "A Political Embarrassment," *The Forum* (July 1919): 120.

58. "An Optimistic Outlook," *The World's Work* (August 1919): 346.

59. "Washington News in Brief," *Chicago Tribune* (June 24, 1919), 2; See also Charlton Bates Strayer, "Ratification with Reservations," *Leslie's* (July 12, 1919): 70.

60. "The Passing of the Treaty," *The World Tomorrow* (November 1919): 295.

61. Stone, *The Irreconcilables,* 38.

62. "U.S. Senate Adopts 'Open Covenant,'" *Editor & Publisher* (July 31, 1919): 8.

63. "Bitter Debate on Treaty of Peace Opens in Senate," *New York Tribune* (May 24, 1919): 3.

64. "'Pitiless Publicity' Is Expensive, Capital Correspondents Find," *Editor & Publisher* (August 21, 1919): 9.

65. "Full Publicity," *Editor & Publisher* (August 28, 1919): 28.

66. "Half and Half Publicity," *New York Tribune* (May 27, 1919): 14.

67. "Treaty Battle on in Senate," *Chicago Daily News* (September 15, 1919): 1.

CHAPTER 13. THE PRO-TREATY CAMPAIGN

1. "Shall the Peace League Include Germany?" *Literary Digest* (October 12, 1918): 11. The same phrase can be found in Sir John Macdonell, *The Contemporary Review,* reprinted in "The League of Nations in Jeopardy," *The Living Age* (October 12, 1918): 65.

2. William Allen White, *Emporia Gazette,* quoted in "The Republican Opportunity," *Literary Digest* (November 23, 1918): 14.

3. Cooper, *Breaking the Heart of the World,* 27.

4. "Birth and Growth of League of Nations Reads Like Arabian Nights Tale," *Editor & Publisher* (April 3, 1919): 18.

5. "A Peripatetic Pilgrimage," *The Outlook* (February 19, 1919): 298.

6. "Answers to Three Big Objections," *Sunset* (April 1919): 5. See also "A Great American Statesman," *The World's Work* (April 1919): 612.

7. See, for example, "Let Critics Consider," *Chicago Daily News* (April 5, 1919): 8.

8. Cooper discusses Gus Karger in *Breaking the Heart of the World,* 123. The quote is from Seward Livermore, *Politics Is Adjourned,* 193. For more on the Scripps' waning support for Wilson, see Zacher, *The Scripps Newspapers Go to War,* 217–223.

9. Bartlett, *The League to Enforce Peace,* 129–130.

10. Cooper, *Breaking the Heart of the World,* 91. Cooper draws heavily from Bartlett's discussion as well.

11. Stone, *The Irreconcilables,* 41, 82; Cooper, *Breaking the Heart of the World,* 83, 90.

12. Bartlett, *The League to Enforce Peace,* 127; Cooper, *Breaking the Heart of the World,* 91.

13. Bartlett, *The League to Enforce Peace,* 143.

14. The president's statement is printed in the *New York Tribune* (December 19, 1918), 2, and is contained in "Statement," December 18, 1918, *Papers of Woodrow Wilson,* ed. Arthur S. Link, vol. 53 (Princeton: Princeton Univ. Press, 1986), 420.

15. "Ironically, one of the most significant and crippling constraints that could be placed on public opinion is not a result of strong leadership, but is rather the result of lack of leadership. . . . Nothing could be more detrimental to the democratic process than the inability to focus discussion because of inadequate leadership" (Manfred Landecker, *The President and Public Opinion* [Washington, D.C.: Public Affairs Press, 1968], 3).

16. "The Lodge-Lowell Debate," *The Outlook* (April 2, 1919): 547.

17. "Lessons of the Lowell-Lodge Debate," *Chicago Daily News* (March 21, 1919): 8.

18. "Both Lodge and Lowell in World League Debate Say Pact Needs Changes," *New York Tribune* (March 20, 1919): 1.

19. "League Is Growing in Favor: Hitchcock," *Chicago Daily News* (March 26, 1919): 1.

20. Advertisement, "Which Shall It Be?" *Survey* (January 11, 1919): back page.

21. "The New League of Free Nations Association," *The Survey* (November 30, 1918): 250. See the "cordial welcome" offered in "The Progress of the Month," *The World Tomorrow* (December 1918): 312.

22. Bartlett, *The League to Enforce Peace,* 111.

23. Editorial, "Senate and Treaty," *New York Times* (May 25, 1919): 1. The paper's shrill dogmatism did not sit well with many critics, *The New Republic* asking "'Must?'" *The New Republic* (May 31, 1919): 133.

24. "Stand by the President," *The Independent* (April 19, 1919): 84.

25. "Republican Contribution to the Covenant," *The Independent* (May 24, 1919): 275. Hamilton Holt repeated this fact to readers in an angry editorial, "The Senate Versus the People," *The Independent* (June 7, 1919): 351. Holt noted that in Senator Lodge's March 19 debate with A. Lawrence Lowell of Harvard University, Lodge had described five suggestions, all of which the president subsequently adopted.

26. "The Republican Congress and the Democratic President," *The Independent* (May 31, 1919): 308.

27. "Wilson Race Hinges on League Success," *Chicago Daily News* (May 28, 1919): 1.

28. Hamilton Holt, "The Senate Versus the People," *The Independent* (June 7, 1919): 352.

29. Hamilton Holt, "The League and the Senate," *The Independent* (June 7, 1919): 387. "[W]hat I cannot understand is how the American people can forget his supreme leadership during the war, and the great achievements he is now accomplishing at the peace table" (Holt, "The People and the President," *The Independent* [June 28, 1919]: 477).

30. "Compromising," *Saturday Evening Post* (June 14, 1919): 26.

31. David Lawrence, "Taft Action Causes White House Dismay; League Friends Do Not Think He Has Helped Cause by Offering Changes," *Chicago Daily News* (July 24, 1919): 4. The *Daily News* may have forgotten Taft's critical remarks when it wrote in an editorial later that month that unlike the position of the former president, the newspaper's stance was not to "accept any old league" ("The League and the President," *Chicago Daily News* [July 26, 1919]: 8).

32. Frederick M. Davenport, "The Senate Should Ratify, With Reservations," *The Outlook* (July 16, 1919): 426.

33. Herbert Hoover, "Our Responsibility," *Sunset* (November 1919): 14.

34. "There is no longer any doubt that the League of Nations covenant will be accepted in principle by the Senate" ("The Treaty's Chance in the Senate," *The Independent* [July 12, 1919]: 39). "I have never had a moment's doubt as to where the heart and purpose of this people lay. When any one on the other side of the water has raised the question, 'Will America come in and help?' I have said, 'Of course, America will come in and help.' She cannot do anything else" ("The President as Conquering Hero," *The Independent* [July 19, 1919]: 71).

35. "Can Congress Compromise?" *The Independent* (August 2, 1919): 139.

36. Considering the fact that critics had been attacking the league concept and Wilson relentlessly since December 1918, it seems odd that administration supporters such as the *Chicago Daily News* would term Swanson's endorsement as an 'opening' in the treaty debate ("Battle on in Senate over World League," *Chicago Daily News* (July 26, 1919): 1.

37. Frederick M. Davenport, "What the Pacific Northwest Thinks about the League and the Treaty," *The Outlook* (August 6, 1919): 538.

38. "The President and the Senate," *The Independent* (September 20, 1919): 381.

39. "The 'Moral Obligation' to Ratify," *Literary Digest* (August 30, 1919): 11.

40. "'Ratification with Reservations' Predicted," *Literary Digest* (August 9, 1919): 46. The *Literary Digest* was paraphrasing Tracy H. Lewis of the *New York Morning Telegraph*.

41. Editorial, *The New Republic* (July 23, 1919): 371.

42. Tumulty to Wilson, June 16, 1919, in *Papers of Woodrow Wilson*, ed. Arthur S. Link, vol. 60 [Princeton: Princeton Univ. Press, 1989], 611.

43. *The Dial* (October 19, 1918): 311.

44. Harold Stearns, "The American Press since the Armistice," *The Dial* (February 1919): 131.

45. "The League of Nations," *The Crisis* (November 1919): 336.

46. "Leadership," *The Crisis* (February 1920): 173.

47. Charlton Bates Strayer, "Wilson Pushed It Over," *Leslie's* (April 5, 1919): 510.

48. "Public Pays for League Propaganda," *New York Tribune* (August 29, 1919): 5; "Administration Propaganda," *New York Tribune* (September 3, 1919): 8. Senator Smoot, of Utah, chairman of the Printing Committee, ordered the propaganda stopped and reprimanded the government bureaucrats involved.

49. George W. Egerton, "Britain and the 'Great Betrayal': Anglo-American Relations and the Struggle for United States Ratification of the Treaty of Versailles, 1919–1920," *Historical Journal* 21 (1978): 908–909. See also Quincy Wright, "The Control of Foreign Relations," *American Political Science Review* 15 (February 1921): 3.

50. Ronan Brindley, "Woodrow Wilson, Self Determination and Ireland, 1918–1919: A View from the Irish Newspapers," *Eire-Ireland* 23 (1988): 62. Brindley uncovers a peculiar immunity Wilson enjoyed in the Irish press, a tendency by Irish nationalist writers to take out their occasional frustrations with the American president on Great Britain by badgering Lloyd George in the pages of their press.

51. Knock, *To End All Wars*, 49; Ambrosius, *Woodrow Wilson and the American Diplomatic Tradition*, 228.

52. "For Mr. Wilson is at once the foremost statesman of the world and its greatest artist. We know of no more enjoyable treat than to hear him at any time. But now he comes to us at the very peak of his fame, his skill, his self-confidence, wearing, as it were, the sheaves of victory in his buttonhole. . . . The President beguiles the intellect and soothes the senses of his hearers. . . . No matter how carefully prepared his speeches have been, they sound extemporaneous and effortless. . . . Orderly, convincing, logical, blandly humorous, he yet continues to suggest strong feeling managed by a stronger mind" ("The Magician," *Collier's* [July 12, 1919]: 14).

53. Carter Field, "Wilson to Be Urged to Cancel Tour," *New York Tribune* (July 6, 1919): 5.

54. "The President's Callers," *New York Tribune* (July 21, 1919): 6.

55. Caner Field, "Wilson Not in Hurry for Treaty Vote," *New York Tribune* (August 5, 1919): 1.

56. "President Wilson Carries the Treaty to the People," *Current Opinion* (October 1919): 205.

57. "Covering President Wilson's Tour," *Editor & Publisher* (September 18, 1919): 14.

58. Quoted in "Wilson's Appeal to the West," *Literary Digest* (September 13, 1919): 14.

59. Quoted ibid., 14.

60. *Boston Herald* [Indiana], quoted ibid., 15.

61. See "Covering President Wilson's Tour," *Editor & Publisher* (September 18, 1919): 14; and "Reporters Marveled at Pres. Wilson," *Editor & Publisher* (October 9, 1919): 14. The press enjoyed Wilson's experimental use in California of a new "[e]lectrical apparatus for transmitting . . . words": a public address system ("Wilson's Voice Will Be Carried to 50,000," *Chicago Daily News* [September 19, 1919]: 1).

62. "The President's 'Fighting' Speeches," *Chicago Daily News* (September 8, 1919): 8.

63. David Lawrence, "Wilson Draws Line in Treaty Criticism," *Chicago Daily News* (September 17, 1919): 3.

64. "The Administration program met a definite setback on September 23 in a test vote which lined up the opposing Senate forces 43–40 in favor of Senator Lodge's side" (in "Speaking of the Treaty," *The Independent* [October 4, 1919]: 6).

65. Charlton Bates Strayer, "Mild Reservationists Hold Key," *Leslie's* (September 20, 1919): 464. This is also the conclusion of Robert C. Hilderbrand, in *Power and the People,* 196.

66. "A Strange Reversal," *New York Tribune* (September 26, 1919): 6; "The Interrupted Tour," *New York Tribune* (September 27, 1919): 6.

67. Carter Field, "Treaty Backers Urge Wilson to Accept Changes," *New York Tribune* (September 27, 1919): 2.

68. "The Threat to Withdraw the Treaty," *Literary Digest* (October 11, 1919): 14. Angrier critics thought the trip brought Wilson low ("The President at His Worst," *North American Review* [October 1919]: 433).

69. "Lest We Forget," *Editor & Publisher* (December 25, 1919): 36.

70. *Chicago Daily News* (October 3, 1919): 8.

71. *Chicago Daily News* (September 26, 27, 29, October 2, 3).

72. "The President's illness . . . helps us to understand and excuse certain otherwise inexplicable sins of omission and commission in his speeches on the treaty during the tour which ended with breakdown" ("The Passing of the Treaty," *The World Tomorrow* [November 1919]: 295). The editorial went on to predict ratification.

We will probably never know exactly whether Wilson's illnesses, including his stroke(s), impaired his political reasoning. For more on that debate, see Edwin A. Weinstein, *Woodrow Wilson: A Medical and Psychological Biography* (Princeton: Princeton Univ. Press, 1981); Juliette L. George, Michael F. Marmor, and Alexander L. George, "Issues in Wilson Scholarship: References to Early 'Strokes' in the Papers of Woodrow Wilson," *Journal of American History* 70 (March 1984): 845. Weinstein contends that the president suffered several strokes, while Marmor and the Georges simply argue that the evidence is inconclusive. For useful summaries of this issue, see Robert M. Saunders, "History, Health and Herons: The Historiography of Woodrow Wilson's Personality and Decision-Making," *Presidential Studies Quarterly* 24 (winter 1994): 57–77; Lloyd E. Ambrosius, "Woodrow Wilson's Health and the Treaty Fight, 1919–1920," *International History Review* 9 (1987): 73–84; Dorothy Ross, "Woodrow Wilson and the Case for Psychohistory," *Journal of American History* 69 (December 1982): 658–668.

73. "The President's Illness," *Chicago Daily News* (October 3, 1919): 8.

74. Small, *Democracy and Diplomacy,* 37–48; Daniel D. Stid, *The President as Statesman: Woodrow Wilson and the Constitution* (Lawrence: Univ. of Kansas Press, 1998), 152.

75. Press Conference, July 10, 1919, Robert C. Hilderbrand. "The Complete Press Conferences," in *The Papers of Woodrow Wilson,* ed. Arthur S. Link, vol. 50 (Princeton: Princeton Univ. Press, 1985), 793.

CHAPTER 14. THE PRINTERS' STRIKE AND OTHER DISTRACTIONS

1. "The March of Events," *The World's Work* (October 1919): 568.

2. See, for example, *Chicago Daily News* (September 26, 1919): 1.

3. "The Public Comes First," *Leslie's* (October 4, 1919): 530.

4. *Greenville Piedmont* (S.C.), quoted in "Topics in Brief," *Literary Digest* (October 4, 1919): 18.

5. David Lawrence, "Wilson Calls Labor Conference Oct. 5." *Chicago Daily News* (September 3, 1919): 1.

6. "A Printers' Strike," *The Outlook* (September 24, 1919): 120. "Book and Job Printers Lock Pressmen Out," *New York Tribune* (October 1, 1919): 1. "By stretching your imagination a little," joked *The Trades Unionist* of Washington, D.C., "you might refer to the New York pressmen's strike as a 'typographical error'" (quoted in "Topics in Brief," *Literary Digest* [November 15, 1919]: 20). Not all printers supported the strike—indeed, more the opposite. As the *Literary Digest* pointed out in October, the chiefs of some half a dozen New York City printers' unions rebuked the walk-out ("New York's Publishing Crisis," *Literary Digest* [October 4, 1919]: 13).

7. "To Our Subscribers: An Explanation," *Printers' Ink* (October 9, 1919): 3.

8. "The Labor Crisis and the People: What Does the Present Industrial Crisis Mean?" *The Outlook* (October 29, 1919): 223.

9. "Effects of the Printers Strike," *Literary Digest* (October 25, 1919): 14. See also "Magazines Out Despite Strike of Pressmen," *New York Tribune* (October 17, 1919): 4.

10. The magazine crowed often about its resourcefulness in continuing to publish in the face of adversity. "As a result of the New York strike, nearly all the well-known magazines printed there have been compelled to suspend publication temporarily, at least, and it was only by adopting an untried process that THE LITERARY DIGEST has been able to appear uninterruptedly. This process consists of first typewriting the manuscript, pasting the sheets on cardboard, and making a photo-engraving of each page. The pages are printed from electro-type plates of the engraving, as in the case of a full-page advertisement, and sometimes in the case of books which are to be reprinted" ("Effects of the Printers Strike," Literary Digest [October 25. 1919]: 14). *The Independent* printed its November 8, 1919, issue in "callitypy," a format similar in appearance to that used by the *Literary Digest.*

11. *The New Republic* (October 8, 1919): 275.

12. "This Issue," *The Survey* (November 8, 1919): 52.

13. "An Explanation," *The World Tomorrow* (November 1919): 295; "Interpreting the Vote," ibid., 327a.

14. *Literary Digest* (October 18, 1919): 9.

15. "Collier's Resumes Publication," *Collier's* (November 8, 1919): 13.

16. "Our Ninth Birthday," *The Crisis* (November 1919): 335.

17. "As We Go to Press," *The Independent* (October 4, 1919): 4.

18. "To Our Readers and Our Advertisers," *The Independent* (November 29, 1919): 115.

19. "A Word to Newsprint Manufacturers," *Editor & Publisher* (October 9, 1919): 22.

20. Frank Crane, "Back to Small Towns," *Chicago Daily News* (October 17, 1919): 8.

21. A rare exception was the socialist paper *The Call,* which described the dispute as "a struggle involving the most vital right of the toilers everywhere. If the pressmen lose the Junker forces will have won a great victory against democracy" ("Effects of the Printers Strike," *Literary Digest* [October 25, 1919]: 15).

22. Quoted in "Effects of the Printers Strike," *Literary Digest* (October 25, 1919): 15.

23. Quoted in "Topics in Brief," *Literary Digest* (October 18, 1919): 15.

24. William L. Chenery, "The Printers' Strike," *The Survey* (December 13, 1919): 231.

CHAPTER 15. THE PRESS AND THE SENATE

1. My survey examines virtually all of the major magazines of the time, about forty in all; four newspapers, the *New York Tribune,* the *New York Times,* the *Chicago Daily News,* and the *Chicago Tribune*; as well as a selective look at several other newspapers. Many dailies, including the preceding four, published their own informal surveys and samples of press opinion. See, for example, *New York Tribune* (August 31, 1919): section VII, page 3; (October 26, 1919): section VII, page 9.

For *Current Opinion,* see especially its March, April, and October 1919 issues. For the *Literary Digest,* see the following issues: (April 5, 1919): 13; (April 26, 1919): 9; (June 7, 1919): 22; (July 19, 1919): 9; (August 9, 1919): 7; (August 30, 1919): 11; (September 20, 1919): 4; (November 11, 1919): 14; (November 29, 1919): 11. The April 5, July 19, August 9, and November 1 issues contain the best compendia.

See also James D. Startt, "Early Press Reaction to Wilson's League Proposal," *Journalism Quarterly* 39 (1962): 301–308; Startt, "The Uneasy Partnership," 67–69; James D. Startt, "Wilson's Trip to Paris: Profile of Press Response," *Journalism Quarterly* 46 (1969): 737–742.

2. Startt, "Early Press Reaction to Wilson's League Proposal," 303.

3. "'Ratification with Reservations' Predicted," *Literary Digest* (August 9, 1919): 7.

4. Leroy T. Vernon, "Senate Treaty Vote Points to Approval," *Chicago Daily News* (October 3, 1919): 5.

5. "Far West Is in Favor of Ratification." *Sunset* (September 1919): 9.

6. "The Treaty About to Be Ratified," *Sunset* (December 1919): 10.

7. "Still Trembling Over the Fate of the Monroe Doctrine," *Current Opinion* (June 1919): 346.

8. Robert T. Barry also drew this conclusion. "The Senate gallery divided on the treaty along much the same lines as did the Senate floor. There were 'irreconcilables' and 'the battalion of death' and 'reservationists' both 'mild' and 'wild.'" Barry detected a few more bitter-enders among the Senate gallery (Robert T. Barry, "Press Gallery Played Important Part in Shaping Treaty Struggle," *Editor & Publisher* [December 4, 1919]: 9).

9. See, for example, "Partisanship," *New York Tribune* (May 12, 1919): 12.

10. "Americanizing the Covenant," *New York Tribune* (August 24, 1919): III, 2.

11. "How the Press Answer the President's Plea," *Literary Digest* (July 19, 1919): 9.

12. Victor S. Yarros, "Study of Article 10," *Chicago Daily News* (October 3, 1919): 8.

13. *The Dial* (March 22, 1919): 309.

14. When Henry Watterson, editor of the *Louisville Courier-Journal,* stepped down in the summer of 1918, his peers wondered where Americans would turn to find "a great editor." "He is the last representative of the great era of personal journalism in this country," the *Baltimore Sun* mourned (quoted in "Col. Watterson, Last of the Great Editors, Leaves Courier-Journal," *Literary Digest* [August 31, 1918]: 85).

15. Robert T. Barry, "Press Gallery Played Important Part in Shaping Treaty Struggle," *Editor & Publisher* (December 4, 1919): 9, 33.

16. For more on Lippmann's contributions toward the treaty's defeat, see Steel, *Walter Lippmann and the American Century,* 158–166.

17. Ritchie, *Press Gallery,* 207.

18. Ibid., 207–208.

19. Robert T. Barry, "Press Gallery Played Important Part in Shaping Treaty Struggle," *Editor & Publisher* (December 4, 1919): 33. Barry also added that the "'regulars' in the Senate gallery

came to enjoy intimate personal relations with Senators and their families. The Senators' wives sat through most of the debates and [there] was a comradeship between the three groups."

20. Ibid., 9.

21. Nord, *Communities of Journalism,* 147.

22. Quoted in "Editorially Speaking," *The Independent* (August 30, 1919): 284.

23. Ritchie, *Press Gallery,* 208.

24. "The Peace Treaty as the World's Greatest Advertising Failure," *Literary Digest* (December 20, 1919): 130.

25. Leroy T. Vernon, "Senate Co-operation Only Hope for Pact; Treaty Up to Democrats and Republicans as Wilson Withdraws Guidance," *Chicago Daily News* (December 15, 1919): 1.

26. Frank L. Cobb, "The Press and Public Opinion," *New Republic* (December 31, 1919): 147.

CONCLUSION

1. Schudson, *Discovering the News,* 165.

2. "And neither side came very close to leading any substantial permanent public opinion. The real public opinion of America went into seclusion and far away from technical bickerings" ("Looking Back On It," *Collier's* [November 29, 1919]: 13).

3. "Wilson's Ripost," *The Independent* (October 19, 1918): 75.

4. *Advocate of Peace* (September/October 1919): 277. For a less impressed, obviously sarcastic aside, see Maurice Francis Egan's brief comment in "The Trimmings of Diplomacy," *Collier's* (September 6, 1919): 7. "If in the Bad Old Diplomacy, which, of course, has entirely passed away under the magic wand of the New Democracy, diplomatists believed that language was given them to conceal thoughts, it is probable that their apparent critical attitude toward one another is intended to hide an undying affection."

5. "President Says He Is a 'Crusader,'" *New York Tribune* (January 26, 1919): 1.

6. The phrase comes from Vicente Blasco Ibañez, "The New Diplomacy," *Saturday Evening Post* (July 19, 1919): 42.

7. K. Shide Kara [*sic*], "The Platitude in Diplomacy," *The Forum* (March 1921): 249. Shidehara's name was misprinted in this article.

8. "The World Partnership of the Press," *Editor & Publisher* (December 11, 1919): 28.

9. Keenan, *American Diplomacy,* 72–73.

10. Senator Bert M. Fernald, "Will Nationality Survive?" *The Forum* (October 1919), 465.

11. W. F. Clark, "Statesmanship the Backward Profession," *The Public* (February 22, 1919), 181.

12. "Reorganizing the State Department," *The World's Work* (August 1919), 350, 351. See also "Mr. Bullitt and a Reform of the State Department," *The World's Work* (November 1919), 16. "The events of the last five years have for the first time in this generation given the public sufficient evidence of the value of knowledge in dealing with foreign affairs to create some public sentiment for the support of a proper State Department and foreign services."

13. Walter Lippmann, "For a Department of State," *The New Republic* (September 17, 1919): 194.

14. "Give the Nation Real Diplomats," *Chicago Daily News* (November 22, 1919): 8.

15. Ilchman, *Professional Diplomacy in the United States,* 177, 184, 200.

16. William G. Shepherd, "Newspaper Men Will Reach New Heights of Importance Where Nations Meet to Barter," *Editor & Publisher* (August 28, 1919): 6.

17. Ibid., 6.

18. "The League of Nations and a New Era," *The World's Work* (August 1919): 345.

19. "Communication and Peace," *Chicago Daily News* (June 17, 1919): 8.

20. "Stone Praises Newspapers as Aid to Peace," *New York Tribune* (April 23, 1919): 3.

21. Riddell, *Lord Riddell's Intimate Diary of the Peace Conference and After,* 219–220, 338.

22. Donald S. Birn, "Open Diplomacy at the Washington Conference of 1921–1922: The British and French Experience," *Comparative Studies in Society and History* 12 (1970): 297–319.

23. Melvin Small, "Historians Look at Public Opinion," in *Public Opinion and Historians: Interdisciplinary Perspectives,* ed. Melvin Small (Detroit: Wayne State Univ. Press, 1970), 20–21.

24. Mott, *American Journalism,* 579–581, 705–706.

25. Many diplomats do, too. See Henry Kissinger, *Diplomacy* (New York: Simon and Schuster, 1994), 671. For more on Cronkite's influence following Tet, see Stanley Karnow, *Vietnam: A History* (New York: Penguin, 1983), 547–48; George C. Herring, *America's Longest War: The United States and Vietnam, 1950–1975,* 4th ed. (New York: McGraw-Hill, 2002), 232, 241; and Clarence R. Wyatt, *Paper Soldiers: The American Press and the Vietnam War* (Chicago: Univ. of Chicago Press, 1995), 168, 187. These authors make clear that while Cronkite did not change the direction of American public opinion at the time (he simply followed it), the broadcast journalist's comments did have a profound impact on President Johnson's opinion.

26. James Reston, "In Defense of Leaks," *New York Times* (June 21, 1974): 37.

27. The clearest recent example is probably the *New York Times* correspondent-turned-columnist-turned-pundit-turned-authority Thomas Friedman, a recognized expert on the Middle East, and the author of such books as *From Beirut to Jerusalem* (1988) and *The Lexus and the Olive Tree* (1999).

28. Steven Livingston, "Diplomacy and Remote Sensing Technology: Changing the Nature of Debate," *iMP Magazine* (July 23, 2001): 1–7; Jonathan H. Spalter and Kevin Moran, "Toward New Digital Diplomacy: Information Technology and U.S. Foreign Policy in the 21st Century," *iMP Magazine* (May 21, 1999): 1–7; Steven V. Roberts, "New Diplomacy by Fax Americana: Technology Can Win Friends and Influence People," *U.S. News and World Report* (July 19, 1989): 35.

29. Marzolf, *Civilizing Voices,* 106; Ritchie, "The Loyalty of the Senate," 590.

30. "Lawrence Dispatches Widely Syndicated," *Editor & Publisher* (September 4, 1919): 39.

31. "Publicity, Public Opinion, and the Wily Press-Agent," *Literary Digest* (October 2, 1920): 58. "Out of press-agenting has grown the vast amount of propaganda that to-day floods the whole world. Every movement has its propaganda, from Bolshevism to the prophet who prognosticates the end of all created things at an early date. Governmental affairs have especially been made the subject of airing through propaganda methods since the war."

32. G. Hanet Archambault, "L'Indépendance Belge" (October 2, 1921), reprinted in "Publicity, An American Obsession," *The Living Age* (November 26, 1921): 546.

33. Herbert C. Ridout, "Another War Would End Civilization—The Press Is World's Hope," *Editor & Publisher* (November 13, 1919): 7.

34. Will Irwin, "If You See It in the Paper, It's—?" *Collier's* (August 18, 1923): 11. See also Marzolf, *Civilizing Voices,* 116.

35. Solomon Bulkley Griffin, "Journalism and Service," *North American Review* (January 1920): 30.

36. See, for example, Donald Wilhelm, "The Failure of the Fourth Estate," *The Independent* (December 28, 1918): 432; and George Rothwell Brown, "The Lynching of Public Opinion," *North American Review* (June 1919): 795.

37. Herbert C. Ridout, "Press of the World Is Drawing Closer Together," *Editor & Publisher* (December 4, 1919); 14; "The World Partnership of the Press," *Editor & Publisher* (December 11, 1919): 28.

38. H. F. Harrington, "Journalism Has Taken on a New Dignity Because of Professional Courses," *Editor & Publisher* (December 11, 1919): 9; Ritchie, *Press Gallery,* 227.

39. For an editorial in support of "foreign propaganda and advertising," see "Plenipotentiaries to the People," *The Independent* (February 22, 1919): 243.

40. Marzolf, *Civilizing Voices,* 116.

41. "Editorially Speaking," *The Independent* (July 12, 1919): 48.

42. Walter Lippmann, "The Press and Public Opinion," *Political Science Quarterly* 46 (June 1931): 166.

43. Arthur L. Salmon, "As to Public Opinion," *Chicago Daily News* (September 1919): 8.

44. "The Press and Public Opinion," *Literary Digest* (January 3, 1920): 32.

45. For more on the connection between objectivity and the professional ethos, see Schudson, *Discovering the News,* 7–9, 141–144.

BIBLIOGRAPHY

MANUSCRIPT COLLECTIONS

Library of Congress, Washington, D.C.
  Herbert Corey Papers.
  W. E. B. Du Bois Papers.
  Edwin M. Hood Papers.
  William Allen White Papers.

Lilly Library, Bloomington, Indiana
  Samuel McClure Papers.

Newberry Library, Chicago, Illinois
  Edward Price Bell Papers.
  Charles H. Dennis Papers.
  Paul Mowrer Papers.
  Melville Stone Papers.

OFFICIAL DOCUMENTS

Link, Arthur S., David W. Hirst, John E. Little, Manfred F. Boemeke, et al., eds. *The Papers of Woodrow Wilson.* 69 vols. Princeton: Princeton Univ. Press, 1966–1994.

Mantoux, Paul. *The Deliberations of the Council of Four (March 24–June 28, 1919): Notes of the Official Interpreter.* 2 vols. Translated and edited by Arthur S. Link and Manfred F. Boemeke. Princeton: Princeton Univ. Press, 1992.

U.S. Department of State. *Papers Relating to the Foreign Relations of the United States, 1918.* 2 vols. Washington, D.C.: Government Printing Office, 1933.

U.S. Department of State. *Papers Relating to the Foreign Relations of the United States, 1919.* 13 vols. Washington, D.C.: Government Printing Office, 1942–1947.

PERIODICALS

Advocate of Peace. 1918–1919.
American Magazine. 1918–1919.
Atlantic Monthly. 1918–1919.
Bookman. 1918–1919.
Century Magazine. 1918–1919.
Collier's. 1918–1919.
Cosmopolitan Magazine. 1918–1919.
The Crisis. 1918–1919.
Current Opinion. 1918–1919.
The Dial. 1918–1919.
Editor & Publisher. 1918–1919.
Everybody's Magazine. 1918–1919.
Forum. 1918–1919.
Good Housekeeping. 1918–1919.
Harper's Bazar. 1918–1919.
Harper's Monthly. 1918–1919.
Independent. 1918–1919.
Ladies' Home Journal. 1918–1919.
Leslie's Weekly. 1918–1919.
Liberator. 1918–1919.
Lippincott's Magazine. 1918–1919.
Literary Digest. 1918–1919.
Living Age. 1918–1919.
McClure's Magazine. 1918–1919.
Metropolitan. 1918–1919.
Munsey's Magazine. 1918–1919.
The Nation. 1918–1919.
The New Republic. 1918–1919.
New Statesman. 1918–1919.
North American Review. 1918–1919.
Outlook. 1918–1919.
Pearson's. 1918–1919.
Printer's Ink. 1918–1919.
Red Cross Magazine. 1918–1919.
Saturday Evening Post. 1918–1919.
Scribner's Magazine. 1918–1919.
Seven Arts. 1918–1919.
Stars and Stripes. 1918–1919.
Sunset. 1918–1919.
Survey. 1918–1919.
World's Work. 1918–1919.
The World Tomorrow. 1918–1919.

NEWSPAPERS

Chicago Daily News. 1918–1919.
Chicago Tribune. 1918–1919.
New York Times. 1918–1919.
New York Tribune. 1918–1919.

MEMOIRS

Angell, Norman. *After All: The Autobiography of Norman Angell.* New York: Farrar, Straus and Young, 1952.

———. *America and the New World-State: A Plea for American Leadership in International Organization.* New York: Putnam, 1915.

———. *The Dangers of Half-Preparedness: A Plea for the Declaration of American Policy.* New York: Putnam, 1916.

———. *Foreign Policy and Our Daily Bread.* London: W. Collins Sons, 1925.

———. *The Fruits of Victory.* New York: Century, 1921.

———. *The Great Illusion: A Study of the Relation of Military Power to National Advantage.* London: Heineman, 1910.

———. *Human Nature and the Peace Problem.* London: W. Collins Sons, 1925.

———. *If Britain Is to Live.* New York: Putnam, 1923.

———. *Nationalism, War and Society.* New York: Macmillan, 1916.

———. *The Peace Treaty and the Economic Chaos of Europe.* London: Swarthmore Press, 1919.

———. *The Public Mind.* New York: Dutton, 1927.

Atherton, Gertrude Franklin Horn. *Adventures of a Novelist.* New York: Liveright, 1932.

———. *Can Women Be Gentlemen?* Boston: Houghton Mifflin, 1938.

———. *Life in the War Zone.* New York: System Printing, 1916.

Baker, Ray Stannard. *Adventures in Contentment.* New York: Grosset and Dunlap, 1907.

———. *Adventures in Friendship.* New York: Grosset and Dunlap, 1910.

———. *Adventures in Understanding.* Garden City, N.Y.: Doubleday, Page, 1925.

———. *American Chronicle: The Autobiography of Ray Stannard Baker.* New York: Charles Scribner's Sons, 1945.

———. *Under My Elm: Country Discoveries and Reflections.* Garden City, N.Y.: Doubleday, Doran, 1943.

———. *What Wilson Did at Paris.* Garden City, N.Y.: Doubleday, Page, 1919.

———, ed. *Woodrow Wilson: Life and Letters.* 8 vols. Garden City, N.Y.: Doubleday, Page, 1927–1939.

———. *Woodrow Wilson and World Settlement.* 3 vols. Garden City, N.Y.: Doubleday, Page, 1922.

Baruch, Bernard M. *The Making of the Reparation and Economic Sections of the Treaty.* New York: Harper and Brothers, 1920.

Bass, John Foster. *America and the Balance Sheet of Europe.* New York: Ronald Press, 1921.

———. *The Peace Tangle.* New York: Macmillan, 1920.

Baukhage, Hilmar Robert. *I Was There with the Yanks on the Western Front.* New York: G. P. Putnam's Sons, 1919.

Becker, Carl L. *America's War Aims and Peace Program.* War Information Series, no. 21. Washington, D.C.: Government Printing Office, 1918.

Bender, Robert J. *"W. W.": Scattered Impressions of a Reporter Who for Eight Years "Covered" the Activities of Woodrow Wilson.* New York: United Press Association, 1924.

Bernays, Edward L. *Biography of an Idea: Memoirs of Public Relations Counsel Edward L. Bernays.* New York: Simon and Schuster, 1965.

———. *Crystallizing Public Opinion.* New York: Boni and Liveright, 1923.

———. *Propaganda.* New York: Liveright, 1928.

———. *Public Relations.* Norman: Univ. of Oklahoma Press, 1952.

Blankenhorn, Heber. *Adventures in Propaganda: Letters from an Intelligence Officer in France.* Boston: Houghlin Mifflin, 1919.

Bonsal, Stephen. *Suitors and Suppliants: The Little Nations at Versailles.* New York: Prentice-Hall, 1946.

———. *Unfinished Business.* Garden City, N.Y.: Doubleday, Doran, 1954.

Bourne, Randolph S. *The History of a Literary Radical.* New York: Huebsch, 1920.

———. *Untimely Papers.* New York: Huebsch, 1919.

———. *War and the Intellectuals: Essays by Randolph S. Bourne, 1915–1919.* Edited by Carl Resek. New York: Harper and Row, 1964.

———. *Youth and Life.* Boston: Houghton Mifflin, 1913.

Brisbane, Arthur. *The Book of Today.* New York: International Magazine, 1923.

———. *Editorials from the Hearst Newspapers.* New York: Albertson Publishing, 1906.

———. *Today and the Future Day.* New York: Albertson Publishing, 1925.

Bullard, Arthur. *ABCs of Disarmament and the Pacific Problem.* New York: Macmillan, 1921.

———. *American Diplomacy in the Modern World.* Philadelphia: Univ. of Pennsylvania Press, 1928.

———. *The Diplomacy of the Great War.* New York: Macmillan, 1917.

Butler, Nicholas Murray. *Across the Busy Years.* New York: Charles Scribner's Sons, 1935.

Cahan, Abraham. *The Education of Abraham Cahan.* 2 vols. Philadelphia: Jewish Publication Society of America, 1969.

———. *Grandma Never Lived in America.* Bloomington: Indiana Univ. Press, 1985.

Call, Arthur Deerin. "The Doom of War" (pamphlet). Washington, D.C.: American Peace Society, 1916.

———. "The Patriotic Duty Facing the Americas" (pamphlet). Washington, D.C.: American Peace Society, 1916.

———. *War for Peace.* Washington, D.C.: Committee for Public Information, 1918.

Cecil, Lord Robert. *A Great Experiment: An Autobiography.* New York: Oxford Univ. Press, 1941.

Chafee, Zechariah, Jr. *Freedom of Speech.* New York: Harcourt, Brace and Howe, 1920.

Cobb, Frank I. *Cobb of "The World": A Leader in Liberalism.* Edited by J. L. Heaton. New York: Dutton, 1924.

Coggeshall, Reginald. "Paris Peace Conference Sources of News, 1919." *Journalism Quarterly* 17 (March 1940): 1–10.

Creel, George. *How We Advertised America.* New York: Arno Press, 1922.

———. *Rebel at Large: Recollections of Fifty Crowded Years.* New York: G. P. Putnam's Sons, 1947.

———. *The War, the World and Wilson.* New York: Harper and Brothers, 1920.

———. *Wilson and the Issues.* New York: Century, 1916.

Croly, Herbert. *Progressive Democracy.* New York: Macmillan, 1914.

———. *The Promise of American Life.* New York: Macmillan, 1909.

Daniels, Josephus. *The Cabinet Diaries of Josephus Daniels, 1913–1921.* Edited by E. David Cronon. Lincoln: Univ. of Nebraska Press, 1961.

Davis, Oscar King. *Released for Publication: Some Inside Political History of Theodore Roosevelt and His Times, 1898–1918.* Boston: Houghton Mifflin, 1925.

Dennis, Charles Henry. *Newspapers and Crime Prevention.* Chicago: Chicago Daily News. 1927.

Dillon, Émile J. *The Inside Story of the Peace Conference.* New York: Harper, 1920.

Dunn, Arthur Wallace. *From Harrison to Harding: A Personal Narrative Covering a Third of a Century, 1888–1921.* 2 vols. New York: G. P. Putnam's Sons, 1922.

Duranty, Walter. *I Write as I Please.* New York: Simon and Schuster, 1935.

———. *Europe: War or Peace?* New York: Foreign Policy Association, 1935.

Essary, Jesse Frederick. *Covering Washington.* Boston: Houghton Mifflin, 1927.

———. *Reverse English: Some Off-side Observations upon Our British Cousins.* New York: Rudge, 1928.

Gallagher, Patrick. *America's Aims and Asia's Aspirations.* New York: Century, 1920.

Gannett, Lewis S. *Discoveries of a Week-end Countryman.* New York: Viking Press, 1949.

Gilbert, Clinton W. *Behind the Mirrors.* New York: Putnam, 1922.

———. *The Mirrors of Washington.* New York: Putnam, 1921.

———. *The Oracle That Always Says "No."* New York: Putnam, 1925.

[Gilbert, Clinton Wallace.] "Anonymous." *The Mirrors of Washington.* New York: G. P. Putnam's Sons, 1921.

Grasty, Charles H. *Flashes from the Front, 1918.* New York: Century, 1918.

Grew, Joseph C. *Turbulent Era: A Diplomatic Record of Forty Years, 1904–1945.* 2 vols. Edited by Walter Johnson. Boston: Houghton Mifflin, 1952.

Hammond, Percy. *But—Is It Art?* Garden City, N.Y.: Doubleday, Page, 1927.

———. *This Atom in the Audience.* New York: Ferris Printing, 1940.

Hansen, Harry A. *The Adventures of the Fourteen Points.* New York: Century, 1919.

———. *Midwest Portraits.* New York: Harcourt, Brace, 1923.

Harris, H. Wilson. *The Peace in the Making.* New York: Dutton, 1920.

Harrison, Marguerite Elton Baker. *Marooned in Moscow: The Story of an American Woman Imprisoned in Russia.* New York: Doran, 1921.

———. *There's Always Tomorrow: The Story of a Checkered Life.* New York: Farrar and Rinehart, 1935.

Haskins, Charles Homer, and Robert Howard Lord. *Some Problems in the Peace Conference.* Cambridge, Mass.: Harvard Univ. Press, 1920.

Hearst, William Randolph. *Selections from Writings and Speeches of William Randolph Hearst.* Edited by E. F. Tompkins. San Francisco: San Francisco Examiner, 1948.

Holt, Hamilton. *Commercialism and Journalism.* Boston: Houghton Mifflin, 1909.

———. "In League to Enforce Peace" (1915) and "Giving the Public What it Wants" (1915), in *The Coming Newspaper,* edited by Merle Thorpe (New York: Henry Holt and Company, 1915).

Hoover, Irwin H. *Forty-Two Years in the White House.* Boston: Houghton Mifflin, 1934.

House, Edward M., and Charles Seymour, eds. *What Really Happened at Paris: The Story of the Peace Conference, 1918–1919.* New York: Charles Scribner's Sons, 1921.

Houston, David F. *Eight Years with Wilson's Cabinet, 1913–1920.* 2 vols. Garden City, N.Y.: Doubleday, Page, 1926.

Howe, Frederic C. *The City: The Hope of Democracy.* New York: Charles Scribner's Sons, 1906.

———. *Confessions of a Reformer.* New York: Charles Scribner's Sons, 1925.

Huddleston, Sisley. *In My Times: An Observer's Record of War and Peace.* New York: Dutton, 1938.

———. *Peace-Making at Paris.* London: Unwin, 1919.

Hungerford, E. *With the Doughboy in France.* New York: Macmillan, 1920.

Hunt, Frazier. *Blown in by the Draft.* Garden City, N.Y.: Doubleday, Page, 1918.

———. *One American and His Attempt at Education.* New York: Simon and Schuster, 1938.

Irwin, Will. *The American Newspaper.* Ames: Iowa State Univ. Press, 1969.

———. *The House That Shadows Built.* Garden City, N.Y.: Doubleday, Doran, 1928.

———. *The Making of a Reporter.* New York: G. P. Putnam's Sons, 1942.

———. *Men, Women and War.* London: Constable, 1915.

———. *The Next War: An Appeal to Common Sense.* New York: Dutton, 1921.

———. *Propaganda and the News; or What Makes You Think So?* New York: Whittlesey House, McGraw-Hill, 1936.

Johnson, Severance. *The Enemy Within.* New York: McCann, 1919.

Johnson, Thomas M. *Our Secret War, 1917–1919.* Indianapolis: Bobbs-Merrill, 1929.

———. *Without Censor.* Indianapolis: Bobbs-Merrill, 1928.

Keynes, John Maynard. *The Economic Consequences of the Peace.* London: Macmillan, 1919; reprint, New York: Harcourt, Brace, and Howe, 1920.

Krock, Arthur B. *The Consent of the Governed and Other Deceits.* Boston: Little, Brown, 1971.

———, ed. *The Editorials of Henry Watterson.* New York: Doran, 1923.

———. *Memoirs.* New York: Popular Library, 1968.

———. *Myself When Young: Growing Up in the 1890s.* Boston: Little, Brown, 1973.

———. *A Responsible Press Is a Free Press.* Tucson: Univ. of Arizona Press, 1967.

Lamont, Thomas W. *Across World Frontiers.* New York: Harcourt, Brace, 1951.

Lansing, Robert. *The Big Four and Others of the Peace Conference.* Boston: Houghton Mifflin, 1921.

———. *The Peace Negotiations: A Personal Narrative.* Boston: Houghton Mifflin, 1921.

———. *War Memoirs of Robert Lansing, Secretary of State.* Indianapolis: Bobbs Merrill, 1925.

Lawrence, David. *Diary of a War Correspondent.* New York: Kinsey, 1942.

———. *Nine Honest Men.* New York: D. Appleton-Century, 1936.

———. *The Other Side of Government.* New York: Charles Scribner's Sons, 1929.

———. *The True Story of Woodrow Wilson.* New York: Doran, 1924.

———. *Who Were the 11 Million?* New York: D. Appleton-Century, 1937.

Lippmann, Walter. *Drift and Mastery: An Attempt to Diagnose the Current Unrest.* New York: Kennerley, 1914; reprint, Madison: Univ. of Wisconsin Press, 1985.

———. *An Inquiry into the Principles of the Good Society.* Boston: Little, Brown, 1937.

———. *Liberty and the News.* New York: Harcourt, Brace and Howe, 1920.

———. *Men of Destiny.* New York: Macmillan, 1927.

———. *The Method of Freedom.* New York: Macmillan, 1934.

———. *Mr. Kahn Would Like to Know.* New York: Foreign Policy Association, 1923.

———. *The New Imperative.* New York: Macmillan, 1935.

———. *The Phantom Public.* New York: Harcourt, Brace, 1925.

———. *A Preface to Morals.* New York: Macmillan, 1929.

———. *A Preface to Politics.* New York: Kennerley, 1913.

———. "The Press and Public Opinion." *Political Science Quarterly* 46 (June 1931): 161–170.

———. *Public Opinion.* New York: Free Press, 1922.

———. *The Stakes of Diplomacy.* New York: Holt, 1915.

———. *U.S. Foreign Policy: Shield of the Republic.* Boston: Little, Brown, 1943.

Lloyd George, David. *The Truth about the Peace Treaties.* London: Gollancz, 1938. Published in the United States as *Memoirs of the Peace Conference* (2 vols., New Haven, Conn.: Yale Univ. Press, 1939).

Lowell, Abbott Lawrence. *Public Opinion and Popular Government.* New York: Longmans, Green, 1913.

———. *Public Opinion in War and Peace.* Cambridge, Mass.: Harvard Univ. Press, 1923.

Lowry, Edward. *Washington Close-Ups: Intimate Views of Some Public Figures.* Boston: Houghton Mifflin, 1921.

Marcosson, Isaac Frederick. *Adventures in Interviewing*. New York: Lane, 1920.

McClure, Samuel S. *My Autobiography*. New York: Frederick A. Stokes, 1914; reprint, Ungar, 1963.

———. *Obstacles to Peace*. Boston: Houghton Mifflin, 1917.

———. *The Purpose and Aim of the McClure's Magazine*. Valparaiso, Ind.: Meyers, 1925.

McCutcheon, John T. *Cartoons by John T. McCutcheon*. Chicago: McClurg, 1903.

———. *Drawn from Memory*. Indianapolis: Bobbs-Merrill, 1950.

———. *An Heir at Large*. Indianapolis: Bobbs-Merrill, 1923.

———. *John McCutcheon's Book*. Chicago: Caxton Club, 1948.

———. *The Restless Age*. Indianapolis: Bobbs-Merrill, 1921.

Miller, David Hunter. *The Drafting of the Covenant*. 2 vols. New York: G. P. Putnam's Sons, 1928.

Mowrer, Paul Scott. *And Let the Glory Go By*. Sanbornville, N.H.: Wake-Brook House, 1955.

———. *Balkanized Europe*. New York: Dutton, 1921.

———. *The Foreign Relations of the United States*. Chicago: American Library Association, 1927.

———. *On Going to Live in New Hampshire*. Sanbornville, N.H.: Wake-Brook House, 1953.

———. *Our Foreign Affairs: A Study in National Interest and the New Diplomacy*. New York: Dutton, 1924.

Nicolson, Harold. *Peacemaking 1919*. Boston: Houghton Mifflin, 1933; reprint, New York: Gosset and Dunlap, The Universal Library, 1965.

Noble, George Bernard. *Policies and Opinions at Paris, 1919: Wilsonian Diplomacy, the Versailles Peace, and French Public Opinion*. New York: Macmillan, 1935.

Older, Fremont. *My Own Story*. New York: Macmillan, 1926.

Page, Walter Hines. *The Life and Letters of Walter Hines Page*. Edited by Burton J. Hendrick. 3 vols. Garden City, N.Y.: Doubleday, Page, 1922–1925.

Pasvolski, Leo. *World War Debt Settlements*. New York: Macmillan, 1926.

Pearson, Drew, and Robert S. Allen. *Washington Merry-Go-Round*. New York: Liveright, 1931.

Prince, Morton. *The American Versus the German View of the War*. London: Unwin, 1915.

Riddell, George A. *Lord Riddell's Intimate Diary of the Peace Conference and After, 1918–1923*. New York: Reynal and Hitchcock, 1934.

Robertson, William R. *Soldiers and Statesmen*. 2 vols. London: Cassell, 1926.

Rodd, James Rennell. *Social and Diplomatic Memories*. 3 vols. London: Arnold, 1925.

Ross, Edward A. *Seventy Years of It: An Autobiography*. New York: D. Appleton-Century, 1936.

———. *Social Control: A Survey of the Foundations of Order*. New York: Macmillan, 1916.

Ross, Ishbel. *Ladies of the Press: The Story of Women in Journalism by an Insider*. New York: Harper and Brothers, 1936.

Russell, Charles Edward. *Bare Hands and Stone Walls: Some Recollections of a Side-Line Reformer*. New York: Charles Scribner's Sons, 1933.

Schiff, Victor. *The Germans at Versailles, 1919*. London: Williams and Norgate, 1930.

Seibold, Louis. *Japan: Her Vast Undertaking and World Expansion*. New York: New York Herald, 1921.

Seymour, Charles. *Geography, Justice, and Politics at the Paris Conference of 1919*. New York: American Geographical Society, 1951.

———. *Letters from the Paris Peace Conference*. Edited by Harold B. Whiteman Jr. New Haven, Conn.: Yale Univ. Press, 1965.

Seymour, Charles, ed. *The Intimate Papers of Colonel House*. 4 vols. Boston: Houghton Mifflin, 1926–1928.

Shotwell, James T. *At the Paris Peace Conference*. New York: Macmillan, 1937.

Simonds, Frank H. *The ABCs of War Debts and the Seven Popular Delusions About Them*. New York: Harper and Brothers, 1933.

———. *American Foreign Policy in the Post-War Years*. Baltimore: Johns Hopkins Univ. Press, 1935.

———. *Can Americans Stay at Home?* New York: Harper and Brothers, 1932.

———. *Can Europe Keep the Peace?* London: Harper and Brothers, 1931.

———. *How Europe Made Peace without America*. Garden City, N.Y.: Doubleday, Page, 1927.

———. *They Shall Not Pass*. Garden City, N.Y.: Doubleday, Page, 1916.

Sinclair, Upton. *The Brass Check: A Study of American Journalism*. Pasadena, Calif.: Upton Sinclair, 1919.

Steed, Henry Wickham. *Through Thirty Years, 1892–1922*. 2 vols. Garden City, N.Y.: Doubleday, Page, 1924.

Steffens, Lincoln. *The Autobiography of Lincoln Steffens*. New York: Harcourt, Brace, 1931.

———. *The Letters of Lincoln Steffens*. Edited by Ella Winter and Granville Hicks. New York: Harcourt, Brace, 1938.

———. *Lincoln Steffens Speaking*. New York: Harcourt, Brace, 1948.

———. *The Shame of the Cities*. New York: McClure, Phillips, 1904.

———. *The Struggle for Self-Government*. New York: McClure, Phillips, 1906.

———. *Upbuilders*. Garden City, N.Y.: Doubleday, Page, 1909.

Stoddard, Henry Luther. *As I Knew Them: Presidents and Politics from Grant to Coolidge*. New York: Harper and Brothers, 1927.

Stone, Melville E. *Fifty Years a Journalist*. Garden City, N.Y.: Doubleday, Page, 1921.

———. *"M.E.S." His Book*. New York: Harper and Brothers, 1918.

———. *News-gathering*. New York, 1918.

Sullivan, Mark. *The Education of an American*. New York: Doubleday, Doran, 1938.

———. *The Great Adventure at Washington: The Story of the Conference*. Garden City, N.Y.: Doubleday, Page, 1922.

———. *Our Times: The United States, 1900–1925*. New York: Charles Scribner's Sons, 1926–1935.

Tarbell, Ida M. *All in the Day's Work: An Autobiography.* New York: Macmillan, 1939.

———. *The Business of Being a Woman.* New York: Macmillan, 1912.

———. *Peacemakers Blessed and Otherwise.* New York: Macmillan, 1922.

———. *Reporter for Lincoln: Story of Henry E. Wing, Soldier and Newspaperman.* New York: Macmillan, 1927.

Tardieu, Andre P. *The Truth About the Treaty.* Indianapolis: Bobbs-Merrill, 1921.

Temperley, H. A. W., ed. *A History of the Peace Conference of Paris.* 4 vols. London: Henry Frowde and Hodder and Stoughton, 1920–1924.

Thompson, Charles Thaddeus. *The Peace Conference Day by Day.* New York: Brentano's, 1920.

Thompson, Charles Willis. *Presidents I've Known.* Indianapolis: Bobbs-Merrill, 1921.

Tumulty, Joseph P. *Woodrow Wilson as I Know Him.* Garden City, N.Y.: Doubleday, Page, 1921.

Villard, Oswald Garrison. *Carl Schurz Als Journalist.* 1929.

———. *The Disappearing Daily: Chapters in American Newspaper Evolution.* New York: Knopf, 1944.

———. *Fifty Years: Memoirs of a Liberal Editor.* New York: Harcourt, Brace, 1939.

———. *Lincoln on the Eve of '61: A Journalist's Story.* New York: Knopf, 1941.

———. *Oswald G. Villard: The Dilemmas of the Absolute Pacifist in Two World Wars.* Edited by Anthony Gronowicz. New York: Garland, 1983.

———. *Prophets True and False.* New York: Knopf, 1928.

———. *Some Newspapers and Newspaper-Men.* 1926; reprint, Freeport, N.Y.: Books for Libraries Press, 1971.

Watson, James E. *As I Knew Them.* Indianapolis: Bobbs-Merrill, 1936.

White, William Allen. *The Autobiography of William Allen White.* New York: Macmillan, 1946.

———. *Conflicts in American Public Opinion.* Chicago: American Library Association, 1925.

———. *The Editor and His People: Editorials by William Allen White.* New York: Macmillan, 1924.

———. *God's Puppets.* New York: Macmillan, 1916.

———. *In Our Town.* New York: McClure, Phillips, 1906.

———. *Letters of William Allen White as a Young Man.* New York: Day, 1948.

———. *The Martial Adventures of Henry and Me.* New York: Macmillan, 1918.

———. *Masks in a Pageant.* New York: Macmillan, 1928.

———. *The Old Order Changeth: A View of American Democracy.* New York: Macmillan, 1910.

———. *Politics: The Citizen's Business.* New York: Macmillan, 1924.

———. *Selected Letters of William Allen White, 1899–1943.* Edited by Walter Johnson. New York: Holt, 1947.

———. *Woodrow Wilson: The Man, His Time, and His Task.* Boston: Houghton Mifflin, 1924.

Whitlock, Brand. *Forty Years of It.* New York: Appleton, 1914.

Wile, Frederic William. *News Is Where You Find It: Forty Years' Reporting at Home and Abroad.* Indianapolis: Bobbs-Merrill, 1939.

Wilson, Woodrow. *Constitutional Government in the United States.* New York: Columbia Univ. Press, 1908; reprint, 1961.

———. *The New Freedom: A Call for the Emancipation of the Generous Energies of a People.* Garden City, N.Y.: Doubleday, Page, 1913.

———. *The Public Papers of Woodrow Wilson.* Edited by Ray Stannard Baker and William E. Dodd. New York: Harper, 1925–1927.

SECONDARY SOURCES

Abbott, Andrew. *The System of Professions: An Essay on the Division of Expert Labor.* Chicago: Univ. of Chicago Press, 1988.

Adams, Henry. *The Education of Henry Adams.* Boston: Massachusetts Historical Society, 1918; reprint, Boston: Houghton Mifflin 1961.

Altschull, J. Herbert. *From Milton to McLuhan: The Ideas Behind American Journalism.* New York: Longman, 1990.

Ambrosius, Lloyd E. "Secret German-American Negotiations during the Paris Peace Conference." *Amerikastudien* 24 (1979): 288–309.

———. *Wilsonian Statecraft: Theory and Practice of Liberal Internationalism during World War I.* Wilmington, Del.: Scholarly Resources, 1991.

———. *Woodrow Wilson and the American Diplomatic Tradition: The Treaty Fight in Perspective.* New York: Cambridge Univ. Press, 1987.

———. "Woodrow Wilson's Health and the Treaty Fight, 1919–1920." *International History Review* 9 (1987): 73–84.

Anderson, Alexis J. "The Formative Period of First Amendment Theory, 1870–1915." *American Journal of Legal History* 24 (January 1980): 56–75.

Anderson, George L., ed. *Issues and Conflicts: Studies in Twentieth Century American Diplomacy.* Lawrence: Univ. of Kansas Press, 1959.

Aron, Daniel. *Men of Good Hope: A Story of American Progressives.* New York: Oxford Univ. Press, 1951.

Bailey, Thomas. *The Man in the Street: The Impact of American Public Opinion on Foreign Policy.* New York: Macmillan, 1948.

———. *Woodrow Wilson and the Great Betrayal.* New York: Macmillan, 1945.

———. *Woodrow Wilson and the Lost Peace.* New York: Macmillan, 1944.

Baillie, Hugh. *High Tension.* New York: Harper and Brothers, 1959.

Baldasty, Gerald J. *The Commercialization of News in the Nineteenth Century.* Madison: Univ. of Wisconsin Press, 1992.

———. *E. W. Scripps and the Business of Newspapers.* Urbana: Univ. of Illinois Press, 1999.

Banning, Stephen A. "The Professionalization of Journalism: A Nineteenth-Century Beginning." *Journalism History* 24 (winter 1998/1999): 157.

Bartlett, Ruhl J. *The League to Enforce Peace.* Chapel Hill: Univ. of North Carolina Press, 1944.

Beisner, Robert L. *From the Old Diplomacy to the New, 1865–1900.* New York: Thomas Y. Crowell, 1975; reprint, Arlington Heights, Ill.: Harlan Davidson, 1986.

Bell, Sidney. *Righteous Conquest: Woodrow Wilson and the Evolution of the New Diplomacy, 1917–1919.* Port Washington, N.Y.: Kennikat Press, 1972.

Bemis, Samuel Flagg. *Diplomatic History of the United States,* 4th ed. New York: Holt, 1955.

Benda, Julien. *The Betrayal of the Intellectuals.* Boston: Beacon Press, 1959.

Bent, Silas. *Newspaper Crusaders: A Neglected Story.* New York: McGraw-Hill, 1939.

Birdsall, Paul. *Versailles Twenty Years After.* New York: Reynal and Hitchcock, 1941.

Birkhead, Douglas. "The Power in the Image: Professionalism and the 'Communications Revolution.'" *American Journalism* 1 (winter 1984): 1–12.

Birn, Donald S. "Open Diplomacy at the Washington Conference of 1921–1922: The British and French Experience." *Comparative Studies in Society and History* 12 (1970): 297–319.

Bjork, Ulf Jonas. "The First International Journalism Organization Debates News Copyright, 1894–1898." *Journalism History* 22 (summer 1996): 56.

Blancké, W. Wendell. *The Foreign Service of the United States.* New York: Praeger, 1969.

Bledstein, Burton. *The Culture of Professionalism: The Middle Class and the Development of Higher Education in America.* New York: Norton, 1976.

Bleyer, Willard Grosvenor. *Main Currents in the History of American Journalism.* Boston: Houghton Mifflin, 1927.

Blum, John M. *Joe Tumulty and the Wilson Era.* Boston: Houghton Mifflin, 1951.

———. *The Progressive Presidents: Roosevelt, Wilson, Roosevelt, Johnson.* New York: Norton, 1980.

———. *Woodrow Wilson and the Politics of Morality.* Boston: Little, Brown, 1956.

Boyer, Paul. *Urban Masses and Moral Order in America, 1820–1920.* Cambridge, Mass.: Harvard Univ. Press, 1978.

Braeman, John, et al., eds. *Twentieth-Century American Foreign Policy.* Columbus: Ohio Univ. Press, 1971.

Brown, Daniel P. *Woodrow Wilson and the Treaty of Versailles: The German Leftist Press Response.* Ventura, Calif.: Golden West Historical Publications, 1978.

Brown, JoAnne, and David D. van Keuren, eds. *The Estate of Social Knowledge.* Baltimore: Johns Hopkins Univ. Press, 1991.

Buehrig, Edward H. *Wilson's Foreign Policy in Perspective.* Bloomington: Indiana Univ. Press, 1957.

———. *Woodrow Wilson and the Balance of Power.* Bloomington: Indiana Univ. Press, 1955.

Buenker, John D. "Sovereign Individuals and Organic Networks: Political Cultures in Conflict during the Progressive Era." *American Quarterly* 40 (June 1988): 187–200.

———. *Urban Liberalism and Progressive Reform.* New York: Charles Scribner's Sons, 1973.

Buenker, John D., John C. Burnham, and Robert M. Crunden. *Progressivism.* Cambridge, Mass.: Schenkman Publishing, 1977.

Buenker, John D., and Edward R. Kantowicz, eds. *Historical Dictionary of the Progressive Era, 1890–1920.* Westport, Conn.: Greenwood Press, 1988.

Calhoun, Frederick S. *Power and Principle: Armed Intervention in Wilsonian Foreign Policy.* Kent, Ohio: Kent State Univ. Press, 1986.

Carey, James W. "Commentary: Communications and the Progressives." *Critical Studies in Mass Communication* 6 (1989): 264–281.

Cater, Douglass. *The Fourth Branch of Government.* New York: Vintage Books, 1959.

Ceaser, James W., Glen E. Thurow, Jeffrey K. Tulis, and Joseph M. Bessette. "The Rise of the Rhetorical Presidency." *Presidential Studies Quarterly* 11 (1981): 158–171.

Chambers, John W., II, ed. *The Eagle and the Dove: The American Peace Movement and U.S. Foreign Policy, 1900–1922.* New York: Garland, 1976.

Chatfield, Charles. *For Peace and Justice: Pacifism in America, 1914–1941.* Knoxville: Univ. of Tennessee Press, 1971.

Clements, Kendrick A. *The Presidency of Woodrow Wilson.* Lawrence: Univ. Press of Kansas, 1992.

———. *Woodrow Wilson: World Statesman.* Boston: Twayne Publishers, 1987.

Coogan, John W. *The End of Neutrality: The United States, Britain, and Maritime Rights, 1899–1915.* Ithaca, N.Y.: Cornell Univ. Press, 1981.

Cooper, John Milton, Jr. *Breaking the Heart of the World: Woodrow Wilson and the Fight for the League of Nations.* Cambridge: Cambridge Univ. Press, 2001.

———. "The British Response to the House-Grey Memorandum: New Evidence and New Questions." *Journal of American History* 59 (March 1973): 958–971.

———. *The Vanity of Power: American Isolationism and the First World War, 1914–1917.* Westport, Conn.: Greenwood, 1969.

———. *The Warrior and the Priest: Woodrow Wilson and Theodore Roosevelt.* Cambridge, Mass.: Belknap Press of Harvard Univ. Press, 1983.

Cooper, John M., Jr., and Charles E. Neu, eds. *The Wilson Era: Essays in Honor of Arthur S. Link.* Arlington Heights, Ill.: Harlan Davidson, 1991.

Cornebise, Alfred E. *War as Advertised: The Four Minute Men and America's Crusade, 1917–1918.* Philadelphia: The American Philosophical Society, 1984.

Cornwell, Elmer E., Jr. *Presidential Leadership of Public Opinion.* Bloomington: Indiana Univ. Press, 1965.

Couperie, Pierre. *Paris Through the Ages* (Paris au fils du temps). Translated by Marilyn Low. New York: Braziller, 1968.

Cranston, Alan. *The Killing of Peace.* New York: Viking, 1945.

Crunden, Robert M. *Ministers of Reform: The Progressives' Achievement in American Civilization, 1889–1920.* New York: Basic Books, 1982.

———. *American Salons: Encounters with European Modernism, 1885–1917.* New York: Oxford Univ. Press, 1993.

Czitrom, Daniel J. *Media and the American Mind: From Morse to McLuhan.* Chapel Hill: Univ. of North Carolina Press, 1982.

Danborn, David B. *"The World of Hope": Progressives and the Struggle for an Ethical Public Life.* Philadelphia: Temple Univ. Press, 1987.

Davis, Allen F. "Welfare, Reform and World War I." *American Quarterly* 19 (1967): 516–533.

Davis, Elmer. *History of the* New York Times, *1851–1921.* New York: New York Times, 1921; reprint, New York: Greenwood Press, 1969.

DeBenedetti, Charles. *Origins of the Modern American Peace Movement, 1915–1929.* Millwood, N.Y.: KTO Press, 1978.

Desmond, Robert W. *Windows on the World: The Information Process in a Changing Society, 1900–1920.* Iowa City: Univ. of Iowa Press, 1980.

Devlin, Patrick. *Too Proud to Fight: Woodrow Wilson's Neutrality.* New York: Oxford Univ. Press, 1975.

Drucker, Peter F. "The Rise of the Knowledge Society." *Wilson Quarterly* 17 (spring 1993): 52–66.

Egerton, George W. "Britain and the 'Great Betrayal': Anglo-American Relations and the Struggle for United States Ratification of the Treaty of Versailles, 1919–1920." *Historical Journal* 21 (1978): 885–911.

Eisenach, Eldon J. *The Lost Promise of Progressivism.* Lawrence: Univ. Press of Kansas Press, 1994.

Ellis, Mark. "'Closing Ranks' and 'Seeking Honors': W. E. B. Du Bois in World War I." *Journal of American History* 79 (June 1992): 96–124.

Emery, Edwin, and Henry Ladd Smith. *The Press and America.* New York: Prentice-Hall, 1954.

Feiger, C. C. *The Era of the Muckrakers.* Chapel Hill: Univ. of North Carolina Press, 1932.

Ferrell, Robert H. *Woodrow Wilson and World War I, 1917–1921.* New York: Harper and Row, 1985.

Filene, Peter. "An Obituary for 'The Progressive Movement.'" *American Quarterly* 22 (1970): 20–34.

Filler, Louis. *Appointment at Armageddon: Muckraking and Progressivism in the American Tradition.* Westport, Conn.: Greenwood Press, 1976.

———. *Crusaders for American Liberalism: The Story of the Muckrakers.* New York: Harcourt, Brace, 1939.

———. *Randolph Bourne.* Washington, D.C.: American Council on Public Affairs, 1943.

Fleming, Denna F. *The United States and the League of Nations.* New York: Putnam, 1932.

Floto, Inga. *Colonel House in Paris: A Study in American Policy at the Paris Peace Conference, 1919.* Princeton: Princeton Univ. Press, 1981.

Flower, B. O. *Progressive Men, Women, and Movements of the Past Twenty-Five Years.* Boston: The New Arena, 1914,

Forcey, Charles. *The Crossroads of Liberalism: Croly, Weyl, Lippmann, and the Progressive Era, 1900–1925.* New York: Oxford Univ. Press, 1961.

Ford, Guy Stanton. "America's Fight for Public Opinion." *Minnesota History* 3 (February 1919): 3–26.

Fowler, W. B. *British-American Relations, 1917–1918: The Role of Sir William Wiseman.* Princeton: Princeton Univ. Press, 1969.

Fredericks, Pierce G. *The Great Adventure: America in the First World War.* New York: Dutton, 1960.

Gardner, Lloyd C. *Safe for Democracy: The Anglo-American Response to Revolution, 1913–1923.* New York: Oxford Univ. Press, 1984.

Gelfand, Lawrence E. *The Inquiry: American Preparations for Peace, 1917–1919.* New Haven, Conn.: Yale Univ. Press, 1963.

———. "The Mystique of Wilsonian Statecraft." *Diplomatic History* 7 (spring 1983): 87–101.

———. "Where Ideals Confront Self-Interest: Wilsonian Foreign Policy." *Diplomatic History* 18 (1994): 125–134.

George, Alexander L., and Juliette L. George. *Woodrow Wilson and Colonel House: A Personality Study.* New York: Dover, 1954.

George, Juliette L., Michael F. Marmor, and Alexander L. George. "Issues in Wilson Scholarship: References to Early 'Strokes' in the Papers of Woodrow Wilson." *Journal of American History* 70 (March 1984): 845–853.

Gilbert, Martin. *The First World War: A Complete History.* New York: Holt, 1994.

Ginsberg, Benjamin. *The Captive Public: How Mass Opinion Promotes State Power.* New York: Basic Books, 1986.

Gleason, Timothy W. "Historians and Freedom of the Press since 1800." *American Journalism* 5 (1988): 230–247.

Goldberg, George. *The Peace to End Peace: The Paris Peace Conference of 1919.* New York: Harcourt, Brace and World, 1969.

Goldman, Eric. *Rendezvous with Destiny.* New York: Knopf, 1952.

Gould, Lewis L., ed. *The Progressive Era.* Syracuse, N.Y.: Syracuse Univ. Press, 1974.

———. "Theodore Roosevelt, Woodrow Wilson, and the Emergence of the Modern Presidency: An Introductory Essay." *Presidential Studies Quarterly* 19 (winter 1989): 41–50.

Graebner, William. *The Engineering of Consent: Democracy and Authority in Twentieth-Century America.* Madison: Univ. of Wisconsin Press, 1987.

Grimes, Alan P. *The Political Liberalism of the New York Nation, 1865–1932.* Chapel Hill: Univ. of North Carolina Press, 1953.

Hammack, David C., ed. *Making the Nonprofit Sector in the United States: A Reader.* Bloomington: Indiana Univ. Press, 1998.

Hanna, Martha. *The Mobilization of Intellect: French Scholars and Writers during the Great War.* Cambridge, Mass.: Harvard Univ. Press, 1996.

Hargrove, Edwin C. *Presidential Leadership: Personality and Political Style.* New York: Macmillan, 1966.

Haskell, Thomas L., ed. *The Authority of Experts: Studies in History and Theory.* Bloomington: Indiana Univ. Press, 1984.

———. *The Emergence of Professional Social Science: The American Social Science As-*

sociation and the Nineteenth-Century Crisis of Authority. Urbana: Univ. of Illinois Press, 1977.

Hatch, Nathan O., ed. *The Professions in American History.* Notre Dame, Ind.: Univ. of Notre Dame Press, 1988.

Hays, Samuel P. *The Response to Industrialism, 1885–1914.* Chicago: Univ. of Chicago Press, 1957.

Herman, Sondra R. *Eleven Against War: Studies in American Internationalist Thought, 1898–1921.* Stanford, Calif.: Stanford Univ. Press, 1969.

Hess, Stephen, and Milton Kaplan. *The Ungentlemanly Art: A History of American Political Cartoons.* New York: Macmillan, 1968.

Hilderbrand, Robert C. *Power and the People: Executive Management of Public Opinion in Foreign Affairs, 1897–1921.* Chapel Hill: Univ. of North Carolina Press, 1981.

Hilton, O. A. "Public Opinion and Civil Liberties in Wartime, 1917–1919." *Southwestern Social Science Quarterly* 28 (December 1947): 201–224.

Hirschfeld, Charles. "Nationalist Progressivism and World War I." *Mid-America* 45 (July 1963): 139–156.

Hobson, Wayne K. "Professionals, Progressives and Bureaucratization: A Reassessment." *The Historian* 39 (1977): 639–658.

Hofstadter, Richard. *The Age of Reform: From Bryan to F.D.R.* New York.: Vintage Books, 1955.

———. *The American Political Tradition.* New York: Knopf, 1948; reprint, New York: Vintage Books, 1989.

———. *Anti-Intellectualism in American Life.* New York: Knopf, 1962.

Hogan, Michael J. *Informal Entente: The Private Structure of Cooperation in Anglo-American Diplomacy, 1918–1928.* Columbia: Univ. of Missouri Press, 1977.

Hogan, Michael J., and Thomas G. Paterson, eds. *Explaining the History of American Foreign Relations.* Cambridge: Cambridge Univ. Press, 1991.

Hohenberg, John. *Foreign Correspondence: The Great Reporters and Their Times.* New York: Columbia Univ. Press, 1964.

Holborn, Hajo. *The Political Collapse of Europe.* New York: Knopf, 1960.

Hollinger, David A. *In the American Province: Studies in the History and Historiography of Ideas.* Baltimore: Johns Hopkins Univ. Press, 1985.

Hollinger, David A., and Charles Capper, eds. *The American Intellectual Tradition.* 2 vols. New York: Oxford Univ. Press, 1993.

Hooker, Helene Maxwell, ed. *History of the Progressive Party, 1912–1916.* New York: New York University Press, 1958.

Hopkin, Deian. "Domestic Censorship in the First World War." *Journal of Contemporary History* 5 (1970): 151–169.

Hunt, Michael H. *Ideology and U.S. Foreign Policy.* New Haven, Conn.: Yale Univ. Press, 1987.

Ilchman, Warren Frederick. *Professional Diplomacy in the United States, 1779–1939: A Study in Administrative History.* Chicago: Univ. of Chicago Press, 1961.

Israel, Jerry. *Progressivism and the Open Door: America and China, 1905–1921.* Pittsburgh: Univ. of Pittsburgh Press, 1971.

Israel, Jerry, ed. *Building the Organizational Society: Essays on Associational Activities in Modern America.* New York: Free Press, 1972.

Johnson, Donald. "Wilson, Burleson, and Censorship in the First World War." *Journal of Southern History* 28 (February 1962): 46–58.

Johnson, Robert D. *The Peace Progressives and American Foreign Relations.* Cambridge, Mass.: Harvard Univ. Press, 1995.

Johnson, Walter. *William Allen White's America.* New York: Holt, 1947.

Jones, Robert W. *Journalism in the United States.* New York: Dutton, 1947.

Joost, Nicholas. *Years of Transition: The Dial, 1912–1920.* Barre, Mass.: Barre Publishers, 1967.

Josephson, Matthew. *The President Makers: The Culture of Politics and Leadership in an Age of Enlightenment, 1896–1919.* New York: Harcourt, Brace, 1940.

Juergens, George. *News from the White House: The Presidential-Press Relationship in the Progressive Era.* Chicago: Univ. of Chicago Press, 1981.

Kahn, E. J., Jr. *The World of Swope.* New York: Simon and Schuster, 1965.

Kaplan, Richard L. *Politics and the American Press: The Rise of Objectivity, 1865–1920.* Cambridge: Cambridge Univ. Press, 2002.

Kaufman, Burton K. *Efficiency and Expansion: Foreign Trade Organization in the Wilson Administration, 1913–1921.* Westport, Conn.: Greenwood Press, 1974.

Kelley, Stanley, Jr. *Professional Public Relations and Political Power.* Baltimore: Johns Hopkins Univ. Press, 1956.

Kennan, George F. *American Diplomacy, 1900–1950.* Chicago: Univ. of Chicago Press, 1951.

———. *Soviet-American Relations, 1917–1920.* Princeton: Princeton Univ. Press, 1956.

Kennedy, David M. *Over Here: The First World War and American Society.* New York: Oxford Univ. Press, 1980.

———, ed. *Progressivism: The Critical Issues.* Boston: Little, Brown, 1971.

Kernell, Samuel, and Gary C. Jacobsen, "Congress and the Presidency as News in the Nineteenth Century." *Journal of Politics* 49 (1987): 1016–1035.

Kimball, Bruce A., ed. *The Professions in America.* Boston: Houghton Mifflin, 1965.

———. *The "True Professional Ideal" in America: A History.* Cambridge, Mass.: Blackwell, 1992.

Kirschner, Don S. *The Paradox of Professionalism: Reform and Public Service in Urban America, 1900–1940.* Westport, Conn.: Greenwood Press, 1986.

———. "'Publicity Properly Applied': The Selling of Expertise in America, 1900–1929." *American Studies* 19 (spring 1978): 65–78.

Kloppenberg, James T. *Uncertain Victory: Social Democracy and Progressivism in European and American Thought.* New York: Oxford Univ. Press, 1986.

Knightley, Phillip. *The First Casualty: From the Crimea to Vietnam: The War Correspondent as Hero, Propagandist, and Myth Maker.* New York: Harcourt Brace Jovanovich, 1975.

Knock, Thomas J. *To End All Wars: Woodrow Wilson and the Quest for a New World Order.* New York: Oxford Univ. Press, 1992.

Landecker, Manfred. *The President and Public Opinion.* Washington, D.C.: Public Affairs Press, 1968.

Larson, Magali Sarfatti. *The Rise of Professionalism: A Sociological Analysis.* Berkeley: Univ. of California Press, 1977.

Lasch, Christopher. *The American Liberals and the Russian Revolution.* New York: Columbia Univ. Press, 1962.

———. *The New Radicalism in America, 1889–1963: The Intellectual as a Social Type.* New York: Norton, 1965.

Launay, Michel. *Versailles, Une Paix Baclée? Le XXème Siècle Est Mal Parti.* Bruxelles: Editions Complexe, 1981.

Lazo, Dimitri D. "A Question of Loyalty: Robert Lansing and the Treaty of Versailles." *Diplomatic History* 9 (winter 1985): 35–53.

Lee, Alfred McClung. *The Daily Newspaper in America.* New York: Macmillan, 1937.

Lee, James Melvin. *History of American Journalism.* Garden City, N.J.: Garden City Publishing, 1917.

Leigh, Michael. *Mobilizing Consent: Public Opinion and American Foreign Policy, 1937–1947.* Westport, Conn.: Greenwood Press, 1976.

Lentin, A. *Lloyd George, Woodrow Wilson and the Guilt of Germany: An Essay in the Pre-History of Appeasement.* Baton Rouge: Louisiana State Univ. Press, 1984.

Leonard, Thomas C. *The Power of the Press: The Birth of American Political Reporting.* New York: Oxford Univ. Press, 1986.

Leuchtenberg, William E. "Progressivism and Imperialism: The Progressive Movement and American Foreign Policy, 1898–1916." *Mississippi Valley Historical Review* 39 (December 1952): 483–504.

Levering. Ralph B. *The Public and American Foreign Policy, 1918–1978.* New York: Morrow, 1978.

Levin, Gordon, Jr. *Woodrow Wilson and World Politics.* New York: Oxford Univ. Press, 1968.

Link, Arthur S. *The Higher Realism of Woodrow Wilson, and Other Essays.* Nashville, Tenn.: Vanderbilt Univ. Press, 1971.

———. *Wilson: Campaigns for Progressivism and Peace.* Princeton: Princeton Univ. Press, 1965.

———. *Wilson: Confusions and Crises.* Princeton: Princeton Univ. Press, 1964.

———. *Wilson the Diplomatist: A Look at His Major Foreign Policies.* Baltimore: Johns Hopkins Press, 1957.

———. *Wilson: The New Freedom.* Princeton: Princeton Univ. Press, 1956.

———. *Wilson: The Road to the White House.* Princeton: Princeton Univ. Press, 1947.

———. *Wilson's Diplomacy: An International Symposium.* Cambridge, Mass: Schenkman Publishing, 1973.

———. *Woodrow Wilson and the Progressive Era.* New York: Harper and Row, 1954.

————. *Woodrow Wilson: Revolution, War, and Peace.* Arlington Heights, Ill.: AHM Publishing, 1979.

Livermore, Seward W. *Politics Is Adjourned: Woodrow Wilson and the War Congress, 1916–1918.* Middletown, Conn.: Wesleyan Univ. Press, 1966.

Loewenheim, Francis L. *The Historian and the Diplomat: The Role of History and Historians in American Foreign Policy.* New York: Harper and Row, 1967.

London, Kurt. *Backgrounds of Conflict: Ideas and Forms in World Politics.* New York: Macmillan, 1947.

Lynn, Kenneth S., ed. *The Professions in America.* Boston: Houghton Mifflin, 1965.

Macmillan, Margaret. *Paris, 1919: Six Months That Changed the World.* New York: Random House, 2001.

Mamatey, Victor S. *The United States and East Central Europe, 1914–1918: A Study in Wilsonian Diplomacy and Propaganda.* Princeton: Princeton Univ. Press, 1957.

Margulies, Herbert F. *The Mild Reservationists and the League of Nations Controversy in the Senate.* Columbia: Univ. of Missouri Press, 1989.

Markowitz, Gerald E. "Progressivism and Imperialism: A Return to First Principles." *The Historian* 37 (February 1975): 257–275.

Marzolf, Marion Tuttle. *Civilizing Voices: American Press Criticism, 1880–1950.* New York: Longman, 1991.

May, Henry F. *The End of American Innocence.* New York: Knopf, 1959.

Mayer, Arno J. *Political Origins of the New Diplomacy, 1917–1918.* New Haven, Conn.: Yale Univ. Press, 1959.

————. *Politics and Diplomacy of the Peacemaking: Containment and Counterrevolution at Versailles, 1918–1919.* New York: Vintage, 1970.

McCormick, Richard L. "The Discovery That Business Corrupts Politics: A Reappraisal of the Origins of Progressivism." *American Historical Review* 86 (April 1981): 247–274.

————. *From Realignment to Reform: Political Change in New York State, 1893–1910.* Ithaca, N.Y.: Cornell Univ. Press, 1981.

McGerr, Michael. *The Decline of Popular Politics: The American North, 1865–1928.* New York: Oxford Univ. Press, 1986.

Mervin, David. "Henry Cabot Lodge and the League of Nations." *Journal of American Studies* 4 (February 1971): 201–214.

Milkis, Sidney M., and Jerome M. Mileur, eds. *Progressivism and the New Democracy.* Amherst: Univ. of Massachusetts Press, 1999.

Mindich, David T. Z. *Just the Facts: How "Objectivity" Came to Define American Journalism.* New York: New York Univ. Press, 1998.

Mitchell, David. "Woodrow Wilson as 'World Saviour.'" *History Today* 26 (1976): 3–14.

Mock, James R., and Cedric Larson. *Words That Won the War: The Story of the Committee on Public Information, 1917–1919.* Princeton: Princeton Univ. Press, 1939.

Mott, Frank Luther. *American Journalism: A History, 1690–1960,* 3rd ed. New York: Macmillan, 1941; reprint, 1962.

————. *A History of American Magazines.* 5 vols. Cambridge, Mass.: Harvard Univ. Press, 1968.

Mowry, George. *The Era of Theodore Roosevelt.* New York: Harper and Brothers, 1958.

————. *Theodore Roosevelt and the Progressive Movement.* Madison: Univ. of Wisconsin Press, 1946.

Murphy, Paul L. *World War I and the Origin of Civil Liberties in the United States.* New York: Norton, 1979.

Murray, Robert K. *Red Scare: A Study in National Hysteria, 1919–1920.* Minneapolis: Univ. of Minnesota Press, 1955.

Nevins, Allan. *American Press Opinion: A Documentary Record of Editorial Leadership and Criticism, 1785–1927.* Boston: Heath, 1928.

————. *The Evening Post: A Century of Journalism.* New York: Boni and Liveright, 1922.

————. *Henry White: Thirty Years of American Diplomacy.* New York: Harper and Brothers, 1930.

Nord, David Paul. *Communities of Journalism: A History of American Newspapers and Their Readers.* Urbana: Univ. of Illinois Press, 2001.

————. *Newspapers and New Politics: Midwestern Municipal Reform, 1890–1900.* Ann Arbor: UMI Research Press, 1981.

O'Brien, Frank M. *The Story of "The Sun," 1833–1918.* New York: Doran, 1918.

O'Grady, Joseph P. *The Immigrants' Influence on Wilson's Peace Policies.* Lexington: Univ. of Kentucky Press, 1968.

Osgood, Robert Endicott. *Ideals and Self-Interest in America's Foreign Relations.* Chicago: Univ. of Chicago Press, 1965.

Parsons, Edward B. *Wilsonian Diplomacy: Allied American Rivalries in War and Peace.* St. Louis, Mo.: Forum Press, 1978.

Payne, George Henry. *History of Journalism in the United States.* New York: Appleton, 1920.

Pearlman, Michael. *To Make Democracy Safe for America: Patricians and Preparedness in the Progressive Era.* Urbana: Univ. of Illinois Press, 1984.

Peters, John Durham. "Satan and Savior: Mass Communication in Progressive Thought." *Critical Studies in Mass Communication* 6 (1989): 247–263.

Peterson, Horace C. *Propaganda for War: The Campaign Against American Neutrality, 1914–1917.* Norman: Univ. of Oklahoma Press, 1938.

Peterson, Horace C., and Gilbert C. Fite. *Opponents of War, 1917–1918.* Madison: Univ. of Wisconsin Press, 1957.

Pimlott, J. A. R. *Public Relations and American Democracy.* Princeton: Princeton Univ. Press, 1951.

Pollard, James E. *The Presidents and the Press.* New York: Macmillan, 1947; reprint, New York: Octagon Books, 1973.

Ponder, Stephen. "Federal News Management in the Progressive Era: Gifford Pinchot and the Conservation Crusade." *Journalism History* 13 (summer 1986): 42–48.

———. *Managing the Press: Origins of the Media Presidency, 1897–1933.* New York: St. Martin's Press, 1998.

Porter, Theodore M. *The Rise of Statistical Thinking: 1820–1900.* Princeton: Princeton Univ. Press, 1986.

———. *Trust in Numbers: The Pursuit of Objectivity in Science and Public Life.* Princeton: Princeton Univ. Press, 1995.

Read, James Morgan. *Atrocity Propaganda, 1914–1919.* New Haven, Conn.: Yale Univ. Press, 1941.

Ritchie, Donald A. "'The Loyalty of the Senate': Washington Correspondents in the Progressive Era." *The Historian* 51 (August 1989): 574–591.

———. *Press Gallery: Congress and the Washington Correspondents.* Cambridge, Mass.: Harvard Univ. Press, 1991.

Rivers, William L. *The Adversaries: Politics and the Press.* Boston: Beacon Press, 1970.

Roberts, Chalmers M. *The Washington Post: The First 100 Years.* Boston: Houghton Mifflin, 1977.

Rodgers, Daniel T. *Atlantic Crossings: Social Politics in a Progressive Age.* Cambridge, Mass.: Belknap Press of Harvard Univ. Press, 1998.

———. "In Search of Progressivism." *Reviews in American History* 10 (December 1982): 113–132.

Rogers, Jason. *Newspaper Building.* New York: Harper and Brothers, 1918.

Rosenau, James N. *Public Opinion and Foreign Policy: An Operational Formulation.* New York: Random House, 1961.

Rosenberg, Emily S. *Financial Missionaries to the World: The Politics and Culture of Dollar Diplomacy, 1900–1930.* Cambridge, Mass.: Harvard Univ. Press, 1999.

Rosewater, Victor. *History of Cooperative News-Gathering in the United States.* New York: Appleton, 1930.

Ross, Dorothy., ed. *Modernist Impulses in the Human Sciences, 1870–1930.* Baltimore: Johns Hopkins Univ. Press, 1994.

———. *The Origins of American Social Science.* Cambridge: Cambridge Univ. Press, 1991.

———. "Woodrow Wilson and the Case for Psychohistory." *Journal of American History* 69 (December 1982): 658–668.

Rosten, Leo C. *The Washington Correspondents.* New York: Harcourt, Brace, 1937.

Roth, Jack J. *World War I: A Turning Point in Modern History.* New York: Knopf, 1967.

Rothblatt, Sheldon. "How 'Professional' Are the Professions? A Review Article." *Comparative Studies in Society and History* 37 (January 1995): 194–204.

Rothwell, V. H. *British War Aims and Peace Diplomacy, 1914–1918.* Oxford: Clarendon Press, 1971.

Rourke, Francis Edward. *Secrecy and Publicity: Dilemmas of Democracy.* Baltimore: Johns Hopkins Press, 1961.

Rudin, Harry R. *Armistice 1918.* New Haven, Conn.: Yale Univ. Press, 1944.

Salmon, Lucy Maynard. *The Newspaper and the Historian.* New York: Oxford Univ. Press, 1923.

Saunders, Robert M. "History, Health and Herons: The Historiography of Woodrow Wilson's Personality and Decision-Making." *Presidential Studies Quarterly* 24 (winter 1994): 57–77.

Scheiber, Harry N. *The Wilson Administration and Civil Liberties.* Ithaca, N.Y.: Cornell Univ. Press, 1960.

Schiesl, Martin J. *The Politics of Efficiency: Municipal Administration and Reform in America 1880–1920.* Berkeley: Univ. of California Press, 1977.

Schlesinger, Arthur M., Jr. *The Imperial Presidency.* Boston: Houghton Mifflin, 1973.

Schudson, Michael. *Discovering the News: A Social History of American Newspapers.* New York: Basic Books, 1978.

———. *The Good Citizen: A History of American Civic Life.* New York: Free Press, 1998.

———. *Origins of the Ideal of Objectivity in the Professions: Studies in the History of American Journalism and American Law, 1830–1940.* New York: Garland, 1990.

———. *The Power of News.* Cambridge, Mass.: Harvard Univ. Press, 1995.

Schulzinger, Robert D. *American Diplomacy in the Twentieth Century.* New York: Oxford Univ. Press, 1994.

Schwabe, Klaus. *Woodrow Wilson, Revolutionary Germany, and Peacemaking, 1918–1919: Missionary Diplomacy and the Realities of Power.* Trans. by Rita and Robert Kimber. Chapel Hill: Univ. of North Carolina Press, 1985.

Seideman, David. *The New Republic: A Voice of Modern Liberalism.* Westport, Conn.: Praeger, 1986.

Shapiro, Stanley. "The Twilight of Reform: Advanced Progressives after the Armistice." *The Historian* 33 (May 1971): 349–364.

Shi, David E. *Facing Facts: Realism in American Thought and Culture, 1850–1920.* New York: Oxford Univ. Press, 1995.

Sigal, Leon V. *Reporters and Officials: The Organization and Politics of Newsmaking.* Lexington, Mass.: Heath, 1973.

Sklar, Kathryn Kish. *Florence Kelley and the Nation's Work: The Rise of Women's Political Culture, 1830–1900.* New Haven, Conn.: Yale Univ. Press, 1995.

Skocpol, Theda. *Protecting Soldiers and Mothers: The Political Origins of Social Policy in the United States.* Cambridge, Mass.: Belknap Press of Harvard Univ. Press, 1992.

Small, Melvin. *Democracy and Diplomacy: The Impact of Domestic Politics in U.S. Foreign Policy, 1789–1994.* Baltimore: Johns Hopkins Univ. Press, 1996.

———, ed. *Public Opinion and Historians: Interdisciplinary Perspectives.* Detroit: Wayne State Univ. Press, 1970.

Smith, Bruce Lannes, Harold D. Lasswell, and Ralph D. Casey. *Propaganda, Communication, and Public Opinion: A Comprehensive Reference Guide.* Princeton: Princeton Univ. Press, 1946.

Smith, Daniel M. *American Intervention, 1917: Sentiment, Self-Interest, or Ideals?* Boston: Houghton Mifflin, 1966.

———. *The Great Departure: The United States and World War I, 1914–1920.* New York: Wiley and Sons, 1965.

Smith, Gene. *When the Cheering Slopped: The Last Years of Woodrow Wilson.* New York: Morrow, 1964.

Smith, Mark C. *Social Science in the Crucible: The American Debate over Objectivity and Purpose, 1918–1941.* Durham, N.C.: Duke Univ. Press, 1994.

Smith, Tony. "Making the World Safe for Democracy in the American Century." *Diplomatic History* 23 (spring 1999): 173–188.

Startt, James D. "Early Press Reaction to Wilson's League Proposal." *Journalism Quarterly* 39 (1962): 301–308.

———. "The Uneasy Partnership: Wilson and the Press at Paris." *Mid-America* 52 (January 1970): 55–69.

———. "Wilson's Trip to Paris: Profile of Press Response." *Journalism Quarterly* 46 (1969): 737–742.

Steel, Ronald. *Walter Lippmann and the American Century.* New York: Vintage Books, 1980.

Steigerwald, David. "The Synthetic Politics of Woodrow Wilson." *Journal of the History of Ideas* 50 (1989): 465–484.

———. *Wilsonian Idealism in America.* Ithaca, N.Y.: Cornell Univ. Press, 1994.

Stid, Daniel D. *The President as Statesman: Woodrow Wilson and the Constitution.* Lawrence: Univ. of Kansas Press, 1998.

Stillman, Edmund, and William Pfaff. *The Politics of Hysteria: The Sources of Twentieth-Century Conflict.* New York: Harper and Row, 1964.

Stone, Ralph. *The Irreconcilables: The Fight Against the League of Nations.* Lexington: Univ. of Kentucky Press, 1970.

Stuart, Graham H. *American Diplomatic and Consular Practice.* New York: Appleton-Century-Crofts, 1952.

Swados, Harvey, ed. *Years of Conscience: The Muckrakers.* Cleveland: World Publishing, Meridian Books, 1962.

Swanberg, W. A. *Citizen Hearst: A Biography of William Randolph Hearst.* New York: Charles Scribner's Sons, 1961; reprint, New York: Galahad Books, 1996.

Taylor, A. J. P. *The First World War: An Illustrated History.* London: Hamish Hamilton, 1963; reprint, New York: G. P. Putnam's Sons, 1972.

———. *Politics in Wartime and Other Essays.* New York: Atheneum, 1965.

———. *The Struggle for the Mastery in Europe.* Oxford: Clarendon Press, 1954.

Teaford, Jon C. *City and Suburb: The Political Fragmentation of Metropolitan America, 1850–1970.* Baltimore: Johns Hopkins Univ. Press, 1979.

———. *The Unheralded Triumph: City Government in America, 1870–1900.* Baltimore: Johns Hopkins Univ. Press, 1984.

Tebbel, John. *The American Magazine: A Compact History.* New York: Hawthorn Books, 1969.

———. *The Compact History of the American Newspaper.* New York: Hawthorn Books, 1963.

———. *The Media in America.* New York: New American Library, 1974.

Thelen, David P. *The New Citizenship: Origins of Progressivism in Wisconsin, 1885–1900.* Columbia: Univ. of Missouri Press, 1972.

Thompson, John A. "American Progressive Publicists and the First World War, 1914–1917." *Journal of American History* 58 (September 1971): 364–383.

———. *Reformers and War: American Progressive Publicists and the First World War.* Cambridge: Cambridge Univ. Press, 1987.

———. "Woodrow Wilson and World War I: A Reappraisal." *Journal of American Studies* 19 (1985): 325–348.

Tillman, Seth P. *Anglo-American Relations at the Paris Peace Conference of 1919.* Princeton: Princeton Univ. Press, 1961.

Trask, David F. *Victory without Peace: American Foreign Relations in the Twentieth Century.* New York: Wiley and Sons, 1968.

———. *World War I at Home: Readings on American Life, 1914–1920.* New York: Wiley and Sons, 1970.

Trattner, Walter I. "Progressivism and World War I: A Re-Appraisal." *Mid-America* 44 (July 1962): 131–145.

Tuchman, Barbara W. *The Guns of August.* New York.: Macmillan, 1962.

———. *The Zimmerman Telegram.* New York: Macmillan, 1958.

Tulis, Jeffrey K. *The Rhetorical Presidency.* Princeton: Princeton Univ. Press, 1987.

Vaughn, Stephen L. *Holding Fast the Inner Lines: Democracy, Nationalism, and the Committee on Public Information.* Chapel Hill: Univ. of North Carolina Press, 1980.

Vinson, John Chalmers. *Referendum on Isolation: Defeat of Article Ten of the League of Nations Covenant.* Athens: Univ. of Georgia Press, 1961.

Waldrop, Frank C. *McCormick of Chicago: An Unconventional Portrait of a Controversial Figure.* Englewood Cliffs, N.J.: Prentice-Hall, 1966.

Wallace, James M. *Liberal Journalism and American Education, 1914–1941.* New Brunswick, N.J.: Rutgers Univ. Press, 1991.

Wallach, Glenn. "'A Depraved Taste for Publicity': The Press and Private Life in the Gilded Age." *American Studies* 39 (spring 1978): 31–57.

Walworth, Arthur. *America's Moment, 1918: American Diplomacy at the End of World War I.* New York: Norton, 1977.

———. *Wilson and His Peacemakers: American Diplomacy at the Paris Peace Conference, 1919.* New York: Norton, 1986.

Weingast, David Elliott. *Walter Lippmann: A Study in Personal Journalism.* Westport, Conn.: Greenwood Press, 1949.

Weinstein, Edwin A. *Woodrow Wilson: A Medical and Psychological Biography.* Princeton: Princeton Univ. Press, 1981.

Weisberger, Bernard A. *The American Newspaperman.* Chicago: Univ. of Chicago Press, 1961.

Westbrook, Robert B. *John Dewey and American Democracy.* Ithaca, N.Y.: Cornell Univ. Press, 1991.

White, Morton G. *Social Thought in America: The Revolt against Formalism.* New York: Viking Press, 1949.

Widenor, William C. *Henry Cabot Lodge and the Search for an American Foreign Policy.* Berkeley: Univ. of California Press, 1980.

Wiebe, Robert H. *The Search for Order, 1877–1920.* New York: Hill and Wang, 1967.

Wikander, Ulla, Alice Kessler-Harris, and Jane Lewis, eds. *Protecting Women: Labor Legislation in Europe, the United States, and Australia, 1880–1920.* Urbana: Univ. of Illinois Press, 1995.

Willert, Arthur. *The Road to Safety: A Study in Anglo-American Relations.* New York: Praeger, 1953.

Williams, Sara Lockwood. *Twenty Years of Education for Journalism: A History of the School of Journalism of the University of Missouri—Columbia, Missouri, U.S.A.* Columbia, Mo.: Stephens Publishing, 1929.

Williams, William Appleman. *The Tragedy of American Diplomacy.* New York: Dell, 1959; reprint, 1972.

Wilson, Christopher P. *The Labor of Words: Literary Professionalism in the Progressive Era.* Athens: Univ. of Georgia Press, 1985.

Wilson, Harold S. *McClure's Magazine and the Muckrakers.* Princeton: Princeton Univ. Press, 1970.

Winter, Ella, and Herbert Shapiro, eds. *The World of Lincoln Steffens.* New York: Hill and Wang, 1962.

Wilcox, Delos F. "The American Newspaper: A Study in Social Psychology." *Annals of the American Academy of Political and Social Science* 16 (July 1900): 56–92.

Wolper, Gregg. "Wilsonian Public Diplomacy: The Committee on Public Information in Spain." *Diplomatic History* 17 (winter 1993): 17–34.

Wreszin, Michael. *Oswald Garrison Villard: Pacifist at War.* Bloomington: Indiana Univ. Press, 1965.

Wright, Quincy. "The Control of Foreign Relations." *American Political Science Review* 15 (February 1921): 1–26.

Wriston, Henry Merritt. *Executive Agents in American Foreign Relations.* Baltimore: Johns Hopkins Univ. Press, 1929.

———. *Diplomacy in a Democracy.* New York: Harper, 1956.

Yarros, Victor S. "A Neglected Opportunity and Duty in Journalism." *American Journal of Sociology* 22 (September 1916): 203–211.

Yost, Charles. *The Insecurity of Nations: International Relations in the Twentieth Century.* New York: Praeger, 1968.

Zacher, Dale E. *The Scripps Newspapers Go to War, 1914–1918.* Urbana.: Univ. of Illinois Press, 2008.

INDEX